Languages in America

BILINGUAL EDUCATION AND BILINGUALISM
Series Editors: Professor Colin Baker, *University of Wales, Bangor, Wales, Great Britain* and Professor Nancy H. Hornberger, *University of Pennsylvania, Philadelphia, USA*

Other Books in the Series
At War With Diversity: US Language Policy in an Age of Anxiety
    James Crawford
Bilingual Education and Social Change
    Rebecca Freeman
Continua of Biliteracy: An Ecological Framework for Educational Policy, Research, and Practice in Multilingual Settings
    Nancy H. Hornberger (ed.)
Cross-linguistic Influence in Third Language Acquisition
    J. Cenoz, B. Hufeisen and U. Jessner (eds)
Dual Language Education
    Kathryn J. Lindholm-Leary
Foundations of Bilingual Education and Bilingualism
    Colin Baker
Identity and the English Language Learner
    Elaine Mellen Day
An Introductory Reader to the Writings of Jim Cummins
    Colin Baker and Nancy Hornberger (eds)
Language and Literacy Teaching for Indigenous Education: A Bilingual Approach
    Norbert Francis and Jon Reyhner
Language Minority Students in the Mainstream Classroom (2nd Edition)
    Angela L. Carrasquillo and Vivian Rodriguez
Language, Power and Pedagogy: Bilingual Children in the Crossfire
    Jim Cummins
Language Rights and the Law in the United States: Finding our Voices
    Sandra Del Valle
Language Socialization in Bilingual and Multilingual Societies
    Robert Bayley and Sandra R. Schecter (eds)
The Languages of Israel: Policy, Ideology and Practice
    Bernard Spolsky and Elana Shohamy
Learning English at School: Identity, Social Relations and Classroom Practice
    Kelleen Toohey
Learners' Experiences of Immersion Education: Case Studies of French and Chinese
    Michèle de Courcy
The Native Speaker: Myth and Reality
    Alan Davies
Power, Prestige and Bilingualism: International Perspectives on Elite Bilingual Education
    Anne-Marie de Mejía
Reflections on Multiliterate Lives
    Diane Belcher and Ulla Connor (eds)
The Sociopolitics of English Language Teaching
    Joan Kelly Hall and William G. Eggington (eds)
Teaching and Learning in Multicultural Schools
    Elizabeth Coelho
World English: A Study of its Development
    Janina Brutt-Griffler

Please contact us for the latest book information:
Multilingual Matters, Frankfurt Lodge, Clevedon Hall,
Victoria Road, Clevedon, BS21 7HH, England
http://www.multilingual-matters.com

BILINGUAL EDUCATION AND BILINGUALISM 42
Series Editors: Colin Baker and Nancy H. Hornberger

Languages in America
A Pluralist View

2nd edition

Susan J. Dicker

MULTILINGUAL MATTERS LTD
Clevedon • Buffalo • Toronto • Sydney

Library of Congress Cataloging in Publication Data
Dicker, Susan J.
Languages in America: A Pluralist View/Susan J. Dicker. – 2nd ed.
Bilingual Education and Bilingualism: 42
Includes bibliographical references and index.
1. Multilingualism–United States. 2. Pluralism (Social sciences)–United States.
I. Title. II. Series.
P115.5.U5 D53 2003
404'.2'0973--dc21   2002153765

British Library Cataloguing in Publication Data
A catalogue entry for this book is available from the British Library.

ISBN 1-85359-652-3 (hbk)
ISBN 1-85359-651-5 (pbk)

Multilingual Matters Ltd
UK: Frankfurt Lodge, Clevedon Hall, Victoria Road, Clevedon BS21 7HH.
USA: UTP, 2250 Military Road, Tonawanda, NY 14150, USA.
Canada: UTP, 5201 Dufferin Street, North York, Ontario M3H 5T8, Canada.
Australia: Footprint Books, PO Box 418, Church Point, NSW 2103, Australia.

Typeset by Wordworks Ltd.
Printed and bound in Great Britain by the Cromwell Press Ltd.

Contents

Acknowledgments

A book may have the name of one author on its cover, but a writer is always dependent on others for inspiration and aid. I have been blessed with friends and colleagues who have supported me throughout the writing of this book, who have lent an ear when I needed to talk something out, and who have made valuable suggestions. I have also been blessed with a generous and thorough editor, Colin Baker. Colin helped me organize and clarify my thoughts, and often posed questions that pushed me to think and write about the subject matter more deeply. In addition, his superb knowledge of bilingualism and bilingual education led me to the sources I needed to give some sections of the text a better-rounded discussion. Finally, I am grateful to Mike and Marjukka Grover for their decision to publish the book and for their continued support during its production.

I was extremely pleased and honored when Multilingual Matters asked me to produce a second edition of Languages in America, in light of the positive response the original has received. I am glad to know that the book is being used to educate future teachers and those interested in language issues. At a time when bilingual education is under growing attack, the promotion of a balanced view of bilingualism and its place in society is critical. I would especially like to thank Terrance Wiley, whose review of the first edition offered invaluable constructive criticism, as well as the anonymous reviewer of the second edition.

Introduction

THE VALUE OF DIVERSITY

Diversity is a natural phenomenon. It exists in animals, in plants, in topography. Biodiversity supports human survival; people around the world depend on it for food, shelter, and clothing, and much medical research is based on the curative powers of natural compounds. In specific environments, the balance between living organisms and certain physical factors regulates the climatic systems that provide clean air and water and needed oxygen. When this balance is thrown off, as happens when a species disappears, the environment and its remaining residents suffer. Biodiversity also enriches human lives esthetically. We enjoy seeing and learning about all forms of animal life, eagerly anticipate the blossoming of color in the spring, and value trips to places whose scenery differs from the places where we reside.

For these reasons, many of us express sorrow over those instances in which biodiversity is threatened. We hear of an animal about to become extinct and rally to its cause; we lament the loss of rain forests. However, threats to diversity are often generated by human needs, such as industrial development, living space, and food production. It is at these times that the course that is best taken for human survival is not at all clear.

Like biodiversity, linguistic diversity helps sustain human existence. At times, medicinal cures are found in plants and flowers native to a particular region; knowledge about these cures comes from natives speaking the local language. If the language disappears, the medical knowledge will disappear as well. Languages contain other types of knowledge; they express particular ways of viewing life. Natural phenomena are viewed differently, as are familial and social relations. A wealth of information about human survival and adaptation is embedded in the many languages of the world. Linguistic diversity offers writers a wide range of artistic expression. In addition, research has shown that multilingual people have advantages over monolinguals in creative and divergent thinking, intelligence, and cognitive flexibility; investment in multilingualism thus means an investment in potential solutions to the problems humans face.

Just as biodiversity is threatened today, linguistic diversity is threatened as well. Of the roughly 6,000 languages that currently exist, half may be dead or dying by the year 2050. While the extinction of some languages is natural, language loss has accelerated in modern times. The same factors that are responsible for the loss of biodiversity, such as increased industrialization and population pressures, are responsible for diminished linguistic diversity. The global economy pushes small, non-industrialized communities to abandon local cultures and languages for participation in the larger world. The Internet, in particular, has introduced people far and wide to an enticing, globally-based source of knowledge that may compete with particular and local ways of seeing the world. Not surprisingly, there is a high correlation between biodiversity and linguistic diversity; in places where biodiversity is strong, linguistic diversity is also strong, and in places where biodiversity has been compromised, languages have been lost. In a similar way, a loss of linguistic diversity throws off the balance of life.

Whether the preservation or sacrifice of linguistic diversity best serves human survival is as difficult to answer as the same question regarding biodiversity. Linguistic diversity poses problems of communication. It may divide populations and pit them against each other in political struggles over rights and resources. However, because linguistic divisions often reflect other divisions by which society categorizes individuals, such as race, wealth, and power, different groups may see greater or lesser linguistic diversity as beneficial to their particular needs.

In some societies, the majority-language group attempts to maintain control over minority-language groups by suppressing their languages and imposing the majority language. In other societies, the majority-language group may foster minority languages and block those who speak them from learning the majority language for fear that it may help unite the groups and foster challenges to those in power. A minority-language group that gains control of a territory may limit the use of the majority language as a means of protecting its own language. In addition, minority-language communities and individuals within them may differ regarding the way they value linguistic diversity. Some may see the preservation of their languages as necessary for the preservation of their identity and heritage; others may see it as barring access to socioeconomic mobility in the larger world. As we will see, the particular characteristics of a minority-language group help determine the extent to which its language is maintained.

Social and historical change within a society add further complications to the issue of linguistic diversity. Such changes, with their concurrent shifts in population and power distribution, may disturb what is thought to be the linguistic balance or status quo of the society. The United States is in the midst of such a transformation today. People of European ancestry, who have long assumed their right to status and power, are becoming a numerical minority, while the number of people of non-European ancestry increases. In the case of the United States, the cause of this shift is a significant transformation in the source of immigration.

In the past, major waves of immigrants coming from Europe were eventually assimilated with older residents, while non-Europeans faced more resistance. Today, the majority of newcomers are from Africa, Asia, and Latin America. These immigrants are less easily drawn into mainstream American life than their European predecessors were. They are racially distinct from Europeans, which means they are likely to encounter the racial bigotry that is so endemic in American culture. Recent immigrants come from countries that have sometimes been plagued by years of economic distress and political strife, and that have often been dependent on various kinds of international assistance. After moving to the United States, these immigrants are often ill prepared to survive on their own, and many of them fall once again into a state of dependency. There is no longer the abundance of factory jobs which earlier immigrants relied on to support their families, and which required little knowledge of English. Great differences between the immigrants' own cultures and the American culture may make their adjustment even more difficult. In general, then, even though immigrants have never had an easy time of it, for these new immigrants the process of adapting to a new life, and of being accepted by established Americans, often presents obstacles that their European predecessors did not face. In addition, because of their non-European ancestry, their children and grandchildren may encounter similar obstacles to acceptance, even as these generations become Americanized.

Complicating this situation is an economic crisis. The American dream of upward socioeconomic mobility is dying; the middle class has to struggle just to stay where it is. As mainstream Americans lose their sense of security and well-being, they try to find ways to maintain the feeling of control that seems to be slipping away.

Some Americans have found what they believe to be a solution. They hang on to their sense of control by elevating the importance of their language, English, over the languages of minorities, and by insisting that it be the only language of communication. There is little they can do to change those who are different; they can't alter people's skin color or their facial features. Without being labeled racist, they can't prevent them from being hired for coveted jobs or from moving into their neighborhood. But they can try to control their language and culture.

In the process, society applies pressure on immigrants to discard the visible and audible marks of their distinctiveness, their vital links to a foreign land and another life. The dignity and self-respect of these minorities diminish; the message that they are worth less than others comes through clearly. In addition, their access to American life is constrained; their ability to adjust to their new homeland is made more difficult. By debilitating those who have not mastered English, those who have spoken it from birth maintain their advantage. Language diversity is diminished in an attempt to preserve the status quo.

WHY THIS BOOK IS NEEDED

Most Americans are not aware of the consequences of language restrictionism. The idea of declaring English as the official language seems to be a good one. Advocates for official English promise that it will bring greater unity and harmony to American life; no one wants to pass up a chance to improve human relations. They also claim that such a measure will help immigrants adjust to their new home; this humanitarian gesture is welcome. No one will be hurt by official English, they say; it can only help. The idea of improving life for everyone with this one, easy step has tremendous appeal.

Therein lies the need for this book. All of the above arguments for institutionalizing monolingualism are unsupportable. Making the government function in only one language will not bring greater harmony to American life, will not help immigrants adapt to a new society, and in fact will hurt many of the people it promises to help. One goal of this book is to examine the movement for English monolingualism in detail, to put all of its arguments under the microscope and reveal their inherent weaknesses. Another goal is to examine the antithesis of English monolingualism, language pluralism, to show how much it has already enriched American life, and to suggest the promise of a future in which language pluralism is nurtured instead of inhibited.

Support for language pluralism appears often in the media. But what has been missing until now is an extended discourse on the issue from the point of view of a linguist. In linguistics, and especially in the subfields of second-language acquisition and bilingualism, there exists a wealth of scholarly information which should be used to counter the rhetoric of language restrictionists. Unfortunately, American linguists do not have a tradition of sharing their work with the public; mostly, they speak to each other at professional conferences and through academic journals. Perhaps this is because the public has shown little interest in the work. Until recently, second-language learning has been of relatively little importance, and immigrant acquisition of English has not been considered a societal problem. However, with the demographic shifts described above, all matters relating to immigrants have taken central stage in national politics. Linguistics has much to offer to the public discourse on language minorities and their adjustment to American life.

The results of linguistic research are especially important to this discourse in light of the nature of the opposition. The official-English camp is made up of people with a political ideology to maintain. Most of its leaders have little expertise in language learning or actual contact with major immigrant groups. Advocates of monolingualism have little science and scholarship on their side. The few educators and language experts on their side are willing to play havoc with the literature, distorting or lying about research results to support their political viewpoint. This makes objective, scholarly information all the more essential to the discussion.

This book therefore brings what linguists have learned about language acquisition to the issue of how the United States should deal with the language needs of its population. This information is written especially for the layperson. No expertise is needed to understand the concepts. Second-language learning is a common human process, and many of the readers have probably gone through it themselves. Hopefully, they will see their own experiences or the experiences of people they know reflected in the discussion of linguistic research.

A linguistic perspective on the place of languages in American society must intersect with the perspective of other disciplines. Learning a language does not take place in a vacuum. It happens to a particular group of people, in a particular community, at a particular place in time. This book does something that has not been done before. It draws together linguistic, socio-logical, and historical information for a multifaceted view of what language diversity means and what place it has in American society.

THE GENESIS OF THE BOOK

Writers come to their subjects from various routes, some professional and some personal. In the case of this book, I am naturally influenced both by my professional and by my personal lives.

I am a professor of English at Hostos Community College of the City University of New York, in the heavily Hispanic neighborhood of the South Bronx. I am therefore intimately familiar with the obstacles that immigrants face in learning English and adjusting to American life. The competing demands of work, family, and study among adult immigrants are enor-mous, and the determination with which many face these demands is truly admirable. Above and beyond these pressures are a fierce attachment to their native language and culture and an unavoidable physical and psycho-logical separation from mainstream American life, making the acquisition of English and an understanding of American culture even more difficult.

Most Americans do not realize the enormity of the task of changing one's life so completely; if they did, there might be greater compassion for immigrants in society in general and in the halls of state and federal capitols.

But my involvement with this issue – and perhaps my choice of profession – has a strong link to my personal history as well. I am a daughter of multilingual immigrants. Growing up in a small northern city of Italy, my parents learned Italian in school; Yiddish was their home language, and Hebrew the language of prayer. Being routed from Italy as young adults, they picked up other languages along the way. My mother's family lived in Palestine during the Second World War, and my mother became proficient in modern Hebrew. My father came to the United States to join the military; his stay in army camps in the South was his introduction to English. After the war, my parents settled in New York, where my father began an export business, making good use of his knowledge of languages.

I was constantly exposed to different languages during childhood. I did not acquire bilingualism naturally, but the sounds of Italian from my parents' conversations became very familiar, and I could eke out some expressions in Yiddish when conversing with my grandmother and other relatives of her generation. Throughout the 1950s and 60s, members of our family trickled in to the United States, staying with us for the months it took to adjust themselves and filling the house with the sounds of different languages. Business clients from Europe and Latin America often came to visit. When I started studying Spanish in school, I was fortunate to be able to practice the language with dinner guests; both my parents had acquired Spanish as well.

Looking back, I am amazed at my parents' self-taught linguistic proficiency. My father could converse and write word-perfect business letters in several languages. My mother finished the Sunday *New York Times* crossword puzzle every week and was a champion Scrabble player. We even had a Spanish-language Scrabble set. From my parents I learned the joy of reading and playing with words. I also acquired an appreciation of different languages, and of the people who speak them.

Having been the beneficiary of such a rich linguistic upbringing, I can only react to the wave of language restrictionism that has washed over the United States with the greatest dismay. It is difficult to imagine why society would deny children this kind of experience, if it can be so easily and naturally offered to them. When I first heard of a particular piece of legislation proposing that English be the preferred language of Americans, and calling on government to encourage its use among citizens, I could not help thinking how my parents would have reacted. I imagined someone coming to our house and informing them that they should speak only English; I then imagined my mother politely but firmly showing this individual to the door. If this happened to me today, I know I would do the same.

THE PLAN OF THE BOOK

This book proceeds in a logical manner, with each chapter offering information that prepares the reader for the chapter to come. Chapter 1 begins with some basic concepts about the nature of language and the role it plays in identifying people and connecting them to each other. As symbols of nationality, languages have often been targeted for attack as a means of repressing people with low status. This explains the present language-restrictionist movement in the United States. The premises of this movement are presented and challenged.

A major theme of the language-restrictionist movement is the loss of what is known as the melting-pot tradition. In this vision of the nation, newcomers of every stripe willingly jump into a great cauldron; what emerges from this brew is a new kind of American, one who reflects some of the features of all the residents in the country. Chapter 2 shows this tradition to be an illusion. The melting-pot view of America is compared to other paradigms of immigrant adaptation; we discuss the place of all these paradigms in American history. A review of the history of immigrant languages reveals that Americans have always expected immigrants to replace whatever traits make them different with characteristics that make them appear more "American." Rather than becoming part of a prototype American, many immigrant characteristics, including language, have become extinct largely through coercion. The chapter also challenges two premises of the language-restrictionist movement: that language loss is inevitable and desirable, and that present-day immigrants resist the acquisition of English.

If this last premise is false, and immigrants truly do want to learn English, why is it so difficult, and why does it take so long for them to learn it? Most Americans are not experts in second-language learning; indeed, few of them acquire high-level proficiency in a second language. Chapter 3 dispels a number of myths about learning a second language, showing that the process is more complex and time-consuming than most people realize, and offering information about bilingual learning that they may not know.

With this basic knowledge of how language is learned, the reader will be ready to investigate the types of language education available to children in the United States. Chapter 4 analyzes instructional approaches for minority-language children learning English, for English-dominant children learning second languages, and for children of both groups learning both of their native languages together. This analysis includes assessments of these programs in the press, which reveal a clear double standard regarding language education in America: bilingualism for English-dominant children is valued, while bilingualism for minority-language children is discouraged.

The attitudes toward minority languages in American education are mirrored in the attitudes toward these languages in the larger society.

Chapter 5 delves into the modern language-restrictionist movement. A brief review of American language policy puts the present surge of language repression into historical perspective. The chapter then describes the social, political, and economic factors that have provided the optimal conditions for this resurgence. This is followed by an analysis of US English, the organization that has led the movement, and the present state and federal language-restrictionist legislation.

Chapter 6 describes the forces working against language restrictionism. This includes the official bilingualism of two states, resistance to official English in Puerto Rico, and the work of language-pluralist advocates across the nation. The only successful legal challenge to a state official-English law is described. The long tradition of workplace bilingualism is an additional challenge to language restrictionism. Two legal cases asserting the right of minority-language employees to speak a language other than English at work are discussed; their contrasting outcomes reveal the ambiguities of the law with regard to such claims.

Ambiguity is an apt description of what Americans feel about multilingualism. The language-restrictionist movement puts this ambiguity to good use by arguing that multilingualism is divisive. Proponents of the movement contend that the social and political problems of linguistically diverse nations are due to this diversity. Chapter 7 shows that language diversity in itself is not a cause of civil unrest. Rather, the imposition of a single official language and the repression of minority languages are indications of a class system that favors some people and disadvantages others. Several examples demonstrate this to be the case: official multilingualism in Canada and Switzerland, the revival of regional languages in Western Europe, and the struggle to perpetuate minority languages in India.

Chapter 8 brings the book to conclusion by asking one of the fundamental questions that the United States faces: how can a pluralistic, multilingual population live in mutual respect and harmony? This chapter imagines a society in which people cross racial and ethnic boundaries to come together around common interests. A necessary component of this society would be the fostering of universal bilingualism, so that people could connect with and learn from those who are different from them. The benefits of universal bilingualism would reach every level of the community, from individuals to the nation as a whole.

SOME NOTES ABOUT TERMINOLOGY

When I first came up with the title for this book, I struggled over using the word "America." I was acutely aware of the political implications of referring to the United States by this term; certainly, there is more to America than the United States. But using "the United States" for the title didn't seem to work; "America" has a sense of poetry that the other term lacks. It is also the term closely associated with the immigrant experience; Roger Daniels titled his history of immigration *Coming to America*. Seeing that Daniels and other authors use "America" in their titles when referring to the United States, I decided to use it as well.

The same problem occurred during the writing of the book. "The United States" is an awkward adjective, so I opted for "American" as an adjective and "Americans" when referring to citizens of the United States. On this matter, I rely on the indulgence of residents of other nations on the American continents.

I also had to search for a way of identifying Americans whose native language is English. "Native-English-speaking Americans" was rather awkward. Other writers have used "European-American" and "Anglo-American" to refer to this category of Americans. I find these terms too exclusionary. I decided instead to use the terms "mainstream Americans" and "established Americans." These terms are a bit exclusionary also; there are Americans outside the mainstream and the establishment who are native speakers of English. But these terms come the closest to representing this category of Americans.

A note is in order about the terms "immigrants" and "language minorities." When I use the word "immigrants," I refer to those immigrants whose native language is not English; there are of course immigrants who are English-dominant. The immigrants to whom I refer are part of a larger group known as "language minorities." Language minorities include American-born people whose first language is not English. The children of immigrants who speak a language other than English may belong to this group, if their parents' language is used predominantly at home. Also included are Native Americans and Mexican Americans whose home and community languages are not English. Issues of language diversity and language restriction affect all of these people in the same way.

Choosing terms for ethno-racial groups has also been problematic. There has been some discussion about the appropriateness of using the terms "Latino" and "Hispanic." It is argued that Americans and immigrants with roots in the Spanish-speaking Caribbean and in Central and South America have little connection to either Latin or to Spain, from which "Hispanic" is derived. However, there is no satisfactory alternative to these terms; I use them both. Also, two designations are often used to refer to people of African origin: "black" was the preferred term in the 1960s; now, "African American" is popular as well. Both terms are used here.

CHAPTER 1

Language and Identity

INTRODUCTION

In the first part of this chapter, some basic linguistic concepts regarding the nature of language are presented, along with examples. Language is viewed as a shaper of personal and cultural identity. Language and accents may also be the means by which one group of people culturally stereotypes another, whether the two groups speak different languages or speak variations of the same language. Language is then viewed in its role of connecting individuals to each other. As people move through their day and through their lives, changing the style of their language or changing from one language to another is a natural way to express their relationships to the people with whom they interact. Finally, language is viewed in relation to other characteristics that define individuals. Languages and accents are changeable; physical and racial traits are usually not. This is an important concept when considering the situation of immigrants who relocate to a country with a language different from their own. Acquiring proficiency in the new language may not alter the way they are seen and treated by the larger society.

The second part of the chapter applies the above concepts to a larger context: the relative status of cultures throughout the world. As a result of world history, some nations and the cultures that predominate in them have acquired greater power and prestige than others. As a consequence, the languages identified with them also acquire relative status. The discussion then focuses on the situation of non-English speakers in the United States. The low status of many of these groups derives from the low status of their countries of origin and is reflected in the low status conferred on the languages they speak. The history of the United States is marked by periods of repression of immigrant and minority languages. The most recent evidence of this repression is the current official-English movement.

Examination of the rhetoric of this movement reveals its basis in anti-bilingualism, anti-bilingual education, and a melting-pot ideology. The concerns underlying the movement are legitimate: issues of national unity, equality of opportunity, and integration. However, it is argued here that the repression of non-English languages does little to resolve the problems that have fostered these concerns.

LANGUAGE AND PERSONAL IDENTITY

It is not surprising that our native language is often referred to as our "mother tongue," a term that recalls our earliest memories and influences. The term itself has different meanings. The sociolinguist Tove Skutnabb-Kangas (1981) hypothesizes five definitions of "mother tongue" depending on who is defining it. For the sociologist, mother tongue is the language one learns first. For the linguist, it is the language one knows best. For the sociolinguist, it is the language one uses the most. For the social psychologist, it is the language one identifies with and through which one is identified. For the lay person, it is "the language one counts in, thinks in, dreams in, writes a diary in, writes poetry in" (Skutnabb-Kangas, 1981: 18).

For most Americans, there is only one language that fits all of these definitions. But a large part of the world's population makes use of two or more languages during a lifetime. Many people grow up bilingual, perhaps because their parents are native speakers of two different languages, or because the language of their family and community differs from the regional or national language. Many others come into contact with a second or third language as a result of migration to another country. In these cases, defining one's "mother tongue" becomes more complicated. The immigrant, in particular, is often faced with a situation in which the new language begins to supplant the native one. Outside one's home and community, the new language is usually required. But in the most private of thought processes, such as the ones described in Skutnabb-Kangas' (1981) last definition, the speaker must choose between two languages. This dilemma is most acute for immigrant children, whose formative experiences are taking place in a language and culture different from the ones they have previously experienced. This is illustrated in the autobiography of the writer Eva Hoffman, who emigrated from Poland to Vancouver, Canada, at the age of 13:

> As I lie down in a strange bed in a strange house – my mother is a sort of housekeeper here, to the aging Jewish man who has taken us in in return for her services – I wait for the spontaneous flow of inner language which used to be my night-time talk with myself, my way of informing the ego where the id had been. Nothing comes. Polish, in a short time, has atrophied, shriveled from sheer uselessness. Its words

don't apply to my new experiences; they're not coeval with any of the objects, or faces, or the very air I breathe in the daytime. In English, words have not penetrated to those layers of my psyche from which a private conversation could proceed. (Hoffman, 1989: 107)

On her birthday, Hoffman is given a typical gift for a teenage girl, a diary. But this creates a dilemma for the young lady caught between two languages:

If I am indeed to write something entirely for myself, in what language do I write? Several times, I open the diary and close it again. I can't decide. Writing in Polish at this point would be a little like resorting to Latin or ancient Greek – an eccentric thing to do in a diary, in which you're supposed to set down your most immediate experiences and unpremeditated thoughts in the most unmediated language. Polish is becoming a dead language, the language of the untranslatable past. But writing for nobody's eyes in English? That's like doing a school exercise, or performing in front of yourself, a slightly perverse act of self-voyeurism.

Because I have to choose something, I finally choose English. If I'm to write about the present, I have to write in the language of the present, even if it' s not the language of the self. As a result, the diary becomes surely one of the more impersonal exercises of that sort produced by an adolescent girl. (Hoffman, 1989: 120–121)

This experience is not limited to immigrants. A similar dilemma faced Richard Rodriguez, a writer and lecturer of Mexican origin who grew up in a largely non-Hispanic neighborhood of Sacramento, California. He and his siblings were the only Spanish-speakers in their Catholic school. Concerned about his initial reluctance to speak English, his teachers convinced his parents to substitute their mother tongue with English when conversing with their children. The effect on Rodriguez was poignant, and echoes Hoffman's sense of loss: "The special feeling of closeness at home was diminished by then. Gone was the desperate, urgent, intense feeling of being at home; rare was the experience of feeling myself individualized by family intimates. We remained a loving family, but one greatly changed" (Rodriguez, 1982: 22–23). As Rodriguez became more proficient in English, his feeling of separation from his parents grew. Spanish was forbidden at home, but English could not replace it:

The old Spanish words (those tender accents of sound) I had used earlier – *mamá* and *papá* – I couldn't use anymore. They would have been too painful reminders of how much had changed in my life. On the other hand, the words I heard neighborhood kids call their parents seemed equally unsatisfactory. *Mother* and *Father, Ma, Papa, Pa, Dad, Pop* (how I hated the all-American sound of that last word especially) – all these terms I felt were unsuitable, not really terms of address for *my* parents. (Rodriguez, 1982: 24)

Indeed, the *mother* tongue – the language children use with those closest to them – has a deep significance for them. It is the seed of identity that blossoms as children grow. When Hoffman moved to Vancouver and learned a new language, that seed, Polish, was ignored; no one encouraged her to nurture it, to find ways of expressing her new experiences in her most intimate language. In Rodriguez's case, Spanish, the seed of his identity as a family member, was considered an impediment to his intellectual growth and his acceptance into the larger society. The pain that this caused in both cases is apparent. It is also unnecessary. In a society that accepts and nurtures pluralism, there is room for two languages; minority-language children can learn the new language required for their public identity while developing the language that defines them personally. If both languages are allowed to develop to their fullest, both may serve private and public functions.

LANGUAGE AND CULTURAL IDENTITY

Skutnabb-Kangas' social psychological definition of mother tongue brings out the importance of language as part of one's cultural identity. The mother tongue is

> the language through which in the process of socialization one has acquired the norms and value systems of one's own group. The language passes on the cultural tradition of the group and thereby gives the individual an identity which ties her to the in-group, and at the same time sets her apart from other possible groups of reference.... Since this socialization process to a large extent occurs with the aid of language, language itself comes to constitute a symbolic representation of the group. (Skutnabb-Kangas, 1981: 15)

Fellow sociolinguist Joshua Fishman echoes these sentiments: "Almost all of the languages of the world have also come to stand for the particular ethnic collectivities that speak them, for the ethnocultures that traditionally utilize them and, where we are dealing with official languages of nations or regions, for the polities that implement them" (Fishman, 1991: 23).

That the norms and values of a culture are expressed through language becomes apparent to anyone who undertakes the task of learning a second language: this person quickly learns that word-by-word translation from one language to the other just doesn't work. The Portuguese word *saudade* is loosely translated as *melancholy,* but this word fails to capture the quality of *angst* (another word difficult to translate into English) that so typifies the Luzo–Brazilian persona. When the English-dominant author Louise Erdrich began studying Ojibwemowin, the Native American language last used in her family by her maternal grandfather, she learned that objects are designated as either animate or inanimate. As a result, she was forced to see the physical world in a new way: "Once I began to think of stones as animate, I started to wonder whether I was picking up a stone or it was putting itself into my hand ... I can't write about a stone without considering it in Ojibwe and acknowledging that the Anishinabe universe began with a conversation between stones" (Erdrich, 2000: E2).

Kristof (1991) gives a sampling of ways in which the Chinese culture is revealed through language. Chinese has two dozen expressions for *wife*, all of which connote women's various subservient roles in society; until the early part of the century, it was common for peasant women to be referred to by kinship terms instead of by given names. There are two ways of saying *we*, depending on whether the person addressed is being included. The words for *freedom*, *politics*, *democracy*, and *economy* are only a century old; *individualism* and *privacy* are also recent additions, although they still have a negative connotation. Thus, not only does language reflect culture, the changes it undergoes reflect the sometimes slow and painful course of change in the culture itself.

The difficulty of making connections between two languages, of bringing sense and meaning to strange new sounds, is brought to life in this passage by Eva Hoffman:

> There are some turns of phrase to which I develop strange allergies. "You're welcome," for example, strikes me as a gaucherie, and I can hardly bring myself to say it – I suppose because it implies that there's something to be thanked for, which in Polish would be impolite. The very places where language is at its most conventional, where it should be most taken for granted, are the places where I feel the prick of artifice.... The words I learn now don't stand for things in the same unquestioned way they did in my native tongue. "River" in Polish was a vital sound, energized with the essence of riverhood, of my rivers, of my being immersed in rivers. "River" in English is cold – a word without an aura. It has no accumulated associations for me, and it does not give off the radiating haze of connotation. It does not evoke. (Hoffman, 1989: 106)

LANGUAGE AND CULTURAL STEREOTYPING

As both Skutnabb-Kangas (1981) and Fishman (1991) point out, language not only gives people a way of identifying with their cultures, but also constitutes a means by which they identify people and cultures different from their own. Hearing a language other than one's native language can trigger a set of thoughts and impressions associated with the culture to which it gives voice. Likewise, hearing one's native language spoken with a regional accent different from one's own, or hearing one's native language spoken in a variety associated with a particular sub-culture, can trigger thoughts and feelings about the people who speak that way. Language is therefore a means by which cultural stereotypes are transmitted. We will explore these two aspects of language and cultural stereotyping: people's reactions to foreign languages and foreign accents, and Americans' reactions to variations of English.

Cultural Stereotyping by Language Group

No one is immune to the phenomenon of stereotyping by language group. For many Americans, the sound of French conjures up a romantic, sophisticated Parisian scene: young lovers, sidewalk cafes, art galleries. The Russian language may trigger negative thoughts: repression, gloom, uniformity. The images of foreign cultures and minority cultures prevalent in any country are distorted by the mass media, which influences perceptions through pervasive stereotyping.

Much linguistic research has been conducted into the effect of both foreign language and foreign accent. Researchers use the *matched guise* technique, in which subjects listen to taped voices reading a text in two different languages or with two different accents, without being told that the same person has recorded both versions. The subjects then rate the speaker of each reading on a variety of personal characteristics. Consistently, the studies show that choice of language or accent, being the only variable factor, greatly affects the subjects' evaluations. In a Canadian study, Lambert *et al.* (1960) found that both English- and French-speaking college students from Montreal rated the speakers using English more favorably than those using French. In an Israeli study, Lambert *et al.* (1965), the ratings given by Arab and Jewish teenagers listening to bilingual speakers reflected the antagonistic relationship between the two populations: each language group gave low marks to speakers of the other language on a range of personality traits. In a study of American-accented French, Ensz (1982) found that errors in pronunciation, vocabulary and grammar typical of Americans learning French negatively affected the attitudes of French listeners toward the speakers' competence, personal integrity, and social attractiveness. These studies indicate the powerful effect of language and accent on the way people judge each other.

In the United States, animosity toward Spanish-speakers is widespread; its roots can be traced to the country's imperialist relationship with Puerto Rico and the absorption of part of Mexico into the southern region of the nation. Many Americans view Spanish-speakers as second-class citizens, and the Spanish language itself has suffered negative stereotyping as a result. A 1995 custody battle exemplifies this (Gross, 1995; Verhovek, 1995). An English-dominant father requesting visitation rights with his five-year-old daughter complained that she knew very little English because her Spanish-dominant mother spoke to her mainly in Spanish. Texas judge Samuel Kiser agreed with the father, labeling the use of Spanish a form of child abuse. According to Kiser, speaking Spanish would retard the girl's educational progress when she started school, and would relegate her to life as a maid. He threatened the mother with loss of custody if she did not speak English to her child.

The story appeared in a local newspaper and was picked up by the national media, producing enraged responses from numerous organizations and individuals and, obviously, causing Kiser some embarrassment. While he let the order stand, he retracted the use of the word "abuse" to describe the mother's use of Spanish and apologized to those in the housekeeping profession. Sadly, he did not see fit to apologize to Spanish-speaking Americans. In failing to do so, he missed the opportunity to erase some of the stain that has unfairly fallen on the language and the people for whom it is a mother tongue.

Cultural Stereotyping Within English

The symbolic nature of language not only explains attitudes toward foreign languages, but can just as easily be applied to attitudes toward different forms of a particular language. In the United States, the way English is spoken by those with prestige and power is referred to as *standard English*, while variations spoken by groups at the lower end of the socioeconomic scale are called *non-standard*. Traditionally, non-standard forms of English were referred to as *dialects*; however, linguists prefer to call different forms of a language *varieties*, avoiding the stigma attached to the word *dialect*.

Perhaps the most well-known non-standard variety of English in America is Black English, now popularly called African American Vernacular English (AAVE). There are several misconceptions about this variety. Both terms suggest that it is a variety used exclusively among African Americans. However, not all African Americans speak it, and many who are not African Americans are conversant in it. Many speakers of AAVE speak standard English as well; they are bidialectical, and can move back and forth from one to the other as the situation warrants.

To many speakers of standard English, AAVE sounds like a corruption of the standard, English spoken in a lazy or uneducated way. However, a significant body of research exists which links the features of AAVE to those of English-based Caribbean creoles (Edwards, 1991). A creole is the more developed, second-generation version of a pidgin, a language created when speakers of mutually unintelligible languages come into contact.

The importation of African slaves to English- and French-speaking Caribbean islands created just such a situation.

Studies of this variety (Wolfram, 1969; Labov, 1972; Fasold, 1972) show that it follows its own rules and has its own logic, however different the rules and logic may be from standard English. For instance, AAVE follows the rule of the double negative (*I don't have nothing*) which appears in other languages. There are different meanings attached to the uninflected verb be (*He be sick*) and the inflected verb be (*He is sick*): the uninflected form indicates a permanent state, while the inflected verb indicates a temporary condition, a distinction which also differentiates the Spanish verbs *ser* and *estar*. AAVE is a valid and expressive means of communication used among people belonging to a subculture of America, one that has had a significant influence on the larger culture, especially in the music world. However, because AAVE is identified with this subculture, it is a variety that is stigmatized by the larger society.

This stigmatizaton became particularly evident in a California city in December, 1996. The Oakland School Board faced a contentious problem: a large population of African American children entered school speaking a variety of English that was difficult for their teachers to understand. As a result, the schools were unable to give these children an adequate education, and they persistently got poor scores on standardized tests. Based on a report and recommendations by its African-American Task Force on the Language Stature of African-American Speech, the Board passed the Resolution on Ebonics (a new term for Black English that combines the words *ebony* and *linguistics*), calling for training in Ebonics for teachers, and its use in classroom instruction. The resolution pointed out that, just as bilingual programs are tailored to children whose first languages are not English, African American children deserve programs tailored to their own needs (*Black Scholar*, 1997). The idea proposed by the resolution was not new. Rickford and Rickford (1995) explain that the development of AAVE reading texts began in the 1970s, and the classroom use of AAVE showed promise in helping students bridge the gap between the children's variety of English and standard English. However, this instructional method was stopped by the negative reactions of parents and teachers, who feared that the non-standard variety would only be reinforced and that the learning of standard English would be stymied.

A large part of the linguistic community supported the resolution. Labov (1997) explains that plans like Oakland's have largely been misunderstood; people believe that the goal of the program is to teach children to speak AAVE, rather than helping them make the transition from AAVE to standard English. Most current instructional methods are based on the viewpoint that recognition of the non-standard English as a legitimate means of expression will confuse students and reinforce their use of it; as Labov

(1997) points out, these methods have been unsuccessful. More promising is the concept that children learn reading and writing in their own language quite rapidly, and can benefit from doing so in motivation and achievement. On this basis, Labov (1997) believes the Oakland resolution is on the right track and deserves a chance.

Adger (1997) challenges the idea that AAVE is "bad" or "malformed" English. Rather, she explains, it is a system with certain features that differ from the features of other varieties of English. The critics of the Oakland resolution ignore what educators know: that students' implicit knowledge of their own dialect can be used to contrast its features to those of the standard. Teachers' knowledge of the structure of AAVE allows them to draw on students' linguistic proficiency in the process of teaching the standard. In addition, when educators call students' speech "slang" in order to convince them not to use it, the opposite may actually happen, since the attack hits the students' sense of identity and social solidarity as well as the language. Programs like Oakland's also have the potential for improving language education for all students: "In a diverse society, permitting dialect myths to persist contributes not only to language ignorance but to social factionalism" (Adger, 1997: 1).

The Linguistic Society of America concurred with Oakland in its own resolution, stating that "the Oakland School Board's decision to recognize the vernacular of African American students in teaching them Standard English is linguistically and pedagogically sound" (Linguistic Society of America, 1997: 1). Perry and Delpit (1998) point out that children's confidence is affected when they are made to feel ashamed of their home language and, implicitly, their parents and community. They also point to the advantage of knowing two linguistic codes.

Despite the educational support for the resolution, it touched on a sensitive nerve for many, especially for middle class African Americans. Hutchinson (1997) is disturbed by the impression given in the resolution that Ebonics is the primary language of all blacks, noting that there is as much variation in the speech of blacks as there is in the speech of other ethnic groups. He insists that Ebonics is represented only by some young people who mispronounce words, misplace verb tenses, or code switch with each other. To Hutchinson, the Oakland plan merely reinforces negative stereotypes about blacks: that they are chronic educational failures, that they are mentally inferior to whites, or social misfits needing special help to learn. Black students have excelled in the past, he insists, not as a result of special programs, but as a result of having dedicated teachers who were determined to see them do well and who held them to the same standards and accountability as whites.

In the end, however, the program does appear to be successful. At the Prescott School in Oakland, after three years of Ebonics training for teachers and the use of Ebonics in the classroom, scores improved significantly on the California Test of Basic Skills (*The Post-Standard*, 1998). As we will see, the arguments for and against the Oakland plan sound very similar to those heard in the debate over bilingual education. This is not surprising, considering the other similarities in the cases: both involve children of low socioeconomic status and with a culture and language different from those of the mainstream. Both groups of children face similar challenges in school, and the programs that show promise in helping them succeed academically, in part by making use of the children's languages, are viewed with suspicion.

Although we have been discussing standard English as if it were a monolithic entity, the concept of one standard English – used by all people of power across the country – is a myth. A single standard English exists only in theory, in the pages of English grammar textbooks. In actuality, various factors influence the way people of wealth and status express themselves. Perhaps, at some time in the past, when status could be acquired only through the inheritance of "old money," many of those in positions of power could be identified by a particular variety of English. The same does not hold true today. Professional athletes, for example, are praised for their achievements and admired for their wealth and power; many, however, are not exemplars of standard English.

All of this does not prevent people from having subjective reactions to certain varieties of English. For people who grow up in immigrant neighborhoods and, through education and job advancement, move into the larger society, the realization that others judge them by the way they speak can be painful. Some make the effort to adapt, to fit in. The following passage was written by Anne Marie, a New York student in a graduate-school sociolinguistics class. It is taken from the journal in which she was required to apply what she was learning in the class to her own life. Here, Anne Marie reflects on the role that her Bronx accent has played in her life:

> It was only after graduating from high school and traveling to Manhattan to attend Katherine Gibbs Business School that I began to realize more clearly differences in speech. I noticed that students from New Jersey, Long Island, Brooklyn and Manhattan did not all necessarily sound the same, and that from the way I spoke they had an image of me. I heard things like, "You sound tough when you speak." ... By the time I reached the business world, I realized that the way a person spoke could limit their opportunities because there were stereotypes associated with sounding as though you were from "the Bronx," "Brooklyn," or "Connecticut." I began to be more conscious of the way I spoke so that I would not be perceived as "low class," "uneducated" or "tough," which were the Bronx stereotypes I was aware of.

In time, however, Anne Marie started to resent the pressures on her to alter her speech in order to improve her standing in the business world. As she matured, affirming her pride in her background and being her true self began to take precedence over accommodating others:

> Over the past 10 years I have become much more comfortable with who I am and how I sound. I am proud of my Bronx heritage and see it as an aspect of who I am the same way that my French heritage is a part of who I am.... What I've noticed is that although it's true that through being myself I may turn some people "off," those people and their attitudes would probably be turned "off" by me at some time anyway. The reason being that my Bronx heritage is not only for me a way of talking but really a part of who I am, so that if the way I talk doesn't do it – something about the way I act will probably alienate that person.

The difficulty of separating who we are from how we sound is evident once again in this example. Society persists in sending messages about how to respond to different varieties of English. American young people pick up these messages readily, as has been illustrated in a number of matched-guise experiments. Arthur *et al.* (1974) asked Anglo-American college students to evaluate the voices of Mexican Americans using varieties of English ranging from the local standard to Chicano English. The subjects gave the voices using Chicano English the most negative ratings on scales related to success, ability, and social awareness. In Ryan and Carranza (1975), Mexican American, black, and Anglo adolescent females listened to standard English and Mexican American-accented English. All the subjects rated the standard-English speakers more favorably, although the accented speakers were rated higher when the passage read referred to a home context rather than a school context. Sadly, these studies show the effect of cultural stereotyping on both majority- and minority-group members.

These messages are also sufficiently strong to be picked up by new-comers to the language. Two studies by Eisenstein (1982, 1986) investigated the reactions of adult learners of English as a second language from a wide socioeconomic range to three varieties of English: standard, New York non-standard, and Black English. She found that learners at all levels of proficiency were able to distinguish among these varieties, and that those who had acquired a high degree of proficiency had also adopted the same attitudes and stereotypes toward these varieties as those of native speakers. Eisenstein and Verdi (1985) found that when intermediate-level, working-class learners of English listened to the three different varieties of English, they reported having the most difficulty understanding Black English, even though they had had considerable contact with speakers of Black English. When asked to make judgments regarding the friendliness, appearance, and job status of speakers of each of these varieties, the learners demonstrated attitudes very similar to those of native speakers, rating the standard-English speakers the highest and the speakers of Black English the lowest. It appears that these students had learned a lesson outside their language class: how to judge people by the features of their speech.

LANGUAGE AND MAKING CONNECTIONS

The above discussion shows us how language is used to separate people, by serving as a symbol of a set of features that distinguishes one group from another. By the same token, language is also used to unite people, by symbolizing the common bonds that hold groups together. In modern society, individuals generally belong to a number of groups: we may work with one group, play with another, worship with a third, share a cultural heritage with a fourth. One of the ways we express our membership in these various groups and our relative status to others in the group is through language. Moving from one group to another, our language changes to express these multiple allegiances. We can make these various connections in two ways: by moving from one variety of a language to another variety, or by moving from one language to another language. We will discuss these two means of making connections through language as they relate, respectively, to native speakers of English and to immigrant and US-born minority-language speakers.

Making Connections Through Variation Within a Language

Linguists have two terms to refer to individual variations in speech. *Register* refers to the type of language used in a particular context (a courtroom, synagogue, or laboratory) by the people functioning in that context (judges and lawyers, rabbis, or scientists). We expect the language used in a courtroom to be different from language used in a science lab. *Style* is defined as a situational variation of language. Speaking in front of a large audience in a formal setting requires a different style than that of speaking to an intimate group of friends. Style and register influence how we speak and determine the set of rules we follow concerning what is appropriate and inappropriate speech in given situations. These rules are also guided by the *status distance* and the *social distance* between the speakers.

How does this work for most of us on a typical workday? On waking up, we go through our daily morning routines while engaging in conversations with partners and children. These are people we are intimate with; we may express ourselves in only a few words at a time, supplementing talk with gestures and actions like kissing, hugging, and waving goodbye. We get to work and greet our co-workers, whom we see every day, in a familiar manner but without the physical expressiveness we show our family members. The level of familiarity expressed is conditioned by our relative status. We may call our secretary "George," but George may respond by using a title: "Professor Garcia" or "Ms Chin." We sit down at our desks to work. Making and receiving phone calls, we may use a formal or familiar manner depending on the intimacy and relative status of our relationship with the party on the other end of the line. Our speech may also switch to the register of our particular profession. If the boss calls us in to her or his office, we may straighten our tie or dress and switch to more formal speech. After work, our activities may call for a reserved tone if we need to visit a child' s teacher, or a more comfortable, casual tone if we meet friends for a drink. Finally, back home, we switch to our most intimate style as we greet our family members once again.

In all social situations, specific groups of people settle on a shared way of talking and behaving. Teenagers in particular find satisfaction in indulging in a language specific to their peer group. Each generation of adolescents creates a style of speech that is difficult for outsiders to understand. This style offers teenagers a sense of individuality, filling a need adolescents have to grow away from their parents and to grow into their adult selves. They realize, however, that the distinctive style that they use with friends is inappropriate in other situations – in the classroom or with their families. When only one person involved in a conversation is capable of using a particular style, communication breaks down.

The style of speech we adopt may also be determined by our desire to be a member of a group from which we are excluded. A ground-breaking sociolinguistic study of the speech styles of Lower East Side New Yorkers was conducted by William Labov (1966). One of his findings was that, among the nine social classes identified there, lower-middle-class women were the most likely to adopt elements of speech associated with higher-class speakers when engaged in formal communication, even resorting to hypercorrection in order to approximate this speech style. Labov noted that men in the same class were more likely to value the tough talk associated with blue-collar occupations, a kind of talk identified with masculinity and physical strength. Finding similar evidence in a study in Norwich, England, Peter Trudgill (1972) suggested that the reason for this difference was that women, lacking occupations with which to identify themselves, relied on the way they presented themselves in public for self-esteem and a sense of value. They tended to model their behavior on what they believed to be the norms of a better-situated class.

Today, this explanation may still apply. Although most American women work outside the home, only a small percentage work in high-status, high-paying jobs. The privileges enjoyed by men based on their gender are still a fact of life, and women may still feel more of a need than men to present themselves in a socially-acceptable manner. Even among men of relatively high status, the "rough" language of blue-collar speakers is considered suitable in certain situations, particularly in all-male conversations focused on personal bonding. Public revelations of private conversations among people in power exemplify how coarse means of expression typify the speech of even the highest government officials in the nation (who are still predominantly male). Using this type of speech appears to give them a sense of shared identification and intimacy that they find satisfying. Of course, these speakers change their way of address in more formal situations, when they are being judged by the public.

Making Connections by Moving From One Language to Another

Just as monolinguals change style and register within their language, people who are bilingual or multilingual switch languages according to the situations they are in and the people they encounter. Americans who trace their history in this country within the last two or three generations often see this situation reflected in their own families. First-generation immigrants gain some proficiency in English, but many rely heavily on their native language. Family members who come here as children or who are the first to be born here often become bilingual, and the third generation is often monolingual in English. Thus, within one family, the language of communication may shift depending on the configuration of people present at any one time. Where family members live plays a role in the language used; those residing in ethnic neighborhoods maintain the first language when interacting with friends in the community. Choice of occupation is also an important factor. Those working in a family-run store, or who are employed within the ethnic enclave, may use the native language. Those who move into the mainstream workforce outside the neighborhood adapt to the demands of that situation and communicate in English. The younger generation's choice of social contacts also affects its language of communication. As with style-shifting English speakers, the desire to establish bonds of solidarity and be accepted by different groups of people determines language choice at any given moment.

There are different degrees of second-language proficiency that a person may achieve. A bilingual person may have a high proficiency in her native language, but proficiency in the second language may not be exactly native-like. Linguists refer to the ideal of native-like competence in two languages as *balanced bilingualism*. Those who approximate this ideal have a distinct advantage in life. They benefit professionally by having control over the registers of their occupations in two languages. They also have control of the various speech styles in both languages. They can therefore identify and act appropriately with a range of people in a variety of settings. As we will see in a later chapter, people who have a high level of literacy in their native language are more likely to achieve a high degree of proficiency in a second language, and are therefore more likely to acquire balanced bilingualism.

Immigrants to America who come from the upper classes of their countries and have had a good educational background often become balanced bilinguals and enjoy the benefits that come with it.

THE RELATIVE IMPORTANCE OF LANGUAGE AS A MEANS OF CULTURAL IDENTIFICATION

We have been considering the roles that language plays in how individuals identify themselves and how others identify them. However, the importance of the latter role of language should not be overstated. Language is only one trait among many that society uses to assign people to different cultural groups. It is also not indelible or unchangeable. A non-native English-speaker may learn English proficiently, and, if she begins to learn it early enough, may even speak it without a trace of foreignness. But other, permanent traits – physical and racial features – may still identify her as belonging to a culture different from the prototypical American (read "European"). Thus, while many Americans stress the importance of immigrants and language minorities acquiring English (which most do not contest), they fail to admit to the reality that learning English will not offer instant entrée into American society.

Students whose native language is not English are certainly not the only children who do poorly in American schools. The key factor is not the language of the children, but the quality of the schools they attend and the type of neighborhoods they live in, which reflect the position of these children and their families in the socioeconomic hierarchy of American life. For example, many African American children who are native speakers of English live in inner-city neighborhoods and attend poorly-funded schools that disregard the cultural values and ways of learning that they bring with them from home. Many of these children are likely to receive little benefit from their education. The same can be said for children of Hispanic origin who grow up with English as their native language. Jim Cummins points out that many of these children perform as poorly in American public schools as their Spanish-dominant peers do. According to Cummins (1987), this suggests that "status and power relations between majority and minority groups constitute the source of minority students' under-achievement, with linguistic and other factors playing an important, but secondary or intervening, role." School failure occurs among minority groups "who have experienced persistent racism and who have been denied opportunities to validate their cultural and linguistic traditions" (Cummins, 1987: 31) both at school and in the larger society.

The implementation of bilingual education for language minorities is considered one means of balancing this power relationship. Substantial research evidence points to the benefits of extensive use of the first language in the schooling of minority-language children (e.g. Cummins, 1979; 1983; Willig, 1985; Ramirez *et al.*, 1991). However, native-language instruction has lost significant ground in public education. Through three decades of re-authorizations of federal bilingual education law, native-language instruction has invariably been de-emphasized while alternate pedagogical approaches have received increasing support. Current law stresses the rapid teaching of English and makes no reference to the enhancement of native-language skills as a valued goal. Several states have even passed laws mandating the mainstreaming of English-language learners after a one-year English immersion program.

In many states, the most common bilingual program is short-term or "quick-exit," which is considered by many language-education experts to be the weakest variety. According to Cummins, these "quick-exit" programs have been shown to be much less effective in producing high academic achievement than programs aimed at biliteracy and biculturality. Since quick-exit programs "do not require any personal or institutional role redefinitions on the part of educators," the result is that "institutionalized racism ... is preserved even more effectively because there is the appearance of change to meet 'the needs' of language-minority students" (Cummins, 1987: 33).

Despite the shortcomings of this type of program, it appeals to many Americans, including many educators, because it taps into a widespread belief about the way that immigrants should adapt to life in the United States. Lily Wong Fillmore explains:

> As a people we have a hard time tolerating differences among us. Immigrants are expected to adopt American ways as soon as they can, with as little resistance as possible. The expectation is that newcomers will learn and use English immediately. There has never been much recognition of the fact that it takes people, even children, time to learn a language, or that some cannot learn it well despite their best efforts. For most Americans, to suggest that immigrant children should learn initially through their native language, rather than be made to bite the linguistic bullet and start learning exclusively in English, seems tantamount to saying they don't have to learn English at all. (Wong Fillmore, 1992: 369–370)

American society is largely defined by the existence of a racially-determined class system, one that has little to do with native language. At various times in our history, Americans have been forced to come face to face with this system; a look at one of these times, as described by Chan (1991), illustrates the minor role that language really plays. In June of 1982, a 27-year-old Chinese American named Vincent Chin, out for a drink with some friends, was confronted by two European American men in a Detroit bar. The two men were auto workers; one of them had been laid off. They picked a fight with Chin and his friends because they thought they were Japanese, and harbored the notion that Japan was responsible for the depressed state of the industry in which they worked. Following Chin out of the bar, they pursued him and beat him to death with a baseball bat. Although both men admitted to the murders, a local trial and two civil-rights trials resulted in their acquittal; neither man spent a day in jail for their crime, to the horror and dismay of the country's Asian-American community and many others.

That Chin was an English-speaking American citizen was not significant to the men who accosted him. Race, and not language or nationality, was the means by which they identified him. This incident illustrates how easily racial fears are touched off in America, how ready people are to identify an individual as a symbol of an entire ethnic group, how ignorant Americans can be in making this identification, and how tragic the consequences can be.

It would therefore benefit Americans to question the common belief that acquiring English is the only key to acceptance for immigrants in America. This type of thinking illustrates the denial that Americans indulge in in order to avoid their own responsibility in the erection of barriers that shut minorities out of mainstream society. If learning English were the only necessity for enjoying the good life of America, the onus would fall solely on minority-language groups. But the reality is that the ingrained intolerance of the country poses a much more formidable obstruction.

LANGUAGE AND THE RELATIVE STATUS OF CULTURES

As we have seen above, language helps to shape an individual's personal identity, and is one way in which a person may be categorized as belonging to a culture. From an objective viewpoint, no culture or language can be said to be more or less valuable than another. However, as a consequence of world history, cultures have acquired statuses relative to one another: cultures that have enjoyed wealth and power are preferred over those that are poor and powerless. The languages identified with these cultures are valued relatively by the same measuring stick.

The fact that today English is the pre-eminent international language is therefore not accidental. The rise of Great Britain as a colonial power established English as a language of import across the globe. The subsequent domination of the United States in politics and technology further insured its status. There are approximately 300 million native speakers of English; at least as many native speakers of other languages use English as an additional language. About forty countries use English in an official capacity, and many nations require that their children learn it as a second or foreign language (Wolfson, 1989). In most countries, social and economic advancement are in large part dependent on one's proficiency in English.

Americans grow up speaking the language of power around the world. Learning a second language is sometimes required of them by an educational institution; many Americans take two or three semesters of a foreign language in high school or college. But most will probably have no use for what they have learned once the courses are over; learning that second language is seldom a necessity for their future plans. Consequently, it is easy for Americans to take for granted the power of the language that they learn naturally. Americans traveling to any corner of the world can find people able to communicate with them in English. Many have come to expect all the comforts of home no matter where they are: not only people who speak English, but restaurants that serve American food and hotels that offer the amenities of American life. Indeed, this often leads foreigners to label Americans as insensitive to the languages and cultures of other nations. The image of the "ugly American" persists.

It is therefore not difficult to see why many Americans have little compassion for the plight of immigrants to their shores. They have difficulty understanding why these new arrivals can't learn English, why they cling to their native cultures and ways. This lack of compassion derives in part from the fact that most Americans have had no experience that compares with the American immigrant experience. Most have never had to go to school, practice their professions, or even carry out the daily tasks of life in a language not their own. Most Americans have no means of connecting to what immigrants feel and experience while adapting to American life.

Some Americans do move to other countries. But the circumstances are usually different. They are often motivated by a new job, a promotion, an opportunity to advance their careers. This hardly compares with the motives behind most immigration to the United States: political or religious persecution and economic hardship. Consequently, when Americans emigrate abroad, they usually carry with them the status and power of being American.

Consider, for example, the American colony that was home to the builders and operators of the Panama Canal for much of the twentieth century. The colony, located in the Panama Canal Zone, had its own stores, schools, country club, restaurants; indeed, it operated like a piece of the United States within a foreign country. Generations of American children grew up in the colony as if they were stateside. There was no need for learning the language of Panama; an interviewer was told by one long-time resident about a restaurant "with its wide timber verandas, wicker chairs and a bar where heads might turn at the sound of a conversation in Spanish." Recalled another resident: "I knew one fellow who only left the zone on his way to the airport. And he was here for 30 years" (Borrell, 1987: 8–9). Because of their status in Panama, because they were employed and protected by the United States government, these Americans were never obligated to assume the language and culture of their adopted country. Instead, the locals who wanted to profit from the presence of the Americans, and acquire jobs within the enclave, had to learn English. During preparations for the 1999 transfer of operations to the Panamanian Government, the colony began closing down, and its residents started returning to the United States. There was much nostalgia among the Americans for the privileged life that they were losing, a life that contrasted sharply with that of many native Panamanians.

Not all Americans living abroad work for their government and benefit from the perquisites that this status insures. But being an American carries with it an aura of prestige in many parts of the world, no matter who one's employer is. The American culture that émigrés take with them is often envied and emulated in their adopted countries. They are not expected to abandon their language and culture, but usually find ways to keep in touch with both, by sharing them with the natives of their adopted countries and by bonding with other émigré Americans.

THE STATUS OF NON-NATIVE ENGLISH SPEAKERS IN THE UNITED STATES

Historically, most immigrants to America have enjoyed none of the perquisites described above. They have come from countries plagued by political and economic strife, conditions to which the United States has sometimes contributed. Like Americans resettled in other countries, immigrants to the United States have tried to maintain their languages and cultures as a way of maintaining their identities. Unlike American émigrés, because of who they are and where they come from, their languages and cultures have been the targets of derision and scorn. The same situation has held true for minority groups who are native to the United States but speak a non-English language; relegated to marginal status, largely the result of government policies, their languages and cultures are devalued. At moments in United States history in which economic and/or political insecurity plagues the nation, immigrants and American-born minority-language speakers serve as targets for the fear and anger felt by English-speaking Americans. Allowing non-English languages to flourish appears to jeopardize the status quo of the dominance of English and those who speak it. Several examples of attempts to suppress minority languages follow.

Cherokee Bilingualism

According to Wolfson (1989), the predominant policy of the United States in the early part of its history was to eradicate all traces of Native American cultures and languages. However, the Cherokee, originally from the eastern United States, managed to create a written form of their language. In the early nineteenth century, after being forcibly resettled in Oklahoma, the Cherokee established a system of bilingual education that resulted in high levels of literacy in both Cherokee and English. In fact, the Cherokee had a higher literacy rate in English than the English-speaking populations of neighboring Texas and Arkansas.

However, this highly effective educational system was dismantled when the Federal Government insisted that Native American children be placed in all-English boarding schools away from their reservations. In these schools, any expression of Cherokee language or culture was met with punishment. One reason for this policy was that Native American languages were considered crude and illogical, and thought to be detrimental to cognitive development. Bilingualism was also considered an impediment to intellectual growth, and eradicating the Cherokee language and culture was considered essential to the assimilation of the Cherokee into mainstream American life. As a result of this policy, the literacy rate of the Cherokee plummeted, and they remained marginalized members of society.

German Immigration

As Kloss (1977) documents, Germans represent one of the largest and most influential immigrant groups in United States history. Their presence was particularly significant in Pennsylvania and Ohio, which attracted Germans from the seventeenth century onwards. In Pennsylvania's New Sweden colony, the languages of business and government were German, Swedish, and Dutch. Vital German-language pockets in Ohio appeared in the 1770s. After the War of Independence, German became a major means of governmental communication. In Pennsylvania, laws and constitutional convention proceedings were published in German editions. In 1824, the state began requiring certain legal notices to be published in both English and German newspapers; in 1915, these provisions were extended to Italian and Yiddish. German translators were employed by the legislature and other branches of government. Similarly in Ohio, the state legislature approved the printing of laws of a general nature in German in 1817; the printing of school law in German was approved in 1829. While German never acquired the status that it had in Pennsylvania, where German and English newspapers were on an equal footing as means of communicating governmental information, Ohio did require some legal notices to be published in German newspapers. As in Pennsylvania, this provision was eventually extended to Polish and Czech newspapers, to a lesser degree.

German also flourished as a language of instruction. In both states, German-language schools began as private institutions affiliated with churches. In Pennsylvania, an 1837 state law permitted German-language and bilingual English/German public schools. German Americans also established private higher-education institutions and theological seminaries that functioned in German. In Ohio, public schools offered instruction in English, German and both languages. Germans in other parts of the country also influenced public school systems. The first public schools in Texas are thought to have been the German municipal schools of New Braunfels. An 1867 Colorado law directed school districts with at least 25 German children to establish bilingual schools.

However, public tolerance for the German language began to wane in the latter part of the nineteenth century. Laws passed in Illinois and Wisconsin required that most subject matter be taught in English in both private and public schools, largely as a result of a movement that considered the German language and the Lutheran religion to be alien. These laws were soon repealed, but by this time instruction in English had come to dominate public school systems anyway.

In 1917, with the country's entry into World War I, anti-German sentiment reached its peak. Once Germany became identified as the enemy, its language was also marked as such. The National Council of Defense, established in 1916, directed subordinate councils in states, cities, and counties throughout the country to urge Americans to abandon the private and public use of German. Some cities passed laws suppressing the use of the language. A number of states prohibited instruction in German in both private and public schools. By the end of the war, some measures against the use of German were extended to other languages. However, in 1923 the Supreme Court ruled that states could not criminally punish residents for teaching languages other than English in the schools.

The Present Official-English Movement and the Case of Monterey Park

The most current effort to restrict non-English languages was born in the early 1980s. The movement gained its momentum from the increasing presence of non-European immigrants in the country, whose distinct appearance, languages and cultures stood out against those of "white" Americans. It was at this time that Senator S.I. Hayakawa of California introduced an amendment to the United States Constitution that would for the first time in American history declare English as the country's official language. The effort failed, but Hayakawa joined forces with Dr John H. Tanton, an ophthalmologist from Michigan, to form US English, a national organization dedicated to lobbying for federal and state official-English laws. These laws would prohibit bilingual ballots and voting material, restrict government funding of bilingual education to short-term transitional programs, and curtail the use of languages other than English in both the government and private sectors. Today, the battle continues with language-restrictionist legislation introduced in states around the country.

One of the most telling cases in the present revival of language restrictionism is that of Monterey Park, California. As Crawford (1992) explains, for many years Monterey Park had a predominantly white population; in 1985 it was designated by *USA Today* as an "all-American city." By that time, however, Monterey Park had already seen its character change drastically. In the 1970s, investors from Taiwan and Hong Kong took advantage of a depressed real estate market and the exodus of white residents to begin buying up property and establishing businesses in the city. By the mid-1980s, 50% of the residents were Chinese. Alarmed by the rising Asian power and influence, and disturbed by the proliferation of commercial signs in Chinese, some of the remaining white residents were moved to act. In 1985, the city council adopted a proposal making English the official language. Although one council member was convinced to change his vote, voiding the resolution, the language war continued.

One battle in this war was joined several years later, when the city council voted down the allocation of funds for the purchase of Chinese-language books. Explaining the vote, Councilman Barry Hatch said, "People from other parts of the country should not be faced with volumes of foreign books they cannot read when they come to our city library." When Councilwoman Judy Chu successfully engineered the donation of 1,000 Chinese-language books from the Lions Club International in Taiwan, there was further disagreement about where to house the books. Hatch proposed adding an annex to the library, arguing, "I think our library should house mainly English books. There is definite educational values [*sic*] to these donated books, but the contributors will probably not stop here" (Siao, 1988).

What was at the root of this attack on the Chinese language and the surge in support for English? It had nothing to do with the inherent value of Chinese, which Hatch readily conceded. Rather, Hatch and others saw the encroaching Chinese language as symbolic of the encroaching presence of Asian foreigners in a city that was once predominantly white. Chinese-language books seemed to be taking over the public library in the same way as the Chinese residents appeared to be taking over the city. Hatch's wariness toward the book contributors is telling: they've taken over the library; what will they do next? The spreading influence of the Chinese language not only defined the growing power of the new residents but also highlighted the waning power of the older residents.

However, this power was not absolute. During the seventies and eighties, the entrepreneurial Chinese elite in Monterey Park pushed for policies that encouraged development in the city – development from which this group profited, along with other, white, land developers. Opposition to these policies became a rallying cry for non-Chinese and older, less affluent Chinese residents. Councilwoman Judy Chu advocated for slow growth and general cooperation among all ethnic groups – Chinese, white, and Hispanic. With support from a multi-ethnic coalition, she won re-election in 1992 over a candidate supported by the conservative, nationalistic, and ethnocentric Chinese-voting bloc. Fong (1994) explains that, while the Chinese became a dominant demographic, economic, social, and cultural force in Monterey Park, as evidenced by the strong presence of the Chinese language, they never gained political dominance. Besides the fact that the Chinese elite could not rally all Chinese residents in support of development, the Chinese population of the city was highly mobile, and most of the Chinese were not citizens. Fong explains that, from 1988 to 1992, "the community slowly but surely turned away from the politics of division and isolation, symbolized by Barry Hatch, and came to recognize calls for ethnic unity as a cover for the class interests of a pro-growth faction" (Fong, 1994: 155). It is important, then, not to over-represent the importance of language and ethnicity in the story of this complex, diversely-populated American city. Those who tried to accumulate political support on the basis of language and ethnicity – either by calling on the Chinese to unite against non-Chinese, or by calling on non-Chinese to unite against the presence of the Chinese language – ultimately failed.

The Legacy of Xenophobia Through Generations of Immigrants: A New York Story

A phenomenon that has been widely documented throughout history is the complex reactions of older immigrants toward newer ones. Many Americans feel uncomfortable with their own immigrant roots. Fishman believes that "ethnicity is still so uncomfortable and guilt-laden an area" (Fishman, 1966: 387) for the middle class. This rings true for me. I used to teach a graduate course in sociolinguistics at a suburban New York college. Among the largely middle-class students there were often several second- and third-generation European Jews. Responding to our textbook's section on the demise of Yiddish in America, several of these students reported feeling sad or guilty about their lack of knowledge of their parents' or grandparents' language. Although there was usually little practical need in their lives for knowing Yiddish, feelings of connection to the language as part of their heritage were still evident.

Despite these feelings of guilt, according to Fishman (1966), many second- and third-generation Americans "are likely to have been 'liberated' (intellectually and overtly, if not emotionally) from the claims and constraints of many primordial ties and biases." Some even commit themselves to "assisting various population groups to gain liberation from constraints that impede their full participation in higher levels of sociocultural life" (Fishman, 1966: 372). In other words, having given up – with varying degrees of reluctance and guilt – evidence of their own ethnicity, Americans may become convinced that each new immigrant group is obligated to do the same. Any overt manifestations of the ethnicity of these new immigrants – such as hearing them speak their language to each other, or seeing advertisements in the language displayed in store windows – is likely to bring up complex emotions. In the case of older, European, immigrants confronting evidence of the languages of more recent, non-European, immigrants, the predominant emotion generated may be hostility.

An incident in my own life serves as an example of this type of hostility. During the period of European immigration, the Manhattan neighborhood I live in, Yorkville, was largely populated by Germans, Hungarians, and Irish. Despite the extensive commercial turnover and the increase in new high-rise apartment buildings over the last few decades, signs of this immigrant past are still evident in local stores and churches, and in the languages and accents one hears on the streets. Once, at a holiday party organized by the local block association, I struck up a conversation with an elderly Irish woman who had lived her entire life in the same apartment building. When she asked me what I did for a living, I told her that I taught English as a second language in the Bronx, and that my students were mostly Hispanic. This led her to recount something that had happened to her that had obviously sparked her ire. She was waiting for a subway train and was standing next to two young women conversing in Spanish. One of the women suspended the conversation, turned to the Irish woman, and asked a question about the train in English. The woman responded, the young woman thanked her, and then turned back to her companion to resume their conversation in Spanish. The Irish woman was horrified, she told me. The young woman had demonstrated that she was able to speak English, yet chose to speak Spanish instead. According to the Irish woman, the young Hispanic woman had committed a dire social sin in making this choice.

Given the sociopolitical context of the narrator's life, her reaction is not very surprising. Those who have gone through the immigrant experience and are relatively established Americans often resent the presence of newer immigrants, in this case, immigrants who not only speak a language unintelligible to the older immigrants but who are racially distinct. However, from an objective viewpoint, her anger seems irrational. It is possible that the other young woman didn't know English, and that Spanish was the only language they could communicate in. But even if they were both bilingual, the language they chose to converse in was a purely private decision, and had nothing to do with anyone else who might be within earshot. That two speakers opt to converse in the language that represents the powerful ties that bind them to their culture and to each other is not unusual. It is a phenomenon that the Irish woman must have observed often in her own neighborhood, although in languages other than Spanish.

However, it is clear that the Irish woman was not reacting at all rationally, and would probably have been unmoved by any logical arguments. Whatever combination of factors accounted for her reaction, it was apparently a very potent one. It is probably safe to say that reactions like hers occur more frequently than not in the large urban areas that have become home to new immigrants.

THE PREMISES OF THE MOVEMENT AGAINST NON-ENGLISH LANGUAGES AND RESPONSES TO THEM

The Monterey Park and New York incidents mentioned above and the sentiments they underscore are representative of a strong current of opinion against the proliferation of non-English languages. Central to this movement is the sense that immigrants today are resisting the English language and clinging unnecessarily to their own languages. Bilingualism is considered an evil and a detriment to acceptance into mainstream American life. Immigrant languages are also thought to pose a serious threat to English as the dominant language of the country and to the unity of the nation.

Underneath the rhetoric of this movement lie several legitimate concerns about the well-being of the United States. As a country based on the principles of democracy, the United States has always struggled to balance individual freedoms, such as the right to speak as one wishes, with the need for national unity and identity. In this section, after the premises of the movement are explained, the concerns on which they are based will be explored and responses will be offered. We will see that, while these concerns are legitimate, attempting to resolve them by restricting language freedom fails to solve the underlying problems. In subsequent chapters, each of these issues will be discussed in greater depth.

The Arguments Against Bilingual Education and Bilingualism

US English has been extremely vocal in its opposition to bilingual education. A major argument it has advanced is that previous immigrants to this country were not educated bilingually and were able to learn English without native-language instruction. Gerda Bikales, for example, a one-time director of the organization, recalls her own experience in a New York high school after fleeing Germany. Except for a few encouraging teachers, she received no extra attention, and graduated in 19 months. Many others like her, she claims, are offended by long-term bilingual education and "don't see what the big fuss is" (Keyser, 1986: 52) in acquiring English.

The position of the organization is that bilingual education impedes the learning of English. In 1989, at a time when the state of New York was considering strengthening its bilingual programs, the organization paid for a full-page newspaper advertisement urging opposition to the plan. Above a photograph of a man washing dirty dishes, the ad read, "If some NY educators get their way, this is the kind of future many of our children will face." Underneath the photograph, the ad proclaimed that "English is the key to opportunity. A young person who cannot communicate effectively in English faces a bleak future." It also warned that bilingual education "will handicap, not help, children with a limited knowledge of English" (*The New York Times*, 1989: A7).

Opposition to bilingualism comes from the academic sector as well. Arthur Schlesinger, Jr, a noted historian, contends that bilingualism "shuts doors. It nourishes self-ghettoization, and ghettoization nourishes racial antagonism.... Using some language other than English dooms people to second-class citizenship in American society" (Schlesinger, 1992: 108). Aaron Wildavsky, a professor of political science and public policy, refers to bilingualism as one of the "perennial problems of our time, sure to cause consternation and heartburn" and "symptomatic of a number of elemental conflicts ... that constitute running sores in American public life" (Wildavsky, 1992: 310–311). Wildavsky proposes to solve the "problem" of bilingualism by substituting bilingual education with a universal second-language requirement in elementary school.

Bilingualism and bilingual education pose the possibility of immigrant and minority-language children developing their native languages while they acquire English. This is considered a breach in the obligation of non-English-speaking people to replace their own language and culture with the language and culture of America. A US English membership letter, signed by the British journalist Alistair Cook, quotes Theodore Roosevelt: "Begging the country to stop talking about German-Americans and Italian-Americans and Polish-Americans, he said: 'We have room for but one language here, and that is the English language, for we intend to see that the crucible turns people out as Americans.... No more hyphenated Americans'" (Cook, undated).

The Response

Antagonism toward bilingual education stems from the legitimate concern that children in bilingual programs do not learn English, one of the essential skills needed for success in America. This is indeed what much of the public thinks; major newspapers often print articles on the worst bilingual programs, reinforcing the belief that money is being thrown away "coddling" children in their own language instead of making them confront the need to acquire English quickly and thoroughly. However, if many bilingual programs fail, it may not be because they are bilingual, but rather because they are targeted for minority populations that are looked down on and expected to fail anyway.

Lily Wong Fillmore, who has followed the development of public bilingual education in the United States since its inception, describes the educational system that is responsible for instituting bilingual programs as one that holds the common belief that "people who don't look or act or think in the way Americans do – and most of all, who don't talk the way Americans talk – are suspect." She explains further: "A close examination of bilingual education where it has performed poorly will often show the extent to which it has been sabotaged from within by people who were supposed to make it work" (Wong Fillmore, 1992: 369–370). Such sabotage includes doing as little as possible, staffing programs with the wrong people, not allowing teachers to function bilingually, testing students in English, failing to recruit prospective bilingual teachers from local communities, and pitting bilingual teachers against other faculty members.

Traditionally, there have been two types of bilingual programs in the United States: *transitional*, in which the first language is phased out and replaced with English in a short period of time, and *maintenance*, in which the first language continues to be developed and to be used as a means of instruction while English is phased in and increased gradually. The first model has been the most common type instituted in the public schools. Ironically, however, only the second type is truly bilingual. While the goal of transitional programs is monolingualism in English, the goal of maintenance programs is bilingualism: high levels of literacy in both the native language and English. And, also ironically, the second type has proved to be more successful. Research shows that students who are allowed to develop literacy in their own languages do better than those who have less opportunity to develop their first languages (San Diego City Schools, 1982; Ramirez *et al.*, 1991; Thomas & Collier, 1995). The specter of sabotage rears its head once again.

The experiences of individual immigrants are a poor basis on which to rest the education of large numbers of minority-language children. If Bikales learned English as quickly and effortlessly as she says she did, the circumstances of her life need to be measured against those of present-day language minorities. Having come from Europe, she may have enjoyed the advantages of a rigorous education in her own language; she also admits to being trilingual upon arrival in this country. In contrast, many minority-language children today have little or no native-language literacy and a poor educational background. Just because previous generations of immigrants did not have the advantages of bilingual education does not mean that present-day minority-language speakers should be deprived of it. Indeed, previous immigrant generations did not survive very long in public schools, often dropping out because of poor academic performance or family financial needs; as we shall see later, public education has a history of being unresponsive to the needs of children recently arrived in the United States.

The antagonism expressed toward bilingualism in general needs to be examined. We have previously discussed the advantages of bilingualism, the way that it broadens one's life by increasing the number of people within one's social and professional spheres. How can something as beneficial as bilingualism elicit the harsh judgments passed down by writers such as Schlesinger (1992) and Wildavsky (1992)? A crucial point in understanding these remarks is that they refer not to the literate, balanced bilingualism of the privileged, the kind that characterizes immigrants from the upper classes of their countries. Rather, both these authors are referring to the bilingualism of the growing population of non-English-speaking minorities, largely impoverished people of color.

Schlesinger's definition of bilingualism as a means of self-ghettoization and as a barrier to the enjoyment of first-class citizenship is very telling. It is obvious that he is in fact not referring to bilingualism but to mono-lingualism in a language other than English. Presumably, Schlesinger would be hard-pressed to defend this definition as it relates to those who are able to understand French films as well as English films, or to those who can converse freely with the natives of other countries when traveling. Instead, he refers specifically to the recent "flood of immigration from Spanish-speaking countries" (Schlesinger, 1992: 107–108). The class bias in Schlesinger's definition, and the double standard of bilingualism that it implies, are transparent.

Still, there is a reason why Schlesinger makes this error. It is the fear, shared by many in the United States, that the use and perpetuation of minority languages deters minority groups from acquiring English. For one thing, it is believed that, if non-English speakers can use their own languages, they will not see the need for learning English. For another, minority languages are viewed as taking up too much room; the native language and English must compete for the attention of the non-English speakers, and cannot coexist.

Neither of these premises has any validity. First, there is every indication that immigrants are as eager to learn English as they ever were; in every urban center, low-cost and free English classes fill up quickly and waiting lists are common. It is true that, in neighborhoods where a non-English language dominates, residents can get along without using English by going to minority-run stores and taking advantage of some government services offered in their language. But this is essential for the basic survival of the minority-language community, whose residents are heterogeneous in their command of English. This community may include residents who have mastered English, residents who are in the process of learning English, newly-arrived immigrants with no English; and those too isolated, infirm, elderly, or busy earning a living to enroll in an English class or find English-speakers to converse with. Access to native-language services has traditionally served as a stepping stone to full participation in American life, but has never been considered a substitute for acquiring English.

Second, the idea of languages competing with each other defies the very notion of bilingualism. There are certainly enough examples throughout the world of people who are functionally and happily bilingual. Again, concerns about bilingualism seem to be class- and race-specific. No one has challenged the right of natives of Russia living in the United States to maintain their mother language, nor has anyone considered their use of Russian a deterrence to their acquisition of English; indeed, in Brighton Beach, Brooklyn, more Russian is heard than English.

Like Schlesinger, Wildavsky focuses on the Spanish-speaking populations of this country. Hispanics, he claims, "blame 'the system' for the poor performance of Spanish-speaking children." Bilingual education is considered the best way "to break the existing system's stranglehold over education.... In short, disparity in performance is attributed to systematic bias, which is to be overcome by exerting an equally powerful discrimination from the other direction" (Wildavsky, 1992: 310). Wildavsky, however, insists that instruction in Spanish will only do more harm to the students, as it will prevent them from learning English. He proposes, instead, that the problem of bilingualism be "solved" with a universal second-language requirement in the elementary schools, a requirement that would supersede and abolish all forms of bilingual education.

There are many theoretical weaknesses in Wildavksy's argument (for a complete critique of Wildavsky, see Dicker, 1993). The most glaring is that he fails to acknowledge that the goals of good bilingual education and second-language education are actually the same: bilingualism. In fact, current pedagogical practices in teaching second languages largely fail to produce citizens with high proficiency in those languages; meanwhile, some forms of bilingual education have been successful in promoting high-level bilingualism and high-level academic achievement. However, second-language education is a more acceptable approach to bilingualism for many because, while bilingual education is targeted solely at language minorities, second-language education is aimed at the general student population. A language taught in a second-language course is a "foreign" language, spoken by people living in an exotic location far away; a language used in a bilingual program is a "minority" language, spoken by those living one neighborhood away from established Americans.

Bilingualism is an asset for the general population, but a debit for minorities. Once again, the double standard reveals itself.

Considering the value that society places on second-language learning, it is essentially illogical to insist that non-English speakers give up their own languages. According to Brod and Huber (1991–92), Spanish is still one of the most popular languages chosen by college students fulfilling requirements for a foreign-language course, although languages experiencing the greatest increase in popularity as subjects of study are Chinese, Japanese, Portuguese, and Russian. We have a precious resource for the learning of these languages in the populations for whom these languages are the mother tongue. But it will be necessary to get past the prejudices we have toward minority groups before we see their languages as assets rather than detriments.

The Need for Immigrant Sacrifice

Just as Bikales' personal history attempts to illustrate that bilingual education is unnecessary, the histories of other successful immigrants exemplify the apparent rewards that await those who give up their language and culture while plunging into English and the American way of life. De la Peña traces the rise to fame of one of America's most popular stars, Arnold Schwarzenegger. Schwarzenegger's decision to come to America was based on his desire to seek greater challenges than those offered by his home town in Austria, where his family life was "traditional, regimented, and devoid of high aspirations or expectation" (de la Peña, 1991: 44). Schwarzenegger's eventual triumphs in his adopted country could not have been realized "without a solid command of English and a strong drive to be accepted as an American" (de la Peña, 1991: 47). After a visit home, de la Peña recounts, Schwarzenegger knew that he would never again be an Austrian; "it had become painfully obvious to him that 'I had much more the American spirit'" (de la Peña, 1991: 45).

Another, lesser-known, immigrant described by de la Peña is Stephen Baker, who emigrated from Hungary in the 1940s and became successful as a writer of advertising copy and popular books. When Baker arrived in the United States, his goals were clear: "I never thought of myself as Hungarian. I was a man without a country, trying to make out. My entire ambition, my dream was to become completely Americanized" (de la Peña, 1991: 49). His dedication to all things American culminates in the near deification of his adopted language: "English is my second language, but my first love.... As I said in a recently published article on the subject, 'no doubt, English was invented in heaven. It must be the lingua franca of the angels'" (de la Peña, 1991: 125).

The Response

It is a fact of human psychology that people bond with those who are most like themselves in speech, dress, beliefs, and way of looking at the world. Those who are most like us are readily accepted into our sphere of social acquaintances; those who are different are looked on with suspicion and must prove their affinity to us in some way. If we can connect with these outsiders in one particular way – if we find a common bond in religion, profession, family life, or hobby – we are more likely to bring them into our circle. But outward indications of difference are obstacles that must be overcome.

For this reason, minorities in the United States have always faced and continue to face the pressure to conform to mainstream American life. This means giving up whatever it is about them that makes them appear to be outsiders. A potent example of this is the kind of fever that hits every corner of the nation in the month of December: the celebration of Christmas. Christmas is no longer the religious observation of Christians that it once was. Instead, it is an accepted part of American life. For several generations, people of Jewish ancestry have assumed the trappings of this celebration, putting up Christmas trees and exchanging gifts on December 25th the same as their Christian friends. And the pressure continues. In a recent news article, a non-Christian newcomer to the country explained that he has now incorporated the holiday into his family's life as a way of fitting in; after all, he said, Christmas is an American tradition.

De la Peña's (1991) depiction of the passage of Schwarzenegger and Baker into American life are further examples of the pressures brought to bear on immigrants. True, both these men have achieved what could be called the American dream: wealth, recognition, and acceptance (in Schwarzenegger's case, even adulation). In this particular telling of their stories, only by giving up what made them different and denying their roots were their successes possible. But this telling just doesn't ring true. Of course, learning English well was necessary for each of them – especially since one is an actor and the other a writer. But it is hard to accept the notion that English could not be learned while maintaining their own languages, and that an appreciation of American culture could not coexist with continuing admiration for their native cultures. Baker's purported need to make himself a *tabula rasa* in order to implant all things American onto his being is impossible to believe; one wonders how he gets along with his relatives and fellow Hungarians after supposedly giving up all claims to his birthright. And some time after de la Peña wrote this account of Schwarzenegger, the actor opened up a restaurant in California serving dishes from his native Austria; it was reported, as well, that customers can listen to language-learning tapes in the restrooms. It is a false and damaging image that these stories impart to their readers: this is the way to succeed in America; if you haven't "made it" as these two men have, your sacrifices have been insufficient and less than whole-hearted.

The Threat of Other Languages to English and National Unity

Immigrant languages are not only considered harmful to those who bring them to America, but also pose a threat to English as the dominant language and to the nation as a whole. Bikales warns that Hispanic leaders are responsible for a movement to "implant rival languages" (Keyser, 1986: 52) in the United States. She insists that "foreign languages are useful ... but they are foreign languages, not coequals. They don't have the same relevance or history, and they are not replacements for English" (Keyser, 1986: 53). Gary Imhoff, who has served as a consultant to official-English advocates, writes that linguistic and cultural pluralism "insists that the group and the preservation and development of the group's identity take precedence over both the unity of the nation and the identities of individuals" (Imhoff, 1990: 56). Hayakawa also warns of the threat to national unity. Ethnic chauvinism, he contends, "threatens a division perhaps more ominous in the long run than the division between blacks and whites. Blacks and whites have problems enough with each other, to be sure, but they quarrel with each other in one language" (Hayakawa, 1985: 98).

The Response

For English-speakers living in big American cities, it may seem at times as if foreign languages are taking over. Cities are the magnets for those seeking to better themselves. Large numbers of immigrants flock to these cities and settle in neighborhoods where their languages and cultures flourish. In these enclaves, English is the minority language. A monolingual English-speaker venturing through one of them may feel as if in a foreign land. Outside these enclaves, English may dominate, but other languages continue to be the means of communication among language minorities mingling with the larger society. Might one of these languages actually replace English?

This fear is unfounded. Throughout the United States' history as a nation of immigrants, English has always prevailed as the dominant language. As we shall see later, in most cases the transition from immigrant language to English is rapid and complete. While older immigrants may struggle to learn the language, their children acquire it fully, and in the process learn to denigrate and belittle their native languages. Non-English languages in fact have very little pull: bilingual programs and bilingual voting services, for example, reach only a tiny percentage of language-minority residents.

If the anti-minority-language forces have been so successful at stoking the embers of this fear into a blazing fire, they have done so by preying on American insecurities that go well beyond concerns for the English language. Fishman sees middle-class American support for this movement being engendered by "a wounded *amour propre*" (Fishman, 1988: 130). America's loss of world prestige and economic domination has bred

> attitudes [which] are all sublimations of the sense of being abused, of being taken advantage of, of being denied one's rightful place in the sun.... The Official English/English Only movement may largely represent the displacement of middle-class Anglo fears and anxieties from the more difficult if not intractable real causes of their fears and anxieties to mythical and simplistic and stereotyped scapegoats. (Fishman, 1988: 132)

The same sense of insecurity is taken advantage of in the argument that the perpetuation of minority languages threatens the unity of the nation. Throughout its history, the United States has sought, with varying degrees of success, to maintain its commitment to diversity, to offer its citizens the freedom to speak, believe and live as they choose. It has also legislated against discrimination based on the differences among people. But despite these democratic principles, inequities persist. Wealth is distributed in a wildly uneven manner; people of color face obstacles to socioeconomic security not encountered by those of European ancestry. It seems at times as if the United States is not one nation at all, but separate, unconnected nations: the poor, the working and middle classes, and the rich, with people of color over-represented at the lower end of the scale.

Where does the issue of language come in? The Imhoffs and Hayakawas try to convince us that allowing non-English languages to flourish will further weaken the ties that bind Americans together as a nation. But we have already seen that the dominance of English is not in danger. What these alarmists fail to acknowledge is that non-English languages survive alongside and not in place of English. If Americans supported bilingualism in its truest sense, they would have a nation in which every individual spoke a non-English language as well as, and not instead of, English. This would pose no impediment to communication among different groups, which would all have English as a common language. Bilingualism would also give the nation an advantage it doesn't enjoy today: it would enhance America's ability to deal with other nations, and both international trade and diplomacy would benefit.

Hayakawa's (1985) reference to the divisions between black and white in America is revealing. The reference is clearly being used as a scare tactic: we already have racial conflicts; do we need linguistic conflicts as well? But it also points to the fact that America's greatest internal problems have nothing to do with language differences. Blacks speak the same language as whites, yet are largely relegated to a lower socioeconomic status. The same is true for Hispanics. As we learned earlier from Cummins (1987), there is little difference between the academic performance of English-dominant and Spanish-dominant Hispanic students. The real problems that divide Americans are not as easily mended as the acquisition of a language; they go deep into the role that race and class play in the social structure of American society. The attempt to focus concerns on language differences is a technique for diverting attention away from the more intractable issues that need to be faced.

The Relationship of Pluralism to Integration

The maintenance of culture and language purportedly poses a serious danger to the welfare of minorities, and to the American social structure as a whole. According to Rosalie Pedalino Porter, an educator and one-time member of US English, "retaining ethnic boundaries inevitably reinforces existing inequality. Cultural pluralism in America is uncomfortably linked to ethnic inequalities and exclusion or alienation of certain groups" (Porter, 1990: 189). While acknowledging that the problems of minorities lie deeper than their visible features, and involve economic inequities and public policies, she maintains that diversity works against efforts to unify Americans of different backgrounds, calling cultural pluralism and integration "two quite opposed social goals" (Porter, 1990: 166). Her arguments are grounded in an unshakable belief in the melting pot. Writing that "groups on the margin of the country's economy have kept their ethnic distinctions because they have been isolated and excluded from the larger society" (Porter, 1990: 189–190), she implies that bringing all Americans into the mainstream will inevitably cause their differences to disappear.

The Response

An analysis of Porter's comments calls for an inquiry into the ways immigrants and minority groups come together with the larger society in which they live. Various models of this process exist; a deeper discussion follows in the next chapter. Generally, *assimilation* refers to the absorption of the smaller group into the larger one, the *host* or *core society*. This absorption is not necessarily total and complete; it occurs at various levels. The smaller group may adopt the cultural patterns of the larger group; this is called *acculturation*. The smaller group may move into the institutions of the larger group. The two groups may intermarry: a process called *amalgamation*. The smaller group may adopt the host society's sense of identity. Prejudicial attitudes and discriminatory behavior against the smaller group may disappear. Value and power conflicts may be eliminated.

For any particular minority group, not all of these processes may take place; indeed, few minority groups reach total assimilation into the host society. Additionally, most of these processes can take place without the elimination of ethnic distinctions to which Porter refers. Similar to assimilation, the exclusion and isolation of minority groups is not an absolute concept; exclusion and isolation occur in varying degrees. This brings into question Porter's contention that ethnic distinctions result from exclusion and isolation.

Would eliminating the isolation of ethnic groups, in the form of integration, eliminate ethnic distinctions? There is reason for doubt here. Integration in the United States is a governmentally-initiated effort to remedy the historic inequity in the treatment of different groups of people by bringing them into the same institutions. Thus, children from one school are moved into another; provisions are made so that certain groups may move into neighborhoods from which they have previously been excluded. The results of these initiatives have not been resoundingly successful. In integrated schools, children have often formed cliques based on race, ethnicity or nationality, while viewing those who are different with suspicion. Attempts to integrate neighborhoods have sometimes been met with the flight of the existing group as the new one moves in. Outside of these experiments, race and ethnicity are still controlling forces in the determination of where Americans live. A large federal study of housing discrimination reveals that, despite laws enacted in the 1980s to prevent such discrimination, landlords and real estate agencies still resort to subtle and underhanded maneuvers to steer minorities away from renting or buying houses in white-dominated neighborhoods (Leuck, 1991).

Clearly, something other than integration is necessary for the type of assimilation that results in the disappearance of ethnic differences. Mere contact is not sufficient, and directives from governmental authority may even be detrimental. For ethnic differences to be eliminated, it is necessary for members of the smaller group and the host society to intermarry on a large-scale basis. Amalgamation, then, is the variety of assimilation that most closely fits the metaphor of the "melting pot" for which Porter and others express enthusiastic support.

Whether or not one believes that the elimination of ethnic distinctions is desirable, the feasibility of this type of assimilation is doubtful. Individuals do intermarry across ethnic and racial lines; for instance, black Americans marry white Americans. However, the more common pattern is still intragroup marriage. A large-scale, nationwide "melting pot" would be impossible. It would require the intermarriage of all ethnic groups over an extended period of time, the end result of which would be a new breed of American: everyone would have the same bloodline, the combined ancestries of all the ethnic groups in the nation. The attraction of such a possibility is a powerful one. If everyone looked the same, there would be no basis for discrimination. The idea caught the imagination of *Time* magazine when, in the fall of 1993, it released a special issue on "The New Face of America: How Immigrants are Shaping the World's First Multicultural Society" – a chauvinistic conceit in itself. On the cover is a computer-generated head shot of a woman created by combining selected features of male and female models representing seven ethnicities. In the end, however, she looks surprisingly European, which says much about the ambivalence that most white Americans feel toward this egalitarian biological fantasy.

For most white Americans, the prospect of grandchildren of color is not desirable. Many non-whites likewise prefer intra-marriage to intermarriage. Furthermore, because of varying types and degrees of discrimination in different geographical locations, ethnic groups do not all come into contact with each other at equal rates and in an evenly-disbursed manner across the country. When two or more groups do come together, as in the experiments in integration mentioned above, they do not always form immediate and intimate bonds with each other. When intermarriage occurs, it does not occur in the same proportions for all ethnicities; the Chinese, for example, have very low rates of intermarriage. Nor does such intermarriage cancel out the legacy of discrimination. The children of such mixed marriages often face the same prejudices encountered by their parents, and often worse.

It is unlikely, then, that we will see in the United States the product of true amalgamation, the fruits of the melting-pot process touted by Porter (1990). Cultural pluralism is not at odds with integration; instead, in a truly democratic society, cultural pluralism coexists with integration. It is important for all people to have the same economic opportunities and to live in the neighborhoods of their choice. But to enjoy these opportunities equitably, people shouldn't have to look the same, participate in all the same cultural activities, or share monolingualism in English. True equity can only come about not when differences among people disappear, but when they don't matter. The failure to accept diversity, and not the existence of diversity itself, threatens national unity.

CONCLUSION

The power of language is difficult to deny. In this chapter, we have explored this power. We described the role of language in shaping personal and cultural identity, in defining how people see themselves, as well as how they are seen by others. Through language we connect to each other; consequently, we modify the way we communicate depending on the relationship we have with our conversation partners. However, factors other than language carry significant weight in how people are identified and treated. No matter how well a person speaks English, that person's physical and racial characteristics will affect his or her interactions with English-speaking society.

We then moved our discussion to a larger framework: the relative status of people from different cultures and the languages identified with those cultures. Because of the socioeconomic power that native speakers of English have all over the world, the English language itself has become a language of unrivaled power. In the United States, the hierarchy of language power is reflected in instances of the suppression of minority languages at times when the speakers of these languages appear to pose a threat to the status of the majority. The current official-English movement is just such an instance. In examining the premises of this movement, we concluded that, while the concerns raised (national unity, equality of opportunity, the adjustment of immigrants to American society) are crucial to a discussion of the future of the country, the repression of minority languages will do nothing to relieve the problems underlying these concerns.

Running throughout the rhetoric of the official-English movement is the premise that immigrants need to change, to conform to American ways, in order to be truly accepted and successful in their new country. Advocates for official-English contend that there is a long-established American tradition involved here, one that previous immigrants readily accepted but that present immigrants are resisting. The metaphor that embodies this tradition is that of the American "melting pot." However, the image of the melting pot does not in fact symbolize what Americans actually expect immigrants to do. Furthermore, in contrast to the rather hazy memory of those fondly recalling this alleged tradition, to the extent that immigrants of the past did conform to the expectations of American society, they did so not solely out of their own free will and desire, but also as a result of deliberate tactics of coercion and disparagement. It is these tactics that have constituted an American tradition, a tradition of which Americans need not feel very proud. In the next chapter, the myth of America as a melting pot is examined in greater detail

CHAPTER 2

The Melting-Pot Mythology

INTRODUCTION

The heterogeneous nature of the American population would seem to be obvious. One need only walk down a street in any large city to see and hear the diversity of people who make the United States their home. The image of the melting pot – a great cauldron in which differences among people fade away in the creation of a new type of being – has largely symbolized the American immigrant experience since Europeans first arrived. It has colored the way established Americans view newcomers, the expectations they have concerning immigrants' passage into American life, and their attitudes toward the languages immigrants bring with them.

This chapter traces the roots of this mythology and places it alongside other conceptions of immigrant adaptation: acculturation, assimilation, Anglo-conformity, and cultural pluralism. Viewing American history from this perspective, we find that a melting pot of people of European heritage did take place during colonial times, but that immigrants coming after this period were expected to follow the Anglo-conformity adaptation model. This expectation is contrasted with modern yearnings for a return to a melting-pot America that never actually occurred. We then turn to a brief history of the trajectory of immigrant languages and cultures from the age of exploration to the early twentieth century. The fate of most immigrant languages has been virtual extinction, and the factors responsible for this extinction are explored. First are the internal factors, having to do with the specific characteristics of the immigrant groups. Second are the external factors, the pressures exerted on immigrants from the larger society by the actions of three powerful institutions: the government, public education, and the mass media.

The premise on which American society has justified the actions of these institutions is that language loss is inevitable and desirable. This view, which is illustrated by some present-day writers, is challenged by the view of linguists who have studied the phenomenon of language loss. The premise is also challenged with the example of an immigrant language that has endured: Chinese. Another component of the melting-pot mythology is also disputed: that present-day immigrants fail to follow in the path of their antecedents by refusing to learn English. The desire to acquire English is in fact extremely strong. However, it is not synonymous with a desire for assimilation. Furthermore, while immigrants acknowledge the importance of acquiring some of the traits of mainstream America in order to reach their goals, most realize that the acquisition of these traits will not protect them from second-class citizenship.

THE MELTING POT AND OTHER THEORIES OF IMMIGRANT ADAPTATION

The image of America as a melting pot is imbedded in the nation's history. One early, famous reference came from Michael-Guillaume-Jean de Crevecoeur, an eighteenth-century Norman nobleman who arrived in America with the French army, toured the British colonies and settled in upstate New York. After extensive travels throughout the country, de Crevecoeur came to this definition of the American:

> He is an American who, leaving behind him all his ancient prejudices and manners, receives new ones from the new mode of life he has embraced, the new government he obeys, and the new rank he holds. He becomes an American by being received in the broad lap of our Alma Mater. Here individuals of all races are melted into a new race of men, whose labors and posterity will one day cause great changes in the world. (de Crevecoeur, 1904: 54–55)

However, the melting pot represents only one of several paradigms that have been used to explain and, at times, to attempt to influence immigrant adaptation in America. Two overriding paradigms are *acculturation* and *assimilation.*

According to Redfield, Linton, and Herskovits "acculturation comprehends those phenomena which result when groups of individuals having different cultures come into continuous first-hand contact with subsequent changes in the original culture patterns of either or both groups" (Redfield *et al.*, 1936: 149). Put more succinctly, "acculturation is the study of the cultural transmission process" (Herskovits, 1949: 523). The relative social prestige of the groups determines the direction of acculturation; in Linton's words, "Other things being equal, a group which recognizes its social inferiority will borrow more extensively from its superiors than the superiors will borrow from it" (Linton, 1940: 491–492).

An early, authoritative definition of assimilation is one by Park and Burgess: "Assimilation is a process of interpenetration and fusion in which persons and groups acquire the memories, sentiments, and attitudes of other persons or groups, and, by sharing their experience and history, are incorporated with them in a common cultural life" (Park & Burgess, 1921: 735). Park later modified this definition, explaining that an immigrant in America can be said to have gone through "social assimilation" when "he has acquired the language and the social ritual of the native community and can participate, without encountering prejudice, in the common life, economic and political.... He has shown that he can 'get on in the country'" (Park, in Seligman, 1930: 281).

From these definitions, it is apparent that assimilation describes a type of immigrant adaptation to the larger culture that is deeper and more extensive than that of acculturation. Those who study immigrant life in the United States differ somewhat in the ways that they see these two concepts in relation to each other; however, this essential difference holds.

Gordon (1964), for example, sees assimilation as a broad heading comprising different steps or subprocesses through which the immigrant group adapts to the core society, and which range from the more superficial to the more profound. These are:

(1) *behavioral* or *cultural assimilation* (or *acculturation*): change in cultural patterns;
(2) *structural assimilation*: entrance into the institutions of the core society and the establishment of close personal relations with its members;
(3) *marital assimilation* (or *amalgamation*): large-scale intermarriage;
(4) *identificational assimilation*: the acquisition of a sense of peoplehood based solely on the core society;
(5) *attitude receptional assimilation*: the absence of prejudice on the part of the core society;
(6) *behavioral receptional assimilation*: the absence of discrimination on the part of the core society;
(7) *civic assimilation*: the absence of value and power conflicts between the two groups.

According to Gordon, each of these stages may occur in varying degrees; not all may occur. He posits two abstract, "ideal" types of assimilation in which all the stages are complete. In one, the cultural, structural, and identificational subprocesses are completely one way, the immigrant group adapting to the core society in all these aspects; this is called "adaptation to the core society and culture" (Gordon, 1964: 75). In the second, cultural assimilation occurs in both directions, resulting in

a cultural blend ... which has melted down the cultures of the two groups in the same social container, as it were, and formed a new cultural product with standard consistency. This process, has, of course, also involved thorough social mixing ... and a large-scale process of intermarriage. The melting pot has melted the two groups into one, societally and culturally. (Gordon, 1964: 74)

In this way, assimilation taken to the extreme results in either the disappearance of the immigrant group into the core society or a truly mixed, new society resulting from a melting-pot process. Acculturation may or may not lead to some form of assimilation, but it is a necessary component of it.

Park's and Gordon's definitions do not completely converge. Park's definition of "social assimilation" embraces some of Gordon's stages (acculturation, attitude receptional assimilation and behavioral receptional assimilation), but makes no reference to others, such as marital and identificational assimilation. Other theorists offer further complications. For instance, Weinstock defines assimilation as "the *complete* loss of original ethnic identity in an individual or group of individuals leading to absorption into the dominant culture" (Weinstock, 1969: 4), while Gordon allows for the possibility of the blending of immigrant and dominant cultures into a new culture containing aspects of each. Still, there is significant agreement regarding the basic distinctions between acculturation and assimilation. Weinstock agrees with Gordon that "while assimilation is often the result of acculturation, the two phenomena are not the same" (Weinstock, 1969: 4). Gordon's categorization of acculturation as a type of assimilation parallels Rose's definition of "extrinsic assimilation": "taking on the superficial trappings of the dominant group – speech, dress, musical tastes – while remaining socially separate" (Rose, 1989: 109).

Another form of adaptation has been labeled *Anglo-conformity*. Abramson defines this as a path to assimilation in which "different ethnic groups would become a part of the English Protestants in culture, structure, and identity.... The dominant group, in this case, would not change but would be large enough to receive others into the ethnic background" (Abramson, in Thernstrom, 1980: 151). Because of the influence of the British Empire, Anglo-conformity is applicable to instances of assimilation in many parts of the world. In the United States, advocates of the Anglo-conformity process consider

the development of the American people, with the inevitable exclusion of blacks and Indians, as an assimilation to the ethnicity of the English, transplanted to America. The process would evolve over time, changing Anglo-Saxons and other Europeans and their descendants into what Winthrop Jordan terms "non-English Englishmen." (Abramson, in Thernstrom, 1980: 152)

Gordon describes the central assumption of Anglo-conformity to be "the desirability of maintaining English institutions (as modified by the American Revolution), the English language, and English-oriented cultural patterns as dominant and standard in American life" (Gordon, 1964: 88). He associates Anglo-conformity with behavioral assimilation or acculturation to the core culture, which in this case is Anglo-oriented. In the words of Greer, Anglo-conformity is "the belief on the part of 'Native Americans' that foreigners should give up their past cultural identity to take on the social and cultural habiliments of their new homeland" (Greer, 1972: 87).

A final theory of immigrant adaptation is *cultural pluralism*. The Harvard University philosopher Horace Kallen is credited with the classic statement of what a nation based on cultural pluralism would be:

> Its form would be that of a federal republic; its substance a democracy of nationalities, cooperating voluntarily and autonomously through common institutions in the enterprise of self-realization through the perfection of men according to their kind. The common language of the commonwealth, the language of its great tradition, would be English, but each nationality would have for its emotional and involuntary life its own peculiar dialect or speech, its own individual and inevitable esthetic and intellectual forms. The political and economic life of the commonwealth is a single unit and serves as the foundation and background for the realization of the distinctive individuality of each *natio* that composes it and of the pooling of these in a harmony above them all. (Kallen, 1924: 124)

THEORIES OF IMMIGRANT ADAPTATION AND UNITED STATES HISTORY

We can see that the idea of America as a "melting pot" competes with many other conceptions of what America is or should be. At this point, it is helpful to look back at American history to see which processes of adaptation were theoretically popular, and which actually occurred. As Gordon (1964) explains, from the colonial period through the nineteenth century, the theories of adaptation that predominated were those of Anglo-conformity and the melting pot.

Early colonizers of America were largely from Northern and Western Europe. While English Protestants dominated numerically, other Europeans, such as Germans, Scotch-Irish, Dutch, Swedish, and Swiss, were easily absorbed into the larger group. Since all of these settlers shared cultural and racial characteristics, issues of adaptation were not problematic. Intermarriage was common, and a form of melting pot took place, with English Protestant culture as the norm. Of course, this melting pot excluded Native Americans and blacks, who were not welcome to assimilate. This period of complacency continued through the War of Independence and the establishment of the new nation.

In the next century and a half, however, the make-up of the nation became more complex. Large numbers of immigrants from Ireland, Germany and Scandinavia arrived in the mid-nineteenth century. Native Americans were herded into reservations, the Civil War emancipated blacks, and Asians began arriving in the western part of the country. Then the late 1800s and early 1900s saw the massive arrival of Southern and Eastern Europeans.

There was significant doubt whether these new immigrants could be "melted" into the dominant society, and the concept of Anglo-conformity gained adherence. The theory attracted those who believed in notions of "Nordic" or "Aryan" superiority, as well as others who did not ascribe to such racist ideas. Even leaders such as Presidents Theodore Roosevelt and Woodrow Wilson, who believed that the newcomers could be absorbed into the new society and who held no racist notions, expressed the belief that the melting pot was complete, having been formed in the late 1700s, and that immigrants should be indoctrinated into the canons already established by earlier arrivals. Anglo-conformity reached its highest pitch during World War I and the so-called Americanization movement, which was, as Gordon describes, "a consciously articulated movement to strip the immigrant of his native culture and attachment and make him over into an American along Anglo-Saxon lines" (Gordon, 1964: 99). The excesses of this campaign ended by 1921, but elements of it appeared in materials written for public schools for many years. Anglo-conformist policies continued, aimed at blacks, Hispanics, and Jews.

If it can be said that a melting pot ever existed, then, it ended rather early in the nation's history. Gordon describes American society from his perspective in the middle of the twentieth century:

> A substantial proportion of the descendants of the non-English immigrants of colonial times and the first three-quarters of the nineteenth century (with the exception of the Irish Catholics and the German Jews) have by now been absorbed into the general white "sociological Protestant" sector of American life.... Rather than an impartial melting of the divergent cultural patterns from all immigrant sources, what has actually taken place has been more of a transforming of the later immigrant's specific cultural contributions into the Anglo-Saxon mold. (Gordon, 1964: 126–127)

With regard to these later immigrants, structural assimilation was resisted both by first-generation immigrants and by the core society, and second-generation immigrants who attempted to enter core society institutions were largely rejected. Acculturation was particularly slow for blacks, Puerto Ricans, and Native Americans.

At that time many European Americans found their closest associations across ethnic and nationality lines but within the three major religious groups, Protestant, Catholic, and Jewish, a concept called the "triple melting pot" by sociologist Ruby Jo Kennedy (1944). Gordon defines this as "structural pluralism," an adaptation of the idea of cultural pluralism: "the maintenance of the structurally separate subsocieties of the three major religious and racial and quasi-racial group, and even vestiges of nationality groupings, along with a massive trend toward acculturation of all groups ... to American cultural patterns" (Gordon, 1964: 159).

There is reason to doubt whether the triple melting pot defined in the mid-twentieth century still exists. Religion does not appear to be the center of social life, as it was for many Americans in the past. In a Gallup poll taken in 1988, 65% of Americans identified themselves as members of a church or synagogue, the lowest figure since the poll began in 1937. A 1987 poll found that 26% of Americans attended a place of worship weekly, 14% attended once or twice a month, 30% attended several times a year, and 15% never attended. There is also a large gap between the number of Americans who say they want religious training for their children and the number actually providing their children with such training (Gallup & Castelli, 1989).

The extent to which nationality remains an important means of identification for Americans is also in question. Many children growing up today find other forms of identity more attractive. For example, Newman (2001a, b) explores the attraction of the rap culture for a group of New York City high school boys of various national origins. In addition to downplaying the importance of nationality, a number of these students reject the path of assimilation to the values and practices of mainstream American life. Of course, children's identities go through various transformations as they mature; still, we cannot be sure whether national heritage will figure significantly in their adult lives.

The contrast between the romantic, idealistic notion of the melting pot and the reality of life in America can be seen in the work of Israel Zangwill, a British-Jewish playwright who popularized the phrase in his play *The Melting-pot: Drama in Four Acts*, produced on Broadway in 1908. The play, hugely successful at the time, contains a rousing speech by David Quixano, a Russian-Jewish immigrant musician who is composing a symphony meant to embody the spirit of his new homeland:

> America is God's Crucible, the great melting-pot where all the races of Europe are melting and reforming! Here you stand, good folk, think I, when I see them at Ellis Island, here you stand in your 50 groups with your 50 languages and histories, and your 50 blood hatreds and rival-

ries, but you won't be long like that brothers, for these are the fires of God you've come to – these are the fires of God. A fig for your feuds and vendettas! German and Frenchman, Irishman and Englishman, Jews and Russians – into the Crucible with you all! God is making the American. (Zangwill, 1939: 33)

In many respects, this idealistic yearning is discordant with the play itself and with the life of the Quixano family. The Quixanos experience great consternation at the sacrifices to religious observance they must make in order to survive; David and his uncle, also a musician, must work on Friday nights, the Sabbath. Additionally, at every encounter with society they confront virulent anti-Semitism. This vision of American life was more reflective of the reality of the time, with the great migration from Europe well under way eliciting mounting nativist sentiments, than that of Americans melting into one. In fact, Zangwill was disturbed by the fact that the play was widely interpreted as a call for the dissolution of immigrant cultures and religions. In the Afterword to the play, he describes the melting pot he envisions as "that which takes place in a human brotherhood without any surrender of one's beliefs or ideals. In the eyes of David Quixano the American constitution as it was laid down and built up by the Puritan fathers, by Washington or Lincoln, was a mere modern attempt to set up the Mosaic ideal of a perfect State" (cited in Leftwich, 1956: 253). He also believed that Jews could maintain their religion as Americans, and wrote in 1916, "It was vain for Paul to declare that there should be neither Jew nor Greek. Nature will return even if driven out with a pitchfork. Still more if driven out with a dogma" (cited in Leftwich, 1956: 254). Zangwill's vision of America more closely fits the mold of a cultural pluralist state than one of a melting-pot amalgam.

MODERN YEARNINGS FOR THE MELTING POT

Still, the notion of a melting-pot society creating a new prototype American persists. The longing for a return to such a society, existing in the mind if not in reality, started to appear again in the latter part of the twentieth century, as immigration from the developing world swelled, the American dream of unlimited socioeconomic mobility became doubtful, and concern over the loss of so-called traditional values grew. Rosalie Porter, for example, decries "the renewal of ethnic sensitivities in the 1970s, following on the heels of the civil rights movement of the 1960s" as

a celebration of tolerance, an exaltation of all ethnic groups, and a declaration that the "melting-pot" had never been. From the 1960s to the 1980s sociologists viewed the melting-pot concept – various generations of immigrants merging to form an essentially "American" national character with a core of common values – as a myth, and a repugnant one at that. (Porter, 1990: 159).

Nostalgia for the mythic melting-pot past is often rooted in the fear that ethnic groups will cling to their non-English languages and cultures in place of accepting the dominant language and culture of the United States. In a critique of bilingual education, political scientist Abigail Thernstrom is concerned that "if the students are, say, Puerto Rican, they will learn about Puerto Rico; by ninth grade, Abraham Lincoln may mean nothing to them but they will know that the River Culbrinas is a small tributary in the northwest corner of the island" (Thernstrom, 1990: 44). Dismayed at the prospect of classrooms "in which one feels in a foreign land" (Thernstrom, 1990: 48), Thernstrom professes nostalgia for a time in which "to 'melt' immigrant children had once been central to the mission of public schools" (Thernstrom, 1990: 45).

A further example of present-day yearning for a mythic past comes from Arthur Schlesinger, Jr. Lamenting the loss of national unity, he paraphrases de Crevecoeur more than two hundred years later:

> The United States had a brilliant solution for the inherent fragility of a multi-ethnic society: the creation of a brand-new national identity, carried forward by individuals who, in forsaking old loyalties and joining to make new lives, melted away ethnic differences. Those intrepid Europeans who had torn up their roots to brave the wild Atlantic *wanted* to forget a horrid past and to embrace a hopeful future.... The point of America was not to preserve old cultures, but to forge a new *American* culture. (Schlesinger, 1992: 13)

Like Porter and Thernstrom, Schlesinger is discouraged by the replacement of the goal of a unified America with one that celebrates diversity and a revival of ancestral roots:

> The vision of America as melted into one people prevailed through most of the two centuries of the history of the United States. But the twentieth century has brought forth a new and opposing vision.... A cult of ethnicity has arisen both among non-Anglo whites and among non-white minorities to denounce the idea of a melting pot, to challenge the concept of "one people," and to protect, promote, and perpetuate separate ethnic and racial communities. (Schlesinger, 1992: 14–15)

In this way, the vision of a society that transforms its citizens into a new type of American is seen as challenged by the view of a cultural pluralist society of separate ethnic groups. However, the nearest that the nation ever got to a melting pot occurred four centuries ago, and it seems unlikely that such an experience will ever happen again. Similarly, the vision of a truly cultural pluralist society has been stymied by the pressures of Anglo-conformity and the ever-changing influences of the modern world on the way Americans connect with each other. America today is the sum total of very complex forces, making it difficult to put the nation into one particular category. With this in mind, we turn to the specific topic of the language history of the nation, to see the route through which it came to reach its present linguistic state.

A HISTORICAL OVERVIEW OF IMMIGRANT LANGUAGES: THE AGE OF EXPLORATION TO THE EARLY TWENTIETH CENTURY

The United States has developed in a continent that was never monolingual; numerous Native American languages were thriving when the first explorers arrived. The history of the country is marked by wave after wave of immigration, each one bringing new cultures and languages. While English was most often the language of official mass communication, immigrant languages were always in use as well. What emerges from a study of the history of immigrant languages in America is a kind of multi-layered time line: English is a constant presence throughout, existing with other languages that appear and sometimes die out in different parts of the country at various points along the time line. What also emerges is a complex combination of factors contributing to the lifespan of immigrant languages. The section that follows describes the patterns of linguistic and cultural persistence among the non-English speaking immigrants who helped shape modern America. On the following pages of this chapter, a series of statistical figures enhances our understanding of the patterns of immigration to America.

The Colonial Period

It is estimated that the first Europeans to arrive in North America encountered 1.5 million Native Americans speaking approximately 300 different languages. Given the predominant belief among Europeans in their inherent superiority, they were not about to adapt themselves to the existing culture. As Daniels puts it:

> The newcomers, although learning from observation if in no other way, did not melt into the existing society any more than the Pilgrims became Indians.... Whether one is talking about the sixteenth century or the twentieth, few metaphors are more inappropriate than the melting-pot. (Daniels, 1991: 8)

Instead of acculturating to the ways of Native Americans, the Europeans did just the opposite: they presided over the massive subjugation and annihilation of native populations, languages, and cultures.

The three major colonizing powers in America were the English, the Spanish, and the French. While the English became the dominant power, the languages and cultures of the two other colonizers also left their mark.

The Spanish were the first Europeans to traverse much of the continent and the first Europeans to establish a colony, in present-day northern Florida. In their quest for gold, the early colonists shaped a labor force out of the local Indian populations. When these populations declined, succumbing to foreign diseases as well as to European aggression, the Spanish imported slaves from Africa. Because Spanish immigration was mostly male, sexual relationships between the colonists and women from the subordinate classes were common, and the mixed or *mestizo* race came into being.

As in most colonial societies, the Spanish settlers early on divided the inhabitants of their new home by place of birth; the *peninsulares*, those born in Spain, were considered superior to the *creoles*, those born in the New World. But with the creation of a tri-racial society, the social hierarchy opened up to people of mixed ancestry. Access to power and prestige depended on a person's degree of acculturation: "An individual who spoke Spanish, wore European clothes, and ate European style food was considered, if not Spanish, not any longer Indian. Such *mestizos* were crucial in helping administer the empire" (Daniels, 1991: 10). In contrast to Schlesinger's (1992) view of early settlers shedding their European roots to form a new American society, the history of the Spanish paints a quite different picture: these settlers pressured the lower classes to conform to the culture they had brought with them from Europe.

Besides settling in Florida, Spanish and Spanish Mexicans also established themselves in the Southwest and California. Spanish settlements in Texas were not highly successful, and by the first half of the nineteenth century, Spanish residents of Texas were a small percentage of the total population, dwarfed by the numbers of other immigrants coming into the state. In California, the Spanish population dominated until the gold rush of 1849, which attracted many newcomers and left the Spanish in the minority. The situation in New Mexico was different. There the Spanish–Mexican culture took root, and Spanish Americans remained the majority population until about 1940. Today both English and Spanish are used in official state business.

Daniels (1991) describes the original French settlers as a small group that scattered over an extensive area from Detroit to New Orleans. A second group of immigrants were the Acadians, or Cajuns, who were expelled from present-day Nova Scotia by the British in 1713. Dispersing first to the American colonies, to the West Indies, and some even back to France, they made their way to Louisiana in the mid-1700s. Forming a tightly-knit community with a language and religion (Roman Catholicism) different

Table 2.1 Approximate numbers of European emigrants to America, 1500–1783

Country of Origin	Number	Date
Spain	437,000	1500–1650
Portugal	100,000	1500–1700
Britain	400,000	1607–1700
Britain[1]	322,000	1700–1780
France	51,000	1608–1760
Germany[2]	100,000	1683–1783
Total	1,410,000	1500–1783

1 Includes between 190,000 and 25,000 Scots and Irish.

2 "Germany" refers to emigrants from southwestern Germany and the German-speaking cantons of Switzerland and Alsace Lorraine.

Adapted from Altman & Horn, 1991: 3. Sources: Bailyn, 1986; Gemery, 1980; Altman, 1991; Choquette, 1991; Horn, 1991; Wokeck, 1991.

from those of their neighbors and eschewing formal education, a distinct Cajun culture was established. In the twentieth century, threats to the Cajun culture arrived in the form of the prohibition of French in the schools during Word War I, the enforcement of compulsory school attendance in 1944, and decreased isolation as a result of improved transportation and the intrusion of modern culture. Today, efforts are being made to prevent the further loss of the Cajun language and culture.

A third group of French immigrants was the Huguenots. Fleeing religious persecution in 1680, they settled in small numbers in Massachusetts, New York, and South Carolina. Most of the Huguenots came with work skills and some with capital, and within a short time they achieved substantial social and economic status, acculturating easily into American society. Although they established their own churches, these churches were so similar to those of their Protestant neighbors that they did not last long. For these reasons, Huguenot culture and language did not survive.

Other non-English speaking Europeans came to America in the late seventeenth and early eighteenth centuries. The most prominent among these were the Germans, who established a strong German American culture in Pennsylvania, where by 1790 they constituted a third of the population. The Pennsylvania Germans created their own distinct folk art and produced German-language religious and secular music. German-language religious services were common until as late as 1930.

The prominence of the German population is evident in the use of the language during the War of Independence. The Continental Congress translated a number of publications into German, including the Articles of Confederation. In 1775, a group of prominent German citizens, including the Lutheran and Reformed clergy of Pennsylvania, sent a German-language letter to friends and countrymen in New York and North Carolina encouraging them to enlist in the war effort. Congress formed a number of troop units composed solely of American-born Germans, in which German was the language of command. In 1794, a petition to Congress to continue printing copies of federal laws in German was narrowly defeated. As late as the 1830s, a small group of German-immigrant adherents of political liberalism were petitioning Congress to publish all deliberations and decisions in German; by this point, however, support for such endeavors had waned and the proposals were rejected.

Daniels (1991) also describes other immigrant groups from Europe who made use of their languages in varying degrees. Celts from Ireland used Irish Gaelic as a unifying force, particularly in church services, until the mid-nineteenth century. The Dutch used their native language in their reformed churches for a century. In contrast, the Welsh in Pennsylvania, Delaware and the Carolinas saw their language last only one generation. Swedish settlers of this period lost their language and culture rather quickly. Ladino-speaking Sephardic Jews from Brazil were not a large enough group for their language and culture to leave a significant mark. German-speaking and Yiddish-speaking Jews from Europe were also not a significant group in this era; however, Yiddish would have an important place in immigrant society in the late nineteenth century.

As noted above, these immigrants were not all viewed alike. Some of the first Americans who began to think and write about immigration recognized that newer groups had to adjust to what had already been identified as a core culture. Jesse Chickering is one such person who espoused Anglo-conformity:

> The people of the United States, considered as a whole, are composed of immigrants and their descendants from almost every country. The principal portion of them, however, derive their origin from the British nation, comprehending by this term the English, the Scotch and the Irish. The English language is almost wholly used; the English manners, modified to be sure, predominate, and the spirit of English liberty and enterprise animates the energies of the whole people....

> The New England states, Virginia, Pennsylvania, Maryland and the new Carolinas were principally settled by the English; New York and New Jersey by the Dutch; Mississippi and Louisiana by the French; Florida by the Spaniards. The new states have been settled mainly by emigrants from the older states, with large numbers from foreign

countries.... We have not the means at hand of determining the exact number that have been derived from these various sources. The tendency of things is to mold the whole into one people, whose leading characteristics are English, formed on American soil. (Chickering, 1848: 56)

The Century of Immigration

The century from 1820 to 1924 was one of massive immigration to the United States, most of it from Europe. One of the largest immigrant groups came from Ireland. Between 1820 and 1930, roughly 4.5 million Irish emigrated to the United States (Daniels, 1991: 127). While many think of Irish emigration as stemming from the potato famine of the 1840s, the actual period of exodus from Ireland began before the famine and was still strong after it ended. During the pre-famine years, emigration was stimulated by Ireland's huge population growth, which reduced agricultural holdings and increased poverty. Immigrants from Ireland settled largely in cities in New England, where the men worked as laborers and the women as domestic servants.

By the mid-1800s, the potato had become the major crop of Irish farmers; it was easy to grow and could feed many mouths. But the potato was also highly susceptible to disease, and when the blight of 1844 hit, it devastated the population. The British did little to relieve the suffering that the blight caused, stimulating further emigration. Those who came to America were drawn to the New England cities where their predecessors were living, as well as to New York, New Jersey, and – across the country – to San Francisco. They continued to be over-represented in the trades and in domestic service, although some were able to go into more prestigious professions. Their generally low status is reflected in the fact that Irish immigrants often successfully competed for jobs against blacks, who were at the very bottom of the socioeconomic ladder.

The large numbers of Irish immigrants had a significant impact on the Roman Catholic Church. Although not all of them were religious, they had a fierce loyalty to the church; in Ireland, it had been their sole defense against the English. In America, they knew that attacks against the Roman Catholic Church were largely motivated by the anti-Irish sentiment of established Americans. While the Irish came to dominate the Church, at times they had to compete with other immigrant groups for control. In the early nineteenth century, the Irish entered into such a struggle with the Germans. One part of that struggle was over the acquisition of clergy who could conduct services in the native language.

The bulk of Irish immigration occurred after the famine, from 1860 to 1930. These immigrants took advantage of the growth of cities in the Northeast and found employment in the infrastructure needed to run them. They became firemen, policemen, plumbers, and streetcar drivers. Networks were established to help new Irish immigrants acquire these jobs; these networks went beyond familial connections and resulted in Irish-controlled trade unions.

The Irish also began to mold the Democratic Party. While often remembered for their role in political corruption, Irish politicians also saw to it that their countrymen did not go hungry at Christmas and Thanksgiving and favored governmental spending on social programs. Daniels notes that, at the polls, when Irish Americans cast their ballots for the political bosses and their machines, they "were voting for their interests, supporting those they perceived to be their friends and opposing those they knew were their enemies" (Daniels, 1991: 145).

This kind of ethnic-bloc voting has become a staple of American politics. Today, however, supporters of assimilation dismiss the efforts of language-minority leaders to represent their populations. Chavez, for example, scorns Hispanic leaders who "have convinced politicians and policy makers that Hispanics want and deserve special treatment ... and that they require protection from an alien, Anglo society in which they cannot compete." By doing so, she writes, these leaders have "enhanced their own power, but their methods jeopardize the future integration of Hispanics into this society" (Chavez, 1991a: 61). However, just as the Irish were aware of the anti-Irish sentiments rampant in American society, and depended on their leaders to speak for their interests, so today Hispanics depend on their leaders to fight against the discrimination against them, discrimination that they believe is the real obstacle to their acceptance into society.

German immigrants, who also came in large numbers during the nineteenth century, settled in many of the smaller American cities, like Milwaukee, St Louis, and Cincinnati. There they created ethnic enclaves, *Kleindeutchlands*, replicating the culture of the homeland. Family businesses, such as beer factories and bakeries, served German-American residents in their native language. But Germans also had a significant presence in rural America; in 1870, Germans constituted one-third of all foreign-born farmers (Daniels, 1991: 151). They formed permanent communities throughout the Midwest and Texas, with family farms, as well as German culture and language, being passed down into the fourth and fifth generations. In many communities, they were also able to acquire a significant amount of political control.

The German language dominated cultural and educational institutions in these areas. In the 1880s there were about 800 German-language newspapers nationwide (Daniels, 1991: 162). Like the foreign-language press of many immigrant groups, these newspapers served as links to both cultures: they allowed immigrants to keep informed about their homeland while introducing them to American culture and politics. The German-language press produced autobiographies, histories, poems, novels, short stories, and an encyclopedia. German theater and singing societies were also common in areas with large German populations. Beginning in 1839, a number of states passed laws allowing German to be the language of instruction in the public schools; numerous private schools also offered all instruction in German. Today, the presence of the German language remains strong in some cities, such as Milwaukee and Cincinnati. But the successful adaptation of Germans to American life led eventually to the demise of German-American enclaves and, together with outside political realities, brought about the decline of their culture and language.

Immigration from Scandinavia was also heavy during this century. Swedes settling in the Midwest established their own churches, which in turn opened parochial schools and colleges crucial to the perpetuation of Swedish language and culture. Churches were also largely responsible for the publication of some eleven hundred Swedish-language newspapers and magazines and some ten thousand books; most of the periodicals, however, had tiny circulations and relatively short lives (Daniels, 1991: 172). In Chicago, the Swedish population reached the critical mass needed for the creation of an ethnic enclave called Swede Town, a bustling neighborhood composed exclusively of Swedish-owned businesses. Daniels notes that enclaves such as this one, where the language and customs of the homeland were transplanted, "provided an important way station for immigrants on the road to fuller integration into the larger streams of American life;" they also served as "a brake on the pace of acculturation" (Daniels, 1991: 170).

The Norwegians also established small church-affiliated colleges, and had a burgeoning ethnic press of approximately 800 different publications (Daniels, 1991: 175). Norwegian writers were split over the need to preserve their native language; eventually, pressure to acculturate to American ways won out, and the use of Norwegian declined. This same debate occurred within the different branches of Danish Lutheranism, which split on the issues of assimilation, ethnic heritage, and the role of the Danish language in America. Because Danes were the most geographically dispersed group of Scandinavians, and because the church did not have a significant influence over the lives of Danish immigrants, the Danish language had less of a chance of survival than Swedish or Norwegian.

The Mediterranean was another major source of immigration during this period. The 1850 census showed 3,645 Italians living in almost every state of the country (Daniels, 1991: 192). Half settled in the South, where they were well accepted and mixed easily into mainstream life. Italians were involved in a number of business enterprises and formed relationships that were mutually beneficial; Italian bankers performed services for Italian businessmen in their native language. Ethnic enclaves formed after

1880 in cities such as New York, Chicago, and New Orleans. Urban Italians were largely manual laborers and vendors; newly-arrived immigrants depended on more established compatriots, *padrones*, for jobs and as intermediaries with English-speaking society. However, Italians formed few fraternal organizations and were not regular churchgoers, and therefore lacked the institutions that might have helped preserve their language.

Some 600,000 Greeks emigrated to the United States before 1924 (Daniels, 1991: 201). Greek Orthodox churches encouraged the perpetuation of the Greek language and culture. Like other immigrants, many established small businesses catering to Greek tastes in Greek-dominated neighborhoods. And, like other immigrants, they disagreed about issues regarding assimilation and loyalty to the homeland. Two competing organizations were formed after World War I, one in favor of Americanization and non-sectarianism, the other favoring the cultivation of Greek culture, religion, and language. As with other groups, Americanization won out; most second- and third-generation Greek Americans do not speak their native language.

Two other groups of immigrants came from the Mediterranean. Arab immigrants prior to 1914 were mostly street peddlers. Learning English and being familiar with American culture were imperative, since their livelihood depended on their ability to communicate with the public. Those who were successful at this were able to open their own shops. Christian Arabs were able to found some churches, with services in Arabic or Syriac, mostly in eastern states. But the Muslim minority found it difficult to maintain mosques in the small communities they lived in. Thus, religious institutions did not play a role in perpetuating their language and culture. Armenians began arriving in the United States prior to World War I, coming from Turkey and Russian Armenia. In California, they were forbidden to buy homes in upper-scale neighborhoods. As a result of this and other types of discrimination, they formed their own ethnic communities and worshiped in their own Armenian Apostolic Church.

Eastern Europeans began arriving in the late nineteenth and early twentieth century to work in the factories of northeastern and north-central cities. Poles formed ethnic enclaves in Chicago, New York, and Michigan. Unhappy with the dominance of the Irish in the Catholic Church hierarchy, they pushed for, and eventually acquired, priests who spoke their own language to serve in their parishes. There was strong support for parochial schools, in which instruction was in Polish. Polish ethnic organizations kept an influential hand in homeland politics.

Religious persecution and the desire to improve their standard of living drove Eastern European Jews to the urban centers of the Northeast and Midwest in the late nineteenth century. Immigrants lived in cramped ethnic enclaves, working in the garment and retail industries mostly for other Jews.

Table 2.2 First-generation immigrants from large ethnic groups, 1910 census: Year of immigration

	British	*Irish*	*Scandinavian*
Number in sample	4,490	4,865	4,768
Year of immigration			
Before 1860 (%)	7.06	11.28	1.4
1860–1879	20.38	26.25	16.55
1880–1889	28.98	26.17	30.10
1890–1899	17.39	18.71	20.26
1900–1910	26.19	17.60	31.69
Total	*100.00*	*100.00*	*100.00*
	German	*Italian*	*Polish*
Number in sample	7,638	5,261	3,402
Year of immigration			
Before 1860 (%)	10.28	6.46	0.35
1860–1879	26.25	1.56	3.17
1880–1889	34.25	7.72	12.52
1890–1899	16.90	18.72	18.34
1900–1910	12.32	65.54	65.61
Total	*100.00*	*100.00*	*100.00*
	Jews (CE)[1]	*Jews (EE)*[2]	*FNE*[3]
Number in sample	805	2,989	6,055
Year of immigration			
Before 1860 (%)	0.25	0.03	2.43
1860–1879	1.37	1.20	15.71
1880–1889	13.79	9.23	21.87
1890–1899	29.69	22.35	24.59
1900–1910	54.91	67.18	35.41
Total	*100.00*	*100.00*	*100.00*

1 Central European; 2 Eastern European; 3 Foreign, not European.
Adapted from Watkins & Robles, 1994: 372–373.

Yiddish was the sole language of daily communication for this first generation of Jews, who rarely came into contact with those outside their neighborhoods. Transplanting the communal tradition of the *shtetl*, people from the same hometowns formed local organizations to serve secular and religious needs. Yiddish cultural life thrived. The *Jewish Daily Forward*, founded in 1897, eventually became the largest foreign-language daily of its time and was a powerful institution in Jewish immigrant life. Yiddish film, theater, and literature also had a quite vigorous life.

The eventual demise of Yiddish was due in part to some of the same reasons that saw the demise of other languages: the desire to acculturate and to avoid the stigma attached to the native language, and contempt for immigrant culture from the larger society. An illustration of this contempt is found in the comments of a professor of education, Ellwood Cubberly, regarding southern and eastern European immigrants:

> Everywhere these people tend to settle in groups or settlements, and to set up here their national manners, customs, and observances. Our task is to break up these groups or settlements, to assimilate and amalgamate these people as a part of our American race, and to implant in their children, so far as can be done, the Anglo-Saxon conception of righteousness, law and order, and popular government, and to awaken in them a reverence for our democratic institutions and those things in our national life which we as a people hold to be of abiding worth. (Cubberly, 1909: 15–16)

While Cubberly makes use of the words "assimilate" and "acculturate," he in fact advocates a policy of Anglo-conformity, which entails a wiping out of any vestige of immigrant roots. Howe explains that Jewish culture in America "was largely ignored and dismissed by the Gentile world.... It was also sneered at by many Jews themselves, who could not really believe that anything 'fine' or 'high' could come out of ... those grimy East Side Streets" (Howe, 1976: 643). Given the history of the Jews, it was not surprising that many yearned for acceptance in America, yearned for a time when "no longer pariahs or wanderers, they would live like other peoples" (Howe, 1976: 639).

Another source of immigration was Asia. The California Gold Rush of 1849 marked the beginning of massive immigration from China. The Chinese settled in large cities such as San Francisco (their port of entry), Boston, and New York, where significant Chinatowns were established. Chinatown inhabitants included both the poor and the well-to-do, who were barred from living in other neighborhoods by rampant discrimination. Like most ethnic enclaves, Chinatowns provided for all the needs of their inhabitants in the language of the homeland. The merchant power elite was responsible for forming family organizations, which eventually banded together under the Chinese Consolidated Benevolent Association. This institution virtually governed the Chinatowns and served as intermediary to the white establishment.

Beginning in the mid-nineteenth century, large numbers of Japanese immigrants settled largely on the Pacific Coast and California. In urban areas they became farm laborers and eventually farm owners. In cities like Los Angeles the Japanese dominated the growing wholesale marketing of produce; as late as the 1930s, Japanese radio programs reported market prices. Like the Chinese, Japanese immigrants faced a great deal of discrimination. However, because Japan was a powerful military country, the federal government took pains to avoid institutionalized discrimination against the Japanese. The Japanese government, also concerned about maintaining good relations with the United States, formed the Japanese Association of America to control immigration into the States and to encourage Japanese immigrants to acculturate, urging them to adopt Western dress and educate their children in public schools. Despite the successful acculturation of many Japanese, they were still discriminated against in society and under the law. The World War II placement of Japanese Americans in internment camps on the West Coast is a vivid example. Policy makers called this action a "military necessity." However, as Takaki (1993) points out, the Japanese in Hawaii were not subjected to the same treatment. The island's military community argued that the Japanese were essential to defense, and white business leaders, possessing a long-standing paternal attitude toward the Japanese, also knew that their internment would decimate the island's labor force.

A final wave of immigrants came not from the east or the west but from the north: French Canadians from Quebec. In the latter nineteenth century many Québécois moved to New England to work in the textile mills and other factories in New England. Often they moved into already-established French-Canadian communities. The strength of the Québécois language and culture in this region can be attributed in large part to the steady migration and re-migration from 1860 to the 1920s and to the ease with which people from both sides of the border could visit each other. In some areas, French Canadians had to fight with the Irish-controlled Catholic hierarchy for the appointment of French Canadian priests, in much the same way as the Poles and Germans did. Strong French Canadian parishes led to the establishment of parochial schools. By the turn of the century, four out of ten parochial schools in New England used French as the language of instruction (Daniels, 1991: 262). Compared with other immigrants, the French Canadians maintained a slow rate of acculturation and intermarriage and kept a tenacious hold on their native ways.

FACTORS AFFECTING LANGUAGE LOSS AND MAINTENANCE

The melting-pot rhetoric we hear today tries to convince us that the most recent immigrants to the United States are failing to follow the lead of their predecessors; by refusing to renounce their nativeness, they decline to participate in the creation of one American ethos. We recall a previous citation from Porter:

> The renewal of ethnic sensitivity in the 1970s, following on the heels of the civil rights movement of the 1960s, became a celebration of tolerance, an exaltation of all ethnic groups and a declaration that the "melting pot" had never been. From the 1960s to the 1980s sociologists viewed the melting pot concept – various generations of immigrants merging to form an essentially "American" national character with a core of common values – as a myth, and a repugnant one at that.... The ethnic revival opened up the question of the nature of our nationhood and with it the role of languages in promoting national cohesion or fragmentation. (Porter, 1990: 159)

When the issue is framed in this way, it is possible to understand how resistance to the melting-pot concept can be viewed as dangerous. Dedication to one's ethnicity and native language is set in opposition to national cohesion, a shared system of values, and something that Americans might call a "national character." A United Sates with such characteristics would be a wonderful place, peaceful and harmonious. If everyone looked alike and thought alike, there would be no discrimination, no need for laws to eliminate the vast differences in the ways individuals are now treated because of their race or national origin.

But the reality is quite the opposite. There are and have always been differences among Americans, differences which cause wide disparities in the opportunities open to them. In addition, as we have seen above, immigrants of the past never did "merge" in the name of forming this new national character. First, they were largely kept out of mainstream life by established Americans who viewed them with distrust and disdain. Second, most immigrant groups were not eager to give up their ties to their homelands for the sake of assuming a new identity. Many began their lives in America largely inclined to maintain their languages and cultures.

The extent to which they were able to do this depended on a variety of factors. Some were internal, having to do with the nature of the immigrant groups themselves and the circumstances of their immigration. Others were external, defined by the pressures brought to bear from the larger society.

Internal Factors

The size of the immigrant group and the length of its migration period were certainly determining factors. Their pattern of settlement – whether concentrated in specific urban or rural areas or spread out over the country – was also significant. The degree to which they differed from their neighbors – in race, religion, language – affected their degree of isolation, with greater isolation leading to less loss of nativeness. Immigrants who found rapid economic success were more likely to undergo rapid acculturation into the larger society. The presence of influential religious institutions played a tremendous role in perpetuating language and culture. Those groups that depended on beneficial or cultural organizations within their communities to serve their personal needs were more likely to maintain their languages and cultures.

The relationship of the immigrant group to its homeland also affected the immigrants' degree of loyalty to their culture and language. Immigrants often took positions on the various sides of the political issues that their countries were grappling with. Depending on their views on these issues, immigrants were likely to disassociate from or associate with their homeland, which would in turn influence their desire to use their native language. The political relationship between their homeland and the United States was another important influence. Finally, access to the homeland – the ability to visit and be visited by friends and family left behind – greatly increased the chances of continued ties to language and culture.

External Factors

Just as important as the internal forces acting on language loss and maintenance were the external factors, those aspects of American society that influenced how immigrants felt about themselves. Anti-immigrant sentiment has existed throughout American history and has always had a dampening effect on immigrant enthusiasm for maintaining identification to the homeland. Ole E. Rølvaag, a Norwegian American writer who published a number of books in his native tongue, was an advocate for the preservation of the Norwegian language in America. But he eventually realized that this would not happen; pressures from the larger society, as well as the internalized self-deprecation that these pressures created, were too powerful. In 1922 he expressed his dismay:

> Again and again [second generation Norwegians] have had impressed on them: all that has grown on American earth is good, but all that can be called foreign is at best suspect. Many of our own people have jogged in the tracks of the jingoists. "Norwegian church service? Why should there be Norwegian church service in America? No, talk English.... No full blooded American can be expected to want to belong

to a Norwegian church!"... The young are extremely sensitive in matters of honor, and much more so in their patriotic honor! It has been – and to some extent still is – a point of honor to be able to prove that nothing *foreign* hangs about one' s person. Under such conditions how could anyone expect that young people should show only enthusiasm for their forefathers' tongue – that would be to expect the impossible. (cited in Daniels, 1991: 176)

Extreme, coercive tactics against immigrant culture and language were the particular marks of the Americanization movement during World War I. Higham writes of those who gave themselves over totally to this movement:

By threat and rhetoric 100 % Americanizers opened a frontal assault on foreign influence in American life. They set about to stampede immigrants into citizenship, into adoption of the English language, and into an unquestioning reverence for existing American institutions. They bade them abandon entirely their Old World loyalties, customs and memories. They used high-pressure, steamroller tactics. They cajoled and commanded. (Higham, 1955: 147)

The forces exerting pressure on immigrants were not always this overt or extreme, but their impact was felt. This section will examine three institutions that greatly influenced the lives of immigrants, the way Americans viewed them, and the way they viewed themselves. First and foremost is the government and its policies regarding immigration and minority-language use. Second is public education and the part it played in shaping the identities of immigrant children and their parents. Third is the popular press and its role in creating negative stereotypes of immigrants.

Government Policies

Government policies on immigration had both an overt and a more subtle, covert effect on immigrant languages. The laws of the 1920s, favoring immigration from Northern Europe and excluding the Japanese, directly affected the range of languages brought to the country. Laws restricting immigration from certain parts of the world and laws imposing constraints on the lives of certain immigrants had a more covert effect in discouraging immigrants from openly identifying with their native languages and cultures.

Immigration Legislation

As Daniels (1991) explains, throughout the period of American history discussed above, popular nativist attitudes fostered by the prevailing political realities of the time had a definite influence on the shaping of public policy. After the war of 1812, the United States experienced a period of self-confidence, and demonstrated considerable tolerance toward immigration. Naturalization was encouraged, and in many states non-citizens were allowed to vote and hold office. However, the growing numbers of Irish and German immigrants set off a latent fear of Catholicism, a religion closely associated in many minds with monarchy and considered to be a threat to the republic. A number of states imposed head taxes for immigrants, to be paid by the owners of immigrant vessels; the Supreme Court eventually held these laws unconstitutional. Growing nativist sentiment led to the creation of the American or Know-Nothing Party in the 1840s. Its proposals included a 21-year naturalization period and restrictions on the foreign-born holding major public office. Nativist sentiment grew in the years before the Civil War, becoming complicated with the battle over slavery and the division of North and South. Abraham Lincoln, struggling with his own views on slavery, took a stand against anti-immigrant policies, as he wrote his friend Joshua Speed:

> I now do no more than oppose the *extension* of slavery. I am not a Know-Nothing. That is certain. How could I be? How can any one who abhors the oppression of negroes, be in favor of degrading classes of white people? Our progress in degeneracy appears to me to be pretty rapid. As a nation, we began by declaring that *"all men are created equal."* We now practically read it "all men are created equal, except negroes, *and foreigners and Catholics."* When it comes to this I should prefer emigrating to some country where they make no pretense of loving liberty – to Russia, for instance, where despotism can be taken pure, and without the base alloy of hypocracy [*sic*]. (cited in Thomas, 1952: 162–163)

Despite substantial popular support for these proposals, there was not enough support in Congress for any of them to pass into law. The Know-Nothing Party had its nemesis in the Free Soil Party, which advocated continued immigration and the distribution of land to the landless; this party and its proposals were eventually absorbed into the Republican Party. In addition, the Civil War saw a shift in the focus of animosity away from foreign immigrants and toward the white South; in fact, many immigrants fought with distinction in the war. However, discrimination eventually found a new target in the Asian population. In 1868, the Fourteenth Amendment established uniform national citizenship to protect former black slaves. For a time, it also insured the right of citizenship to second-generation Asians. But in 1870, the law was changed, restricting naturalization to "white persons and persons of African descent," thereby excluding Asians.

The first law to explicitly end immigration from a particular country was the 1882 Chinese Exclusion Act. Racism was a major reason for the legislation, as the Chinese were considered of the same inferior status as other non-Europeans. In 1879, President Rutherford B. Hayes wrote in his diary,

"The present Chinese invasion is pernicious and should be discouraged. Our experience in dealing with the weaker races – the Negroes and Indians – is not encouraging.... I would consider with favor any suitable measures to discourage the Chinese from coming to our shores" (in Williams, 1924: 522; cited in Miller, 1969: 190). However, the legislation was also influenced by a desire to protect the economic interests of white workers who had to compete with lower-paid Chinese laborers. Originally meant to last until 1892, the act was extended to 1902 and then declared permanent. It was only in 1943 that, in a gesture of good will toward its wartime ally, Congress repealed the act and allowed for the naturalization of Chinese citizens.

Because the Chinese population in 1882 was highly male, this act actually made Americanization more difficult for these immigrants. The inability of Chinese men to bring women into the country stopped them from establishing families, an important step in their adaptation to American life. From the very beginning of Chinese immigration to this country, then, strong external forces posed obstacles to their acceptance into society.

Animosity toward Japanese immigrants was as intense as it was toward the Chinese. However, Japan was a strong military country, and it became imperative for the United States to maintain good relations with it. Wishing to avoid legislation barring Japanese immigration, the United States and Japan entered into the Gentlemen's Agreement of 1907–1908, whereby Japan agreed to restrict the availability of passports to laborers who had already immigrated to the country and to the relatives who were coming to join them.

Anti-immigrant sentiment in America was impelled not only by racism, but by religious prejudice as well. Protestant leaders saw the large numbers of Roman Catholic, Greek Orthodox, and Jewish immigrants as posing grave threats. Many believed that these newcomers contributed disproportionately to the crime rate and to other societal ills. Many also subscribed to the theory of the superiority of Anglo Saxons over others of European ancestry. With Henry Cabot Lodge as its leader, the Immigration Restriction League called for a literacy test for incoming immigrants, to be administered in the native language, as a way of stemming the flow of inferior immigrants into the country. The proposal was blocked by presidential veto in 1897, 1913, 1915, and 1917. This last time, however, as America was about to break with Germany, Congress overrode President Wilson's veto. This marked the first significant general restriction of immigration ever passed. In reality, it had little effect on the number of immigrants allowed into the country. It did, however, designate a "barred zone" which prevented all Asians except Filipinos and Japanese from entering the country.

The early part of the century also saw the passage of legislation designed to prevent various categories of undesirables from entering the country: criminals, those with substandard morals, the ill, paupers, and radicals. At the end of the First World War, fear of an onslaught of war refugees and radicals fleeing Europe led to the Dillingham Plan of 1920, a system of quotas favoring Europeans from Britain, Germany, and Scandinavia. The plan was extended in 1922 and again in 1924; the last extension was more restrictive than the previous versions, and included a ban on the entry of all Japanese.

Language-Restrictionist Legislation

Like legislation controlling the flow of immigration, governmental policies regarding the use of immigrant languages also reflected societal attitudes toward immigrants and the political reality of the times. They did much to discourage the natural sense of pride and connection that immigrants felt toward their native languages, and fostered the idea that demon-

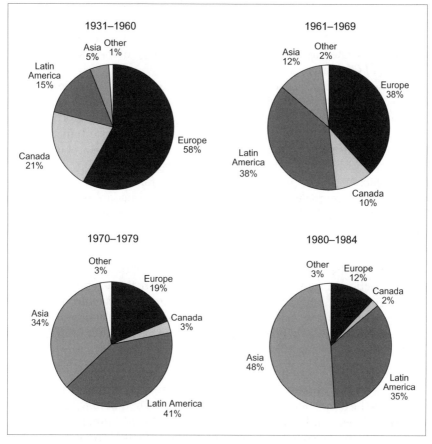

Figure 2.1 Legal immigration to the United States by region, 1931–1984

Adapted from Daniels (1991: 335). Source: Gardner *et al.* (1985)

strating one's desire to be American meant giving up the means of expression that immigrants felt most comfortable with.

Legislation restricting the use of languages other than English was prompted by America's involvement in World War I and the anti-foreign hysteria it engendered. Individual states reacted with laws attempting to wipe out any signs of foreignness, with German as a particular target. In 1918, the governor of Iowa issued a proclamation prohibiting languages other than English in all public places. Iowa, Missouri, and Texas solicited information about clergymen who preached in German. In 1917 federal regulations required all non-English press to submit English translations of any news articles about the war or foreign policy to local post offices.

Language-restrictionist laws greatly affected education in particular. The widespread use of German as the language of instruction in areas with substantial groups of German Americans first met with resistance in the late 1880s, with a number of states curbing the use of German in favor of English in the schools. Later, the anti-German hysteria of World War I largely devastated the use of German as a language of instruction and the teaching of German as a foreign language.

The most famous case of language restrictionism in education was in Nebraska. From 1913 to 1918, a state law required public schools to provide instruction in any European language as long as the parents of 50 students requested it; German was the only language ever requested. In 1918, the law was repealed when the governor labeled it pro-German and un-American. In its place emerged legislation prohibiting any public or private school teacher from teaching any subject in a foreign language or from teaching any foreign language. The law was overturned in the 1923 *Myer v. Nebraska* case, in which the Supreme Court held it to be in violation of the Fourteenth Amendment. But the damage had already been done. According to Daniels,

> In the public schools, the destruction was total: no German-language instruction program survived and, in addition, the teaching of foreign languages in American high schools suffered a setback from which it has yet to recover. And, of course, the demise of instruction in German hastened the death of most of the other cultural institutions of German America. (Daniels, 1991: 161)

Public Education

Earlier in this chapter, we cited a quote by Thernstrom in which she compares the atmosphere of bilingual classrooms to that of a foreign land, and reminisces fondly of a lost time when "to 'melt' immigrant children had once been central to the mission of public schools" (Thernstrom, 1990: 45). This quote reflects the common belief that public education in America is the melting pot for immigrant and US-born minority children, that it is through education that all children gain acceptance into mainstream society. However, the atmosphere of nativist attitudes that created anti-immigration laws and restrictions on immigrant languages in the early part of American history also pervaded the public school establishment. Public education in the early twentieth century contributed to the denigration of foreignness and the glorification of Americanness that marked the rest of society. Rather than making immigrant students feel welcomed as they were, public education taught them that they would not be part of America unless they shed those characteristics that marked them as foreign.

Public schools in the early 1900s served both native and immigrant students poorly. The physical condition of schools was generally dismal. Urban schools were administered by corrupt political systems that controlled every aspect of school life; it was not uncommon for teaching and administrative positions to be bought and sold. Textbooks were of low quality, consisting mostly of plagiarized articles and literary selections that usually had little relevance to the students' own lives. The major pedagogical technique was rote memorization from these texts.

But for immigrant students, schools were a particularly hostile and unwelcome environment. Cordasco characterizes the educational experience of early-twentieth century immigrant children in the following way:

> There is some doubt that the school acted as the main device through which the child was assimilated, and if so, it did its job poorly.... If New York City was typical, the urban school provided no system-wide policy which dealt with the educational needs of immigrant children; and where programs were fashioned to meet these needs, there was no attempt made to differentiate between immigrant groups (e.g. the experience of Italian and Jewish children in New York City strongly documents this failure); instead children were lumped under such rubrics as "native-born" or "foreign-born." If one discounts the multiplicity of dysfunctional programs, rampant discrimination, authoritarian prejudice, it is still difficult to attribute the general pattern of failure to immigrant children or their parents. The blame for the failure lies almost wholly within the schools and the dominant society which shaped its programs and articulated its cultural ideals. (Cordasco, 1976: 36)

The most overt message of the inferiority and unacceptability of foreign traits came with the outright exclusion of one particular immigrant group from participation in public education with other children. In laws passed in 1860 and 1905, Asian children in San Francisco were placed into separate schools. Virulent racism against Asians made acceptable the idea that contact with this minority group would be detrimental to white children.

Early twentieth-century teachers were given little guidance as to how to educate immigrant children, beyond their general charge to "Americanize" them. What this meant was left largely for the teachers themselves to define. In many cities, a major portion of the public school curriculum was devoted to the learning of "good" English and the virtues of cleanliness and health habits, often difficult to put into practice in the tenement houses where city immigrants lived. At the same time, the dress, speech, and personal habits of immigrant children were criticized as "un-American." According to Greenbaum, coercion was the primary means by which children were socialized into American life:

> The main fuel for the American melting pot was *shame*. The immigrants were best instructed in how to repulse themselves; millions of people were taught to be ashamed of their own faces, their family names, their parents and grandparents, and their class patterns, histories, and life outlooks. This shame had incredible power to make us learn, especially when coupled with *hope*, the other main energy source of the melting pot – hope about becoming modern, about becoming secure, about escaping wars and depressions of the old country, and about being equal with the Americans. (Greenbaum, 1974: 431)

Because of the lack of curricular guidance and teacher training, teachers often relied heavily on the textbooks available to them in the classroom. These textbooks made scarce mention of minority groups; however, when mention was made, it was often highly biased. An example is the characterization of Asians in geography texts written in the early part of the century. Redway described the Chinese civilization as stagnant: "We cannot say that the Chinese are a civilized people according to our standard for they are not progressive.... Their way of doing things and thinking about things is today just as we find it in their books to have been 2,500 years ago" (Redway, 1902: 115; cited in Isser & Schwartz, 1985, as are the following textbook and press quotes). The people themselves are portrayed negatively; Robinson contains this description: "[They] are not brave in battle. They have a strong race instinct that breaks out in massacres of foreigners.... They have shown no public spirit, no national patriotism, no readiness to sacrifice self for an ideal" (Robinson, 1910: 310–323). Morris (1909) includes a section on the Chinese in a volume subtitled "Manners and Customs of Uncivilized Peoples." However, a small percentage of geography texts describe China more objectively; an example is the following praise found in Fairgrieve and Young:

> China is another great land which has an old civilization. The Chinese made porcelain dishes long before our European forefathers did and plates and saucers are still called china.... The Chinese had invented gunpowder, discovered how to make silk, paper, found out how to print and invented a kind of taxicab, while some of our ancestors were

living a primitive existence, wandering in the forests of Europe and feeding on berries and wild animals. (Fairgrieve & Young, 1925: 359, 378)

The Japanese were accorded somewhat better treatment in these text-books. Frye views Japanese customs as odd and humorous: "It would amuse you to see the people of Japan eat rice" (Frye, 1898: 156). However, the more favorable evaluation of the Japanese was based in part on their apparent willingness to acquire European habits. According to Frye, "The people of the yellow race living on the islands of Japan have made more progress than any other branch of the race. They are eager to learn how the white men do all kinds of work, and they have been wise enough to adopt many customs of the white race" (Frye, 1895: 36, 172).

Young Asian immigrants were unlikely to find positive images of them-selves and their families in school textbooks. Describing San Francisco, McMurry and Tarr note: "An interesting portion of this city is the section called 'Chinatown.' Many thousands of Orientals landed in the city, living huddled together in hovels, almost like rats" (McMurry & Tarr, 1908: 151). Elson describes San Francisco's Chinatown: "Here may be seen opium dens, idol temples, theaters, dirt, squalor and wickedness" (Elson, 1964: 164). According to Towne, Asians posed a threat to white America compa-rable to that of other minority populations: "The fear is that should we permit the Asiatics to come here as freely as we permit other races, we would soon have on our hands a Japanese problem and a Chinese problem, quite as serious as our present-day negro problem" (Towne, 1916: 53). Not surprisingly, some texts defended laws excluding Asians from entry into the United States.

Besides school textbooks, the use of other classroom material and common classroom practices give further proof of the lack of sensitivity to the diverse student population of the early twentieth century. In many schools, students were required to participate in a daily reading from the Christian Bible, regardless of their religious affiliation. Jewish parents protested against the use of Christian religious material in the public schools, but the practice ended only with a Supreme Court ruling in 1963. No allowances were made for the religious observances of non-Christian children; students who were absent during these holidays were castigated for missing class. Literary selections in the curriculum often included racist, derogatory references to minority groups likely to be represented in the classroom; *The Merchant of Venice*, for example, with its denigrating depic-tion of the Jewish usurer, was required reading for many students.

It becomes clear that the kind of immigrant adaptation promoted by the public schools was that of Anglo-conformity. Immigrant children were taught that their own nativeness was to be despised and cast aside in favor of all that was "American." Language was an inherent part of that nativeness, and the sooner one's native language was replaced by English, the brighter one's prospects for success in the new land would be. It is not surprising that this indoctrination led to serious rifts between parents and children as well as juvenile crime and delinquency.

Isser and Schwartz (1985) point out, however, that not all immigrant groups succumbed to the negative effects of the public school. Asians and Jews, targets of the most intense discrimination, were able to rise above the degrading treatment they received in school to achieve high levels of success in mainstream society. What these groups had in common, and what differentiated them from others, was a set of values that held authority and education in high esteem. The American school system "was an agency that ... parents and community supported, despite all the misgivings. The public school provided, despite its insensitivity to the pupil's cultural diversity, an arena through which they were able to achieve" (Isser & Schwartz, 1985: 60). To counter the influence of an alien environment, the Asian and Jewish communities set up culture- or religion-centered private schools, where "children were constantly inculcated with precepts of duty, respect for their elders, honesty, hard work, and esteem for education" (Isser & Schwartz, 1985: 59). Besides giving the children the principles that would see them through their public school experience, these classes also "provided a familiar haven where immigrant children could retreat to the familiar and traditional while attempting to cross into the American culture, and thus ease the painful and often rebellious feelings that they had" (Isser & Schwartz, 1985: 59).

The Press

Another major conduit through which anti-immigrant sentiment was spread was the press. One particular target of the press was the Jewish immigrant. As noted above, Jewish immigrants achieved fairly rapid economic success, allowing them to venture into the larger society soon after their arrival. However, their attempts to join the mainstream were met with blatant obstacles: exclusion from social clubs, summer resorts, and private schools, and quota restrictions at colleges that also prevented their entry into fraternities and faculties. Justification for this exclusion was the belief that Jews were incapable of assimilating. Sherman wrote of Jews that "their habits are quite incompatible with American standards of life. The persistence of unsanitary conditions for which they are responsible forms a permanent menace to the health of the community" (Sherman, 1904: 675–76). When Jews tried to partake of American life in the most basic ways, they not only met with official resistance, but this resistance was reinforced and sanctioned through its documentation in the press, as exemplified in this passage from *The New York Tribune*:

Numerous complaints have been made in regard to the Hebrew immigrants who lounge about the Battery Park obstructing the walks and
sitting on the chairs. Their filthy condition has caused many of the
people who are accustomed to go to the park to seek a little recreation
and fresh air to give up this practice. The immigrants also greatly
annoy the persons who cross the park to take the boats to Coney Island,
Staten Island, and Brooklyn. The police have had many battles with
these newcomers, who seem determined to have their own way. (cited
in Higham, 1955: 67)

Newspapers and magazines reinforced society's stereotyping of Jewish
immigrants, with ridicule directed at their distinctive physical features and
ways of speaking. For centuries, having been shut out of many professions,
Jews had carved a niche for themselves in the world of business. But this too
found its way into society's anti-Semitism, creating the impression that
Jews were over-concerned with money and survived by exploiting others.
An article in the periodical *Century* offered this evaluation: "The Jews were
a parasitical race, who, producing nothing, fasten on the produce of land
and labor and live on it, choking the breath of life out of commerce and
industry as sure as the creeper throttles the tree that upholds it" (*Century*,
1881–1882: 919).

According to the press, the Chinese were also incapable of adapting to
American life. They were depicted in the press in the basest of ways. The
Montana Post wrote, "The Chinese are so many vampires sucking the life
blood out of any portion in which they remain" (cited in Quinn, 1967: 83).
The New York Times editorialized, "I do not see how any thoughtful lover of
his country can countenance this Mongolian invasion, involving as it does
the subversion of our civilization" (cited in Miller, 1969: 191–192). A
commonly-held fear concerning the Chinese was that their ability to
survive on meager wages threatened the general labor force. This was how
the *Marin Journal* expressed it on April 13, 1876: "We have suppressed rebel-
lion and maintained the integrity of our country for no good purpose what-
soever, if we are not to surrender it to a horde of Chinese simply because
they are so degraded that they can live on almost nothing, and underbid
our own flesh and blood in the labor market" (cited in Sandmeyer, 1939: 38).

During the nineteenth and early twentieth centuries, then, three influential American institutions – the government, public education, and the
press – worked jointly to create an atmosphere inhospitable to new immigrants. The fear and hatred of immigrants that they generated affected the
way older immigrants saw newer ones as well as the way new immigrants
saw themselves. Despite the nostalgia of some contemporary writers for
the good-old melting-pot days, the vision of early immigrants willingly
giving up their native identities to embrace all that is American is a mere

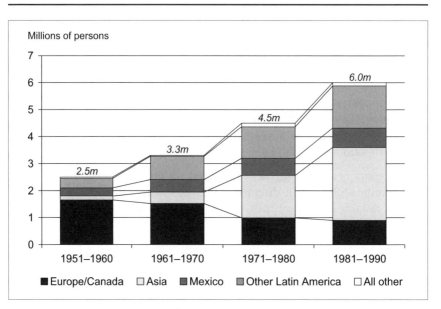

Figure 2.2 Legal immigration by country or region, 1951–1960 to 1980–1990
Adapted from Fix & Passel, 1994: 26. Source: INS, 1993.

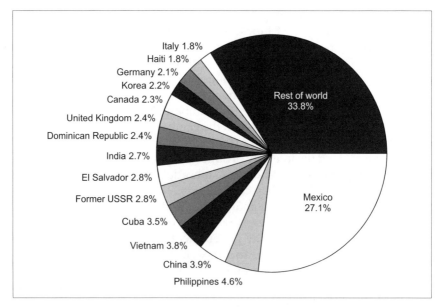

Figure 2.3 Sources of immigrants: the top 15 countries of origin

Source: 1998 *Current Population Survey* (Chart created by the National Immigration Forum)

illusion. If many immigrants did acculturate, it was largely in response to the virulent anti-immigrant atmosphere of society: the repressive legislation of government, the coercive measures of education, and the hate-filled rhetoric of the press. And, when acculturation did take place, the barriers erected by society still prevented them from enjoying the many good things that mainstream America had to offer. America was a country of exclusion rather than inclusion; those who did not possess all the important attributes of the "ideal" American – including, but not limited to, skin color – were effectively shut out of full participation in society. In light of all this information gleaned from the history of our country, the image of a "melting pot" America reveals itself as an illusion. It is this illusion, however, that allows Americans to cling to the belief that we live in a country which is in essence fair, democratic, and free of prejudice.

IS LANGUAGE LOSS INEVITABLE? IS IT DESIRABLE?

For a long time, linguists have documented the fate of immigrant languages in America. Studying the experience of the American continent in general, Haugen writes:

> The native peoples have had bilingualism thrust upon them to a much greater extent than the colonizers. The same is true of the many *immigrant* languages which entered the Americas as the speech of immigrants who settled in areas already occupied by colonial powers. In every country these have remained more or less temporary means of communication among officially unrecognized groups. Political and social pressures have uniformly been unfavorable to their continued use and have gradually whittled down their constituencies. For many of the immigrant groups, bilingualism has been a bridge to membership in the new nation (Haugen, 1956: 11).

Macías writes that in the United States, an immigrant country, "the notions of language and culture change lead one to assume non-English language loss over time. To speak another language is only a temporary phenomenon." This assumption has informed government policy regarding immigrant languages: "Consideration of 'maintenance' language policy, then, is often viewed as temporarily delaying the inevitable loss of the non-English language and is unfairly juxtaposed to not learning English." The government instead settled on "transitional language policies" to help immigrants shift from their native languages to English (Macías, 1979: 96–97).

Both these linguists point out the unwarranted negative assumptions surrounding bilingualism. Macías describes the situation of immigrant languages in the United States in the context of human rights and language rights as defined by international documents; the United States does not fare well in this context. Haugen finds that much of the research showing bilingualism to be a handicap "appears to be based on an unconscious bias against bilingualism as such, at least among immigrant groups;" he also finds in many writings "an emotional attitude of justifying or attacking the practice" (Haugen, 1956: 116). He warns that one should not place a value judgment on bilingualism; what is needed is a way to help people who need to be bilingual reach this goal as easily as possible.

Negative judgments of bilingualism, however, are still with us. Earlier, we noted Arthur Schlesinger's contention that bilingualism "shuts doors. It nourishes self-ghettoization, and ghettoization nourishes racial antagonism.... Using some language other than English dooms people to second-class citizenship in American society" (Schlesinger, 1992: 108). Rosalie Porter offers this:

> For the immigrant recently arrived, bilingualism is an uncomfortable, imperfect phase on the way to somewhere else. Knowing and using a different language at home have been historically seen as signs of being "lower class." Bilingualism that is valued is the elite variety – full competency in two languages among a small percentage of people for the purpose of scholarly work, diplomacy, foreign trade, or travel. The attitude toward "folk bilingualism" in the United States has been negative, with each group that has acquired English tending to look down on the next group to arrive as foreign and inferior. (Porter, 1990: 195–196)

Schlesinger and Porter offer a vivid and disturbing contrast to Haugen and Macías. Porter's class bias is glaring: the bilingualism of the highly literate is an asset, but the bilingualism of the less literate is a burden. It is also not clear where these value judgments come from. Who is it who considers speaking an immigrant language to be "lower class"? Such a statement might surprise the head of US English, Mauro Mujica, a successful businessman of Chilean origin who boasts of speaking Spanish both at home and at work. Schlesinger's comment hints at class bias in a more subtle way. A noted historian and professor, it is likely that he and many of his friends and colleagues know one or two languages in addition to English, but when writing about Hispanics, Schlesinger characterizes bilingualism as confining people to a ghetto existence.

Taking note of Haugen's warning against placing an absolute value on bilingualism, we can still consider its assets and suggest that, when possible, bilingualism should be nurtured and encouraged. An immigrant child of five already has an ability that, allowed to develop, may not only enrich her private life but may benefit the nation. If, however, her language ability is seen as a burden, something to be overcome in time, both she and the country will have missed a valuable opportunity for growth.

A reversal of immigrant language loss may be beneficial to society on a spiritual level as well. Fishman sees language loss as a by-product of our highly technological and mass-market society, an example of "the widespread anomie and alienation that typify so much of modern life among the culturally dominant and the culturally recessive alike" (Fishman, 1991: 6). Many Americans today, the children of immigrants, grew up speaking a language other than English which is no longer part of their daily lives. They experience the pangs of nostalgia and memory on those occasions when hints of that language come back into their lives in a phrase or two heard on the street or over the radio. According to Fishman, the pain felt on these occasions

> deserves attention, if only because it represents a hurt that more people feel than is commonly recognized, and because this hurt (and the lack of recognition for it) is indicative not only of social disorganization but of social injustice as well, the latter being a malady which must not be sloughed off as merely being of interest to the provincial or the antiquarian. (Fishman, 1991: 2–3)

Fishman believes that maintaining immigrant languages offers "a potential contribution to overcoming some of the endemic sociocultural dislocation of modernity," a way of making the present and the future "more meaningful and comfortable for ordinary folk, more creative and humanistically nurturing for all" (Fishman, 1991: 6). In a society in which we are constantly urged to desire the same material goods and services, to think, look and act alike, individuality is threatened. For many, the ability to identify with family roots, a local culture and a hereditary language offers them a needed and comforting sense of who they are.

CHINESE: A LANGUAGE THAT DIDN'T DIE

Of all the immigrant languages transplanted to the United States, one of the most durable has been Chinese. Chinese immigration to this country has a history of over 200 years, allowing more than ample time for American-born generations of Chinese to discard the language of their ancestors in favor of English. In fact, however, the Chinese language is still strong today. Xia (1992) hypothesizes several reasons why Chinese has bucked the trend of many other languages.

With the exception of the period of exclusion of Chinese immigration from 1882 until 1943, the United States has seen a constant flow of new residents from China. Since 1940, the number of Chinese immigrants has increased at a rate of more than 50%. Additionally, with the relatively low birthrate of Chinese in the United States, the proportion of foreign-born to American-born Chinese rose between the 1950s and the 1990s, contributing to the reinforcement of the language.

As Xia (1992) explains, there is no single "Chinese" language; rather, there are numerous varieties with varying degrees of similarity to each other. The earliest immigrants were mostly speakers of Cantonese and Toishanese. These two varieties are not mutually intelligible; as a result, English became the lingua franca. Today, there are more Chinese from Taiwan and other parts of China than from the southern part of the country. Taiwan's *Guo-yu* (national speech) and mainland China's *Pu-tong-hua* (common speech, Mandarin) are similar enough for speakers of these varieties to communicate with each other. Consequently, there is less need for these immigrants to rely on English. This immigration pattern has been aided by political changes. Fear of a takeover by the People's Republic of China harks back to the 1970s. According to Monterey Park architect David Tsai, many Chinese in Hong Kong and Taiwan started emigrating out of fear of Communist China; they did not want their children "to be brought up in war" (Wong, 1977; cited in Fong, 1994: 29). A large exodus from Hong Kong in the late 1980s was motivated by the more imminent takeover in 1997 (Trueba *et al.*, 1993). By the late 1990s, the Chinese community in the United States had grown to over 1.8 million (Kang, 1997).

The residential pattern of Chinese immigrants has also contributed to the longevity of their language. As we have seen, the Chinese settled in a small number of states and cities, creating their own neighborhoods. Since the 1950s, the number of Chinatowns has increased and old established Chinatowns have expanded. Taiwanese communities now exist not only in New York and California, but also in New Jersey, Illinois, and Washington (Ng, 1998). There has also been a substantial growth in Chinese-language mass media.

Cultural forces have contributed to the maintenance of Chinese. The Chinese culture places high value on group support and interaction. Trueba *et al.* (1993) point out that ties of religion, language, business, and neighborhood draw Chinese immigrants together, allowing them to share the information they need as newcomers. The extended family also works as a unit, with older members caring for the young and passing down knowledge of culture and language.

Chinese Americans have a high rate of intra-ethnic marriage, due in large measure to differences between the Chinese and American cultures in matters of sexual behavior and marriage. Statistics show that, while the number of Chinese marrying non-Chinese has increased, owing to increased immigration, when calculated as a proportion of all inter-ethnic marriages, the rate of Chinese inter-ethnic marriage has remained much the same (Sung, 1990). As Xia (1992) points out, parental involvement in marriage is still strong; the tradition of familism requires the subordination of individual feelings for the good of the family. The patrilineal tradition of marriage also discourages Chinese men from choosing non-Chinese wives, who are less likely to accept the unequal distribution of power that is characteristic of the traditional Chinese marriage. Intra-ethnic marriage consequently discourages loss of Chinese language and customs. Sung (1990) predicts that the high rate of Chinese intra-marriage will continue in the future. With the strength of new immigration and the low birthrate of Chinese in the United States, the population will be skewed toward first-generation immigrants, who will probably be more conservative in their marriage patterns.

The passing on of Chinese identity has been bolstered by an increase in the number of privately-run Chinese schools, which teach Chinese language, history, and culture to American-born children. Contributing to the growth of these schools is the fact that immigrants of the past few decades are more educated than previous immigrants were (US Commission on Civil Rights, 1988: 109). They know more about their country, possess stronger national sentiments, and are more conscious of the need for cultural maintenance and ethnic identity.

A final influence on the Chinese language in America is the rising sociopolitical and socioeconomic status of the Chinese. This has had a positive effect on language maintenance; Li (1982) found that Chinese maintenance is highest among the mostly financially successful Chinese Americans. A related study by Koussoudji (1988), of the economic conse-quences associated with English knowledge among Hispanic and Asian men, found that among Asian Americans, English language ability is not a necessary condition of high job status. In this group, minimal knowledge of English is actually associated with managerial positions. The author suggests as probable reasons the availability of jobs in ethnic enclaves, and the economic support systems that allow many to become self-employed. Xia (1992) and others detail these conditions in Chinese neighborhoods throughout the country.

The past few decades have seen an increase in the number of Chinese Americans entering into middle-class professions such as law, medicine, higher education, and industry. This trend has paralleled a change in the media image of the Chinese from the derogatory characterization of "coolies" and "pigtails" to the glorification of the Chinese and other Asians as the "model minority." While this new image is in many respects harmful – it turns a blind eye to the many Asians who fail to fit this image and fosters resentment of Asians by non-Asians who haven't "made it" as far as they'd like – it has to an extent enhanced the status of Asian cultures, as witness the increased interest in the study of Chinese as a foreign language. Lastly, recent efforts toward the modernization of China have heightened the sense of pride that Chinese Americans have in their culture and their desire to identify with it.

Xia's study of Chinatowns in New York City revealed that Chinese

> is maintaining almost all of its functions in intra-ethnic social interaction. It is used in almost all social, political, and cultural activities and in most, if not all, societal domains.... As language maintenance and shift in multi-ethnic or multicultural communities represent, respectively, the persistence and transition of the ethnic or cultural identities of these communities, we can say that the current maintenance of the Chinese language represents a persistence of Chinese culture and ethnic identity. (Xia, 1992: 208)

These findings are confirmed by Pan (1997), who explains that the many Chinese-language resources available in New York City's Chinatown – newspapers, radio and television broadcasts, language schools, bilingual education programs, and churches – "help foster language and cultural awareness and maintenance among the Chinese-American population, and explain partially its ethnolinguistic vitality" (Pan, 1997: 246).

The example of the survival of the Chinese language in America offers two important challenges to the common wisdom about the process of immigrant adaptation. First, it shows that the common belief in the three-generational lifespan of immigrant languages fails to take into account other influential factors involved in language maintenance. The most critical among these is continued immigration: when newcomers arrive, they increase the number of monolingual immigrant-language speakers, reinforcing the use of the language in the community and encouraging the American-born generations to maintain that language as a means of communicating with the most recent immigrants.

Second, the history of the Chinese language challenges the notion that success in America (as measured by economic wealth) necessitates the shedding of immigrant ties and the adoption of an "American" way of life. Our example shows just the opposite: the Chinese who are most successful economically are most likely to maintain their native language. Other immigrants, such as the Germans, largely lost their immigrant identity when they acquired economic success. However, European immigrants were more likely to be accepted socially into mainstream society once they acquired financial stability. Racial prejudice, along with the cultural propensity of the Chinese to live together and maintain community ties, has to an extent kept the Chinese apart from the rest of society. This does not mean that they have rejected all that is "American;" indeed, the ability to deal with English-speaking society is usually a requisite to economic achievement. But knowledge of American language and culture can exist together with knowledge and use of one's native language and culture. As we learned earlier from Gordon (1964), acculturation occurs in varying degrees, leaving open the possibility that an immigrant group's process of adaptation may end in bilingualism and biculturalism. This state can broaden and enrich life on a number of levels: economic, professional, personal, and spiritual.

THE MYTH OF IMMIGRANT REJECTION OF ENGLISH

Those who lament the passing of the mythical melting-pot process of immigrant assimilation often contend that present-day immigrants resist learning English. They paint a picture of language minorities creating neighborhoods in which all their needs are met in their own languages. Insistence on bilingual services in those areas of life that necessitate interaction with the larger world – voting, public assistance, education – is translated as further evidence of immigrant defiance of English. However, hard evidence shows just the opposite. Immigrants are clamoring to learn English, and often find it difficult to find free or low-cost classes. Their children are also learning English, even more rapidly than their parents, and often at the expense of their native languages.

The demand for English-as-a-second-language instruction for adults has actually increased in the last few decades. One reason is the increase in the rate of immigration, which is nearing its highest point since World War II. A second reason is that English literacy has become a more essential tool in the workplace. Immigrants of the past could support themselves and their families with minimal competence in English by working in secure factory jobs or by setting up small family businesses. In the high-tech, service-oriented world of work today, few can sustain a comfortable income without a solid command of spoken and written English.

Unfortunately, the growing number of immigrants wanting to study English has not been matched by increasing funds for such classes. Many large cities to which immigrants are drawn continue to struggle to find ways to meet the demand. Perhaps the most ironic of these cases is Los Angeles. In 1986, the year in which California passed a law making English the official state language, the unofficial estimate of people waiting for English classes in Los Angeles County was 40,000 (Ingam, 1986: 3). While supporters of this legislation argued that such a law would help immigrants learn English, such help did not come in the form of greater access to English instruction. In 1991, Governor Pete Wilson vetoed plans to place $65 million of Federal money into English proficiency classes for immigrants newly legalized under the Immigration Reform and Control Act, insisting that the money would be better spent on medical treatment for them. In protest, 2,500 people staged a march through the predominantly-Hispanic Boyle Heights section of the city. One leader of the march explained the motivation of the protesters: "We want to participate in the economy of the greatest state in the nation" (*The New York Times*, 1991: A12). The marchers clearly understood the connection between their ability to speak English and their prospects for socioeconomic advancement. Whatever motivated Governor Wilson in his action, its consequence was to squelch these aspirations and help maintain the status quo of social and racial stratification.

While California's immigrants were struggling to find ways to learn English, their counterparts in New York were doing the same. A government-financed English language and employment service for immigrants and refugees in New York City served 3,000 people in 1989. In 1990, the Church Avenue Merchants Block Association in Brooklyn offered English classes to 1600 people and had 500 on a waiting list. In the same year, a workplace literacy program organized by ten New York City labor unions served 2,380 immigrants. The Mayor's Office of Adult Literacy had at least 15,000 names on a waiting list for free English classes. The City University of New York, the main provider of free English classes after the Board of Education, taught English to 7,613 people in its regular program and 4,424 in its amnesty program; its waiting list had 5,752 names. (In addition, 40% of the matriculated students at the City University's 16 campuses come from homes in which a language other than English is spoken.) Statewide, the Division of Adult and Continuing Education Programs enrolled 69,200 adults in free English classes in the year ending July 1990, up from 45,000 the previous year (Howe, 1990: 26L).

Since the early 1990s, the demand for adult English classes throughout the country has not diminished. In the fiscal year 1997–1998, New York City provided ESL classes for 22,707 immigrants; 4,139 others were waiting for openings (personal communication, Literacy Assistance Center of the Mayor's Office of Adult Literacy, Sept. 1999). The Aurora, Colorado school district offers adult ESL classes of up to 120 students each; many other potential students report frustration at not being able to attend because of the cost and the shortage of classes (Brovsky, 1998). Teaching ESL has become one of the duties of AmeriCorps Vista volunteers working in public housing developments in Albany, New York (Jackson, 1998). In the Atlanta, Georgia metropolitan area, which has roughly 500,000 immigrants and refugees, public libraries are providing adults with ESL classes and textbooks (Kurylo, 1998). In Loudoun County, Virginia, the number of students attending free adult English classes climbed steadily in the mid 1990s; the 1998 enrollment of 275 was its largest (Nakamura, 1998). Massachusetts steadily increased its funding for adult ESL classes throughout the 1990s, concerned about the business sector's need for highly-skilled workers. Despite this increase, the state has been able to meet only 3–4% of the need for ESL training (Franklin, 1998).

Once they find a place in an English class, the struggle is only just beginning. Adults juggle low-paying, physically-demanding jobs and family responsibilities along with their classwork. Often, the demands of family and work during their first difficult years in America mean that formal study of English is delayed. When adults begin to study English five or ten years after arriving here, they have to confront the fact that the "survival English" they have picked up informally has to be transformed into more grammatically-correct standard English. The linguist Larry Selinker (1972) labels the state of arrested language development that characterizes the informally-learned English of many immigrants *fossilization*, a term that helps to explain the difficulty of breaking through familiar habits of expression to a higher plane of language proficiency.

Another difficulty that many students have is finding the opportunity to speak English outside class. Many live and work in immigrant neighborhoods; their lack of proficiency in English precludes their finding jobs in which their co-workers are English-speaking. Many also find English-speaking Americans to be impatient and unfriendly when they do try to communicate with them. Faced with this dilemma, a resourceful student in one English class in Brooklyn collected mail-order catalogues and called all the 800 (free) numbers he found in them, just to be able to practice speaking in English (Rimer, 1992).

The determination of many immigrants to learn English flies in the face of unsupported contentions that they are unwilling to acquire the language of the country and are content to get by with bilingual services and reliance on bilingual relatives. A second student in the Brooklyn class claimed as one of her triumphs that she could now go to the doctor's office, the store, or her children's schools without bringing her nephew along to translate. Another classmate regretted that, several years before, she didn't know enough English to tell her American factory boss that it was unfair of him to lay her off while keeping on a younger employee with far less seniority (Rimer, 1992). Immigrants are well aware that lack of English leaves them highly vulnerable to exploitation.

Despite the difficulties of learning a new language, all the evidence shows today's immigrants acquiring English at an unprecedented rate. Atchison (1894, cited in O'Neill, 1992) estimates that, at the turn of the century, roughly 25% of immigrants could not speak English. In contrast, according to the US Census Bureau's 1990 figures, only 8% of immigrants over the age of five spoke no English at all. The census results also attest to immigrants' self-confidence in their ability to speak English. Of those who arrived in the 1960s, 80.5% claimed to speak English "well" or "very well." Of those who arrived before 1950, 92% spoke English "well" or "very well" (Rodriguez, 1999: 18–19).

Many immigrants who master the language feel that the foreign accent detectable in their speech is a further deterrent to full acceptance by American society. Even in a city like Miami, where Spanish has gained a high degree of status, accent-reduction classes attract many. Miami-Dade

County Community College offers a three-course workshop taught by two speech pathologists. The students, from Cuba, Jamaica, China, Haiti, and Russia, are mostly business and professional people concerned about how Americans see them. One student explained, "If you have no accent or only a slight accent, you are considered better-educated." Another added, "If you are in sales, and you have to go to speak with a person with a high position in the company, it will be in your interest if you speak with the most polished English that you can. They have to feel they can relate to you" (Castillo, 1992: A3). Students attend workshops like this one because they believe that employers are less likely to hire people with accents if the jobs that they are trying to fill require then to deal with customers from other parts of the country, either directly or by phone. It is clear that these immigrants have not bought the melting-pot theory of America; they understand that their success is dependent on their coming as close as possible to the image of the average native-English-speaking American.

What of the children of these immigrants? Children are in a different situation. They are required to attend school and to learn English, and they do this quite rapidly. According to the 1990 US Census Bureau, self-confidence in English increases for children and grandchildren of these immigrants, and English takes over the native languages. Nearly half of second-generation Asian Americans aged five to seventeen reported speaking English exclusively. While Latino households are more likely than Asian households to be bilingual, two-thirds of third-generation Latino children reported speaking English exclusively (Rodriguez, 1999: 20).

Similar results were found in a study by John Hopkins University, which documented the attitudes toward language and ethnicity of 5,000 eighth- and ninth-grade immigrant children in Miami and San Diego (Sontag, 1993a: A10). In Miami, 99% of the children said they spoke English well or very well; in San Diego, 90% said they spoke it well. There was evidence that these children's attachment to their native languages is waning. A large majority of the Cuban, Haitian, and Filipino children said they preferred English to their parents' languages; 44% of Mexican children and 51% of Vietnamese children admitted to this preference. In only two of these groups, the Cubans and the Mexicans, the majority claimed to know their parents' languages well. However, the children were aware that acquisition of English does not guarantee instant acceptance into American society; a majority of all the groups, except the Cuban Americans, admitted to experiencing discrimination. Nor does acquiring English mean a loss of pride in and identification with their ethnicity: most of the children interviewed preferred to think of themselves as hyphenated Americans ("Haitian-American," "Mexican-American") or as "Haitians,'" "Mexicans," and so on, rather than as merely "Americans."

CONCLUSION

The image of the United States as the great melting pot of the world's peoples has been indelibly stamped on the consciousness of the nation. The thrust of the present chapter has been to analyze the melting-pot paradigm and to show that it is a false representation of the immigrant experience. First, we distinguished the melting pot from other concepts of immigrant adaptation. The expectation of most Americans is that immigrants will acculturate to mainstream Anglo-oriented society; they will take on the superficial aspects of being American: wearing the proper clothing, eating the proper food, speaking the proper language.

We then reviewed the history of immigration from the early seventeenth century to the early twentieth century. In analyzing the country's period of mass immigration from 1820 to 1924, we saw that many factors were involved in the persistence of native languages and culture. These factors relate to the nature of the immigrant groups themselves, and to the pressures placed on them from the larger society to disassociate from their homeland roots. We explored the question of whether the loss of language and culture is inevitable and desirable, and examined the case of the Chinese language, one particular language that has managed to endure. Finally, we challenged the common notion of those lamenting the loss of the melting-pot tradition that current immigrants resist the acquisition of English. We offered evidence that immigrants are generally eager to learn English. However, learning English does not have to mean giving up one's native language and culture, and does not insure automatic acceptance into mainstream society.

We have learned in this chapter that most immigrants do acculturate to American life to a degree, as a necessary part of survival in their adopted homeland. Acquiring English is of course part of this acculturation process. However, many established Americans find it difficult to understand why immigrants have such a hard time learning the new language, and why some never acquire true mastery of it. In the next chapter, we will cull the knowledge acquired from years of linguistic research to shed light on the very complex process of learning a second language. In doing so, it is hoped that those who have never had to function in a language other than their mother tongue will gain some compassion for and understanding of what language minorities go through in adjusting to a new language.

CHAPTER 3

Common Misconceptions About Language Learning

INTRODUCTION

A major source of antagonism toward language minorities today is the belief of mainstream Americans that these groups resist the learning of English. In the last chapter, evidence was given of the great need for English classes, and the eagerness with which non-native English speakers approach such classes. However, whether or not individuals are able to enroll in these classes, the acquisition of English is a slow and arduous task. The characteristics of this task are explored in the present chapter.

First, the chapter examines the attitudes of Americans toward second-language learning in general. It explores the source of their failure to view compassionately the process that language minorities go through in learning English. Then, various myths about language learning are examined from the viewpoint of what linguists presently know. The following topics are covered: the process of first-language acquisition, the age factor in second-language learning, the relationship of first-language acquisition to second-language acquisition, the determinants of successful second-language acquisition, the optimal time of initial exposure to and the optimal amount of exposure to the second language, the process of learning two languages at the same time, the role of first-language literacy in second-language acquisition, and the optimal length of bilingual education programs. An understanding of these issues is crucial before one can critically examine the types of instruction that the American school system offers non-native speakers of English.

AMERICANS AND SECOND-LANGUAGE LEARNING

By the time most US-born Americans reach adulthood, they have had some experience learning a language other than English. It may happen in an informal situation, for instance, by picking up some conversational expressions from a foreign-born co-worker, friend, or spouse. More often, though, it happens through formal education. As Americans have become more educated, staying in school longer than they have ever done in the past, it is likely that a number of them have gone through at least the elementary stages of second-language learning.

The American education system, however, is not usually geared to producing high levels of proficiency in second languages. Students study languages for one or two years, attending class two or three times a week and taking paper-and-pencil exams that require minimal familiarity with the language. In most cases, they can fulfill the second-language require-ments of their institutions without having to demonstrate real proficiency or fluency in the language. People often say that they "took Spanish" or "took French" in school; "taking" a language, however, is not synonymous with being able to speak it. As Lambert suggests, "There is nothing more damaging to the American capacity to cope in a global society than the abysmally low level of foreign language competency of most Americans" (Lambert, 1987: 10).

The educational system should not take sole responsibility for this. American society in general does not place high value on the ability to speak a second language. And why should it? Most Americans can get through life pretty well without having to speak a language other than English. Required second-language courses are viewed in much the same light as required courses in calculus: they are necessary if you want to get your degree, but you probably won't have a use for what you've learned in "real life."

Because Americans rarely need to acquire proficiency in a second language, they find it difficult to understand why recent immigrants struggle so much with learning English. By their own calculations, it should not take newcomers very long to acquire English. Wildavsky, for example, refers to "the worldwide experience of children taking not much more than half a year to get the hang of the language" (Wildavsky, 1992: 313). In the minds of many Americans, if they don't manage to do this, it means they probably haven't tried hard enough, or they aren't getting the right kind of instruction.

Americans often support these beliefs with stories about their own ancestors: how their grandparents' or great-grandparents' success was a result of their mastery of English. In defending the importance of English, the late Senator S.I. Hayakawa, an early advocate of official English, wrote of his family:

> My parents came from Japan to Canada, brought in part by my father's love of the English language and his dream of becoming a writer. Although he never realized that dream, his fluency in the language stood him in good stead throughout his life. At a time when many immigrant Japanese in Western Canada worked as field hands on farms, my father was able instead to organize crews of workers and negotiate their conditions of employment, because of his fluency in English. (cited in de la Peña, 1991: 11–12)

Hayakawa's tale is revealing in that what made his father stand out among Japanese immigrants was his English fluency; mastery of the English language was not common among his compatriots. Also, despite the fact that his father's English was better than that of others, it was not good enough to allow him to fulfill his greatest aspiration: to be a writer. The experience of the majority of Japanese immigrants hinted at in this story is typical of most immigrants of the early twentieth century: they relied heavily on their native languages. Learning English has always been an important part of the process of adjusting to a new life, but few immigrants have had the opportunity to acquire it fully.

There is a huge difference between past immigrants and the immigrants of today in terms of the consequences of not acquiring English. In the past, the industrial sector offered plentiful work opportunities for first-generation immigrants with only minimal knowledge of English. Such jobs were fairly stable, and provided workers with the means to raise their families, however modestly. Today's immigrants, faced with the same stresses of job and family responsibilities, face a greater burden than their predecessors, since the current job market demands both higher-level English literacy skills and higher-level technological skills than ever before. A report by the United States Chamber of Commerce found that one out of every five American workers has literacy skills below the fifth-grade level; it warned of a shortage of 23 million "technologically literate" workers by the year 2000 (Armbruster, 1992: 3A). Irwin Kirsch, the project director of a comprehensive study of American literacy conducted by the Department of Education, notes that the definition of illiteracy has changed. The word used to refer to people who couldn't sign their own names or who had only a few years of elementary-school education. Today, says Kirsch, "many people can read in the technical sense that they can decode words, but they lack the strategies and skills needed to use the information" (cited in Kaplan, 1993: 44–45). Using this latter definition of literacy, the study found that half of the individuals scoring in the lowest 20% had graduated from high school. White Americans scored higher than most other ethnic groups; among those scoring the lowest were the elderly, prison inmates, and immigrants. There has always been pressure placed on immigrants to learn English, but the stakes have never been as high as they are now.

If Americans know little about second-language learning from their own direct experience, they don't learn much more from other sources. Research in the field has existed for decades, yet is rarely communicated to the general public; you don't find articles on the latest studies in the science section of your local newspaper. Whatever information the public does get, through the print and television news media, tends to project the biases of groups with vested political interests. Crawford explains how this applies to the most prominent linguistic issue today, bilingual education:

> As yet, we have no Carl Sagan of linguistics ("Billions and billions of sentences..."). Many otherwise informed Americans seem oblivious to the field's existence. Journalists, frequently unable to determine who the experts are, tend to spread more confusion than enlightenment. Because bilingual education is controversial, it is reported less as a pedagogical field than a political issue.... The result has been to lend credibility to critics whose expertise approximates that of the Flat Earth Society. "We think native language instruction holds kids back," says Kathryn Bricker of US English, and her words are broadcast to the millions via network television. Yet Bricker has no training or expertise in the subject; her career has consisted of advocacy for English Only and immigration restrictions. By contrast, bona fide experts in second-language acquisition tend to have little patience with these simplistic debates or their media impresarios, and thus avoid them. This is unfortunate. (Crawford, 1992: 210)

In fact, language is one of the few topics that all people seem to feel entitled to discuss authoritatively. Donna Christian, the president of the Center for Applied Linguistics, explains, "People would never pontificate about a physics issue, because they would acknowledge that you need to consult an expert. But they wouldn't hesitate to pontificate about language" (cited in Fox, 1999: 40). The study of grass-roots opinions about language, known as "folk linguistics," has begun to interest some language researchers. By examining what ordinary people believe to be true about language, they are able "to identify some of the deeper impulses beneath the public battles: among them, fear of the unfamiliar, insistence of language 'standards' as a way of preserving the social status quo and the condemnation of 'substandard' speech as a coded expression of prejudice against the speaker" (Fox, 1999: 40).

With the growing population of language minorities in American public schools and colleges, knowledge about the process of language learning should no longer be limited to experts who speak only to each other.

Everyone, especially those involved in public education, needs information that is clear and unbiased. Misconceptions about language learning are spread widely in the press and are used by those who have political motives for attacking programs that might benefit non-native speakers of English. The following section challenges some of these misconceptions.

MYTH 1: CHILDREN ACQUIRE THEIR FIRST LANGUAGE QUICKLY AND EFFORTLESSLY

It is true that children of normal abilities and in normal circumstances learn their first languages thoroughly. However, the process of first-language acquisition is neither quick nor effortless. Instead, it is a time-consuming and demanding task that children work at throughout their formative years.

McLaughlin (1978) explains that learning to communicate begins immediately. Babies discover the ability to express their needs and emotions through crying, which brings an adult eager to relieve whatever discomfort they are experiencing, and cooing, which communicates contentedness. They show an awareness of sounds by turning their heads in the direction of their origin. They begin to differentiate sounds after a few weeks, responding more readily to high-pitched human voices (their mothers') than to any other sound. Upon observing mothers and infants as they grew from ten weeks to eighteen months, Holzman (1997) found that four kinds of communicative development – gestures, conversation, and the perception and pronunciation of speech sounds – occur simultaneously. As she describes, "Mothers behave toward their infants as though their infants' arm and body movements and babbles, cries, and vegetative noises were intended by the infants to be meaningful and to communicate meaning" (Holzman, 1997: 60).

According to McLaughlin (1978), babbling represents babies' first attempts at producing language. During the second half of their first year, they produce an increasing variety of vocalizations in increasingly complex combinations, including sounds that are not used in the particular language they are exposed to. The adults around them encourage this activity by repeating and reinforcing these sounds. Babies' first words are those which connect to things in the real world: "milk," "daddy," "mama." As children's language develops, two-word and three-word strings represent certain semantic intentions that can only be understood in context. For example, "Mommy push" might mean that a child sees her mother pushing something, or that she wants her mother to push her. At times, even an awareness of the context may not be enough for an adult to understand what the child wants to express. But children are usually surrounded by adults who will expend any amount of effort necessary to understand what their vocalizations mean. At every step in their language development, children tend to get just the right kind of reinforcement, encouragement, and understanding they need from the adults who take care of them.

An important step occurs when children learn that words have meanings beyond those attached to the immediate moment. As Holzman explains, words are first learned "as components of gestures and rituals.... Then, slowly or suddenly, the child gains the insight that everything has a name, and words become abstract symbols for the child rather than utterances tied to particular gestures or occasions" (Holzman, 1997: 84).

By the time children reach their third year, they are able to verbalize fairly complex utterances, showing, for example, an awareness of the difference between declarative sentences and questions, and the ability to express negation (McLaughlin, 1978). The grammatical correctness of sentences, the naturalness with which they are spoken, and the placement of key words affect children's understanding of what they hear (Gerken & McIntosh, 1993; Shady & Gerken, 1999). They can also formulate complex sentences using subordination (with words such as *because* and *when*) and relative pronouns (*that, which,* and *who*). However, syntactic errors (such as *What did you did?*) are still evident, Also, while their speech shows that they have acquired many of the rules of the language, children will often overgeneralize these rules to new instances in which they are inappropriate. This process produces words like *comed* and *gived, mouses* and *womans* (McLaughlin, 1978). Such errors are frequently corrected by those closest to the children: siblings, mothers, and fathers (Penner, 1987; Strapp, 1999).

When children enter school at the age of five or six, their language is still evolving. Errors produced by rule over-generalization have been reduced, but vocabulary and syntactic development continues. Six-year-olds have difficulty understanding passive-voice sentences (*The apple was eaten by John*), and more difficulty producing them. At age seven, some children begin producing passive sentences when shown pictures illustrating the event, but only after being given an example and only when the object acted upon (*the apple*) is shown in the picture. Much of the progress in language acquisition happens in school, as it becomes necessary for children to deal with increasingly complex and abstract subject matter. As McLaughlin explains, "The acquisition of language is a dynamic process, reflecting the child's changing experiences with the linguistic and non-linguistic environment [and] reflecting the gradual expansion and exercise of the child's cognitive capacities" (McLaughlin, 1978: 46).

MYTH 2: AGE IS A DISADVANTAGE IN SECOND-LANGUAGE LEARNING: YOUNGER LEARNERS ARE BETTER AT ACQUIRING A SECOND LANGUAGE THAN OLDER LEARNERS

Common wisdom and experience suggest that young children have the least trouble acquiring a second language. Take an average six-year-old French child, put him in a playground with English-speaking children his own age, and he will soon be conversing happily with his playmates. Adults look on wistfully and wish that they could pick up a language so easily and naturally.

However, this idyllic image of child second-language learning is only a fantasy, and the adults' envy is greatly misplaced. Just as children spend a great deal of time and effort learning their first language, learning a second language requires comparable exertion. This is illustrated in a study carried out by Valette (1964), who observed her American-born, English-speaking three-year-old son Jean-Michel acquire French after her family moved to Paris. Enrolled in a French nursery school, Jean-Michel interacted with French children five days a week, eight hours a day, for nine months. He first learned to understand what was said to him, then began to invent a language vaguely resembling French, and gradually replaced the invented language with actual French words and phrases. At home, he relied on English to ask his parents about words he didn't yet know. He acquired French intonation patterns before mastering pronunciation, grammar, and vocabulary. According to Valette, it took Jean-Michel nine months to acquire accurate French pronunciation. At the end of these nine months, at the age of four, he had acquired only the equivalent language proficiency of a three-year-old native speaker of French. Clearly, he had made progress in his mastery of French, but was still at the beginning of this long and complex task.

One reason why people assume that children learn second languages easily is that, because of their tender age, less language proficiency is asked of them. In a nursery-school setting, young children spend most of their time interacting in the here-and-now, physical environment. Much of their communication occurs while manipulating objects: playing with toys, drawing pictures, playing games in which actions are repeated over and over. In this environment, body signals are an alternative mode of communication to language, and perhaps a more efficient one. That Jean-Michel was not able to catch up to his French-speaking peers in the physically-oriented environment of a nursery school attests to the difficulty of learning a second language even at an elementary stage. It also suggests that older learners, facing the demands of more complex language proficiency, have a more difficult task confronting them.

Aside from the greater demands for proficiency faced by older learners, a popular theory of several decades ago contended that, as the learner gets older, biological constraints make language learning more difficult. A major proponent of the *critical period argument* was Lenneberg (1967), who claimed that the peak period for second-language learning occurs between the ages of two and puberty. Before puberty, according to Lenneberg (1967), the functions of the brain are not set into the left and right hemispheres; the brain has *cerebral plasticity.* After puberty, mental functions become specialized into one of the two hemispheres. This argument purportedly accounts for the inability of most language learners beyond puberty to acquire a second language automatically, from mere exposure to the language, and to acquire a native-like accent in the second language.

However, a wealth of linguistic research from around the world and making use of different methodologies challenges the notion of the critical period (e.g. Singleton, 1989); a few will be mentioned here. Snow and Hoefnagel-Hohle (1978) followed for one year the acquisition of Dutch by 81 Americans, ranging in age from three to adulthood, who had moved to Holland. The children were exposed to more Dutch than the adults were, since they were attending school in Dutch and playing with Dutch children. In contrast, the American adults were able to speak more English with their counterparts than their children, since many Dutch adults speak English; also, most of the American adults were taking language courses that were no more than 26 hours long. However, when the subjects were tested on aspects of Dutch ranging from pronunciation to grammar to translation and storytelling, the age differences almost consistently favored the older subjects over the younger ones. In another case of Americans abroad, Smith (1935) studied the diaries of an American woman who recorded the development of her eight children, all born in China, from the birth of her first child to some time after the family moved back to America. Part of the data recorded was the speech development of the children in both Chinese and English. Smith's analysis of the diaries showed that, when the family returned to America, the older children had much less difficulty adjusting to an all-English environment than the younger children did.

Some of the studies focus on the formal second-language learning of children of different ages. Genesee (1981) investigated the effects of three different French immersion programs for English-speaking children in Canada. In these immersion programs, the second language was used as the medium of instruction for all courses. In the periods before and after the immersion instruction, students took French-instruction courses, and after immersion they also had one or two courses given in French. Genesee compared a two-year late-immersion program for seventh and eighth graders, a one-year late-immersion program for seventh graders, and an early total-immersion program from kindergarten to sixth grade. He found that, by the ninth grade, the early-immersion group scored higher than the one-year immersion group on only two tests, and scored comparably to the two-year immersion group. Starting intensive second-language learning at an early age did not prove to be advantageous; the older students learned faster and eventually caught up with the younger ones. Politzer and Weiss (1969) tested American children in the first, third, fifth, seventh, and ninth grades with no knowledge of French on their ability to discriminate between French vowel sounds, to repeat the pronunciation of French words, and to recall those words. Again, the older children achieved consistently higher scores than the younger children, suggesting that they had a greater state of readiness for learning the language.

Linguists believe that the greater efficiency of older second-language learners is linked to their more developed cognitive skills and their greater knowledge of their first language. According to Ervinn-Tripp, the older learner "has a fuller semantic system, so he merely needs to discover a new symbolic representation." He also "has more efficient memory heuristics, related to his greater knowledge.... The older learner is smarter. The child's capacity to solve problems, to make sub-rules, to carry in mind several principles increases with age" (Ervinn-Tripp, 1974: 122). The older learner's metalinguistic knowledge – that is, knowledge about language – gives him an advantage in learning a second language, and can be called on beneficially in second-language instruction. As Masny indicates:

> In second-language acquisition, metalinguistic awareness as reflected in the ability to make language judgments may well interact with different aspects of second-language competence, such as listening and speaking.... The heightening of metalinguistic awareness in the classroom may well facilitate second-language development and lead to greater control over speaking, reading, and writing competence. (Masny, 1984: 71)

Wenden (1998) conducted a selective review of the theoretical and research literature on cognition. She concluded that language learning can be facilitated when teachers gain an understanding of their learners' beliefs and acquired knowledge about language learning, and when they help learners develop a more reflexive approach to learning a new language. When learners begin to understand their own language-learning process, "they can begin to use these new insights to experiment with different approaches to learning without guidance, i.e. autonomously – drawing upon solutions and knowledge that have been validated and looking critically at or even discarding what has not" (Wendon, 1998: 531). Clearly, older learners are better able to do this than younger ones.

There does seem to be one area in which children excel over their elders: the ability to acquire native-like pronunciation of a second language. For instance, in a study by Asher and Garcia (1969), Cuban children in the

United States, between the ages of seven and nineteen, all in this country for about five years, were judged on the nativeness of their spoken English by Americans listening to tapes of the children repeating sentences. In this case, the younger children performed better than the older children. The authors concluded that the younger children are when they come to this country, the greater their probability of acquiring near-native pronunciation in English, and that this probability increases the longer they live here. Linguists attribute the ability of children to acquire the sound system of a second language to their greater malleability, suggesting that Lenneberg's (1967) critical-period hypothesis contains a piece of the truth. Mägiste argues:

> There seems to be no critical age for second-language learning, but rather there appears to be an optimal age. If the language task allows for the students' cognitive level, younger students will generally acquire that task with greater ease, because of their greater spontaneity, flexibility, and imitative ability. With increasing age the students become more conscious and reserved. Their readiness to make contacts and to imitate other people decreases considerably. (Mägiste, 1984: 56)

Fathman explains the difference between younger and older learners in this way: "The preteen years may encompass a period during which the ability to discriminate, to interpret or to imitate sounds is manifested more fully; whereas, after puberty the ability to learn rules, to make generalizations or to memorize patterns may be more fully developed" (Fathman, 1975: 251). Of course, many older children and adults do acquire native-like pronunciation in a second language, sometimes with the aid of advanced courses or speech therapy. But, in general, young children do seem to acquire a native-like accent more easily and naturally than older children and adults do.

Recent brain research supplies further evidence that language learning is a different experience for children and adults (Kim *et al.*, 1997; Blakeslee, 1997). It has been known for some time that languages and language abilities reside in different areas of the brain; bilingual adults who are stroke victims or who have epilepsy often retain only one language. However, it was not known how or when these separate areas are formed. Using functional magnetic resonance imaging (a non-invasive procedure), researchers have been able to compare the brains of subjects who learned two languages in infancy with those who learned their second language around the age of eleven. Two parts of the brain were examined: Wernicke's area, which is dedicated to understanding word meanings and subject matter, and Broca's area, which is responsible for the execution of speech and some grammatical aspects of language. All the subjects had only one Wernicke's area, which was activated when they spoke either language. However, the subjects who had acquired bilingualism as infants had one Broca's region; the subjects who had acquired it later had two such regions, each of which was activated for a single language. According to the researchers, this suggests that babies learn to talk using all their faculties – hearing, vision, touch, and movement – which feed into hardwired circuits such as Broca's area; this region functions for both languages. Learners who acquire a second language at a later age have to acquire new skills for generating the sounds of the new language. However, learning the semantic aspects of the second language may be less difficult for them.

From the body of research on age and second-language acquisition, we can conclude, along with Singleton, that "given the right learning conditions, learners exposed to early second-language instruction probably have some advantage in the very long run over those whose exposure begins later." However, for those who start instruction at a later age, "there is every reason to believe that, again given suitable learning conditions, such learners can in most respects be as successful in acquiring a second language as their juniors" (Singleton, 1989: 267). With respect to the situation of minority-language children in the United States, the research suggests that they should not be expected to learn English quickly and effortlessly; if they begin studying English a few years after their arrival, their learning rate and efficiency will increase. Discussions of the various options for educating minority-language children need to be based on this crucial information.

MYTH 3: SECOND LANGUAGES SHOULD BE LEARNED IN THE SAME WAY AS FIRST LANGUAGES, BY BEING USED IN NATURAL, EVERYDAY SITUATIONS

Regardless of the age of the learner, learning a second language is different from learning a first language. As discussed in Myth 1, first-language learning takes place in an optimal environment. Babies are exposed to the sounds of their language as soon as they are born. Their every effort to communicate is met with an appropriate response. The adults around them correct them and encourage and reward their progress, which is allowed to proceed at its own pace. Also, first-language learners are constantly exposed to a stream of input from different speakers communicating at different levels of proficiency in different situations. As they grow, these language learners make use of all this exposure in formulating hypotheses about the language, hypotheses that are constantly tested and reformulated as the learners interact with all the people in their lives.

In contrast, second-language learners often live in an environment in which access to the second language is limited; language minorities, for example, usually hear and speak their first languages in their homes and communities, and often at work. Their efforts to speak the second language are less likely to be met with correction, encouragement, or reward. When they do hear the second language, they are less likely to be exposed to the range of speakers, levels of proficiency, and situations that the first-language learner is, which limits their ability to create and test hypotheses about the new language. While babies spend a great deal of time listening and becoming accustomed to the sounds of their first language before they speak their first words, second-language learners are expected to begin speaking immediately. In addition, they may find themselves in second-language situations that are well beyond their proficiency, such as a newly-arrived teenage immigrant placed in an all-English tenth-grade history class. Finally, they are no longer babies when they begin learning the language; having developed cognitive abilities that babies don't have, the process of second-language learning is qualitatively different from that of first-language learning.

In light of this, formal instruction offers second-language learners advantages that may not be readily available in their daily lives. It can duplicate some of the conditions that make first-language learning possible. Krashen (1982) notes that a language, be it the first or second, is acquired when the language input available to the learner contains struc-tures that are slightly beyond the learners' level of competence. Learners make use of their own store of knowledge, extra-linguistic cues, and the context of the communication to understand what is said and to move to a higher level of proficiency. As children learn their first language, the people who speak to them, called *caretakers*, modify their language roughly to the children's level of competence. Contained in their language are structures that the children have already acquired and structures that they have not acquired and are not ready for. Neither of these will teach the children anything new. But caretaker language also includes structures just beyond the children's competence, which Krashen (1982) calls *comprehensible input*; it is from this component of caretaker speech that children acquire a higher level of proficiency. As they progress, the caretakers increase the level of language difficulty. This is not done consciously, but is done efficiently and effectively. In a second-language classroom, the same conditions can be deliberately replicated.

According to the literature that Krashen reviews, classroom instruction in a second language is more beneficial to some learners than to others: "Language teaching helps ... for beginners and for foreign language students who do not have a chance to get input outside the class. It will be of less help where rich sources of input are available" (Krashen, 1982: 34). For those who need classroom instruction, Krashen and Terrell (1983) advocate what they call the *Natural Approach*. The teacher exposes learners to "natural, communicative, roughly-tuned comprehensible input" that "take[s] advantages of the acquirer's knowledge of the world" (Krashen, 1982: 25); the input is made more understandable with the use of realistic pedagogical aids such as pictures, photographs, and objects used in everyday life. The learners use their already-acquired world knowledge and their knowledge of the language they are learning to understand the material presented to them; in doing so, they acquire new knowledge about the language. The teacher then pushes up a notch the level of comprehensible input of the classroom.

Minority-language speakers who live and work with English-speaking Americans are more likely to get exposed to comprehensible input. These Americans, invested in understanding and being understood by the language learners, may act as the newcomers' caretakers, modifying their speech to the appropriate level. In many cases, however, minority-language speakers do not get the kind of English input they need. The English-speakers with whom they come into contact, those who are most likely to live in their neighborhoods, may speak a non-standard variety of English themselves.

Also, even when language learners do come into contact with standard-English speakers, the situations in which they interact may not be conducive to the language learners' improvement in English. The learners are often low-level employees in their places of work; there is little incentive for their co-workers or bosses to help them master the language. Often, the English these learners acquire is very simplified and telegraphic, understandable but lacking the finer grammatical nuances such as verb tense (*He go yesterday*), verb agreement (*She like ice cream*), and plurality (*I have two dollar*). Selinker calls this an *interlanguage*: "a separate linguistic system ... which results from a learner's attempted production of a [target language] norm" (Selinker, 1972: 214). In characterizing this type of English as a system, Selinker points out its stability and predictability; an interlanguage is resistant to change. As we mentioned in the previous chapter, Selinker labels speech of this nature *fossilized*, composed of "linguistic items, rules and subsystems which speakers of a particular [native language] will tend to keep in their [interlanguage] ... no matter what the age of the learner or amount of explanation and instruction he receives in the [target language]" (Selinker, 1972: 215). Despite Selinker's pessimism, formal instruction may be the only way that learners can push through this stagnant stage. The classroom may be the only place that comprehensible input is made available to them, and where the input is constantly regulated to meet their progress.

Children and young adults may find themselves in either situation. One important factor is the proficiency level of their parents and other family members with whom they are in daily contact. If the important people in their home lives speak no English or have only low proficiency in English, comprehensible input is obviously not available to them. If their family members do speak English well, much language learning will take place outside any formal instruction they receive. A second factor is the amount of comprehensible input available in classes other than their English language courses. If the learners have sufficient knowledge of English to allow them to understand the instruction in these courses, and/or if the level of instruction in these courses is geared to their proficiency, language learning will progress in these courses as well as in language-instruction classes.

Linguists have long advocated access to academic courses for language learners. In describing bilingual programs, Gaarder notes the importance of using the students' second language "as a means to an end rather than an end in itself" (Gaarder, 1967: 111). Texas' Statewide Design for Bilingual Education called both for content instruction in children's dominant language, "encouraging the child to enter immediately into the classroom activities, drawing from all his previous experiences as a basis for developing new ideas and concepts," and also for content instruction in the second language, "providing the vocabulary and concepts which are needed for communication while the second language is being learned" (cited in Harvey, 1976: 232). In a study of 24,000 minority-language children and the factors that affect their academic achievement, Thomas and Collier found that "students achieve significantly better in programs that teach language through cognitively complex content, taught through problem-solving, discovery learning in highly interactive classroom activities" (Thomas & Collier, 1995: 5).

A second advantage of formal language instruction is that it meets the cognitive needs of second-language learners. As we noted previously, by virtue of the fact that they are older, second-language learners do not go through the same process that they did when they learned their first language. With their more developed mental capabilities, second-language learners are able to understand the rules and structures of the new language and apply these rules when they use the language. They are also likely to have questions about how the language works and make use of the answers they receive as they develop an understanding of the structure of the new language. Even if these learners get enough comprehensible input in their daily lives, it may be difficult for them to find either the time to ask these questions, or the people willing and able to explain how the new language works. This is of course what language teachers are trained to do, and what language classes are designed for.

Linguists do not all agree on the value of instruction that focuses on the form of a language. Krashen, for one, does not believe that attention to form is productive. He distinguishes between *language acquisition*, a subconscious process in which learners are focused on communication, and *language learning*, a conscious process which results in knowledge of the rules of the language and the ability to talk about these rules. Acquisition and learning have two different roles: "Acquisition 'initiates' our utterances in a second language and is responsible for our fluency.... Learning comes into play only to make changes in the form of our utterance" (Krashen, 1982: 15). According to Krashen, acquisition is more central to the mastery of a language; learning is limited in usefulness. Only simple rules are remembered, indicating that learning is most beneficial at the early stages of acquiring the language. In order to apply a rule, the learner must have sufficient time and must be focused on form rather than on content. These conditions do not exist when the learner is expected to produce language quickly and fluently. The classroom should therefore focus on language acquisition. Language teaching "helps second-language acquisition when it supplies comprehensible input, which is the true cause of second-language acquisition" (Krashen, 1982: 34).

Others contend that discussion of and exercises in the structure of the new language are more beneficial than is suggested by Krashen (1982). In a review of research on the effects of formal instruction in various learning situations, Long concludes that

> instruction is good for you, regardless of your proficiency level, of the wider linguistic environment in which you receive it, and of the type of test you are going to perform on. Instruction appears to be especially useful in the early stages of [second-language acquisition] and/or in acquisition-poor environments, but neither of these conditions is necessary for its effect to show up. (Long, 1983: 379–380)

Many linguists point to the benefit of instruction for older learners in particular. Sharwood Smith, for example, writes that "it is notoriously difficult to deny adult learners explicit information about the target language since their intellectual maturity as well as their previous teaching/learning experience makes them cry out for explanations" (Sharwood Smith, 1981: 159–160). Sharwood Smith also points out that there is probably an interface between learning and acquisition:

> From learner performance in tests and interviews we may observe that some rules are acquired but the learner is quite unable to account for them in any explicit way, i.e. they are not part of learned competence. In other cases, rules are verbalized by the learners but may not turn up in spontaneous speech.... This and other research ... is strongly suggestive of the fact that two knowledge sources exist. (Sharwood Smith, 1981: 163)

One possible route to second language acquisition is through self-instruction, in which the learner finds materials on her own and studies it by herself. However, Jones (1994, 1998) found that for adult learners, the best method is a combination of instruction types: classroom instruction used in the beginning, self-instruction phased in at the point at which the learner attains intermediate proficiency, followed by the two types of instruction continuing simultaneously. For the learner to attain high second-language proficiency, then, classroom instruction seems to be an important element, and focus on language rules remains a staple of such instruction. Krashen's theories about language and acquisition have inspired greater research into this area; his ideas continue to be examined and developed (Barasch & James, 1993).

MYTH 4: PEOPLE WHO FAIL TO LEARN A SECOND LANGUAGE WELL HAVE ONLY THEMSELVES TO BLAME; THEY JUST AREN'T TRYING HARD ENOUGH

As mentioned previously, many adult immigrants to the United States acquire a kind of English which allows them to communicate in the most basic manner, but which falls far short of what most Americans consider good or proper English. But why do some people stop at this stage while others progress through it? If, as we said above, adults are just as capable as children of acquiring a second language, why don't all adult immigrants learn English well?

One reason may be that their life situations don't provide the circumstances conducive to improving their English. As mentioned above, many immigrants are socially isolated from the rest of society, and are quite capable of leading their lives speaking their own languages and a very basic form of English. But, it may be argued, there are always opportunities for language minorities to seek out contact with English-speakers if they are willing to look for them. Joining a different church, becoming familiar with a different part of town, finding an English-speaking friend, looking for a job outside one's neighborhood are all possibilities. So, of course, is finding an English class. Looked at this way, learning a second language appears to be largely dependent on the deliberate and conscious choices of the language learner.

However, language learning is a much more complex process than this point of view suggests; even under optimal circumstances, language learning may fail. Linguists have long pondered the many variables that influence the outcome of language learning, such as age, intelligence, language aptitude, and classroom methodology. Some linguists have come to realize that these factors may not be the crucial ones, that in fact subtle social and psychological forces may have more to do with success than anything else.

Schumann (1978) is a proponent of this theory. He and several colleagues undertook a ten-month study that followed the untutored acquisition of English by six native speakers of Spanish. On the basis of this study as well as evidence from other research studies, Schumann (1978) came to believe that what matters most in language acquisition is the *social distance* and the *psychological distance* between second-language learners and native speakers of the target language. He theorizes that the greater the social and psychological distance between the two groups, the more difficult second-language acquisition is. There is an assumption that these two groups have an established relationship – certain feelings and attitudes toward each other based on direct contact or information gleaned about each other from various sources. Consequently, according to Schumann (1978), this situation applies less to a foreign-language learning setting and more to one in which the language learners are living in the country where native speakers of the target language live.

The social distance between the two groups is determined in part by the relative status of the groups: whether the second-language group is dominant, equal, or subordinate to the target-language group. The life-style strategy chosen by the second-language group is crucial. Is the goal of the group to adopt the target-language culture, preserve its own culture, or maintain its own culture while adapting to the new culture? The degree to which social interaction is approved, by either or both groups, is also important; this includes attitudes toward intermarriage and the integration or segregation of social institutions such as schools and recreational facilities. The size and cohesiveness of the second-language group come into play, as well as the length of time the group intends to stay in the new country. The degree of difference or similarity between the two cultures is another factor. Finally, the attitudes of the groups toward each other will also affect social distance.

While social distance depends on the characteristics of and decisions made by the language group, psychological distance depends on the way in which individuals react to their new life situation. According to Schumann (1978), the primary problem for those living away from home is alienation. The solution to alienation (joining the target-language community and learning the new language) is often frustrated by fears, anxieties, and insecurities. The learners may feel suspicious of the target-language group, or may be pressured by their own community to maintain their native identity. A general sense of disorientation is caused by *language shock* (the inability to express oneself fully in the second language), *culture shock* (fatigue from the huge resources of energy expended trying to cope with the new culture), and *culture stress* (issues of identity loss when the learners' status in the new country is different from what it was in their own country).

The connection between anxiety and language acquisition is illustrated in a study by MacIntyre *et al.* (1997) of young adult English-dominant students learning French in Canada. Students who exhibited anxiety about speaking a new language tended to underestimate their proficiency in the language and to communicate less often. By communicating less often, they were likely to diminish the opportunity to advance their proficiency, and possibly intensify their existing level of anxiety, in a kind of vicious cycle. In contrast, students with a more relaxed attitude toward speaking French overestimated their proficiency level and communicated in the language to a greater extent. MacIntyre *et al.* (1997) suggest that such over-estimation may not be problematic; with their greater willingness to communicate, these students were more likely to advance their proficiency than their more anxious peers. While this study did not deal with immigrants, the results are applicable to the situation of individuals who are newly arrived in a country with an unknown language, since anxiety about the new language is a likely characteristic.

Two other psychological forces can also affect an individual's ability to learn the language of the target group. The presence or absence of *motivation* on the part of the learner can influence the success of language learning. Motivation takes two forms: *integrative* (the desire to become a member of the target-language group), and *instrumental* (the desire to learn the target language to attain a particular goal, such as getting a better job or going to college). Finally, Schumann (1978) refers to the learner's degree of empathy, or *ego permeability*, as a determinant in language learning. People with permeable egos are those able to let down their guard on their own identities so that the new way of speaking and behaving characteristic of the target-language group can enter. These people are also sensitive to the subtle cues of behavior and feeling on the part of others and can therefore emulate the behaviors they see in speakers of the target language. Ego permeability is thought to diminish with age for some language learners, and this may contribute to the ease that younger learners have in picking up the rhythm and accent of a new language.

Besides Schumann, the prominent linguists William Gardner and Richard Lambert were in the forefront of the study of the psychological factors in second-language learning. Gardner and Lambert (1972) identified the different attitudinal bases behind the motivation necessary for successful second-language acquisition: parental support and encouragement, identification with the language teacher, sensitivity to other people's feelings, a personal interest in the people and culture represented by the language group (integrative orientation), a belief in the usefulness of knowing the language (instrumental orientation), positive attitudes toward the group speaking the language, and the absence of an ethnocentric attitude. After studying second-language learning in Canada, the United States, and the Philippines, Gardner and Lambert (1972) suggested that, for speakers of a dominant language studying a foreign language (such as American children learning French), an integrative outlook is more important. For speakers of minority languages learning a language of national importance (such as Filipinos learning English), both instrumental and integrative orientations are necessary. Gardner and Lambert also pointed out the importance for this latter group of becoming confident bilinguals and maintaining their national identity while acquiring the second language.

The study of attitudes and motivation has continued into the present, expanding the original work of the 1970s. For example, Gardner and MacIntyre (1991) found that even for those learning a foreign language in a clinical setting (English-dominant, Canadian psychology students studying and being tested in French vocabulary) both integrative and instrumental motivations affected the outcome. Similarly, Clément et al. (1994), studying eleventh-grade Hungarian students learning English, found that, despite the students' isolation from native speakers of the target language, both instrumental and integrative orientations were important factors, along with self-confidence and a feeling of group cohesion in the classroom. Findings such as these lead us to revisit the hypothesis of Schumann, Gardner and Lambert that a desire to connect with the speakers of a second language is more essential for learners who reside in a country where the language is being spoken. Integrative motivation appears to be a strong factor in successful second-language learning in general.

All of the variables mentioned above are likely to interact with each other, making language learning easier or more difficult. In the case of most minority-language speakers in the United States, the cumulative effect is negative. They usually find themselves in a position subordinate to English-language speakers; this low status restricts the amount of social interaction with English-speakers and encourages negative attitudes and suspicion on the part of both groups toward each other. The large size and cohesiveness of many minority-language and immigrant groups further deter social interaction. Differences between the native and target-language cultures inevitably exist, but may be exaggerated in the minds of members of both groups because of the lack of interaction between the two groups. Minority-language speakers are likely to opt for preserving their cultures or adapting to both lifestyles rather than substituting the new culture for their own, and there is often pressure on individuals to maintain their cultural identity. Integrative motivation may not be strong, although instrumental motivation may operate. The sense of alienation from American mainstream culture leads many immigrants to make plans to return to their countries when conditions are right, for instance when they have saved enough money or when the political outlook improves (indeed, trips to and extended stays in their countries are common among many immigrants from the Caribbean and Central America). A further effect of the interaction of these variables is high ego permeability: a determination to keep the native identity intact. These conditions also tend to aggravate culture shock, culture stress, and language shock.

This is, of course, a generalization. Not all these conditions hold for all language minorities, and many individuals do break out of the strictures that prevent them from forming relationships with English speakers and adapting to the American culture. But it is difficult to deny the reality of life for most immigrants, a reality that works against their learning English. It is also impossible to ignore the fact that language learners are not responsible for all aspects of this reality. America situates many of them in a subordinate social position, and treats them as such. The American media creates and spreads negative stereotypes of many minority-language groups, which fosters suspicion toward them and encourages Americans to avoid contact with them. This in turn discourages them from wanting to become members of mainstream society. So, while most language minorities try as hard as possible to learn English, fully aware that the achievement of their goals depends largely on how successful they are in mastering it, they are not conscious of the variety of obstacles in their way, obstacles constructed by their own psyches and by the larger society.

There are ways of countering the factors that impede second-language acquisition. Schumann writes:

> Successful adult second-language acquisition might be explained by the fact that under certain conditions adults can overcome the social and psychological barriers of their learning. External factors such as finding a surrogate family (Larsen & Smalley, 1972) or finding language instructors who have a deep understanding and acceptance of the learner's inadequacies, anxieties and insecurities (Curran, 1972) could enable the learner to overcome the trauma of language shock and culture shock. In addition, internal factors such as the development of an integrative motivation (Lambert *et al.*, 1970) might foster ego permeability such that the learner is able to partially and temporarily give up his separateness of identity from the speakers of the target language (Guiora *et al.*, 1972) and to incorporate a new identity so essential to bilingualism. (Schumann, 1975: 230–231)

Krashen (1982) echoes Schumann's (1975) concern for the affective variables influencing language learning, and also suggests ways to facilitate language learning. He targets three factors (motivation, self-confidence, and anxiety) which regulate what he calls an *affective filter*. Krashen explains:

> Those whose attitudes are not optimal for second-language acquisition will not only tend to seek less input, but they will also have a high or

strong Affective Filter.... Those with attitudes more conducive to second-language acquisition will not only seek and obtain more input, they will also have a lower or weaker filter. They will be more open to the input and it will strike "deeper." (Krashen, 1982: 31)

The classroom is one place where the atmosphere can be manipulated to allow for optimal conditions for language acquisition. Krashen suggests that "language teaching helps when it is the main source of low filter comprehensible input" (Krashen, 1982: 34). By regulating the type of input learners receive and incorporating factors which lower the affective filter, teachers and schools can create an atmosphere conducive to language learning.

In addition, Dörnyei (1994) suggests ways in which motivation can be fostered in the language classroom. At the language level, Dörnyei recommends such strategies as developing learners' cross-cultural awareness, promoting contact with speakers of the second language, and developing instrumental motivation. At the learner level, the instructor is urged to develop students' self-confidence, teach learning and communication strategies, and create a supportive environment to decrease anxiety. At the learning-situation level, Dörnyei suggests creating relevant course syllabi based on student needs, making course content attractive and understandable, using authentic materials, and involving students in the choice of teaching materials.

Finally, much can be done to create a school atmosphere that is conducive to successful language learning. Students often view school administrators and teachers as representatives of American culture; for some, they are the only Americans that the learners know. The way educators behave toward their students therefore affects the students' attitudes toward Americans in general: Is a sense of superiority and condescension being transmitted to the students, or do the students feel that they are equal to other members of the school community? Do teachers and administrators hold total control over school life, or do students have some sense of empowerment? The goals that are set for students and the expectations that the school has for them tell the students a lot about how they are regarded. Are students steered toward jobs that will keep them at the margins of American society, or are they encouraged to prepare for professions that offer them full participation in American life? The subject matter used in courses also sends messages. Does the school show respect for the learners' cultures, or is American culture valued over others? These questions will be crucial later on in this book, when we discuss the different models available for educating language minorities.

MYTH 5: IT IS NECESSARY FOR SOMEONE LEARNING A SECOND LANGUAGE TO USE IT AS SOON AS POSSIBLE AND TO BE EXPOSED TO AS MUCH OF IT AS POSSIBLE

Second-language learners are often urged to begin using the language upon their first exposure to it. This may seem to be a practical and efficient way to learn a second language, but in fact it may not be the best way. Research in child second-language acquisition in a natural setting shows that children often go through a *silent period* before trying to express their thoughts in a second language. For example, Ervin-Tripp (1974) observed 31 English-speaking children between the ages of four and nine enrolled in a French school in Geneva, Switzerland. She discovered that some children did not say anything in French for many months; some began speaking six to eight weeks after their enrollment in the school. In a study of a five-year-old Chinese boy learning English, Huang and Hatch (1978) found that, during the first month of his exposure to the language, the only English he uttered consisted of words and phrases he had memorized after hearing others say them. The silent period has its parallel in first-language acquisition: as we learned from McLaughlin (1978), babies hear a great deal of language before they begin to speak, and proceed slowly from babbling sounds to vocalizations to short word-strings to whole sentences.

Studies have also shown that delaying oral practice in second-language learning classes has benefits both for child learners (Gary, 1975) and for adult learners (Potovsky, 1974; Asher, 1969; Asher *et al.*, 1974; Swaffer & Woodruff, 1978). Dulay, Burt, and Krashen conclude from such studies that

> communication situations in which students are permitted to remain silent or respond in their first language may be the most effective approach for the early phases of language instruction. This approach ... appears to be more effective than forcing full two-way communication from the very beginning of [second-language] acquisition. (Dulay *et al.*, 1982: 25–26)

The silent period "is believed to help build up some competence through listening – enough to permit some spontaneous speech production without relying on the first language" (Dulay *et al.*, 1982: 109). For language development to occur successfully during the silent period, the language environment must provide "concrete referents – subjects and events than can be seen, heard, or felt while the language is being used;" these extra-linguistic clues "aid the learner in grasping the meaning of the strange sounds of the new language" (Dulay *et al.*, 1982: 26). It has been my own experience that sitting through a movie in French, a language that I don't know, leaves me with some feel for its sound and rhythm. Even though I do not consciously attend to the words – I'm busy reading the subtitles so that I won't miss anything – the language is entering my awareness at a certain level; I begin to recognize and understand some expressions that are repeated several times. By the time I leave the theater, the 90 minutes of exposure to French has left me feeling that I know what the language is supposed to sound like, even though I probably can't replicate it.

Another misconception about language learning is that the optimal learning situation is one in which the learner is exposed to the greatest amount of language possible. But this is not the case. In Krashen's (1982) theory of language acquisition, the learner may be exposed to many different levels of language input, but it is only that input just above the learner's level of competence that allows for progress. Any language input above that level is too sophisticated for the learner to make use of. So, if you know no Russian at all and you decide to attend a university class in Russian history given in that language, you are unlikely to learn any Russian by the time the course is over. In all probability, there will be very little extra-linguistic clues as to what is going on in the class, other than a map or two, that would allow you to connect the words you hear to something you can understand. If your knowledge of Russian history is minimal, you will be at a further disadvantage.

The notion of the importance of language quantity is often applied to the situation of children enrolled in schools that conduct classes in their second language. This line of reasoning is often called the *time-on-task argument*: the more time spent studying the second language and studying in the second language, the better. Yet the research fails to support this argument. We have previously mentioned a Canadian study by Genesee (1981), which showed that English-speaking students enrolled in French immersion programs from kindergarten to sixth grade did not score significantly higher on French tests than did students who were in one- or two-year immersion programs in the seventh and eighth grades. This occurred despite the greater cumulative exposure to French of the first group by the time all the students were evaluated in the ninth grade.

In another study refuting the time-on-task argument, Siegel (1997) looked at the effect of a preschool program conducted in Tok Pisin, an English-based pidgin learned by children in Papua New Guinea as a second language at an early age or simultaneously with an indigenous language. In that country it is widely believed that instruction in pidgin is a waste of time, and that standard English, the language of upward mobility, should be the medium of instruction. Comparing children who attended the preschool program with children who had not, Siegel (1997) found that children with early literacy instruction in the pidgin learned standard English more easily than those who had not. In addition, they did better in other academic subjects, had a lower drop-out rate, and continued to outperform their peers in the upper grades.

American studies have found similar results. Ramirez *et al.* (1991), for example, conducted an eight-year study comparing Spanish-speaking students in three types of programs: English immersion (from kindergarten to third grade), early-exit bilingual (from kindergarten to third grade), and late-exit bilingual (from kindergarten to sixth grade). All the students in all three programs improved in the areas measured – math (tested in English), English language arts, and English reading. However, students in the late-exit bilingual programs were able to decrease the gap between their own test scores and those of the mainstream population (English-speaking students in regular classes). The late-exit students who were most successful academically were those in the program that had the most consistent use of Spanish, were least likely to have been in all-English preschool programs, and were from families with the lowest incomes. Students in the three-year programs were not deemed ready to be mainstreamed at the end of the third year and were held in them longer than anticipated. Also, students who were abruptly transferred out of bilingual programs using substantial amounts of Spanish and into all-English programs did not fare as well as their counterparts who stayed in the bilingual programs. Greater exposure to English did not mean better performance; indeed, those students who had the most exposure to their first language (Spanish) had the best performance in English.

MYTH 6: WHEN CHILDREN LEARN A SECOND LANGUAGE AT THE SAME TIME THAT THEY LEARN THEIR FIRST LANGUAGE, THEY CONFUSE THE TWO AND DON'T LEARN EITHER ONE WELL

There have been a number of case studies of children who acquire two languages at the same time. These studies follow children in the first few years of their lives, as they learn to speak two languages from the people around them. The studies suggest that whether or not balanced bilingualism is achieved depends greatly on the circumstances in which the children learn to use the two languages. They also indicate that for many children there is a period in which they mix elements of the two languages. However, this mixing is often a phase that children go through on their way to bilingualism.

One way in which a child can become bilingual is when each person in the child's life consistently speaks one of the two languages and the child has an equal opportunity to use both languages. An early case study was undertaken by Ronjat (1913). Ronjat and his German-born wife decided to train their son Louis to speak two languages; Ronjat spoke only French to his son, his wife spoke only German, and other household members were identified as speakers of one of the two languages. By the age of two, Louis was aware of the difference between the two languages. He would test each new word by speaking it with either a German or a French accent, until he was prepared to assign it to his mother's or his father's language. He attempted to learn words in both languages simultaneously, often using one language to ask for the equivalent of a word in the other language. On occasions when he used a French word in German, he gave the word a German accent, doing the same with German words used while speaking French. He never showed any confusion, switching easily from one language to the other depending on the person he was addressing. The results of this upbringing were long lasting: at the age of 15, he was equally fluent in the two languages, preferring German for literature and French for technology.

This kind of balanced bilingualism maintained during childhood is unusual. It is more often the case that one language becomes dominant. Leopold (1939–1949) wrote a detailed, multi-volume study of the speech development of his daughter Hildegard from her birth until the age of 12. Hildegard spoke German to her father and English at all other times. During her first two years she began to develop the ability to express herself in both languages. But as she got older and her father's influence diminished, English became her dominant language. Her German suffered from interference with English. She tended to pronounce it with an English accent, and her sentences in German were interlaced with English words onto which she attached German prefixes and suffixes. Leopold contended that his daughter was aware of the existence of two separate languages early in her third year. However, because she had more opportunity to develop competence in English than in German, her German became increasingly passive; she did not become a balanced bilingual.

Bilingual children may go through a phase of mixing the two languages. Totten (1960) observed the development of his children, who were raised speaking Swedish and English, each the native language of one parent. After an initial period of mixing the two languages, the children developed an awareness of two separate language systems, and the mixing disappeared. Eventually, they acquired the accent of the more fluent parent in each language. When the languages that the children are acquiring are similar, mixing may be more likely to occur. Ruke-Dravina (1965) noted the sound confusions in the speech of two children learning Swedish and Latvian. The children tended to use the Swedish pronunciation of /r/ over the Latvian pronunciation of /r/ in words that were similar in the two languages. The mixing of languages can also occur when parents do not consistently speak a particular language. We have already discussed the study by Smith (1935) of an American missionary family living in China. A great deal of language mixing was noted in the children's speech until the age of three. The children heard Chinese from their Chinese acquaintances and English from their non-Chinese acquaintances; however, both parents spoke both languages at home, which was probably the cause of their early period of language mixing.

It appears from these studies that creating the optimal conditions for bilingual language development results in a very unnatural kind of life, one in which each person in a child's life must speak to the child in a particular language. But the studies can be interpreted in a broader way: bilingualism develops when children have ample opportunity to use each language in clearly-defined situations. There are variations on the one-parent-one-language theme: one language being used downstairs and the second one upstairs, or one language on Mondays, Wednesdays and Fridays, and the other on Tuesdays, Thursdays and Saturdays. In many cases in which children learn two languages, these clearly-defined situations occur naturally. For example, they may speak one language at home and another when visiting grandparents and older relatives. Children respond to routine, and, in terms of bilingualism, they adapt to using different languages in different contexts when this becomes habitual and expected.

In another view, raising bilingual children need not be as regimented as suggested by the studies mentioned here. Skutnabb-Kangas gives more general advice:

> Talk to the child as much as possible and as early as possible.... Try to organize for the child as many varied linguistic situations as possible in both languages.... Play linguistic games with the child.... Try to arrange for the child to get mother tongue instruction in both languages.... Try to show the child in practical situations, not only by discussions, how splendid it is, how useful and rewarding, to be able to participate as a native in two different cultures. Try to give the child a chance to be proud of her bilingualism and her cultural competence. (Skutnabb-Kangas, 1981: 152)

Existing school programs demonstrate that when children's simultaneous acquisition of two languages is properly supported, positive results accrue. Clark (1995) describes a kindergarten class in San Antonio, Texas, with predominantly low-income, Mexican-American students. While instruction was mostly in Spanish, students heard English from staff members in the school; for most students, both English and Spanish were used at home. As the children developed their Spanish writing ability, they voluntarily tried out English writing. Inventive spelling was used for both languages, with first-language knowledge applied to second-language writing. There was no indication that the children were confusing the languages and, given the school's commitment to supporting both languages, the students seemed well on their way to biliteracy.

Students might go through the stage of mixing the languages, or may resort to using one language to learn a word in the other language; they should be able to count on teachers and other students to help in their dual-language development. But it should be clear what language is to be spoken in each situation, and there must be ample opportunity to develop both languages. As we shall see later, this type of bilingual program is a rarity in the United States.

MYTH 7: CHILDREN WHO COME INTO THE AMERICAN SCHOOL SYSTEM WITH LITTLE OR NO LITERACY IN THEIR FIRST LANGUAGE SHOULD BE PLUNGED DIRECTLY INTO AN ALL-ENGLISH EDUCATION

American public schools in large urban areas have been experiencing an increase in the population of children for whom English is not the first language. In fall 1992, the US Census Bureau reported that 6.3 million children, or 14% of the total school-age population, did not speak English at home (*NABE*, 1993: 25). It is impossible to make generalizations about the children in this population, and one of the crucial ways in which they differ is their degree of native-language literacy. Some possess a native-language literacy comparable to the English literacy of their mainstream counterparts; others have little or no literacy in their own languages. Because public schools are often ill-equipped to evaluate native-language literacy, and because acknowledging this as an important factor in their education would necessitate programs tailored specifically to the different needs of different children, a common response to this wide range of native-language literacy levels is to merely ignore it and to insist that all children be instructed in English. This practice leads to what many believe to be predictable results. Children who enter American schools with a high degree of literacy in their own languages acquire English well and succeed academically; those who are illiterate or semi-literate in their native languages do not become highly literate in English and generally do poorly in school.

Cummins (1979) advances the theory that native-language literacy is an important factor in the achievement of second-language literacy. One piece of evidence that he points to is the difference in the outcomes of *immersion* and *submersion* programs. In immersion programs, children whose first language is the majority language of the community spend the first five or six years of school being instructed in a minority language. These children become highly biliterate and reach a high level of academic achievement. In submersion programs, minority-language children are placed together with majority-language children in classes conducted in the majority language. Minority-language children in these programs lose their first language but do not reach a high level of literacy in the majority language, leading to general academic failure.

Cummins (1979) believes that one of the crucial differences in these programs is the degree to which the children are able to develop first-language literacy. In immersion programs, while the children are not using their first language at school, they are exposed to written and oral forms of their language in their lives outside school. An important facet of immersion programs is that parents are committed to encouraging bilingualism and biliteracy in their children. In contrast, minority-language children in submersion programs have no opportunity to develop native-language literacy. Their teachers are often monolingual in the majority language, and the children's first language is treated as if it were an impediment to their learning of the majority language and to academic success. In addition, their parents may not encourage native-language literacy at home; the stresses and constraints of their life may leave them with little time and energy to do so, or the parents may be minimally literate themselves.

These two educational programs reflect two forms of bilingualism: *additive*, in which a second language is added to native-language knowledge, and *subtractive*, in which a second language gradually replaces the native language. A major differentiating factor of these programs is the relative social status of the students and the consequent value placed on their native languages: in additive bilingualism, the students' first language is socially prestigious, and they are not expected to lose it once they learn the second language. In subtractive bilingualism, the native language of the students lacks prestige; the second language is expected to replace the first one.

Cummins describes the outcomes of these two different approaches: "The bilingual child in an additive situation is likely to have relatively high levels of competence in both languages whereas in subtractive situations many bilinguals may be characterized by less than native-like levels in both languages" (Cummins, 1979: 229). He also points to a number of studies which show that additive bilingualism "can positively influence academic and cognitive functioning.... Significant differences have also been reported between bilinguals and unilinguals on measures of both general intellectual development ... and divergent thinking" (Cummins, 1979: 228–229).

This research evidence leads Cummins to posit what he calls the *threshold hypothesis*: "There may be threshold levels of linguistic competence which bilingual children must attain both in order to avoid cognitive deficits and to allow the potentially beneficial aspects of becoming bilingual to influence their cognitive growth" (Cummins, 1979: 229). Minority-language children will reap the greatest cognitive benefits of bilingualism if they are allowed to develop their native-language skills in increasingly complex cognitive tasks in both speaking and writing, just as majority-language children are urged to do in their native language.

Cummins (1979) believes that skills acquired in one language transfer to a second language. There is evidence, for example, that native-language and second-language reading scores correlate very highly. In immersion programs, the grade level at which native-language reading is introduced makes little difference to reading achievement in that language; even if native-language reading is introduced late, students do well. This suggests that the ability to extract meaning from the printed text transfers from one language to another. Further evidence of this is the difference in reading performance between majority-language and minority-language children. Majority-language children in immersion programs have little difficulty learning to read in the second language; in contrast, minority-language children in majority-language programs generally do poorly on reading tests in the majority language.

There is additional support for Cummins' hypothesis in countries where English is an important language, but not the native language of most of the people. Williams (1996) studied the reading ability in native language and English of fifth-grade students in Zambia and Malawi. These two African countries are similar in linguistic, cultural, historical, and socioeconomic backgrounds; in addition, they both consider English an important element in national unification and modernization. However, the countries differ in their educational policies. In Zambia, English-medium instruction begins in the first grade, and one of seven local languages is taught as a subject. In Malawi, the national language, Chichewa, is the medium of instruction for the first to fourth grades, with English taught as a subject; after that, the roles of the languages are reversed. Williams (1996) gave reading tests in both English and the local languages to fifth-grade students in these countries. He found no difference in scores on the English reading test, but on the tests of local-language reading, the Malawian students scored significantly higher than the Zambian students. First-language instruction had no ill effects on second-language reading; in addition, the Malawian students gained the advantage of having more advanced bilingual reading ability than their Zambian counterparts.

Cummins (1979) points out that, before children learn to read, they must first acquire two important insights: that print is meaningful, and that written language differs from speech. Secondly, they must be able to assimilate decontextualized language, that is, language that is not tied to the physical here-and-now. Finally, if they have already acquired the concepts that are represented in their first texts, reading will be easier. Majority-language children in immersion programs, living in an environment permeated with print in their native language, are generally ready to learn to read when they begin school. Even though they may be learning to read in a second language, they will probably have acquired the concepts they will read about because their parents have read to them in their first language; the essential task for them will be to apply new labels to concepts they already understand. Minority-language children being instructed in the majority language are much less likely to learn to read successfully. They may not have been read to in their native language, and so have not acquired the insights that print is meaningful and that written language differs from speech. Not having been exposed to a literate environment, they may not be able to assimilate decontextualized language and may not have acquired the concepts represented in their reading texts. All of this will make learning to read in the majority language extremely difficult, and may result in low levels of literacy and poor academic achievement.

From his insights into the existing research evidence, Cummins offers the *developmental interdependence hypothesis*: "The level of [second-language] competence which a bilingual child attains is partially a function of the type of competence the child has developed in [the native language] at the time when intensive exposure to [the second language] begins" (Cummins, 1979: 233). Many minority-language children have limited literacy skills in their native language when intensive instruction in the majority language begins. If the development of native-language literacy skills is ignored, this in turn limits the development of second-language literacy skills. This explains why so many minority-language children in the United States do poorly in school. And it should cast doubt on an educational system that pays little attention to the level of native-language literacy of its minority-language students.

MYTH 8: BILINGUAL PROGRAMS SHOULD BE SHORT-TERM AND THE FIRST LANGUAGE SHOULD BE PHASED OUT AS QUICKLY AS POSSIBLE

Where bilingual programs exist in American schools today, the prevalent form is the short-term, transitional one. Students remain in the program from six months to two years before being mainstreamed into regular classes; English is introduced early on and predominates as the first language is quickly phased out. This type of program is the easiest to implement, because it is likely to get the greatest support from the public. Everyone believes minority-language children need to learn English as quickly as possible. Allowing use of the native language in the early stages of schooling makes the educational system appear to be sensitive to the needs these children have adjusting to a new school system; limiting the extent of native-language use avoids the appearance that educators are coddling them too much. A short-term program also reassures the public that only a small portion of the public's tax dollars are going to meet the needs of this special student population.

However, all of the debunking of myths that has taken place in this chapter argues against short-term bilingual education. First, we have learned that the acquisition of a language is a long process that develops over an extended period of time (McLaughlin, 1978). Short-term programs do not give students the opportunity to develop their first languages to any significant degree, casting doubt on how "bilingual" they really are.

Second, there appear to be cognitive advantages to being bilingual (Cummins, 1979; Cummins & Gulutsan, 1974; Bain & Yu, 1978; Carringer, 1974; Landry, 1974). In order to become a balanced bilingual, however, it is necessary to have the time and opportunity to use both languages separately. Long-term programs provide the conditions necessary for balanced bilingualism to be achieved.

Third, the evidence suggests that the second-language learning of language minorities will not suffer if attention is paid to first-language development (Ramirez et al., 1991; Skutnabb-Kangas & Toukomaa, 1976; Collier, 1989; Thomas & Collier, 1995; Williams, 1996; Siegel, 1997). Delaying all-English instruction will not be detrimental to the learning of English, since neither the amount nor the immediacy of exposure to a second language is crucial to second-language learning, and older language learners are more efficient than younger ones (Snow & Hoefnagel-Höhle, 1978; Smith, 1935; Genesee, 1981; Politzer & Weiss, 1969; Burstall, 1975; Lapkin et al., 1980). It is more likely the case that first-language development enhances rather than deters second-language learning. There is much in the literature to suggest that skills learned in the first language transfer to the second language, and that those who attain high-level literacy in their first language are likely to achieve high-level literacy in a second language (Cummins, 1979; Gonzalez, 1977; Ramirez & Politzer, 1976; Modiano, 1968; Tucker, 1975; Hornberger, 1989; Swain & Lapkin, 1991; Clark, 1995).

Fourth, long-term use of native language may offer some affective advantages to the learning of English, as discussed by Gardner and Lambert (1972), Schumann (1978), and Krashen (1982). Fear of losing their native language may play a significant part in the psychological distance that immigrant and minority-language children sense between themselves and speakers of English. Reinforcement of the learner's native language and culture may alleviate this fear. Social distance, determined by the relative status of the language learners and speakers of the target language, is also a deterrent to language learning. Minority-language children often get strong signals from the larger society that their languages and cultures are inferior to English and the American culture. Long-term bilingual programs give these children a sense of the legitimacy of their native languages and cultures. When children know that they do not have to choose between one language and the other, that they can be members of two speech communities and two cultures, there is likely to be less resistance to learning English. Their parents are also more likely to feel better, knowing that their children will not lose their native language, and are more likely to be supportive of and involved in their children's education.

Long-term bilingual instruction is only one viable avenue of education for minority-language children. It works best in schools that have a large number of children who speak the same minority language, and it is most necessary when these children enter the American school system with a low level of first-language literacy. There is also a possible downside to such instruction: it separates children from their English-speaking peers and the social interaction that they need to become comfortable with a new language and culture (Toohey, 1998). However, if students are unavoidably isolated from such peers – if their school and neighborhood are dominated by people of their language and culture – interaction with English speakers may already be limited, and long-term bilingual education may be their best route to preparation for full participation in the wider society.

CONCLUSION

In this chapter, we began with the claim that Americans are largely ill-informed about the process of language learning. Although many Americans study a second language during their schooling, very few achieve proficiency. Also, there is little information available to the average American about the process of language learning.

In light of this, eight common myths about first- and second-language learning were offered and then debunked through a discussion of major linguistic theories and examples of relevant research studies. We dealt with the perception that children learn their first languages with little effort; we found instead that acquiring one's native language is a lengthy and complex process. Although many people believe that younger learners are better at acquiring language than older learners, we discovered that, while youth is an advantage in acquiring native-like pronunciation and oral fluency, older learners are in fact more efficient language learners than younger ones. While everyone acquires his or her native language naturally and without formal instruction, most second-language learners, by virtue of being older and cognitively more mature than they were when they were acquiring their mother tongues, benefit from formal language instruction. We learned that successful acquisition of a second language is not just a matter of will and determination; subtle social and psychological barriers often need to be overcome, especially when the language learners have a subordinate place in society.

We then tackled the issue of optimal timing and quantity of exposure to a second language. We found that there are some benefits to delaying the start of language instruction until a sufficient degree of native-language literacy is acquired, the delay naturally cutting down on the amount of language to which the beginning learner is exposed. Children who are learning two languages at once are often perceived as being put into an unduly confusing situation; however, if it is done correctly, children can acquire two languages very successfully. While many believe that minority-language children should be plunged quickly into all-English instruction, research shows that initial instruction through the native language helps children develop cognitive skills that are later transferred to the second language, leading to high-level literacy in the second language as well as in the first. Finally, bilingual instruction that is short-term and quickly phases out use of the first language has received substantial support in society. However, the sum total of our discussion here leads us to conclude that, when bilingual instruction is the method of choice, it is most likely to succeed if there is substantive use of the first language in a program that lasts over an extended period of time.

The understanding gained in this discussion has prepared us for the next chapter, in which we will analyze the role that languages other than English play in the educational system today. We will look at the types of instruction given to English-dominant children learning a second language and to minority-language children learning English. We will look at examples of how these programs are described in the press. In light of the linguistic findings in this chapter, it will become apparent that society values bilingualism for the former group of children over bilingualism for the latter group, and that the most prevalent instructional methods used for minority-language children are not conducive to high academic achievement

CHAPTER 4

Languages in the Schools

INTRODUCTION

Having established in the previous chapter an understanding of how language is learned, we are now ready to examine the role of language as a means of instruction and as a subject of study in the American school system. The first part of the chapter consists of an analysis of different types of instruction. The instructional approaches are categorized according to the students for whom the instruction is designed: instructional approaches for students whose native language is not English, instructional approaches for English-dominant students learning a second language, and an instructional approach for students of both groups. Each section includes definitions of the program types, a description of selected studies of their effectiveness, reactions to the program types and/or to the studies in the mass media and in academia, and an evaluation of these reactions. The section on programs for minority-language children includes a politico-historical overview of bilingual education.

Analyzing these types of instruction in this manner reveals a salient truth: in terms of language acquisition, society supports different educational goals for different kinds of students. Any program that is successful at teaching English-dominant children a second language is lauded. Bilingualism for these children is additive; learning a second language does not mean sacrificing the first language. In contrast, minority-language children are expected to acquire English as a replacement for their native language; bilingualism for them is of the subtractive variety. When majority-language and minority-language children learn together, the benefits of additive bilingualism for the first group accrue to the second group. English continues to be a language of prestige worthy of being learned, but the native language of the minority group gains prestige as well, by virtue of its standing as a second language worthy of acquisition by the majority group.

The second part of the chapter reviews the work of several linguists which supports this analysis. Tove Skutnabb-Kangas (1990) offers an international perspective on the education of minority-language children. She shows that the typical educational goal for this group is mono-lingualism in the majority language, a goal that leads inevitably to low academic achievement. Rolf Kjolseth (1973) and Joshua Fishman (1966) describe two possible sources of the animosity toward the languages of minority groups in the American educational system. Kjolseth (1973) explains that when a minority group is of low socioeconomic status the stigma that clings to the group attaches to the group's language as well. Fishman (1966) points out that many middle-class Americans, including those who administer and teach in the schools, have immigrant roots and ancestral languages themselves. However, in the process of acculturating to mainstream society, they have largely cut their ties to these roots. The ethnic languages that newer immigrants bring to school remind them of what they have left behind, causing feelings of guilt and discomfort.

PROGRAMS FOR MINORITY-LANGUAGE CHILDREN

Definitions

The first type of instruction to be defined in this category, *submersion*, can in fact be described as a lack of any particular approach to the education of minority-language children. Submersion is the term used to describe the situation in which such children are placed in mainstream classes without regard to their degree of readiness. No special help is given to the children nor does their presence affect the manner in which the classes are taught. This situation is representative of the one faced by most minority-language children in past generations.

In *structured immersion* programs, minority-language children are placed in classes separate from those of their English-dominant peers. They are given all their instruction in English by teachers who have received special training; the teachers gear the level of English used to the students' degree of proficiency. The goal of these programs is to prepare the students for transfer into mainstream classes. The linguistic goal for the students is therefore monolingualism in English. (It should be noted that, in the United States, the term *structured immersion* applies exclusively to English-language instruction for minority-language children. It is distinguished from *immersion*, instruction in a second language for majority-language children, based on the Canadian model, which was mentioned in Chapter 2 and which will be discussed in greater detail in the next section.)

Transitional bilingual programs are the most common form of bilingual instruction. Here, initial academic instruction is given in the native language. Content instruction in English is phased in as the students demonstrate greater proficiency, with a parallel decrease in instruction in the native language. The purpose of this method is to allow students to continue their academic development in their native language while learning English. Like structured immersion, the goal is eventual mainstreaming into all-English classes and monolingualism in English.

Maintenance bilingual programs (also called *developmental* or *enrichment* programs) are a rarer breed. In this approach, the native language is used as a medium of instruction and as a subject of study for an extended period of time. Instruction in the English language is mandatory, and English as a medium of instruction increases in the upper grades. The linguistic goal of these programs is bilingualism: maintenance and development of the native language as well as high-level literacy in English.

It should be noted that an important component of the education of minority-language children is instruction in *English as a Second Language (ESL)*, sometimes called *English to Speakers of Other Languages (ESOL)*. ESL classes are usually taught by instructors specially trained in the language needs of this population. At times such classes are the only special help given to these children. At other times, these classes constitute one part of the structured immersion and bilingual programs mentioned above.

A Politico-Historical Overview

As Crawford (1999) explains, the United States has struggled with the issue of educating minority-language children for a long time, with politics and racial issues inevitably playing major roles. Early on, as we will see in the next chapter, an attempt by Native Americans to educate their children bilingually showed signs of promise but was squelched by the government. In the Southwest, Hispanic children and teachers found to be using Spanish in class were punished. After World War II, educators based federal policy on the theory that children whose first languages were not English were victims of cultural and linguistic deprivation; this could be remediated only by teaching them English as a replacement for their native languages; despite this assessment of the problem, few students actually received instruction in ESL.

Some minority-language groups, however, had a different idea of how their children should be educated. In the 1960s, as Crawford (1999) describes, Cuban American refugees in Miami set up a successful experiment in two-way bilingual education, the Coral Way Elementary School, which brought together English-dominant and Spanish-dominant children in a program that valued and developed both languages. Despite the promise of Coral Way, government intervention transformed its focus to conform to its own view of bilingual education as a "poverty program" for disadvantaged children who needed to learn English.

Del Valle (1998) defines the two tracks along which the federal government guided educational policy for minority-language children. On the legislative track, the 1968 Bilingual Education Act defined the problems facing these children as a lack of English-language proficiency and general educational underachievement, but framed the solution as merely teaching students English. Local districts were left with few guidelines, and the racial segregation of poor children into underfunded "compensatory" programs in Latino-dominated schools was reinforced. On the judicial track, in 1974, the US Supreme Court decision *Lau v. Nichols* sent the message to San Francisco schools that Chinese-dominant children must be taught English. While no particular methodology was mandated, the decision was read as an endorsement of transitional bilingual education.

Like the Cuban-American community before it, the Puerto Rican community of New York City attempted to institute its own idea of education in an effort to address the unmet needs of its children. Its goals were a better overall education, respect for the Puerto Rican language and culture as well as all other cultures represented by the student population, and a transformation of the unequal relationship between minority and majority groups. This campaign resulted in the ASPIRA consent decree of 1975 (ASPIRA is the command form of "to aspire" in Spanish). Unfortunately, this decree severely compromised the original demands of the community. It called for transitional bilingual programs and defined the targeted population as Spanish-surnamed children needing remediation in English. According to Del Valle (1998), the ASPIRA decree institutionalized transitional bilingual education, making it more vulnerable to criticism when it failed to educate its students adequately. In addition, it left no legal strategy with which to address educational needs other than remediation in English, and failed to address the already-neglected needs of English-dominant Latino students. Once again, true educational reform was thwarted.

As government support for bilingual education waned, there was a concurrent demand for proof of its efficacy. Keith Baker and Adriana de Kanter (1981) undertook a review of existing studies, sponsored by the US Department of Education, with the goal of finding out if transitional bilingual education led to better performance in English and other subjects. Out of 300 documents, they selected 28; eliminations were based on design flaws or inapplicability to the researchers' questions. From these 28 studies, Baker and de Kanter found structured immersion to be superior to ESL instruction and transitional bilingual education in a number of cases; mixed findings regarding the efficacy of transitional bilingual education led them to suggest that federal policy should not rely on this method exclusively.

Baker and de Kanter's study was widely criticized. The authors were accused of bias in their selection of studies: they had rejected studies which showed bilingual education to be superior to other methods, and had accepted others which showed the opposite, despite flaws in all these studies. They failed to isolate the criteria for successful and unsuccessful bilingual programs. As Colin Baker (1993) points out, several factors interact in determining whether bilingual programs succeed or fail. These include the location of the school (rural or urban), the characteristics of the students (age, social class, motivational level), the characteristics of the parents (level of interest and involvement in their children's education), the characteristics of the teachers (enthusiasm, commitment), and material support (computers, books). Baker and de Kanter's focus on transitional bilingual education excluded discussion of the most successful bilingual models: maintenance and two-way bilingual programs. The way the authors labeled programs was criticized for being misleading. For example, programs that were called "structured immersion" were actually based on the Canadian immersion model. Cummins (1994) points out that the instructional model studied by Legaretta (1979) was labeled by Baker and de Kanter as "alternative immersion," when in reality it made equal use of English and Spanish; it proved to be more effective at teaching English than other programs that made greater use of English.

This latter example points to another serious flaw in Baker and de Kanter's review. Cummins (1994) faults the authors for failing to examine the data with respect to their relationship to the theoretical assumptions underlying the different program types. If they had done so, they would have seen that all the data were inconsistent with the assumptions underlying structured immersion (for example, that more English leads to better learning of English) and consistent with the assumptions underlying maintenance bilingual education (for example, that the development of native-language literacy supports the development of second-language literacy).

In view of the criticism of the Baker and de Kanter study, Willig (1985) set out to conduct a similar study that corrected its flaws. She eliminated studies of Canadian immersion, and used a statistical approach called meta-analysis to tease out the variables accounting for the differences in the results among the various programs. Willig concluded that bilingual programs showed significant superiority to non-bilingual programs in outcomes on tests in English and math. While she found weaknesses in many of the studies, Willig also discovered that the better the design of the study, the greater was the advantage of the bilingual treatment over the non-bilingual treatment.

Government regulation regarding bilingual instruction has undergone various alterations. Changes made in the 1978 Bilingual Education Act called specifically for transitional bilingual education. In the early 1980s, the anti-bilingual voice in Washington was a strong one; Senator S.I. Hayakawa held bilingual instruction accountable for the failure of language minorities to achieve full participation in American society, while he pushed for an official-English constitutional amendment. But in 1984, some ground was gained for native-language instruction. While some funds were set aside for non-bilingual programs, money was also promised for family literacy programs, special education and gifted programs for minority-language children, exemplary instructional models, and developmental bilingual instruction. In addition, educational goals shifted from English-language remediation alone to improved overall academic achievement.

During the Clinton administration, a group of experts in bilingual education, under the leadership of Kenji Hakuta of Stanford University, issued a report offering recommendations for the education of limited-English proficient children. Heeding these recommendations, the administration's 1994 proposed re-authorization of Title VII included for the first time the development of bilingual skills and multicultural understanding as means of helping minority-language children meet the same standards of academic performance expected of other children. This re-authorization was approved by the full Congress (Crawford, 1999). However, in 2002, after the election of President George W. Bush, the Bilingual Education Act was renamed the English Language Acquisition, Language Enhancement, and Academic Achievement Act; in the text of this law, bilingual skills receive no mention.

Clearly, research into the best methods of educating minority-language children is never viewed in a purely objective way; politics and public opinion have an effect on how it is received. It is perhaps not surprising that Baker and de Kanter's study came to the conclusions it did, since it was sponsored by a government inherently ambivalent about bilingual education. Thorough, scientific criticisms of the study did little to change this position. While subsequent studies have had better research design than the earlier ones, and continue to show the positive effects of native-language instruction, resistance to bilingual education in the public sector is still strong, as we will see later on in this chapter.

Cummins (1994) offers an explanation for this. The government has maintained an inherently contradictory stance: at one level, it professes commitment to educational equity, while at another, it is equally dedicated to maintaining the current power structure, in which resources are divided along the lines of class, ethnicity, race, and gender. This accounts for its minimal support for the most effective programs for minority-language students, those which promote additive bilingualism through "empowerment pedagogy" (Cummins, 1994: 162). Empowerment pedagogy nurtures self-respect, self-sufficiency, fearlessness, ability for independent learning, and confidence in one's own academic and personal talents. For minority-language students, most schools do just the opposite: they convince these children of their own inferiority, which encourages submissiveness, dependency, and fear.

Cummins (1994) draws a parallel between the United States' dis-empowerment of minority-language children and its disempowerment of developing countries. Less powerful entities are told that the treatment bestowed on them by the more powerful entity is for their own good, while the true result is the maintenance of the unequal power structure, continued benefits for the more powerful entity, and continued dependency by the less powerful ones. Examples of this are the United States' assistance in the over-throw of democratically-elected governments in Guatemala in 1954, Brazil in 1964, and Chile in 1973.

In addition, Cummins (1994) delineates the tactics used in the process of disempowerment by politicians and members of the public who are committed to the destruction of native-language instruction. One is the limitation of the framework of discourse, as in Baker and de Kanter's focus on transitional bilingual education. A second is the denial or distortion of empirically documented counter-examples, as in the government's re-shaping of two-way bilingual instruction in Miami. A third is the disregard of logical inconsistencies in positions taken, as in the use of French immer-sion results in Canada to argue for structured immersion. In the following section, we will see further examples of strategies used to discredit successful models of instruction for minority-language children.

Selected Studies

Two studies comparing structured immersion and transitional bilingual instruction are discussed here. The first is typical of a number of local, small-scale projects carried out in the 1980s. The second is a large-scale research project covering several cities. Both studies are complex and their results have been interpreted in different ways. In analyzing these studies and the reactions to them, we see how easy it is for opponents of native-language instruction to skew the results to their favor while clouding evidence of the positive effects of such instruction. The discussion of these two reports is followed by a description of a successful maintenance bilin-gual program and its outcomes.

The Dade County, Florida Study (Rothfarb et al., 1987)

Dade County, Florida, which includes the city of Miami, has one of the highest concentrations of Spanish-dominant speakers in the United States. Since the early 1960s, it has been the policy of the Dade County Public Schools to recognize and use the home language and culture of the students as instructional tools during the period in which students are being prepared to enter all-English classes. In 1976, the use of the home language as the medium of instruction for content courses was established as an instructional strategy in the elementary schools. Dade County has therefore been a pioneer in American bilingual education, and its use of native-language instruction has been a source of interest for educators and researchers in bilingual education.

In 1983, the Dade County School Board directed the research division of the school system to conduct a study to determine the effectiveness of native-language content instruction as compared to that of all-English instruction. The three-year study was conducted from 1983 to 1986. One cohort of students was followed from their kindergarten year, when they totaled 287, to the end of first grade, when they totaled 110. A second cohort of 221 kindergarten students was followed until they completed first grade, at which time they numbered 138 (Rothfarb *et al.*, 1987: 6–7). There were various reasons for this attrition, including referral to an exceptional-student program, loss of qualification for the program based on English-proficiency level, and family relocation. Although the sample sizes were small, the study was representative of locally-administered research carried out to determine the effectiveness of bilingual instruction during a period in which such instruction was coming under close scrutiny and was the object of much criticism.

In each cohort, one group of students was enrolled in a program called Bilingual Curriculum Content (BCC). The goal of this program was "to enable [limited-English proficient] students to maintain their academic standing at a level equivalent to their English-speaking peers, while in the process of learning English" (Rothfarb *et al.*, 1987: 2); in other words, it was a transitional bilingual program. The children had daily classes in math, science, and social studies conducted in both English and Spanish, with Spanish used for a maximum of one-half the instruction time. A second group received the same instruction in a structured immersion program, that is, taught in English geared to the proficiency level of the students. The rest of the day was the same for both groups: a Spanish-language class, a class in ESOL, and a class in art and music taught in English. The results showed no significant differences in the two groups on tests of content-area achievement and language arts in both Spanish and English. However, students who left the BCC component after one year did better on content-area tests than those who left after two or three years of BCC. Students in both groups who left ESOL after one year also did better on content-area tests than those who left ESOL after two or three years.

An additional one-year project involved a seventh-grade comprehensive science course in which students were also divided into BCC and structured immersion classes. The academic results were mixed: advanced ESOL students in the BCC class performed better in science than advanced ESOL students in the structured immersion class, but the structured immersion students performed better in English. There were also significant differences between the two groups in measures of teacher and student attitudes and student progress. Structured immersion students were more likely to be retained or to require summer school before being promoted. BCC teachers had more positive attitudes toward their students' progress and were more positive about their own and their students' enthusiasm. Structured immersion teachers expressed greater frustration than their BCC counterparts, reporting more disciplinary problems and complaining about students' lack of motivation and inability to understand English. The implications of these results are that, while students in the immersion program may have performed better on English-language tests, their mastery of English did not seem to be sufficient to allow them to succeed in their academic courses. In addition, the BCC program seemed to have some affective advantages over the immersion program for both teachers and students.

The teachers in the two programs also differed in their suggestions for improving their respective programs. BCC teachers had fewer suggestions but noted the need for more time to emphasize English, easier texts, more materials and films in Spanish, and smaller classes. Structured immersion teachers also cited the need for more simplified texts in English and more bilingual materials. However, they also suggested more extensive changes. Noting the lack of preparedness of their students, they suggested either that students demonstrate greater proficiency in English before being mainstreamed into the science class, or that the class be taught by a special bilingual or ESOL teacher.

The authors of the study conclude that bilingual instruction should be supported, but that the form used needed revision. They note that budget constraints hampered their ability to control the language use of the teachers, and suggest greater initial use of Spanish and more gradual decrease in its use than was actually practiced. The lack of such control resulted in too much similarity between the two groups, which may have contributed to the lack of significant difference in the performance of the groups. The dearth of sufficient bilingual texts and materials is cited as a contributing factor. The authors also note that the use of both languages in the same class might not be the most efficient method of instruction, and they provide evidence that separating languages (teaching different subjects in different languages or using one language in the morning and the other in the afternoon) might lead to better proficiency in both languages.

A Reaction to the Dade County Study

A study with mixed results such as this one offers the critic of native-language instruction the opportunity to pick out bits and pieces of the results that put the value of the approach into question. Porter (1990), who is quoted extensively in this book and has a decided political bias against bilingual instruction, resorts to this tactic in her discussion of the Dade County study.

Porter professes amazement that the authors conclude by recommending increased instruction in Spanish "rather than conclude, as logic would suggest, that no good reason existed for continuing native tongue teaching in the subject areas" (Porter, 1990: 73). Porter's own conclusion is based on two pieces of information gleaned from the results: students who left the BCC component after one year did better on content-area tests than those who left after two or three years and, in the main part of the study, there was no difference between the two groups in teachers' ratings of student attitudes toward learning and toward school.

In regard to the first point, Porter (1990) ignores the section of the report in which the authors give possible reasons for the better performance of students with only one year in the BCC class. First, the students who needed only one year of BCC may have been higher achievers than those who needed two or three years. Second, these students may have been the same students who needed only one year of ESOL, since enrollment in and exit from BCC were determined by English proficiency. (With reference to these two points, it is also probable that these students came into the program with better general academic preparation than those who needed more time in BCC.) Third, the authors point out that the BCC methodology used in the second and third years may not have been meeting the needs of the students who required more than one year in the program.

It is significant that Porter (1990) bases her conclusion on the data regarding years in BCC, but does not mention the data regarding years in ESOL instruction. She reasons that, if students with one year of BCC did better than those with two or three years of BCC, then BCC is ineffective. But students with one year of ESOL instruction also did better than those with two or three years of ESOL instruction. Porter doesn't conclude, however, that ESOL instruction is ineffective. This would indeed go against her very strong conviction that English proficiency is essential to success in the academic areas. This logical inconsistency typifies one of the tactics described by Cummins (1994) in efforts to discredit native-language instruction.

As to the second piece of information on which she rests her conclusion, Porter fails to take into account the data on attitudes and progress from the study of the seventh-grade science classes. In this case there did seem to be a significant difference between the BCC and the structured immersion approach. However, by ignoring this data Porter is able to cling to her belief that "from an educational and an emotional standpoint, instruction in the native language added no benefit" (Porter, 1990: 73).

Porter's (1990) conclusion that native-language instruction has no value is not in fact supported by this study. Neither method in the form implemented by the Dade County Public Schools was superior to the other; in the kindergarten-to-second-grade part of the study, there was little difference in the academic achievements of the two groups. The results of the seventh-grade part of the study suggest that each method has its own strengths and weaknesses; students in the BCC component performed better in science, but those in the structured immersion class performed better in English. However, the seventh-grade teachers in both components appeared to argue for a stronger bilingual approach. They both asked for more appropriate materials in the two languages. In addition, the non-bilingual teachers recognized that they were not prepared to teach science to students who did not have the necessary proficiency in English to handle the subject matter.

This latter point is especially important, since it raises serious questions about the viability of structured immersion. The success of this approach depends on the adequate training of teachers of academic subjects. In order for science or math teachers to be able to instruct limited-English proficient students in English, they have to develop an ability to adjust the language of instruction to the needs of the students. They should receive training before the school term and be given support while they are teaching. This clearly was not the case here.

However, merely training content teachers before they meet their students does not solve all problems. Valdés (1998) explains what happened after academic-content teachers at a California school were instructed in how to adapt their language and techniques for the newly-arrived Mexican children who had become a large part of the school's population. The teachers found themselves attempting to instruct students at all levels of English acquisition, including those with no knowledge of English, and they experienced significant frustration at their inability to teach the mandated course content. Some students, placed into these courses on the basis of their English ability, found the course content too easy. In addition, differences between expected teacher behavior in the Mexican and American cultures caused behavioral problems. Valdés (1998) joins Rothfarb et al. (1987) in supporting other language experts such as Wink, who states that "often, structured immersion is nothing more than submersion dressed up in new language" (Wink, 1991/1992: 17).

If neither of the treatments in the Dade County study was successful, what then is the solution? Optimal instruction for these students appears to lie in another model, one which perhaps incorporates elements of these two methods. But the study in no way proves the inefficacy of native-language instruction.

The Ramirez Report (Ramirez et al., 1991)

This project, supported by the US Department of Education, ran from

1982 until 1989. It involved approximately 2,000 Spanish-dominant students in 9 school districts, 51 schools and 554 classrooms. Five states were represented: New York, New Jersey, Florida, California, and Texas. It was the most comprehensive survey of language-minority education since the 1970s, when Spanish/English bilingual programs were evaluated under the federal Elementary and Secondary Education Act (Dolson & Mayer, 1992: 105–106).

The subjects were enrolled in one of three types of programs. In the English immersion programs, instruction in all the content areas was given in English by instructors with training in bilingual education or ESL. The programs began in kindergarten, and it was expected that the students would be ready for mainstreaming after the first or second grade. In the early-exit bilingual programs, also taught by instructors with special training, there was some initial instruction in Spanish in the introduction of reading skills and for the purposes of clarification. Spanish-language instruction was quickly phased out over the following two years. Like the immersion programs, children were expected to be mainstreamed after two or three years. In the late-exit bilingual programs, students received a minimum of 40% of their total instruction time in Spanish. Students were to remain in the program until the sixth grade even if they were determined to be fluent in English before that time.

Ramirez *et al.* (1991) found little difference in the academic achievement of the students in the immersion and early-exit bilingual programs by the end of the third grade, as measured by tests in math, English language arts, and English reading. Students in these programs progressed at the same rate as students in the general population, but remained significantly behind the general population in achievement. Also, while these students were expected to be mainstreamed by the end of the second grade, many were not deemed ready for this move and were held in the programs longer than anticipated.

In contrast to the students in the first two programs, late-exit students were able to decrease the achievement gap between themselves and the general population. In particular, students in the late-exit program with the greatest use of Spanish, and who began with the lowest academic skills, improved in all three skills faster than the norming population used in the study. Compared to students in the two other programs, these students were less likely to have been in all-English preschool programs, and came from families with lower incomes. In another late-exit program, students who were transferred into mainstream classes before the expected time – the end of the sixth grade – fared worse than those who remained in the program. An additional advantage of the late-exit programs was the high degree of parental involvement: parents of children in these programs were more aware that their children had homework and more likely to help their children with their homework than were parents in the two other programs.

The authors conclude that, since students in all the instructional programs improved academically, "providing substantial instruction in the child's primary language does not impede the learning of English language or reading skills" (Ramirez *et al.*, 1991: 40). The results regarding immersion and early-exit programs indicate that limited-English proficient students may need assistance for longer than two or three years before being mainstreamed into all-English classes. Long-term native language instruction has the effect of lessening the achievement gap between these students and the general population; the authors speculate that if the students using the most Spanish continued in this program, they would eventually catch up with their English-dominant peers. The authors also note the advantages of using the home language of students to engage parents in their children's education.

Mass Media Responses to the Ramirez Report

Because of the Department of Education sponsorship of this study, its results were reported in major newspapers. However, these reports were culled from a summary, released by the government, which tended to obscure the findings. Subsequent newspaper reports were truncated and often misleading. Cooper, for example, cites the department's conclusion that "Spanish-speaking pupils learn at about the same rate, regardless of how much English their teacher uses" (Cooper, 1991: A17), a statement that ignores the positive effects of long-term instruction in Spanish. Cooper refers to all three programs as "bilingual," further blurring the distinction between the treatments.

In addition, the bias of the government report against the use of funds for bilingual instruction is evident in the following quote:

> Most of the $121 million in federal funding supports bilingual instruction that is supposed to end use of native languages, and no more than 25% can go to "immersion" classes taught primarily in English. Rita Esquivel, director of bilingual education, said that policy would be reevaluated in light of the study. (Cooper, 1991: A17)

The implication here is that the emphasis on support for bilingual education, in the form of transitional programs in which the use of native languages terminates, is unwarranted, and that more funds should be freed for immersion programs. But there is no support for this view in the actual results of the report. While short-term transitional bilingual programs did not prove to be more effective than immersion programs, neither approach turned out to be particularly successful. One of the most crucial conclusions of the study is totally overlooked: that sustained native-language instruction may be the most beneficial form of instruction for children with limited English proficiency and low academic achievement.

In another press article, Toth also offers a misinterpretation of the study. Like Cooper, she refers to all three methods as "bilingual." According to the report, Toth states, "the English-only program seemed just as effective as those that provided a great majority of classes in Spanish" (Toth, 1991: A18). The difference in outcomes of the three methods is further blurred by a quote from Ted Sanders, an undersecretary of education, who offers the view that "bilingual education benefits students, and school administrators can choose the method best suited to their students, confident that, if well implemented, it will reap positive results" (Toth, 1991: A18). Writing in a California newspaper, Toth relates the findings to education in that state. While correctly stating that the best effects were achieved when students remained in the programs more than four years, Toth cites the California Department of Education's claim that most students in transitional bilingual programs "are able to enter the main stream of education with native English-speaking children within three or four years" (Toth, 1991: A18). She makes no attempt, however, to reconcile these two conflicting pieces of information. She claims that "the preferred method of teaching non-fluent English students throughout the country has been complete immersion in the English language" (Toth, 1991: A18), a statement also at odds with the results of the Ramirez study. As with Cooper, the effect of the article is to impart the impression that all three methods studied were equally successful, an impression that the Department of Education clearly meant to communicate to the public.

Academic Responses to the Ramirez Report

Researchers and academics took greater care in their analyses of this project. Some described the limitations of the study. Meyer and Finenberg (1992) noted that the design of the study resulted in many variables among students, teachers, and programs. The programs chosen for the study were already in existence, and the students and teachers in them already assigned, before the study began; in a more controlled experiment, students and teachers would have been randomly assigned to programs. The authors of the study acknowledged many of the differences that did exist. For example, teachers in the late-exit programs were more likely to be Hispanic, to know more Spanish, to be better educated, and to have been specially trained to work with language-minority students. The early-exit and immersion programs observed were often in different schools and in different districts, making it difficult to generalize about their effectiveness. Also, late-exit programs were in districts that did not have immersion and early-exit programs, making comparisons between late-exit programs and the other two program types difficult.

While the authors of the study took these differences into account in their analysis of the data, Meyer and Finenberg note that there might have also been hidden biases that were not detectable in the data. For example, one compelling result of the study was that, in one particular school, kindergarten to first-grade students in the early-exit program scored significantly higher on a reading test than their peers in the immersion program. However, write Meyer and Finenberg, "there are unavoidable sources of uncertainty in nonexperimental studies of this sort, and the report falls short of addressing all of these sources of uncertainty" (Meyer & Finenberg, 1992: 78). For example, many students left the early-exit program during the course of the school year. The report did not examine how these students were similar to or different from the students who remained. A simple analysis might have reduced the possibility that a difference between these two groups of students may have affected the difference in reading scores.

Despite the weaknesses in the study, the fact remains that the interpretation given in the press, with its bias against native-language instruction, does not coincide with the results of the report. Cazden (1992) offers a quite different interpretation than that of the press. One of the conclusions Cazden draws from the study is one not clearly articulated in the newspaper articles: "the amount of time spent using a second language in school can no longer be considered the most important influence on learning it" (Cazden, 1992: 6). Students in the immersion programs received more instruction in English than those receiving bilingual instruction, but did not achieve greater proficiency in English. This argues against the idea that immersion is superior to bilingual instruction. Further, recalling Baker's (1993) point about the many factors that contribute to the success of bilingual programs, Cazden (1992) points to two characteristics found to be critical in the high academic achievement of minority-language children: better teacher qualifications and greater parental involvement, both of which were characteristics of the late-exit bilingual programs. Finally, while acknowledging the variety of bilingual programs in existence and avoiding overgeneralizing the study's results, Cazden (1992) reaffirms the finding that late-exit programs similar to those in the study are beneficial to the students they serve. It becomes obvious that the general public reading accounts of the Ramirez report in the press came away with a quite different impression of the results than the small group of academics who had access to Cazden's analysis.

The Rock Point Community Day School: An Example of Maintenance Bilingual Education

Maintenance bilingual programs are not as numerous as other means of teaching minority-language students. They are also not suited to comparison to other instructional methods. One reason is that they are designed to last much longer than other methods. But a more substantial reason is that their goals are distinct from the goals of other approaches. Proficiency in the native language is one of these goals; in other means of instruction, the native language is phased out quickly or not used at all, and is therefore not even measured. Also, achievement in the academic areas is often tested in the native language, which further sets evaluation techniques for this approach apart from other approaches. In light of this, instead of attempting to compare maintenance bilingual instruction to other methods, we will focus on a description of one particular program (Holm & Holm, 1990).

The Rock Point Community Day School, in the interior of the Navajo Reservation, serves a student population of mostly Navajo-dominant or Navajo-monolingual children. The program that came into existence in the mid-1980s was the culmination of more than 25 years of experimentation in providing an education based on three principles: quality education in two languages, the incorporation of Navajo ways into instruction, and the control and involvement of parents and community in the school. A system of "coordinate bilingual" instruction was instituted. In the elementary grades, classes were taught by two teachers (one speaking English and the other Navajo) working with different groups of students. The teachers were of equal status; in addition, there were two co-principals and parallel sets of teacher trainers and language or materials specialists.

From kindergarten to high school, literacy skills in English and Navajo were developed. Academic content was also taught in both languages. As the grades progressed, instruction in Navajo decreased, from two-thirds of class time in kindergarten to 5 to 10% of instruction in high school. However, the study of Navajo culture was a major part of the curriculum at the high school level, including Navajo social studies, history, social problems, government, and economic development. Parents were often used as sources or informants in the Navajo social studies course and in the Applied Literacy Program, in which students produced their own written materials and videos about Navajo themes. As Holm and Holm note, "Rock Point students were among the few students on the Reservation who left high school with some formal preparation for participating in the Navajo political process" (Holm & Holm, 1990: 178).

Both the type of instruction and the administration of the school had a very Navajo flavor. Holm and Holm describe Rock Point as a "talking school," characterized by the constant interaction among students and teachers working in small groups. They explain that "this low hum of meaningful student talk contrasted markedly with the sometimes deathly silence of some more seatwork-oriented Reservation schools – or the near chaos between classes in some other Reservation schools" (Holm & Holm, 1990: 177). The School Board adapted some of the formal characteristics of

Anglo means of administration, but also reflected certain aspects of Navajo culture. It relied on traditional ways of planning, regarded the running of the school as an almost religious undertaking, made sure that the entire community was represented and served, and insisted on self-sufficiency. Throughout, there was an awareness of the need not just to use Navajo ways and teach Navajo content, but to integrate Navajo ways and content with their Anglo counterparts, creating "a contemporary Navajo way to go to school" (Holm & Holm, 1990: 179). The results of this process were rewarding. Students not only learned to value their Navajoness, but to see themselves as achieving because of, rather than despite, being Navajo. On standardized tests, students succeeded by a greater margin at each successive grade level. Rock Point clearly advocates "empowerment pedagogy" as described by Cummins (1994).

This model may not be wholly applicable to most of the other schools that serve minority-language students. Children living on the Navajo Reservation are much more cut off from the rest of society than the majority of limited-English proficient students are. It is clear that one of the goals of the school was to prepare children for living in their unique subculture; other children do not have to learn about the particular governance structure of their community. But in many respects the model can serve other situations. Many minority-language children live in neighborhoods dominated by people of their own heritage; the schools they go to also largely serve members of the same culture. The maintenance bilingual model encourages students to appreciate that culture and to participate in it. By including the native language and culture in the school curriculum, the school acknowledges that the language and culture have value in the eyes of the larger society. Incorporating the native language and cultural ways of learning into instruction eases the way for the children and allows parents greater participation in their children's schooling. Raising awareness of the realities of life in their neighborhoods can be coupled with instruction in how skills learned in school might be used to solve the problems that exist there. Additionally, instruction in the native language enhances both the acquisition of English and general academic achievement. The model encourages children to appreciate where they come from and where they are, while preparing them for full participation wherever they find themselves in the future.

General Views of Bilingual Education in the Mass Media

In the previous section, we discussed specific types of educational approaches for minority-language children, and we noted journalistic reactions to studies that compare such instruction to all-English instruction. More frequent than press reporting of specific studies on bilingual education are instances of general attitudes toward the teaching of minority children in their own languages. These attitudes are often categorically negative, but offer no evidence to support such an evaluation. For example, the *National Review,* in an editorial labeled "The New Apartheid," claims that "bilingual-education advocates are pressing harder to keep English from taking root" despite the fact that "everyone knows that the younger the child, the more readily and painlessly a new language can be learned" (*National Review,* 1990: 15). Bilingual educators are viewed as doing actual harm to the children they claim to serve because they "trap the children in their native languages" (*National Review,* 1990: 16), forever separating them from English-speaking society.

The press largely fails to present an accurate view of the basis for bilingual education. Typical of the rationale given for native-language instruction is the following: "Immigrant children must first be taught mathematics, science and other subjects in their native languages to avoid the humiliation and loneliness of not comprehending what is going on in class" (Berger, 1993: B4). While this statement acknowledges the need to deal with the sense of alienation that immigrant children face in an English-speaking environment, it fails to mention the more important function of native-language instruction: bolstering the development of the native language, which will eventually lead to better proficiency in English and better academic performance. Indeed, the way Berger (1993) frames the need for bilingual education helps foster the attitude represented in the *National Review* that bilingual education isolates children in an all-immigrant language environment.

Another common viewpoint in the press is that there is no real proof of the benefits of bilingual education. Berger writes that "bilingual theories ... continue to be a matter of fierce debate.... Critics and proponents can cite numerous studies to support their arguments" (Berger, 1993: B4). Perhaps Berger has talked to these critics and proponents and has taken their word that there is valid evidence to support the views of each side. This seems like the lazy way out. A more inquisitive reporter would have looked at the evidence himself, or would have sought out a neutral expert to evaluate contradictory evidence. If Berger had done so, perhaps the scales would not have seemed as balanced as he originally thought. There is in fact valid evidence that for many minority-language children bilingual instruction leads to success, and little proof that such children in all-English programs reach high levels of academic achievement.

What is perhaps more damaging, and extremely dismaying, is that the discussion of bilingual education in the press is used to negatively portray the Hispanic population in the United States. It is a fact that bilingual programs in Spanish far outnumber programs offered in other languages, owing to the large numbers of people from the Caribbean and Central and South America who emigrate here and the low level of academic preparation of many children from these regions. The prevalence of bilingual programs in Spanish, combined with strong resistance to bilingual education and negative stereotyping of Hispanics in general, leads to the targeting of Hispanics as the source of much of the animosity toward, and criticism of, native-language instruction. Berger, for example, negatively compares Puerto Ricans to other immigrant groups:

> Chinese and Russian parents, for instance, generally want their children to learn English as quickly as possible and prefer a cold plunge into regular classes or a brief sojourn in English as a second language. By contrast, many second- and third-generation Puerto Rican parents lament that as children growing up in New York they were forcibly separated from their Spanish heritage by the schools' insistence on English. They are eager to see their children acquire a language they lost. (Berger, 1993: B4)

This passage is unfair and dangerously divisive. It ignores the long history of Chinese bilingual education in the United States. Indeed, it was a 1974 case involving the unequal treatment of Chinese children in a San Francisco school (*Lau v. Nichols*) that spurred legislation insuring federally-mandated bilingual instruction.

Berger (1993) also ignores the importance of native-language literacy in determining the need for bilingual instruction. Russian children are more likely to be literate in their own language than are Puerto Rican children, and they may even be bilingual when they enter American schools. In addition, Berger makes the assumption that bilingual education serves mainland-born children, who are presumably dominant in English. However, bilingual instruction is fashioned for children who know little English, no matter where they come from. Berger (1993) fails to consider that many Puerto Rican children, whether born in Puerto Rico or in mainland United States, are often taken back and forth between these two residences for extended stays, which slows the development of their English proficiency.

Berger (1993) unfairly characterizes Puerto Ricans as choosing bilingual education for selfish reasons, rather than for their desire to give a good education to their children. This is unjust and demeaning. In all likelihood Puerto Rican parents are not the only ones who want to see their languages continue into the next generation. Chinese and Russian parents are probably just as eager as Puerto Rican parents for their children to maintain their native languages. Another implication of this passage is that parents must choose between English literacy and native-language literacy, when in fact good bilingual programs have no trouble helping students achieve both.

Berger cites the fact that students are often held in bilingual programs for four years or more as the cause of the "stubbornly high drop-out rate of 22.5% for Hispanic students" (Berger, 1993: B4). Yet there is no proven correlation between bilingual education and high school drop-out rates. In fact, a study of one English–Spanish high school program in the South Bronx found the drop-out rate among the students enrolled to be lower than that of mainstream students (New York City Board of Education, 1991–92). Furthermore, we have seen in our own review of the research that an extensive period of native-language instruction pays off in the end in high levels of academic achievement.

Similar arguments are offered by Linda Chavez. Like Berger (1993), Chavez unfairly pits Hispanics against other immigrant groups. Hispanic children are "victims of federal, state and local policies that promote teaching Hispanic children in their native language at the expense of teaching them English." Meanwhile, "most Asian and other non-Hispanic children receive such assistance through special courses that provide intensive English instruction so that they can quickly perform regular classroom work" (Chavez, 1991b: 59). Chavez clings stubbornly to the unproven theory that amount of exposure to English is essential: "Learning is directly related to what educators call 'time on task'" (Chavez, 1991b: 59), a theory which she claims is wrongly ignored by bilingual educators. In addition, Chavez accuses the Hispanic leadership of relegating Hispanics to a permanent underclass while claiming to empower them: "Winning court battles to have Hispanic children taught in Spanish in a society in which the best jobs go to people who speak, read, and write English well hardly empowers Hispanic youngsters" (Chavez, 1991a: 83). Besides accusing the Hispanic leadership of harboring malicious intent towards its own children, Chavez demonstrates a marked lack of understanding of the basis for bilingual education.

It is true that there are many poor bilingual programs. Berger (1993) highlights the problems that exist in the New York City school system: many children who are English-dominant but have Hispanic surnames end up in bilingual programs or ESL classes; teachers in bilingual programs do not all have the proper training and some are not proficient in English; some students remain in bilingual programs for years without learning English. Berger also offers one small paragraph on a successful program: the Bilingual Bicultural Minischool, which turns out students comfortably bilingual in English and Spanish. This example, it seems, invalidates Berger's contention that the jury is still out on the efficacy of bilingual instruction, but Berger does not seem aware of this. If he were, it might lead him to ask a crucial question: if we know what works, why are there still so many poor programs? He might find some of the answers in Wong Fillmore (1992), which we discussed in Chapter 1. This line of inquiry would be infinitely more fruitful than blanket criticism of bilingual instruction and the vilification of the Hispanic community.

PROGRAMS FOR ENGLISH-DOMINANT CHILDREN

Definitions

Foreign-language instruction has had a long history in the United States, and there are a variety of approaches. To define the different pedagogical approaches effectively, we will divide them into two categories: those that teach the second language directly through a course of study, and those that teach the language both directly and indirectly, through study of the language and through activities conducted in the language. (The term *foreign language* is relative. Any language may be either foreign or native depending on the perspective of the speaker, and some languages studied in the United States are called foreign even though there are native speakers of those languages living there. However, we will use this term here because it is the one generally applied to the learning of non-English languages by English-speaking Americans.)

Language-as-Subject Methodologies

The most common type of foreign-language instruction is one in which the language is the subject of a course of study; students go to "French class" or "German class." The oldest and most traditional kind of instruction in this category is the *grammar/translation* approach. Derived from the study of classical languages, the grammar/translation method relies on the reading of literature, the discussion of grammar rules, written exercises on these rules, and direct translation from English into the language being studied. The stilted nature of this approach and the emphasis on written language led to a period of experimentation culminating in the *audio-lingual method*. This method, greatly influenced by behavioral psychology, is based on the idea that language is a set of habits, and that learners can be taught a language by mimicry, memorization, and pattern drilling. Spoken language, based not on prescriptive rules of traditional grammar but on the language of contemporary native speakers, is seen as primary. Real-life situations are depicted in the form of dialogues, which students memorize and practice. Grammatical structures are learned by manipulating parts of the dialogue; for example, a change in the time frame of a sentence or a change of subject requires a change in the form of the verb. Dialogues are also transformed to reflect the students' own situations and experiences. Writing exercises are imitative in the beginning, but eventually become more creative. The reading of literature is reserved for the advanced levels.

In the last two decades, a number of new methodologies have appeared on the scene. None has gained the stature of the audio-lingual approach. They are not in widespread use, and are more often implemented in ways that vary from the individual versions; teachers often combine these methods in various proportions with each other and with more traditional methods. However, these methodologies have pushed the field in the direction of more naturalistic learning situations. They encourage the more creative and active involvement of students and less reliance on the teacher, eschew intrusive teacher correction and traditional means of evaluation, and attempt to deal with the obstacles of anxiety, defensiveness, and low motivation that have plagued language learning for so long.

One of these methods, the *Silent Way*, is based on the premise that learners can acquire a language by associating it with another medium: colors. The teacher does very little talking other than initially modeling the language; rather, the teacher gets students to speak by referring to a color-coded chart representing the sounds of the language. Colored rods representing real-life objects aid students in expressing original thoughts and in exploring the language. In *Suggestopedia*, untapped cognitive resources are called into action while psychological barriers are lowered with soft lighting, easy chairs, and pleasant music. Dialogues, question-and-answer exercises, games, songs, and dramatizations encourage active participation, lowered anxiety, and ease of learning.

Community Language Learning also seeks to reduce defensiveness and anxiety. Students sit in a circle. When a student wants to express something, he or she whispers in the native language to the teacher, standing behind the student. The teacher translates the expression into the target language (the language being learned), which the student repeats. The ensuing target-language conversation among the students is taped and becomes the class's text, the source from which work on pronunciation, grammar, and further language development derives. The *Comprehension Approach* to language learning is based on the belief that learners should not be asked to produce the language before they are ready. One version of this approach is *Total Physical Response*. The teacher begins by giving commands in the target language to the students, who respond physically. Students learn to read and write the commands, and, when ready, they take over the role of command-giver to both the teacher and their classmates. In the *Communicative Approach*, the goal is to get students to use appropriate language in given social contexts. Games, role-playing, and problem-solving tasks are some of the techniques through which this is accomplished. In an exercise called "information gap," one speaker has to relay information to another, choosing the linguistic forms appropriate to the status of the speakers and to the particular situation they are in. Textbooks are organized by function, such as expressing disagreement, making promises, and responding to invitations. Comprehensibility and fluency of communication take precedence over language accuracy. Krashen and Terrell's (1983) *Natural Approach*, mentioned in the previous chapter, falls into this category.

Many language teachers have experimented with these various approaches and find each of them wanting in one way or another. When this happens, teachers often resort to an *Eclectic Approach*, using different methodologies in combination with each other. They may find one method helps to improve oral competency while another is suited for teaching writing. As we noted in Chapter 3, direct grammar instruction is still popular, and appears to address the cognitive demands of adult learners in particular. Seasoned instructors incorporate what they learn from both old and new methodologies in a way that suits their individual styles of teaching and takes into account the language needs of the student population they serve.

Whatever method is used, it is safe to say that most foreign-language learning takes place in conventional educational settings: elementary, middle, and high schools, colleges, and universities. But other venues exist and are in fact flourishing. *Preschool language programs* are becoming increasingly popular; in 1986, the Center for Applied Linguistics estimated at least 1,200 programs nationwide (Wells, 1986: 60). At the secondary school level, *language magnet programs* offer two types of specialized education. One is the *International Baccalaureate*, well known in other countries, but only recently popular in the United States. With the goal of enhancing intercultural understanding, the rigorous program prepares students for entry into worldwide universities. The second type of magnet program concentrates on international commerce. Intensive study of a foreign language is combined with courses such as global economics, diplomatic history, marketing, finance, and banking. Lastly, most large cities have an array of *private language schools* for both child and adult learners, all using a wide variety of teaching techniques.

While we have been focusing here on foreign-language instruction, it should be noted that all the techniques mentioned have been applied as well to the teaching of English as a second language. The programs for minority-language children described previously make use of a variety of methodologies in those classes devoted solely to developing English-language skills. However, in immersion and bilingual programs, academic courses in which English is the means of instruction are also expected to provide opportunities for children to improve their proficiency in English.

Language-Through-Context Methodologies

Learning a foreign language by taking a course of study in that language is only one way of acquiring a second language. Another approach is to learn the language while engaged in activities conducted in the language.

A second language can be learned while studying other subject matter in that language. This approach, called *immersion* when applied to English-speaking children in the United States learning a second language, is not widespread but is gaining in popularity. Immersion programs attract children whose parents are eager for them to gain proficiency in a particular second language. They generally last throughout the elementary grades.

Initially, all instruction is in the target language. When students gain a significant degree of proficiency in this language, a class in English language arts is added; some academic courses taught in English may also be added to the students' schedule. Throughout the program, parents are expected to support the goal of bilingualism at home, encouraging their children's English literacy as well as their interest in and development of the target language. It is important to note that this approach is inappropriate for minority-language children learning English. Sometimes, the immersion approach is misapplied to such children, resulting in all-English programs that give no support to the students' native language. In essence, this constitutes what we referred to previously as submersion, which is known to result in poor acquisition of English, rapid loss of the native language, and low academic achievement.

One variation on this theme is *partial immersion*. In this version, students take a limited number of academic courses in a foreign language. There is no specific instruction in the language itself. Instead, students acquire the language as they use it in their math or science class. Of course, the content teachers must be sufficiently trained in how to use the target language as the means of instruction for their disciplines.

Another way to learn a language is to live in the language, to use it on a daily basis in the course of going about one's life. This is the philosophy behind the *language summer camp*. These camps combine formal study of the language with an environment steeped in the language and its culture. Students and teachers use the second language exclusively. Language-learning aids often include signs giving the names of objects tacked to trees and buildings. In some camps, the architecture reflects the country of origin of the language, and students use foreign currency at camp stores. Some offer academic credit to high-schoolers.

Evaluating the Effectiveness of Foreign-Language Instruction

The Current State of Foreign-Language Teaching

Despite the many innovative techniques available for foreign-language study, actual practice relies heavily on traditional methods. Lange, pointing out the overriding influence of the textbook as the basis on which teaching methodology rests, states that "in the context of the textbook, the curricula of foreign language programs are limited to basically one content, grammar, the one content that teachers expect to teach and students expect to learn" (Lange, 1987: 71). Even when newer approaches are adapted, they are often subsumed under the primacy of traditional concerns. Textbook chapters often open with a dialogue based on the audio-lingual approach; some textbooks even come with audiotapes in which dialogues of passages are read aloud. But after practicing the oral passage, students are plunged into specific exercises on vocabulary, reading comprehension, and grammar reminiscent of older pedagogies (see, for instance, VanPatten *et al.*, 1992; Jarvis *et al.*, 1991).

Evaluation of language proficiency, also based on the textbook, focuses largely on grammar as well. If this is the case, how effective has grammar-based instruction been? Unfortunately, the United States rates poorly in its ability to produce citizens proficient in languages other than English. Former US Senator Paul Simon, a long-time champion of foreign-language education, calls Americans "linguistically malnourished" (Simon, 1992: 5) and laments the resulting loss to the nation's cultural life, economic health, and foreign diplomacy. Lambert writes that "there is nothing more damaging to the American capacity to cope in a global society than the abysmally low level of foreign language competency of most Americans" (Lambert, 1987: 10).

Lambert points out that most Americans are "devoutly monolingual" (Lambert, 1987: 10), despite a considerable amount of time and money funneled into second-language instruction. American investment in foreign-language education averages over $2 billion annually, the number of students studying foreign languages is rising, and many colleges and universities now require foreign-language study for admission or gradua-tion. But the problems plaguing foreign-language instruction, according to Lambert (1987), prevent any real success. Too little time is allotted to foreign-language study, the skills taught are too low and scholastic, students see little usefulness in what they learn, techniques for measuring proficiency are outmoded, the language competence of teachers is often inadequate, and there is no knowledge of how long the skills learned will last.

Another critic is Leon E. Panetta, who served in the Clinton administra-tion and was a member of the 1979 President's Commission on Foreign Language and International Studies. That group found that "Americans' incompetence in foreign languages is nothing short of scandalous" (Panetta, 1999: 1), and Panetta uses the same word to describe the situation twenty years later. He notes that the foreign-language education system, from elementary school to university, is disjointed and focused over-whelmingly on the lower skill levels. Motivation to learn languages is low because of the "widespread perception in the United States, reinforced daily by innumerable personnel officers in the hiring market, that foreign language skills are not of great utility" (Panetta, 1999: 6). As a result, US businesses abroad resort to hiring bilingual natives rather than American expatriates, who cannot deal with the local populace; only recently are these companies realizing the need for bilingual American managers at their foreign subsidiaries. In light of the superiority of other nations in foreign-language abilities and world knowledge, Panetta sees a need for "a fundamental national commitment to foreign language training" (Panetta,

1999: 10) if the United States wants to be a leader in the global economy of the twenty-first century.

Added to this is the inability of language experts to scientifically measure the relative effectiveness of different pedagogies. Larsen-Freeman writes: "Over the years, large-scale studies comparing methods have been notoriously unrevealing" (Larsen-Freeman, 1987: 68). Comparing methods wholesale, Larsen-Freeman (1987) notes, has not shed light on which features of which methodologies work best with which students; such research has a long road ahead of it before it can be of any real use to linguists and language teachers.

Evaluating the New Approaches

Aside from the failings of traditional grammar-oriented language instruction, the innovative approaches mentioned above (the Silent Way, the Communicative Approach, etc.) have inherent weaknesses as well, according to Larsen-Freeman (1987). While they all strive to achieve communicative competence, there is little accord about what such competence really means, what its components are, and how it can be achieved. The shift of emphasis from the form of language to its functions has ignored language accuracy. Speaking and listening skills are the objects of focus, to the detriment of writing and reading skills. The innovative methodologies concentrate on the beginning and intermediate stages of learning; they are rarely applied to the advanced levels of language learning which are so desperately needed in American society. Finally, these methodologies are bound within the walls of the classroom and ignore the rich wealth of cultural and linguistic information that exists in the students' own neighborhoods.

Evaluation of a Model Immersion Program

One approach that has proved successful is the language immersion model. The prototype for immersion programs was one created in the early sixties to teach French to English-speaking children in St Lambert, a suburb of Montreal in the French province of Quebec, Canada. In Canada, and especially in the province of Quebec, being bilingual has always been considered an asset; at that time, however, English speakers did not usually acquire proficiency in French. Many English-speaking parents not only wanted their children to learn French for personal reasons, but were also concerned with fostering the mutual understanding between the two ethnic groups that would be essential for peaceful coexistence in the future.

A small group of such parents enlisted the help of linguists at McGill University in devising an experimental bilingual program, then pressured the local school board into allowing the program to exist. This group of parents largely ran the project. One class began in September, 1965; a second one began a year later. The McGill linguists monitored the children's progress from kindergarten to the fourth grade (Lambert & Tucker, 1972). The children's proficiency in French and in mathematics was compared to that of control groups of French-speaking and English-speaking children in conventional, monolingual (French or English) classrooms. Also monitored were the students' self image and their attitudes toward speakers of French.

The English-speaking children were separated from their French-speaking classmates so that their teachers, fluent bilinguals, could use a French modified to the level of ability of the students. In kindergarten and first grade, reading and all other subjects were taught in French. In the second grade, instruction in English language arts was added; English was also used as the language of instruction in music, art, and physical education. This continued through the fourth grade.

As a means of foreign-language learning, immersion proved to be superior to traditional methods of instruction. At each grade level, the students' proficiency in French improved. While they did not become as proficient as the French control group, they did achieve a near-native proficiency that outstripped that of the English control group.

By the end of the experiment, the students expressed appreciation for the French culture and people, and were confident in their ability to communicate and form friendships with French speakers. Their attitudes towards French Canadians as a group remained at a level of wariness comparable to those of the English control students. This was ascribed to two factors. First, societal hostility between the two groups had been increasing. Second, the French-Canadian students in the same school as the students in the immersion program were members of a socially stigmatized class (the linguistic, social, and historical situation of Quebec will be described more fully in Chapter 7). In light of these social factors, however, the students' progress in French was considered more remarkable.

Also remarkable was the fact the students had begun to consider themselves bicultural, both English Canadian and French Canadian. In the words of Lambert and Tucker, "the children are acquiring a second social overcoat which seems to increase their interest in dressing up and reduces the wear and tear placed on either coat alone," indicating "a valuable addition, not a subtraction or cancellation of identities" (Lambert & Tucker, 1972: 214). The authors predicted that the students' ability in French would have a positive effect on inter-group relations in the future: "With their highly developed language skills, the pupils should by now be able to seek out and come into contact with an increasingly diverse sample of both English and French Canadians and this should broaden their sociocultural perspectives" (Lambert & Tucker, 1972: 177).

No less important was the result that instruction in the French language did not deter the students' academic progress. Even though their math classes were given in French, the students did as well as the control group on tests in math given in English. The phenomenon of learners transferring skills from one language to another is one that we have encountered before. In Chapter 3, we discussed Cummins' (1979) views on learning to read: once concepts are acquired in one language, encountering the same concepts in a second language facilitates the learner's ability to read in that language. Also, earlier in this chapter we discussed the Ramirez study (1991), which showed that instruction in Spanish for Spanish-dominant students did not impede their progress in English or math; the students tested well in math even though the tests were in English.

The immersion approach to bilingualism for English-dominant students in Canada is extremely popular today. According to Baker, there are over a quarter of a million English-dominant children in some 1600 French immersion schools (Baker, 1993: 161). Baker (1993) attributes the popularity of immersion to a number of factors, including its goal of additive bilingualism in two prestigious languages, the support and commitment of parents and teachers, the optional nature of the program, and the fact that the second language is acquired through meaningful and authentic classroom communication. Bilingualism also affords these students an economic advantage in the future, in the form of better employment and promotion prospects, over their monolingual-English peers.

Views of Foreign Language Education in the Mass Media

General Support

Despite the proven limitations of most foreign-language instruction in the United States, society largely considers the learning of another language by native speakers of English to be a worthy goal, and any programs designed to further this goal are generally supported. This support does not always translate into financial backing; in reality, when school budgets get squeezed, foreign-language instruction is often one of the areas of study that is sacrificed. However, there is general agreement that proficiency in a second language is both a personal and a professional asset.

Increasing interest in foreign-language instruction is being documented in the press. For instance, Marriott notes that "mounting numbers of students from preschoolers to high-schoolers are being exposed to foreign languages in what some educators are calling a renaissance of second-language interest in American classrooms" (Marriott, 1992: 44). The source of this interest, she explains, is "a widening awareness by educators and parents that the United States is becoming a multicultural nation and that Americans need to improve their ability to communicate with others if they wish to remain globally competitive" (Marriott, 1992: 44). The number of students studying foreign languages is on the rise; reports of such increases come from Illinois (Banas, 1997), Arizona (*USA Today*, 1997), Georgia

(Carter, 1998), and Virginia (O'Hanlon, 1998). In Detroit, Michigan, the International Academy, which offers the International Baccalaureate, received 270 applications for the 120 openings for the freshman class of 1999–2000 (Whitaker, 1998).

The benefits of language instruction spill over into other academic areas, as the media acknowledge. Marriott cites a Louisiana Department of Education study finding that "fifth- and sixth-graders who studied a second language scored higher on reading and mathematics tests than their counterparts who did not study a foreign language"(Marriott, 1992: 45). A study by the College Board found that "students who took foreign languages for at least five years scored better on the Scholastic Aptitude Test for college admissions than those who had little or no second-language instruction" (Marriott, 1992: 45).

Although there is much research suggesting that older children are more efficient language learners than younger children, as we learned in Chapter 2, beginning language classes at an early age has become very popular. Holman (1998) and Vuko (1997) cite brain research to support this practice. Christine Brown, chairperson of the National Standards Task Force on Foreign Language Education, is quoted: "We now know that the better learner is one who starts early – at least before age 10" (cited in Holman, 1998: 40). The Task Force has also developed standards calling for greater instruction time and replacing rote memorization and dry grammar exercises with more lifelike activities.

In New York City, the Spanish language has become a valued commodity. Private language schools are experiencing a boom in interest in the language. The Spanish Institute saw its classes double between 1996 and 1998. Mothers seek out classes for their toddlers; courses also attract teachers, clergy, business people, judges, doctors, and police officers, all of whom acknowledge the growing English/Spanish bilingualism of the city (Ojito, 1999). Of the 47% of public high school students in the city studying foreign languages in the academic year 1998–1999, the largest number (109,121) chose Spanish; those studying the next most popular language, French, numbered 13,505 (*The New York Times*, 1999). When this trend is considered alongside government policy for bilingual education, the irony is apparent: monolingual English-speaking New Yorkers are eagerly investing time, and sometimes money, in learning a language which, when coming from the mouths of native-speaking children, results in their categorization as "disadvantaged."

The benefits of bilingualism for American children are touted in an article called "To help a child become bilingual" (Collins, 1994). Collins offers suggestions on how parents can help their children reach this goal. One way is for each parent to each speak to the children in a different language. For instance, a Connecticut attorney with a doctorate in Romance linguistics speaks only French to his children, while their mother speaks to them only in English. A second method is after-school language classes. According to an early-childhood expert, such classes may not result in immediate proficiency, but they do lay the groundwork for later second-language learning. They may also "enhance a child's overall intellectual abilities" and, in the words of the expert, "provide the skills needed for figuring things out: math, writing, drama, everything" (Collins, 1994: C10). In a related article, Rose (1994), a monolingual English-speaking American, writes of the growing bilingualism of his two young daughters as they spend summer months in France with their French-born mother.

In 1991, the sorry state of foreign-language acquisition was brought to the attention of the United States Congress and, subsequently, the press. The Senate intelligence committee proposed a $180 million National Security Education Program to help provide American intelligence agencies and diplomatic posts with a greater number of personnel proficient in foreign languages. The program would provide one-semester scholarships abroad for undergraduates, grants to colleges and universities to improve cultural and language training, and fellowships abroad for graduate students in exchange for a stint with the government or as a teacher. Senator David Boren, one of the bill's co-sponsors, described his concern "that America is dangerously ill-prepared to meet the challenges of the post-Cold War era.... We urgently need to improve our human intelligence capabilities" (cited in Lardner, 1991: B8). Senator Sam Nunn, another co-sponsor, pointed to the Persian Gulf War as an example of the nation's linguistic shortcomings: "We had to put 500,000 American men and women in our armed forces in harm's way because our intelligence community failed to anticipate an impending military crisis and because our diplomatic and policy communities were unable to avert the need for American military action" (cited in Lardner, 1991: B8). Support for passage of the legislation was reflected in one editorial, which said of the "modest but imaginative program'" that "if administered with care and exacting standards, its monies will fall like rain on a desert" (*The New York Times*, 1993d: A22).

The legislation passed; however, the program has experienced some difficulties since then. In the spring of 1995, it was in danger of being eliminated, but was saved by then Senator Paul Simon (Rubin, 1996). Initially, grant recipients were required to work in any branch of the federal government, but a 1996 Congressional proposal called for students to work for the Defense Department, which funds the program. Eventually, this requirement was modified, requiring students to work in any federal agency with "national-security responsibilities." Still, some college professors were reluctant to identify individuals for the program; they were concerned about the safety of students going overseas under the auspices of a program linked to defense and intelligence activities. Confusion over the provisions led other educators to believe the program had been ended. As a result, applications for scholarships fell (Rubin, 1997).

Support for Immersion Programs Based on the Canadian Model

Foreign-language immersion programs for American children, modeled on the French-immersion programs in Canada, elicit a great deal of enthusiasm in the press. In an article proclaiming that "Tots Do Swimmingly in Language-Immersion Programs," Reitman (1994) describes the Foreign Language Immersion and Cultural Studies School located in Detroit and serving a largely African-American student population. The school offers programs in a variety of languages, but the Japanese program is especially popular; parents choose this language because of the growing influence of Japanese businesses in the United States. Reitman points out that although some parents worry what will happen to their children's English, "standardized tests show that children taught in another language actually do as well or better in English grammar, reading comprehension and vocabulary" (Reitman, 1994: B11). The language director of immersion programs in Kansas City also advertises the programs' ability to "teach a child to put on a perspective – the lenses of another culture" (Reitman, 1994: B1).

Skow (1990) visited a language immersion summer camp in Minnesota. He found a fully developed Bavarian village, including a train station and guesthouse, where American children happily interacted in German with instructors and with each other. Not far away were a French village and a Norwegian village, also with their own authentic architectural styles. There were newer camps as well, including Spanish and Japanese, which were less elaborate. At all the camps, students passed through customs gates and acquired new identities to fit their new surroundings and their total experience in a new culture. Skow explains that more conventional means of instruction are employed in some of the camps, but the emphasis is on acquiring language by using it in a natural setting. The approach is apparently successful, as many of the campers express their desire to return as counselors. Skow was obviously impressed, comparing what he observed to a time in the past when "high-schoolers in the US 'took' language the way you take bad-tasting medicine" (Skow, 1990: 70).

The Double Standard

Analysis of the way the press handles language issues reveals a marked double standard. The efforts of English-speaking Americans to become bilingual by acquiring a second language are met with enthusiasm; the efforts of non-native English-speaking Americans and immigrants to become bilingual by maintaining their native languages while acquiring English are considered counterproductive to their adaptation to American society. The benefits to be derived from the language abilities of those who are native speakers of non-English languages are rarely recognized;

Americans wrack their brains to find better ways to acquire other languages, ignoring the resources they have in their own neighbors.

Foreign-language immersion instruction offers an excellent example of this double standard. Earlier we discussed the Canadian immersion program, in which English-speaking children successfully acquire French. It has been argued that this kind of program can work equally well in other settings. Porter (1990), for instance, claims that the following conclusions drawn from the Canadian study should be the guiding principles for the education of minority-language children in the United States:

(1)   Starting second-language learning early ... with a total classroom immersion in that language promises the best results in learning that language.
(2)   Beginning in their first year of schooling, children are capable of learning subject matter content taught in a second language.
(3)   Children are capable of becoming literate in their home language quickly if it is used in the classroom in later years. (Porter, 1990: 119)

If these principles were followed, minority-language children would be immersed in English from the time they entered American schools, taking up study of their native languages at a later time. This is in essence equivalent to the practices of submersion and structured immersion, both of which fail to produce successful academic achievement for such children. Porter (1990) ignores a very important point: children in foreign-language immersion programs speak the majority language of their community. Before they start school, it is likely that they are read to at home, acquiring the skills that Cummins (1979) calls essential for literacy; these skills are transferred to the second language when they begin their education. While they are being immersed in a second language at school, they continue to speak, read, and write in their own language outside school, where that language is used by everyone around them.

This situation contrasts markedly with that of minority-language children. First, it is possible that the parents of these children may be illiterate or semi-literate in their own language, so that reading in the native language may not take place at home. Such children often come from poor families with few resources for books and, even when parents are literate, they may not be in the habit of reading, either for their own benefit or to their children. This means that many of these children will not start school with the reading readiness that is characteristic of majority-language children. Second, the first language of these children is not supported in the wider community. While it may be the prevalent language of the children's immediate neighborhood, if that locality is socially stigmatized, the language is also likely to have a social stigma in the larger community. The result is that the children are likely to reject their native language, but may not be able to acquire the kind of proficiency in the majority language necessary for academic achievement. That is why Lambert and Tucker offer this advice in the conclusion to their study: "In any community where there is a serious widespread desire or need for a bilingual or multilingual citizenry, priority for early schooling should be given to the language or languages least likely to be developed otherwise, that is, the languages most likely to be neglected" (Lambert & Tucker, 1972: 216).

This statement is significant in that it highlights the difference between the goals that the educational establishment sets for English-speaking and minority-language children in the United States. Bilingualism is a valued goal for the first group, but not for the second; the "desire or need for a bilingual or multilingual citizenry" extends only to native speakers of English. The tunnel vision through which society sees only the need for minority-language children to acquire a basic knowledge of English as quickly as possible blinds it to the methods that work best in accomplishing other, more demanding goals.

Another example of the confusion over immersion is found in Aikman (1992). Aikman describes a partial immersion program in Virginia, in which elementary school children were taught math and science in Japanese. The children in this program scored at the same level on math and science tests as other children, but in other classes they scored eight percentile points higher, which was attributed to the high verbal concentration required for Japanese. There were other benefits as well; according to the school principal, "the kids are more flexible in their analysis and their critical thinking.... They are more open-minded" (Aikman, 1992: 81). Aikman then attempts to apply the principles of this approach to students of English as a second language. Citing a "multicultural language expert," Aikman states that "many students, particularly Asians, who study English in immersion programs back home or upon arrival in the US have the same learning patterns and achievement characteristics" (Aikman, 1992: 81).

What Aikman (1992) fails to note is that there is a big difference between English immersion programs in other countries and those in the United States. Those who study English in their own countries, even in the immersion experience, are still using their native languages; there is no threat of loss to those languages. However, immersion programs for immigrants in the United States make no provisions for maintenance of native languages; they are geared toward monolingualism in English. If the immigrants' languages are not supported either in school or in society, they will be lost. Again, bilingualism is a valued goal for English-speakers only.

It is sometimes startling to see how blind the press can be to this double standard. Wells writes of the trend to start foreign-language study at an early age. Aside from the parents who want to share their heritage with their children, Wells states, "many are enrolling their children in classes that have no connection with family heritage" (Wells, 1986: 60). One African American mother put her child in a Chinese class because "she wants her son to be able 'to communicate with the largest nationality in the world'." As in the other articles discussed here, Wells mentions the many cognitive advantages to bilingualism. However, she warns, "the only drawbacks that experts see in raising a child bilingually are that some might be teased because they're speaking a different language or, if placed in a class with native speakers, might be intimidated by the fluency of others" (Wells, 1986: 60). As an example of child rejection of language, she describes the case of Paúl Duston Muñoz, a young Hispanic boy who, at age three, told his mother that he didn't want to speak Spanish any more because it made him feel different from others. Wells quotes the boy's mother, who explains that "the only time he uses Spanish is when he is sick or thirsty at night or to say words that aren't polite in English" (Wells, 1986: 60).

How did Paúl's example even get into this article about foreign-language instruction? Wells (1986) is apparently blind to the fact that Paúl's case has no relevance to her subject. He was not learning a second language; in all probability, he was in an all-English school that left him with the view that Spanish is a language that doesn't belong in the public sphere. What a contrast this picture poses to that of the young boy learning Chinese, a language his parents tell him will help him in the future; it is unlikely that this child will reject Chinese the way Paúl rejected Spanish. The implications of this comparison are clear: learning a language spoken by "the largest nationality in the world" is an affirming act; speaking the language of one's minority parents and community is a self-denigrating one.

It is not unusual to find the double standard described here reflected in the same forum. One major national newspaper published the editorial supporting the National Security Education Program (*The New York Times*, 1993d) and the articles praising foreign language education by Marriott (1992), Collins (1994), Rose (1994) and Ojito (1999). The same newspaper published the article critical of bilingual education by Berger (1993). While the learning of Spanish by English-speakers is touted in Ojito (1999), Berger (1993) reproves Puerto Rican parents for their desire to see Spanish continue into the next generation. It is also noteworthy that Collins (1994) and Rose (1994) focus on the learning of French, a language associated with sophistication and high culture. (There is one sentence in Collins about Spanish: "Even parents whose foreign language skills are limited to phrases like '*no habla español*' can instill in their children a desire to learn a second language, merely by exposing them to it" (Collins, 1994: C10)). This unequal treatment of languages underlies a parallel unequal treatment of language groups, and hints at currents of racism and discrimination which are extremely disturbing.

A PROGRAM FOR MINORITY-LANGUAGE AND ENGLISH-DOMINANT CHILDREN

In the previous two sections, we described programs designed for children with distinct linguistic backgrounds. We noted the different educational goals generally expected of these two groups: programs geared to minority-language children have as their goal the acquisition of English; programs targeted for English-dominant students value the attainment of bilingualism. We also noted the biased manner in which these programs are written about in the press: bilingual programs for minority-language children are denigrated for their efforts to maintain the children's native languages, while foreign-language programs are extolled for their aims of additive bilingualism. But what happens when these two groups of children are educated together? We now turn to a discussion of a relatively rare but increasingly popular type of program, one that gives a particular spin to the double standard described above.

Definition

A unique educational experience that does not fit into either of the two previous categories is variously called a *dual-language*, *two-way immersion*, or *bilingual immersion* program. Student enrollment in this program aims at a 50:50 mix of English-dominant children and children who all speak the same minority language. Administrators, teachers, and staff are also chosen to represent a balanced mix of the two languages. Both languages are used, independently and for sustained periods of interaction, as media of instruction. Separate language arts instruction in each language is also a part of the model. In this way, all the students are learning a second language while developing their first. Both the school and the parents are committed to the goal of bilingualism. Parents are expected to encourage home use of the native language and to help their children achieve the high academic standards expected by the school. The number of programs of this type is small, but interest is growing. In 1991–92, 76 programs in 13 states were counted; in 1992–93, an additional 29 programs in 11 states were identified (Christian & Mahrer, 1991–92, 1992–93). In 1999, the web site of the Center for Applied Linguistics (www.cal.org) listed 261 programs in 23 states and the District of Columbia. In the next section, two dual-language programs will be described, one in New York City and one in Washington, DC.

Public School 84 in New York City

Spanish has been the most common minority language represented in the New York City public schools over the last three decades. Schools with large concentrations of Spanish-speaking students have dealt with the needs of these students in a variety of ways. But a different kind of program was initiated in one school on the racially-mixed Upper West Side of Manhattan. The school is PS 84. (In New York City, publicly-funded schools are designated in this way and identified by number. They are distinguished from privately-run schools, which require tuition and have selective admissions requirements.)

According to the school's principal, Sidney Morison (1990), the roots of the program can be traced to the 1960s. At that time, minority parents throughout the city were demanding community control of schools that were failing their children. Hispanic parents in particular were demanding bilingual education. At PS 84, parents and teachers combined forces to unseat the existing administration that had been unresponsive to their concerns and selected a principal of their own choice. Guided by a professor at the City College of New York, the new administration organized heterogeneous classes in which students' diverse experiences and languages were factored into the academic content of the curricula. This meant eliminating a tracking system which tended to separate out Hispanic and black children for less-demanding programs and special education instruction, hiring bilingual instructors and other personnel, and inviting Hispanic parents into the classroom to demonstrate aspects of their culture. Teachers devised new pedagogical techniques to deal with the untried experiment of teaching students of different languages in the same class. Simultaneous translation was used when both language groups were together, children were separated into language groups for reading and, in the middle grades, English was increasingly emphasized. However, these practices did not achieve the intended results: Spanish-dominant students were losing their Spanish and English-dominant students were not acquiring it. No one was becoming bilingual.

In the 1980s, with the help of another City College professor, the program reaffirmed its goal of bilingualism for all students. This has resulted in the more linguistically-sound pedagogy that characterizes the program today: the two languages are separated as means of instruction, alternating with each other daily, on half-days, or weekly. Despite the fears of teachers and administrators that the children would not be able to understand content taught in the second language, the students adapt easily. Whatever confusion exists in the beginners' grades is assuaged by the support that the children receive from parents, from the practice of having them work in linguistically heterogeneous groups, and from class activities designed to build vocabulary and develop concepts in each of the languages. Reading and writing skills develop in both languages; as Morison states, "In the middle grades, it is common to see a child who has just had a breakthrough in reading in his or her first language spurt ahead in second-language reading a week or two later.... It is taken for granted that learning to read is one process" (Morison, 1990: 167). By the middle grades, older children are writing plays and poetry in two languages; proficiency and accent in the two languages have by then become quite native-like.

A further positive result of this dual-language program is an increased sensitivity and compassion for members of the other language group. In classes given in English, English-dominant students are in a position to help out their less-proficient Spanish-dominant peers; in classes given in Spanish, the positions are reversed. According to Morison, "those who are or become bilingual often assume the role of translator, helping others even without being asked" (Morison, 1990: 166). Morison also notes the greater attentiveness of children in the dual-language program. He observes children "searching for cues in the context of what is being talked about in the reactions of other children or in the speaker's body language. In the previous setting, where teachers often resorted to translations, children often tuned out the less familiar language and simply waited for explanations in their first language" (Morison, 1990: 166). In 1991, a dual-language middle school program was added in response to parents' desire to continue the bilingual experience for their children (Morison, 1994, personal communication).

Academically, the school has had some problems, In the mid-1990s, the school was not meeting mandated standards, which was attributed to a weak curriculum. In the following years, however, the curriculum was made more rigorous, and performance began to improve. In the process, administrators have made sure that the school's progressive nature and child-centered approach were not compromised (PS 84, 1999, personal communication).

A Press Response to the PS 84 Dual-Language Program

Berger, whose article on bilingual education was discussed earlier, describes dual-language instruction in enthusiastic language; the approach, he writes, "is revolutionizing both language instruction and bilingual education in many parts of the nation" (Berger, 1989: A1). Dual-language instruction "has the lofty aim of giving English-speaking elementary schoolchildren a truly fluent command of a foreign language, both spoken and written. At the same time, it hopes to preserve the native languages of children from Hispanic and other foreign backgrounds, not eradicate them" (Berger, 1989: Al, B8). Berger describes the program at PS 84 and its academic success. Parents are also impressed, not only with the academic results but also with the program's ability to broaden the social perspective and contact of its students. The head of the parents' association recalls an incident during a family stay on Long Island "when Adam [her son] and several friends watched a group of Hispanic workers pruning trees. Not comprehending the workers, the other children walked off. Adam, she said, stayed and talked with them; they in their broken English, and he in his broken Spanish" (Berger, 1989: B8).

It is rather ironic to see the same journalist who derided Puerto Rican parents for allegedly sacrificing the academic careers of their children to their desire to preserve Spanish (Berger, 1993), now praise the goal of preserving the native language of Hispanic children. The only factor which could have changed Berger's perspective is that, in the context of a dual-language program, Spanish is not just the native language of half the students but is also a "foreign language," a desired object of study for the other half of the students. Some of the high status accorded the language of study for English-speaking students has rubbed off on the language of a minority group. It is also noteworthy that the social benefits of the program are illustrated in only one direction: English-speaking students can now communicate with members of a lower social class, people with whom they would usually not interact. There is a decidedly patronizing tone to this example. Certainly more significant is the influence the program has on members of the less-dominant social group: Spanish-speaking children in the program will probably not see themselves as different from or lesser than English-speaking children. This will inevitably affect the way they see themselves in relation to the wider society and will ease their entry into the mainstream world.

The James F. Oyster Bilingual School in Washington, DC

The genesis of the Oyster Bilingual School was similar to that of PS 84: the civil rights movement and the inspired activism of a traditionally marginalized group of Latinos hoping to secure a better education for its children. Freeman (1996, 1998) studied the program from a perspective that went beyond the assessment of language acquisition. Interviewing administrators, teachers, and parents, and observing classes in action, she came to a broader understanding of the underlying social goals of the program and the extent to which these goals have been met.

While the idea for the school originated with the Latino population, the school is meant to encompass the entire range of ethnic groups in the community. Parents, teachers, and administrators collaborate in running the school. Its overarching goal is nothing less than "to promote social change by socializing children differently from the way they are socialized in mainstream US educational discourse" (Freeman, 1996: 558). The mainstream notion of teaching "involves the transmission of a standardized curriculum content to what is assumed to be a homogeneous student population who speak Standard English and behave according to white middle-class norms" (Freeman, 1998: 150). In this model, learning is measured by standardized tests, students are receptors of knowledge transmitted by teachers, competition among students is considered the best way to encourage learning, and children who do not fit the norm (limited-English proficient students) are segregated into transitional bilingual programs and expected to join the mainstream, monolingual population in a short period of time. This policy typifies the common US language-planning orientation of "language-as-problem," as described by Ruíz (1988).

Oyster's goal is to stand this mainstream educational model on its head. Minority-language and majority-language students are socialized to see themselves and each other in a new way. This involves raising Spanish, a generally stigmatized language, to a status equal to that of English, making native speakers of both languages "legitimate participants in educational discourse" (Freeman, 1996: 572). This is done by placing two teachers (each a native speaker of one of the languages) in every classroom, and having them teach in their dominant language. Each team works out the structure of its course: the teachers may divide the class into two groups, with native speakers of both languages in each group, and work simultaneously, or they may each teach the entire class on alternate days. The student, teacher, and staff population is multi-ethnic; the Spanish-dominant faculty come from various countries, which is viewed as helpful in raising the status of Spanish.

The curriculum is a multicultural one, bringing the contributions of numerous ethnic groups into all of the content areas. Students are encouraged to look critically at the ways different groups are represented in the curriculum, relate their own experiences to what they learn and, when possible, propose and implement solutions to any discriminatory practices they identify. Spanish-dominant students in particular benefit from learning "techniques for asserting their right to speak and to be heard in a society that ... regularly refuses minority populations such rights" (Freeman, 1998: 121). Cooperative learning is the normal instructional method, with students negotiating meaning in the two languages. The linguistic goal is, of course, bilingualism for all. In Ruíz's (1988) categorization of language-planning orientations, Oyster represents the "language-as-resource" model.

Opening in 1971, the Oyster Bilingual School quickly gained status and popularity; by 1980, while general enrollment in the District of Columbia's public schools was declining and classroom space was in excess, Oyster was operating at 130% of its maximum physical capacity (Freeman, 1998: 24). By conventional standards of academic assessment, Oyster is an unquestionable success; its students consistently achieve at or above grade level on standardized tests. However, its ambitious social goals have fallen short of realization. This is mostly due to the great status differential in the larger society between English-speakers and English on one hand, and Spanish-speakers and Spanish on the other.

At the time of Freeman's study (1989–90), while all the Spanish-dominant teachers were fluent in English, not all of the English-dominant teachers knew Spanish; as a result, Spanish-dominant teachers code-switched into English more than English-dominant teachers code-switched into Spanish. (Freeman (1998) reports that this situation had improved by 1994.) English-language development was evaluated by standardized tests, while Spanish-language development was not; failing a third-grade English reading test meant not being promoted to the next grade, while failing a third-grade Spanish reading test did not affect promotion. This may have accounted for the fact that English-dominant teachers put more emphasis on skills development, while Spanish-dominant teachers stressed fluency and creativity. Despite the school's commitment to treating all students equally, comments by some teachers and the principal suggested that Spanish-dominant students were seen as poor, disadvantaged, and needing the most attention, while white and African American English-dominant students were seen as rich, advantaged and requiring the least attention.

Freeman (1998) notes that, by their last year of school, the students she observed had not attained the same level of bilingualism. Spanish-dominant students were maintaining their stronger language, but English had become their strongest language. Also, these students had more proficiency in English than their English-dominant classmates had in Spanish. This may be unavoidable, for a number of reasons. When they start school, Spanish-dominant students know some English, while English-dominant students generally know no Spanish. Spanish-dominant students have ample opportunity to use, and are expected to use, English in the outside world; when English-dominant students use Spanish outside of school, it is considered exceptional.

It is therefore ironic, but perhaps not unexpected, that one newspaper editorial on Oyster School focuses on one of the school's lesser accomplishments: the learning of Spanish by English-speaking students. Martin Plissner, an English-dominant writer, marvels at the achievement of his daughter, a student at the school, who by age twelve "could have made herself understood almost anywhere in the Western Hemisphere, something that cannot be said for her college-educated parents." The author takes for granted the linguistic accomplishment of the Hispanic students, stating that "over half the Oyster Bilingual graduates, including many Hispanics, spoke English when they entered. All were up to speed in it when they left." What he sees as a major accomplishment of the school is that "you don't have to be Hispanic to win the gift of bilingualism" (Plissner, 2001: A13). As in Berger's (1993) piece, the success of Spanish-dominant children in mastering English, likely to make a much greater difference in their life chances than the linguistic accomplishment of their English-dominant classmates, receives no mention.

By the end of their education at Oyster, as well, students had formed separate social groups. White English-dominant, white Spanish-dominant, and darker-skinned Spanish-dominant students tended to eat lunch separately, the latter two groups distinguished by family-income differences. Most disturbingly, after entering a mainstream junior high school, several students reported being shunned by their new classmates when they tried to befriend "the ESLs," as Spanish-dominant students were categorized in that school (Freeman, 1998). One can only hope that such peer pressure did not succeed in discouraging their desire to socialize with Spanish-speakers or dampening their enthusiasm for the Spanish language and its related cultures.

In a sense, with Oyster and other schools like it, bilingual education has come full circle. These schools recall the grassroots efforts begun several decades previously, in New York and Miami, to create an education that nurtures a more encompassing, pluralistic vision of American society and expects all students to reach their academic potential. These previous efforts were stymied by the interference of the larger society and its institutions, which, as Cummins (1994) reminds us, have a stake in maintaining the current power structure. We may also recall the elements of what Cummins (1994) terms "empowerment pedagogy," the kind rarely available to minority students: one that teaches them self-respect, self-sufficiency, fearlessness, the ability for independent learning, and confidence in their own academic and personal talents. Two-way bilingual education clearly puts this model into practice, and its continuing growth is encouraging.

A General Academic Evaluation of Dual-Language Programs

The advantages of dual-language programs for minority-language students are now becoming evident. Thomas and Collier (1995) conducted an analysis of the records of 24,000 minority-language students in four school districts in various regions of the United States. The records consisted of six to ten years of data on background variables and academic achievement as measured by standardized tests, performance assessment measures, grade point averages, and high school courses taken by the students. The authors found that for students educated in American schools from kindergarten on, "the elementary school program with the most success in language minority students' long term academic achievement, as measured by standardized tests across all the subject areas, is two-way developmental bilingual education" (Thomas & Collier, 1995: 5). Students in well-taught bilingual classes, which allow for substantial cognitive development of the first language and which continue until the sixth grade, also do well. The program with the least success in terms of long-term academic achievement is one in which students in the early grades are pulled out of English-language content classes for traditionally-taught ESL instruction.

Thomas and Collier (1995) enumerate the characteristics of two-way bilingual programs that differentiate them from many of the other types of instruction available to minority-language students. These characteristics are integrated schooling, with English-dominant and minority-language students learning each other's native language; the perception among staff, students, and parents that the students are in a "gifted and talented" program with high academic expectations; the equal status of the two languages, encouraging self-confidence among the minority-language students; healthy parental involvement; and continuous support for staff development, emphasizing the use of cognitively complex language and interactive classroom activities in all academic courses. The basis for the success of language-minority students in two-way bilingual programs might be stated very simply: these students are being treated the same as their more socially prestigious, English-dominant counterparts. Their language and culture are respected, bilingualism is considered an attainable and desirable goal, the most promising instructional methods are used, and high academic standards are set for them.

What has emerged from this chapter's analysis of the use of languages in the American school system is a very clear double standard: bilingualism is a desired asset for English-dominant children; for minority-language children, it is a phase on the way to monolingualism in English. But if we dig deeper into this phenomenon, we see that the basis is more insidious and widespread. There are usually two kinds of education, one for majority-group children and another for minority-group children. Education teaches children their place in society, and in order to maintain the status quo of the social order, children must be socialized to accept the particular status that has been assigned to them – a status often based on race, nationality, or language. In the next section, we will find that the double standard so prevalent in American thought, as reflected in the press articles we have just discussed, has been the subject of several prominent linguists, and exists outside as well as within the United States.

THE DOUBLE STANDARD: AN INTERNATIONAL AND A NATIONAL PERSPECTIVE

An International Perspective

In a comprehensive study of countries around the world, Tove Skutnabb-Kangas (1990) establishes the role that language plays in the social structure of societies and in the education of language minorities. As Skutnabb-Kangas (1990) tells us, the majority of people in the world possess a native language that is not the dominant or official language of the countries where they live. Those who are native speakers of the dominant language, whether they constitute a numerical minority or a numerical majority of the population, have privileged status compared to native speakers of other languages. They tend to have a higher living standard, more power and resources, and more control over their lives. To them, monolingualism is not a burden; since their native language is the dominant language, they have little need to learn a second. They may learn another language as a means of personal enrichment – and indeed have the financial resources to do this – but they can live perfectly well as monolinguals. Language minorities, however, must become bilingual. They need to know their native language in order to live within their families and to have a sense of their cultural identity, and they need to learn the dominant language in order to participate to some extent in the life of the nation. It is the exigency of this situation that defines their disadvantage. As Skutnabb-Kangas states, "Since they have been forced [to learn another language] precisely because of their powerless linguistic status, this means that they as a group have less power than those whose native language is the official language" (Skutnabb-Kangas, 1990: 6).

During the period of European colonization, those in power instituted language policies that best met their own interests. In India and parts of Africa, the British sought to create an elite class among the natives to serve the state and act as mediators between them and the local population. To this end, they restricted English-language education to the children of the indigenous upper classes. English, considered by the British to be superior to the indigenous languages, became a prized possession. After the colonies gained independence, English continued to be the language of the major societal institutions; in India, English shared its status with Hindi. Upward mobility for the indigenous populations was dependent on their acquisition of English; bilingualism was a must.

In the United States, the forcible takeover of territories where Spanish dominated – Puerto Rico and parts of Mexico – came with a legacy of devaluation of the Spanish language and those who spoke it. In this case, while Spanish/English bilingualism was also a necessity for upward mobility, it became a stigma because of its association with a marginalized people. As Skutnabb-Kangas explains, in the United States "being bilingual has ... been used almost as a synonym for being poor, stupid and uneducated.... Bilinguals are often labeled negatively, in terms that focus on their (actual or suspected) lack of knowledge in the majority language, or their supposed 'foreignness'" (Skutnabb-Kangas, 1990: 14–15). The diatribes against bilingualism and bilingual education penned by Schlesinger (1992), Wildavsky (1992), and others that are documented in this book certainly attest to the low place of bilingualism in American culture, specifically when such bilingualism refers to language minorities. As Skutnabb-Kangas explains, "School bilingualism (learning French in boarding school in England or doing the European baccalaureate at a multilingual school) and bi- or multilingualism in languages useful for business and culture is not seen as negative, especially when the person has the 'right class background'" (Skutnabb-Kangas, 1990: 15).

How does this social structure affect education? Since the dominant monolingual class controls all the social institutions of the nation, and since the values of this class permeate these institutions, it is not surprising that most educational systems see monolingualism in the majority language (with perhaps some knowledge of other major world languages) as a desired goal for all children. There may be some recognition that the country is itself multilingual, and that many children enter school speaking a minority language. However, the overriding educational goal for minority-language children is the acquisition of the majority language. The school exerts pressure on such children to stop using their native language, convincing them that the native language is the cause of their academic failure; conversely, children are rewarded for using and excelling in the majority language. In the past, this was often accomplished by the physical removal of the children from their families; Navajo children in the United States and Kurdish children in Turkey were forcibly taken from their homes to be educated in boarding schools. The result of such tactics is to alienate the children from their families and communities; at the same time, the children may not acquire a high level of proficiency in the majority language, leaving them in a social limbo between the subculture and mainstream society.

In some instances, the educational bureaucracy may make pedagogical concessions to the existence of minority languages. Most European countries include passages referring to bilingualism or multilingualism in their statements of goals for the education of minorities. However, high-level bilingualism is not a common aim, and emphasis is still placed on acquisition of the majority language. In the United States, for example, the prevalent form of bilingual instruction, transitional bilingual education, makes some use of minority languages, but these languages are quickly phased out in favor of English, rendering the term "bilingual" meaningless. In general, bilingualism goes against the best interests of the dominant class. Skutnabb-Kangas writes, "In order to legitimate assimilation, the dominant population, its language and culture have to be seen as superior and the dominated one as inferior.... In addition, the relationship between the groups has to be rationalized, always to the advantage of the dominant group which is seen as doing the dominated a favor" (Skutnabb-Kangas, 1990:17). The failure of the minority group to attain high academic achievement is thus viewed as the group's own fault. *Linguicism* (the justification for and perpetuation of the unequal division of power between language groups) "blames the victim in more subtle ways than biologically based racism, by colonizing consciousness instead of colonizing the body" (Skutnabb-Kangas, 1990: 17).

In doing this, the schools turn a blind eye to the evidence of the benefits of bilingualism. High-level bilinguals have been shown to perform better than monolinguals on tests that measure cognitive flexibility, divergent thinking, and different aspects of creativity and of metalinguistic awareness. However, the educational emphasis on learning the majority language usually prevents minority-language children from attaining high-level bilingualism. Their school failure keeps them locked into the socioeconomic class to which they are born, and the dominance of the language majority remains uncontested.

Examining educational programs for language minorities internationally, Skutnabb-Kangas (1990) finds a relationship between the linguistic goal of the program, the societal goal, and general academic achievement. When the linguistic goal of a program is high-level bilingualism, the societal goal is generally a positive one: integration into the larger society and equity of opportunity; consequently, academic achievement is high. Examples of this are maintenance bilingual and two-way immersion programs. When the linguistic goal is monolingualism, in either the majority or minority language, the societal goal is segregation from the larger society: apartheid, repatriation, or continued ghettoization; academic achievement in this case is low. Most programs fall into the second category, evidence once again of the vested interest of the language majority in the academic failure of language minorities.

A National Perspective

In the late 1960s, bilingual instruction was at a relatively young age in the United States. It was hailed as a new direction in the education of language minorities, a turning away from a policy that had an assimilationist goal to one that favored pluralism. The linguist Rolf Kjolseth (1973), somewhat skeptical about this claim, decided to examine the evidence as it pertained to the largest language minority at the time, Spanish-speakers, and specifically to the education of Mexican Americans in the Southwest. Kjoseth's description of this language group might apply to many of the language minorities in the United States today, including Hispanics: "The overwhelming majority are poor ('lower' class), politically powerless, sharply discriminated against and residentially segregated whether in urban or rural settings" (Kjolseth, 1973: 6–7).

Kjolseth (1973) described two oppositional models of bilingual education against which he could evaluate existing programs. Each consists of a set of factors that have different effects on language use both within and outside the school setting. The *Pluralistic Model* is the ideal one. In this model, the educational program is created through the collaboration of parents and school; it is a political and social issue around which the entire community is mobilized. Research into the varieties of the minority and majority languages spoken in the community is undertaken to determine which varieties will be used as media of instruction, in instructional materials, and in the components of teacher training to be instituted. The program lasts a minimum of nine years. School personnel are of local, ethnic origin; their background and education insure that they are appropriate bilingual and bicultural role models for their students. The student body is composed of both majority- and minority-language members. Instruction begins in the local dialects of both languages; the standard varieties of the languages are introduced gradually but do not supplant the local varieties, since the linguistic goal is maintenance of all four varieties (the standard and local variety of the majority language, and the standard and local variety of the minority language). The content of instruction includes the cultures of both language groups and stimulates community language planning efforts. Parents are involved in the program through extracurricular activities, demonstration classes, and a bilingual adult education program that replicates the design of their children's program. Evaluation of the program includes changes in language skills and attitudes, qualitative and quantitative measures of the use of all four language varieties outside the school, and traditional measures of academic achievement.

At the other end of the scale is the *Assimilation Model*. This bilingual program is created by the educational system; the community is invited to become involved, but has no decision-making power. Teachers are either majority-language members or minority-language members living outside the community. They are trained to teach the standard variety of the minority language and its "high" culture. They tend to look down on local varieties of the minority language and see them as obstacles to be overcome in acquiring the standard variety. The student body is exclusively minority-language. The program, which usually lasts three years, may begin by using the standard variety of the minority language alone or in combination with the majority-language standard as the medium of instruction, but in a short time the minority language is phased out in favor the majority language. The content of the curriculum emphasizes the culture and values of the majority language. If an adult bilingual program is offered to parents, its structure parallels that of the children's program, with the goal of functional literacy in the majority language. Extracurricular activities for children and their parents revolve around the "high" culture of the minority language. Program evaluation focuses on measurement of the quality of individual academic performance.

Kjolseth (1973) then used information provided by the US Office of Education to study the bilingual programs in existence at that time. To little surprise, he found that over 80% of the programs approximated the Assimilation Model in design. Thus, states Kjoseth, "In most cases the ethnic language is being exploited rather than cultivated – weaning the pupil away from his mother tongue through the transitional use of a variety of his mother tongue in what amounts to a kind of cultural and linguistic 'counterinsurgency' policy on the part of the schools" (Kjolseth, 1973: 16). Kjolseth notes that his findings are supported by Gaarder (1970), John and Horner (1971), and Andersson (1971).

Kjolseth also articulates the reason for this phenomenon. Given the low socioeconomic status of Mexican Americans, anything associated with this group suffers from low status as well. As a consequence, "Spanish is only a prestige idiom in the United States where there are irrelevant numbers of Spanish-speakers. Where Spanish-speakers are a relatively large group, it is an idiom held in considerable contempt" (Kjolseth, 1973: 7). This accounts for the fact that in the majority of bilingual programs then in existence, when choosing a variety of Spanish to serve as the transitional medium of instruction, program planners opted for the standard variety of Spanish over the local variety of the community. The entire phenomenon is summed up by Kjolseth in what he calls "the Law of Anglo love of ethnic irrelevance" or the "Disneyland preference for symbolic ethnicity": "The more locally irrelevant an ethnic language and culture is, the higher its social status, and the more viable it is locally, the lower its social status" (Kjolseth, 1973: 7, footnote 14).

Joshua Fishman sees American aversion to signs of ethnicity from another angle. Many American intellectuals who are two or three generations removed from their own immigrant ancestors are themselves thoroughly assimilated. According to Fishman,

> they are likely to have been "liberated" (intellectually and overtly, if not emotionally) from the claims and constraints of many primordial ties and biases. As a result, they are less inclined than most to take kindly to serious consideration of the values of ethno-religious participation, not to mention consideration of ways and means of reinforcing such participation. (Fishman, 1966: 372)

They may even commit themselves to "assisting various population groups to gain liberation from constraints that impede their full participation in higher levels of socio-cultural life" (Fishman, 1966: 372). Consequently, given the influence of Americans of this type in the educational establishment, languages associated with local immigrant groups are not accorded much value in the school:

> As long as these languages and cultures are truly "foreign" our schools are comfortable with them. But as soon as they are found in our own backyards, the schools deny them. However, by denying them we not

only deny a part of ourselves (a dangerous act in any democracy) but we limit the extent to which public school instruction in languages and cultures is live, real, and meaningful. Ethnicity is still so uncomfortable and guilt-laden an area for the essentially middle-class public school teacher, principal, superintendent, and curriculum expert that it is less objectionable to cut pupils off from deep understanding and appreciation than to give ethnically-based linguistic and cultural materials their due recognition. (Fishman, 1966: 387)

Both Kjolseth's and Fishman's words were written decades ago. Yet there is still a great deal of relevance to them. We have seen examples of the difference in society's treatment of foreign-language instruction and bilingual education. Kjolseth's Assimilation Model has prevailed since the government began supporting bilingual instruction. The federal government's Office of Bilingual Education and Minority Language Affairs (OBEMLA) reported that, for the fiscal years 1985–1992, 73.4% of the funding for minority-language children went to transitional bilingual education, 1.6% funded developmental bilingual education, and 12.4% supported programs using only English (Crawford, 1997). The revisions to the education law of 2002, mentioned earlier in this chapter, which renamed the Bilingual Education Act and OBEMLA and deleted any mention of bilingual skills, give further proof of the government's investment in assimilation approaches to instructing minority-language children.

The most innovative and promising programs we have studied approximate Kjolseth's Pluralistic Model. The Rock Point Community Day School is a true bilingual program for minority-language children; the St Lambert experiment had the goal of high-level bilingualism for its majority-language children; and the dual-language programs of PS 84 and Oyster illustrate what can be accomplished when minority-language and majority-language children help each other to achieve bilingualism. All of these programs were created through the ollaboration of parents and school administrators, and were born out of the communities' dissatisfaction with traditional schooling. Yet these programs are the exceptions rather than the rule. Society's need to distance itself from the cultural and linguistic pluralism that is evident at every turn is destructive, for in the end the potential for creating a true democracy with a high-functioning, literate population is lost.

CONCLUSION

In this chapter, we have analyzed the use of language as a means of instruction and as a subject of study in the American school system. Among the programs available for minority-language children, we found that approaches that encourage development of the minority language along with acquisition of English tend to result in high levels of school success. However, these results often get distorted in the press; bilingualism is not seen as a valuable goal for minority-language children, and animosity toward native-language instruction, especially as it applies to Hispanics, is largely evident. In contrast, efforts to promote bilingualism in English-dominant children through foreign-language instruction receive widespread praise and encouragement. This double standard is extremely unjustifiable. In addition, arguments for monolingual English instruction for language minorities based on the positive results of foreign-language immersion programs are misguided and unproductive. The journalistic tactics described here clearly illustrate Cummins' (1994) three categories of strategies for disempowering language minorities.

We also discussed the dual-language program, an innovative educational approach that encourages high-level bilingualism and academic achievement for minority- and majority-language children. Two schools using this approach were described. In press reports on the schools, societal bias is evident: while the positive results of this program are acknowledged, emphasis is placed on the benefits to English-dominant children. An analysis of the second school reveals its ambitious goal to transform the educational system and change social attitudes from the bottom up. In confirmation of the benefits of dual-language programs, a large-scale study of minority-language students has found this educational approach to be the most promising form of instruction for this population.

In the second part of this chapter, we reviewed the work of several linguists which supports the evidence presented here. Tove Skutnabb-Kangas (1990) offers a world view of how school systems perpetuate linguicism (discrimination against those who speak minority languages) through the process of enforced monolingual education for minority-language children and the consequent low academic performance that results. Rolf Kjolseth (1973) and Joshua Fishman (1966) describe the source of animosity toward minority languages in the American school system in the pervasive societal disdain for those whose ethnic distinctiveness is outwardly visible, those who remind assimilated Americans of their own humble ethnic roots.

As we have seen here, systems of education are based on the beliefs and values of the society in general. If minority languages are repressed in the school system, in all likelihood they are objects of repression outside the schoolroom as well. In the next chapter, we will examine current attempts to control minority language use in society. We will examine the perpetrators of these efforts, the alleged and real motives for their actions, and the consequences of language repression for the quality of life in the United States.

CHAPTER 5

The Modern Official-English Movement

INTRODUCTION

In public life, as in public education, attitudes towards language pluralism are generally favorable, but become less so when the languages of immigrants and minority groups are involved. As has happened at various times in our past, we have recently seen a re-emergence of efforts to restrict the use of minority languages in communities where their native speakers reside in large numbers. This phenomenon is the focus of the present chapter.

First, we put the current period of language restrictionism into perspective with a brief review of general attitudes towards languages in American history. Then we explore the reasons for the present resurgence: the changed nature of immigration, fear of the importation of foreign problems, economic insecurity, and territorial issues in multi-ethnic communities. In doing so, we explore the ways in which the official-English movement is both similar to and different from conservative social movements in general. We then analyze the organization that has spearheaded this movement, US English, which lobbies for state and federal legislation making English the official language. We describe its beginnings and its connections to other movements to reveal the ideological basis at its core, which contrasts significantly with the face it presents to the public. We also discuss the problems the organization has faced in the span of its existence.

The last section of the chapter focuses on legislation. First, we describe the status of state official-English laws. Then, we discuss various reactions to the concept of federal official-English legislation which surfaced when the issue came to national attention in 1995, and follow the developments since then. We present the major elements of the legislation, examine the arguments justifying this legislation, and respond to them.

NATIVIST AND LANGUAGE-RESTRICTIONIST MOVEMENTS: PAST AND PRESENT

As we have seen in previous chapters, at various times in the past nativist and language-restrictionist movements grew out of particular political and social realities. The sociolinguist Ofelia García (1985, 1992) defines five historical periods marked by general attitudes toward the use of non-English languages which were shaped by these realities and which informed government policy. In categorizing these periods, she makes use of Heinz Kloss's distinction between *tolerance-oriented* and *promotion-oriented* policy (Kloss, 1977: 21–25). Tolerance-oriented policy protects the right of minorities to cultivate their languages in the private sphere. Promotion-oriented policy regulates the ways in which public institutions may use and cultivate the languages and cultures of minorities. García (1992) also refers to *restrictive policy*, in which languages are intentionally repressed.

The colonial period of American history was marked by *promotional* policies toward non-English languages. While most settlers were English-speaking, the presence of Scots, Welsh, Irish, French, Italians, Swiss, and Germans made multilingualism a necessity for the purposes of trading, teaching, spreading the gospel, and diplomacy. In the eighteenth century, land developers sent pamphlets written in numerous languages abroad, encouraging mass migration from Europe. Some languages, however, were under attack. The languages of Native Americans and African Americans were looked down on because they were spoken by non-white minorities. German became a suspect language in reaction to the size and power of the German-speaking population.

From the 1770s to the 1880s, the United States demonstrated a largely *tolerant* attitude toward other languages. The government made use of these languages when it was necessary, for example, sending French-language literature to Quebec encouraging its involvement in the War for Independence, and publishing the Articles of Confederation in German. But English was by and large the only language that was actively promoted. The use of other languages was seen mainly as a way to integrate new immigrants; the expectation was that eventually everyone would speak exclusively in English. Tolerance for German and for the languages of non-whites diminished, although instruction in the German language proliferated in some parts of the country.

García (1992) describes the period from 1880 to the 1950s as one characterized in general by language *restriction*, with a slight shift in language policies beginning in 1923. The year 1880 marked a significant change in the type of immigration to America; the flow of immigrants from Northern Europe was replaced by one from Southern Europe. Many of these new immigrants, such as Jews and Italians, were considered racially distinct and inferior. In addition, the late nineteenth century was a time of reduced economic opportunity for everyone; restricting minority-language rights was a means of reserving educational opportunities and economic benefits for those in the mainstream. The most explicit language-restrictionist policy was aimed at Native American children, who were separated from their homes and sent to boarding schools where they were expected to acculturate completely to mainstream American customs and language. Other minority-language children were denied schooling in their native languages; by 1923, 34 states allowed only English as the medium of instruction in both private and public schools (Leibowitz, 1978: 6). In the Southwest, where former Mexican regions became part of the United States, use of the English language was enforced. World War I also encouraged language restrictionism. German Americans became associated with the enemy; in some cities, the use of German in public was flatly banned. Minority-language newspapers were required to submit English translations of their periodicals to the government.

A shift in language policy toward greater tolerance began in 1923 with the legal case of *Meyer v. Nebraska*, which we mentioned in Chapter 2. This case overturned a state law prohibiting both instruction in a foreign language and instruction through the medium of a foreign language. The Supreme Court held that the right to teach a heritage language is the same as the right to teach any subject. This was seen as a limited victory, since it recognized non-English languages as foreign languages taught for enrichment purposes, rather than mother tongue languages which minorities had the right to preserve. Similarly in the Southwest, Spanish began to be taught as a foreign language. The federal government made use of some languages for disseminating information about social and economic policies, and subsidized theater in languages such as German and Yiddish through the Works Program Administration (Kloss, 1977: 34).

This trend toward tolerance ended with the American entry into World War II, resuming a period of *restriction* that lasted until 1958. The xenophobia that war inevitably encourages led to the internment of many Japanese Americans. Native American languages and Spanish came under attack, and German continued to be repressed.

García (1992) characterizes the period from 1958 to 1980 as one of *promotion* of foreign languages, leading eventually to a degree of *tolerance* for ethnic languages. With the Soviet launching of the Sputnik satellite in 1957, the United States became concerned about its ability to compete with other technologically advanced nations. Foreign-language study, now viewed as necessary for national defense, was supported by measures such as the National Defense Act of 1958 and the Fullbright-Hays Act of 1961. The connection between bilingualism acquired through foreign-language study and that acquired by maintaining ethnic tongues was not immediately evident to America's leaders. Joshua Fishman (1966), a lone but powerful voice, took up the promotion of the latter type of bilingualism as important and beneficial to the nation.

Support for foreign languages and the Civil Rights movement eventually created a more hospitable climate for ethnic languages. These languages came to be viewed as instruments of access and opportunity for the minority groups who spoke them. The Bilingual Education Act of 1968 recognized native-language instruction as one means of remedying educational inequities; however, the legislation fell far short of supporting bilingualism, since its goal was the mainstreaming of minority-language children into all-English classes. The Court Interpreter's Act of 1978 and the 1975 amendments to the Voting Rights Act of 1965 also recognized the use of non-English languages as a means of addressing the needs of first-generation immigrants and bringing minorities into full participation in American society.

Finally, García (1992) describes the years from 1980 to the early 1990s as a period of *tolerance* toward ethnic languages under the ghost of *restriction*. It began with the birth of the official-English movement and is marked by a decline in support for multilingualism. Governmental promotion of bilingual education, never popular to begin with, faded considerably. President Ronald Reagan, rescinding a proposal supporting native-language instruction written during his predecessor's administration, declared that "it is absolutely wrong and against [the] American concept to have a bilingual education program that is now openly, admittedly dedicated to preserving [minority-language children's] native language" (Feinberg, 1981: C5). A news article described revisions in a California bilingual education bill: "Some language has been added to reassure doubters that the program's purpose is to move limited English speakers into regular classrooms as fast as possible, not to maintain separate languages and cultures" (Trombley, 1980: 6). An editorial insisted that "teaching non-English-speaking children in their native language during much of their school day constructs a roadblock on their journey into English.... A language is best learned through immersion in it, particularly by children" (*The New York Times*, 1981: 24).

During this period, however, federal legislators exhibited a certain level of tolerance for and promotion of Native American languages. The Native American Languages Act, which became law in 1990, amended a previous law to allow for greater funding of tribally-controlled community colleges and technical assistance contracts. In addition, it declared that it was federal policy to promote the rights of Native Americans to use, practice and develop their languages; to encourage and support the use of these languages as media of instruction; to encourage the involvement of Native American parents, educators and governing bodies in the creation of public education programs; and to encourage all levels of public schooling to include the teaching of Native American languages and to give foreign-language credit for competency in the languages. Finally, it declared the right of Native Americans to express themselves in their own languages in public proceedings, including publicly-supported education programs. In 1991, the Alaska Native Language and Preservation and Enhancement Act passed the Senate, but did not proceed beyond a House of Representatives committee. It would have directed the Secretary of the Interior to award grants for the purpose of enhancing, encouraging, preserving and facilitating the ability of Alaska Natives to speak in their own languages, and preserving and expanding knowledge about such languages (http://thomas.loc.gov).

At the beginning of the twenty-first century, the federal government took a promotional step in acknowledging the needs of speakers of native languages other than English. In August, 2000, President Bill Clinton signed Executive Order 13166, "Improving Access to Services for Persons with Limited English Proficiency." This order directed all federal agencies to develop systems for delivering programs and activities to people for whom English is not a native language, in compliance with Title VI of the Civil Rights Act of 1964 (*Federal Register*, 2000). As we have seen above, under President Clinton the Bilingual Education Act recognized bilingual skills as an asset for the first time. However, all mention of bilingual instruction was eliminated from the education law passed early on in the Bush administration. The new century has not seen a significant move toward promotional language policy in education, with the limited exception of its policy toward Native American languages.

Government policies relating to minority languages have largely resulted in the loss of such languages. Second- and third-generation immigrants are usually monolingual English-speakers, and many of them have come to mourn the loss of their heritage languages. As a result, the latter half of the twentieth century witnessed a significant growth in privately-funded ethnic publications, television and radio broadcasts, and language schools, whose purpose is to preserve native languages and cultures (Fishman *et al.*, 1980). Ethnic-language media also addresses the needs of the newest crop of immigrants at the start of the twenty-first century. Print, radio, television, and the Internet speak not only to the largest immigrant groups, such as Hispanics (Schwirtz, 1999; Calvo, 1999; Bixler, 1999), but also to Russians (Bixler, 1999; Barnes, 2000), Africans (Bixler, 1999) Chinese (Zhang & Xioming, 1999), and Bosnians and Croations (Berger, 1999). As in the past, these outlets help immigrants both to maintain links to the home-land and to adjust to their new, adopted country.

García notes the irony in the two contradictory trends of this period: "the restriction of natural bilingualism for the welfare of the minority coupled with the promotion of learned bilingualism for the welfare of the majority" (García, 1985: 155). Cummins points out the logical inconsistency of an education system that "first ensure[s] that schools eradicate students' native 'foreign' language skills and then spend[s] significant amounts of money trying to teach these same 'foreign' language skills using traditional non-bilingual methods that have been demonstrated to be ineffective except for a small elite of students" (Cummins, 1994: 175). In the midst of these two conflicting trends, which we have discussed more fully in Chapter 4, the official-English movement has found fertile ground for growth. We now look at this movement in greater detail.

THE UNDERLYING CAUSES OF PRESENT LANGUAGE RESTRICTIONISM

The Official-English Movement

Today, some of the same social and political forces that fueled past nativist and language-restrictionist movements are at work once again. These forces include resentment of people who are different and often considered inferior, the desire to bring such people into conformity with the rest of the country, the ailing economic status of many Americans, and political strife abroad. One particular organization, US English, launched by John Tanton, has succeeded in gathering the collective anxieties aroused by all these factors and pointing them in the direction of one of the most visible signs of immigrant presence: non-English languages.

Tanton started US English in 1983, as a lobbying group dedicated to making English the official and sole language used by government. However, the route that led him to focus on this particular issue had various stops along the way. They included concern for overpopulation and the diffi-culties of distributing natural resources in an equitable manner, problems that Tanton attributed to the influx of immigrants to America, especially those of color. Thus, we shall see that objection to the use of non-English languages is merely a cover for a more insidious philosophy: the scape-gating of immigrants for the ills of society in general, a dogma which is as old as the United States itself.

Anatomy of a Conservative Movement

In its essence, language restrictionism conforms to the pattern of most conservative social movements. According to sociologist Clarence Y.H. Lo, such movements are attempts "to maintain structures of order, status, honor, or traditional social differences or values" (Lo, 1982: 108). In the rhetoric of the official-English movement, the desire to hold on to established ways and traditions is very evident. Representative Norman Shumway, sponsor of several versions of the English Language Amendment, writes, "English has been the common language of the United States as a result of historical tradition.... That common language has been the 'glue' which has held us together, forging strength and unity from our rich cultural diversity" (Shumway, 1988: 121). Without the legal protection of the law, Shumway fears that "the primacy of English is being threatened, and that we are moving toward the status of a bilingual society" (Shumway, 1988: 122).

Supporters of official English lament the loss of an alleged immigrant tradition, one in which newcomers adapted to American life in a manner that met with the approval of mainstream America. Gary Imhoff, a frequent consultant to US English, describes what he calls the reshaping of the paradigm of the Hispanic experience. Before the civil rights movement, Hispanics were part of the immigrant paradigm, which he characterizes as follows:

> The stereotype of the American immigrant is that he or she learns the language of the new society, its customs and folkways, and the skills that are useful in the new land. Then the immigrant works twice as hard as native-born Americans and succeeds – "achieves the American dream" – by virtue of heroic and bittersweet industriousness, devotion, and discipline. Of course, the success of the immigrant in American society can also be attributed to the openness and accessibility of America, to the free and generous assistance offered to the immigrant in this country, but the primary effort and the primary credit both belong to the immigrant. (Imhoff, 1990: 58).

In the 1960s and 70s, according to Imhoff, Hispanic leaders reconfigured the Hispanic experience from the immigrant paradigm to the minority paradigm, analogous to the experience of African Americans. In this paradigm,

> the problems that arise between a minority and his or her society are presumed to be caused by – to be the fault of – the society. The responsibility for solving those problems, therefore, lies with the society.... If Hispanics in America are a minority and not an immigrant group, then the responsibility for learning a new language lies with the general society and not with Hispanics. (Imhoff, 1990: 58)

In comparing present-day immigrants to those of the past, Imhoff fails to take into account the differences in the experiences of these two sets of newcomers. Sociologist Douglas Massey (1995) argues that it is impossible to expect the assimilation process to be the same, and that it is necessary to overcome what he calls "some of the nation's most enduring myths." Arising from the last period of mass migration, these are myths "about the achievement of economic mobility through individual effort, about the importance of group solidarity in the face of ethnic prejudice and discrimination, and about the inevitability of assimilation into the melting pot of American life" (Massey, 1995: 633–634).

First, the great immigrant wave of the past was overwhelmingly Southern and Eastern European; although different from each other and from Northern Europeans in language, literacy, culture, and economic background, after several generations these differences faded, and all these groups became one large, amorphous class of mixed European ancestry. Second, the period of immigration virtually ended in the 1930s, which lessened the influence of the sending countries and strengthened the influence of the United States in the ways in which ethnic groups defined themselves. Third, this immigrant wave was followed by a period of sustained economic expansion, offering ample opportunities for socioeconomic advancement and allowing first- and second-generation Southern and Eastern European immigrants to reach economic parity with those of Northern and Western Europeans by the latter half of the twentieth century.

The situation of present-day immigrants is quite different. First, they are mostly non-European, making it harder for them to blend in with established Americans. They are also more concentrated in terms of national origin and language: Spanish is spoken by immigrants of twelve sending countries and is the language of 38% of all new arrivals (Massey, 1995: 646). Second, as we noted previously, it is likely that immigration will continue, given the conditions in the sending countries and the availability of low-prestige jobs in the United States that Americans refuse to accept. This means that the character of ethnicity will continue to be influenced by the sending countries, and, with the geographical clustering of Hispanics in a limited number of large, metropolitan areas, insures that Spanish will continue to be "viable as a second language of daily life" (Massey, 1995: 646). Third, the economy of today is the opposite of the one encountered by immigrants of the early part of the twentieth century. It is characterized by stagnant wages, greater income inequality, the end of the decline of poverty rates, decreased occupational mobility, and the growing importance of education paired with the growing neglect of public schools. According to Massey, there is a great likelihood today that second- and third-generation immigrants will remain at the same socioeconomic level as those of the first generation, creating a further impediment to their absorption into the larger mainstream society.

It is important to note that some of the same problems faced by Hispanic immigrants – discrimination, ethnic distinctiveness from Europeans, a faltering economy – are also faced by African Americans; both of these groups have difficulty making it into mainstream society. In addition, some of the same forces have compelled these groups to assert their unique identities and to resist accepting a mainstream culture that neither includes them nor offers them its rewards. Despite Imhoff's view, it is not surprising that similarities between these two groups exist.

Thus, by invoking a mythic past, and misrepresenting the immigrant past, Imhoff is able to create the illusion that a long-time tradition of assimilation has been sullied. In this mythic past, already-established Americans didn't feel threatened or alienated by people who were different from themselves, didn't feel the pressure to adapt their own lives to those of the newcomers. Instead, newcomers were obligated to adapt themselves to a new society. If they failed, it was not because of the nature of this society or its people, but because of their own shortcomings. The rule of mainstream society – its language, culture, and values – was unimpeachable and unchallenged.

During periods of change, it is exactly this sense of comfort, this feeling of being in control, that is taken away. Invasions into the sphere of dominance – invasions into the neighborhood, into the workplace, and especially into the wallet – bring out feelings of vulnerability. According to sociologist Carol Schmid, "Complaints about a breakdown in the process of assimilation seem to be especially prevalent during periods of high immigration, economic restructuring, and recession, providing fertile soil for the growth of nativism" (Schmid, 1992: 202–203). Fishman states, "There is a seriously wounded self-concept involved insofar as mainstream America yearns for 'English Official/English Only' to salvage its sense of propriety and law and order" (Fishman, 1988: 131). Crawford concurs: "English-only flows from feelings of insecurity. Now that demographic changes of all kinds – greater mobility, nontraditional families, mass culture – are disrupting Americans' sense of community, there is a renewed search for unifying institutions" (Crawford, 1992: xii). We now turn our attention to the changes in American life that have affected attitudes towards immigrants.

The Changed Nature of Immigration

Throughout most of American history, immigration policies favored people from European countries wishing to emigrate to the United States. In 1965, laws favoring European immigration were repealed. At the same time, events abroad (the Cuban Revolution, the Vietnam War, unrest in Southeast Asia and Africa, political and economic problems in the Caribbean and Central America) resulted in an influx of immigrants from the so-called "developing world." This has literally changed the face of immigration to America, from one essentially white to one that is largely non-white.

It has also brought to America people with cultures markedly different from the cultures of people of European ancestry.

In numerical terms, this wave of immigration is less daunting than that of the early twentieth century. The total number of legal and illegal immigrants who arrived in the 1980s, roughly 8 million, is not very different from the number of immigrants who arrived between 1900 and 1910, 8.8 million. Since the current population is three times the size of what it was at the turn of the twentieth century, the impact of this immigrant wave is much less significant. In 1910, foreign-born residents made up 14.6% of the population; in 1989, they made up 7% (Woodrow, 1990). In the last year of the century, out of the 270 million people residing in the United States, the foreign-born numbered 25 million, roughly 9% of the total population (US Census Bureau, 1999a). However, much is made in the new nativist movement of the country's inability to deal with the present wave of immigration. Antonio Califa of the American Civil Liberties Union writes, "These new immigrants have caused much concern among immigration restrictionists.... While the economy absorbed millions of immigrants in the late nineteenth century, immigration restrictionists currently contend that the United States cannot sustain this new influx of immigrants" (Califa, 1989: 298–99).

The anti-immigration movement is fueled by the frustrations of those who believe immigration can and should be controlled, but find it impossible to do so. First, no one can foresee the events in other parts of the world that impel people to leave their homelands, attracted by the lure of a better life in the United States. Boatloads of Cubans (Spencer, 1999), Haitians (Norton, 1999), and Chinese (Farrell, 1997) are willing to risk their lives crossing angry seas to get to American shores, even knowing that if they survive, they may be turned back. Parts of the country are often startled by an unexpected change in immigration. For example, in northwestern Colorado (where residents have become accustomed to undocumented immigrants from Asia, Africa, and Central and South America) investigators followed evidence leading to the discovery of illegal workers from the former Soviet bloc countries (Hughes, 1998).

Second, government policies that are intended to stem immigration often end up having the opposite effect. The 1993 North American Free Trade Agreement was supposed to reduce incentives for Mexicans to leave their country. Instead, unemployment in Mexico increased as small farmers, business owners and other workers were displaced. At the same time, the policies of the Mexican government resulted in slowed job growth and an increased wage gap between Mexico and the United States. All of this produced more compelling reasons than ever before for Mexicans to migrate north. Another example is the 1996 law passed by the United States cutting public benefits to immigrants, which was intended to discourage people from coming and encourage those already here to return to their home countries. However, receiving public assistance is rarely the intention of immigrants, who generally expect to find work. The law failed to decrease either legal or illegal immigration. Instead, it encouraged legal immigrants to apply for citizenship, for two reasons: First, they wanted to insure that if they did need public assistance, they could get it. Second, many realized that the only way to prevent lawmakers from passing legislation harmful to immigrants is to actively participate in the political process that chooses those who make the laws (Freedberg & McLeod, 1998).

Massey (1995) believes that continued immigration is inevitable. He writes, "Current knowledge about the forces behind international migration suggests that movement to the United States will grow, not decline." In addition, "these forces are beyond the immediate reach of US policy, particularly immigration policy.... Athough politicians call for even stronger measures, the forces producing and perpetuating immigration appear to be of such magnitude that the new regime of US immigration may continue indefinitely" (Massey, 1995: 644). Illegal immigrants alone numbered more than five million in 1999, with an additional quarter-million expected to arrive each subsequent year (Pan, 1999: C5).

Most observers of the backlash against immigration believe that resistance to the new immigration is based in large part on prejudice. Its most frequent target is Hispanics. According to estimates, in 1998 Hispanics made up 42% of the immigrant population (US Census Bureau, 1999b); they tend to congregate in large communities in southern and western cities, making them highly visible and distinctive. Illegal immigration is a particular source of irritation to many Americans, and most Americans tend to think of undocumented aliens as Hispanic. This is especially true in the two states with the largest number of such immigrants. As Sontag explains, "Chinese boat people and Central American day laborers ... dominate the public perception of New York State's illegal immigrants" (Sontag, 1993b: B1); in California, "the image of illegal immigrants coming across the US–Mexican border dominates the immigration debate" (Simon, 1993: A1).

However, a study by the Immigration and Naturalization Service (INS) based on estimates of undocumented aliens in fall 1992 found that the three largest groups in New York were from Ecuador, Italy, and Poland; Mexicans did not even make the top 20 list (Sontag, 1993b). The 1994 figures showed Italy to be at the top of the list, followed by Ecuador and Poland (Dunn, 1995). In California, while the largest numbers come from North and Central America, significant numbers of undocumented aliens also come from Asia and Europe. Nationally, roughly one third of undocumented immigrants are from Mexico, one third from the Caribbean and Central and South America, and one third from other countries such as Canada, Poland, and the Philippines (Simon, 1993). In addition, while about half of undocumented immigrants arrive by crossing the border with Mexico, the rest come by boat or by airplane armed with forged documents or temporary tourist visas. In a sense, these immigrants may pose more of a threat to ordinary Americans than those who slip into the country from the south, because, in the words of Mike Flynn, the INS chief of enforcement for the western region, "they are more sophisticated and more likely to take those good jobs that US citizens would want because they have skills" (cited in Simon, 1993: A42).

While many Hispanics congregate in large urban communities, they have become more visible for another reason: work often pulls them into the suburbs. In the wealthy counties of Westchester and Fairfield, north of New York City, many men have found work as day laborers on construction and landscaping crews. They have also become suburban residents; in Mount Kisco, a town of 9,100 people, the Hispanic population increased from 401 to 1,180 between 1980 and 1990, and continues to grow. Established residents have responded with wariness. Some of the immigrants say that their neighbors become more welcoming if they speak English, hold steady jobs and have families; those working with the newcomers cite the sources of discomfort as their race and class distinctiveness and their habit of "outdoor socializing" (Gross, 2000). Clearly, the largely white population has no problem relegating their most menial jobs to Hispanics, but would prefer that the workers did not live in their community.

There are other signs of Americans' uneasiness with the presence of Hispanics and their language. In Chapter 4, we mentioned the growing demand for instruction in Spanish among residents of New York City. Ojito (1999) cites the growth of the Hispanic population as the impetus for this demand. However, while the desire of English-dominant speakers to become bilingual might be seen as something positive, Ojito frames it in a way that puts Hispanics in a negative light:

> While in years past, Hispanic immigrants and Puerto Ricans tended to live and work within the boundaries of traditional enclaves like Washington Heights, the Lower East Side, the Bronx and parts of Queens, today's Hispanic residents are moving beyond the barrios, the factories and the bodegas and are flooding the city's service-oriented businesses looking for work and business opportunities, often in Spanish only. (Ojito, 1999: A1, B4)

According to Ojito, it appears that Hispanics are not staying where they belong, but moving into neighborhoods that are not "theirs." The use of the word "flooding" gives the sense that Hispanics are wiping out everything in their way (why is it that the word "flood" is so often used to characterize the arrival of immigrants?). Furthermore, Ojito insinuates that English-speakers may be more willing to learn Spanish than Spanish-speakers are to learn English, an idea which is refuted in research showing the rapid transition to English among Hispanics (Grenier, 1984).

Wariness towards Hispanics and the Spanish language also appears in academic literature. As we discussed earlier, Massey (1995) aptly argues that today's immigrants cannot be expected to assimilate to American life in the same way that the last great wave of immigrants did at the beginning of the twentieth century. He acknowledges that the size, concentration, and continued immigration of the Hispanic population insure that Hispanic culture and language have a permanent place in American society. He even sees bilingualism as an asset:

> Assimilation will become more of a two-way street, with Euro-Americans learning Spanish and consuming Latin American products as well as Latins learning English and consuming Anglo-American products. Increasingly the economic benefits and prospects for mobility will accrue to those able to speak both languages and move in two cultural worlds. (Massey, 1995: 648)

However, he also contends that "large communities of Spanish speakers will emerge in many US urban areas, lowering the economic and social costs of not speaking English while raising the benefits of speaking Spanish. As a result, the new immigrants from Latin America are less likely to learn English than were their European counterparts at the turn of the century" (Massey, 1995: 647). Like Ojito (1999), Massey suggests that bilingualism is a greater lure for English-speakers than for Spanish-speakers; given his belief in the economic and social capital of being bilingual, he fails to explain why the Spanish-dominant should be less eager to acquire such capital than the English-dominant.

Hispanics have largely become the symbol of American immigration and all the ills it has purportedly brought with it; as we shall see later on, much of the anti-immigrant rhetoric produced by the language-restrictionist movement attacks this specific group. Racism is certainly involved. European immigrants share a common heritage with many Americans; Asians are currently thought of as the "model minority." In contrast, Hispanics, representing immigrants from all Spanish-speaking countries in the developing world, comprise the largest immigrant group and have a significant contingent of dark-skinned people. Although they possess a hereditary link to European Americans, this link is rarely acknowledged; as a result, they lack the psychological support that would ease their transition into mainstream society. Unlike Asians, they are not thought of as possessing any particular positive characteristics that would further help their acceptance. Califa contends that, while the issue of maintaining economic and political dominance has fueled the official-English movement, "pure prejudice also plays a part. English Only proponents feel that

Hispanics have objectionable cultural traits which are harmful to the country" (Califa, 1989: 347).

This accounts for the fact that opinions regarding official English break down sharply along ethnic lines. In November 1988, exit polls taken in California and Texas asked voters how they would have voted on making English the official language of the country if that issue had been on the ballot. Studying this poll, Schmid (1992) found that Anglo Americans were largely in favor of this legislation, while Hispanic Americans were largely opposed; ethnicity turned out to be a more accurate predictor of opinion than economic status, education, or gender. Schmid (1992) notes that on this point the official-English movement differs from other conservative social movements. Generally, conservative causes are supported by people who are either fighting to maintain their socioeconomic status, or are rising in status and wish to separate themselves from the group they have left behind. According to Schmid, the high level of support for official English among Anglo Americans of all socioeconomic and educational back-grounds is largely related to the general anxiety about the social and polit-ical problems that seem to be hitting everyone in the country. However, there is an additional factor at work: "Hispanics see the English-Only movement as a new means to justify discrimination, a phenomenon driven by prejudice and fear, and a threat to their ethnic community" (Schmid, 1992: 207).

Fear of the Importation of Foreign Problems

Closely related to Americans' prejudices against those who are different from themselves is their fear that foreign problems will travel with immi-grants and embed themselves into American life. The United States has generally been very fortunate: there have been no wars on its soil for over a hundred years, it has dominated the economic and political world scene for the last half-century, and it has enjoyed a relatively high standard of living. Yet every day in newspapers and television broadcasts, Americans see evidence of misery and unrest in other parts of the world. In response, they are often torn between two competing reactions: compassion and a desire to share some of the advantages they have with those less fortunate, and a sense of relief that such miseries are far away and a desire to keep them there. It is the latter reaction that fuels xenophobia and rejection of all that is foreign on American turf.

An inherent part of this xenophobia is the blurring of boundaries between the troubles occurring in foreign countries and the immigrants who come to the United States to escape them. It is as if the warfare and poverty in other countries were caused by some genetic strain, which immi-grants spread to their adopted homeland upon their arrival. Crawford, for example, writes, "With ethnic warfare spreading in eastern Europe, many are wondering when it will reach our shores. Already there is talk of 'tribal-ism' and 'the disuniting of America' from those who fear that common ties are being frayed by group claims of all descriptions' (Crawford, 1992: xii). In the 2000 presidential race, the Reform Party candidate Pat Buchanan, having previously gained infamy for incendiary remarks about Hispanic and Asian immigrants, blacks and Jews, cited the many social ills inflicted by recent immigrants, including crime, a decrease in wages and the forma-tion of ethnic ghettos. He warned of the increasing splintering of American culture and the "balkanization" of the country (Dine, 2000). However, the reality is that ordinary people are swept up into national turmoil by forces quite outside their control. The nativist movement tends to ignore some basic truths about such conflicts, for example, that the factions at war with each other in Bosnia-Herzegovina lived together peacefully in the same neighborhoods and even in the same families before political forces set them at each other's throats.

The fear among Americans of "others" coming from troubled countries thinly masks the role that the United States has played in creating and stoking these troubles, and the benefits it derives from them. The United States' history of support for dictatorships such as those in Haiti and El Salvador certainly contributed to the poor conditions suffered by those in the lower classes. American companies have long viewed developing nations as opportunities for inexpensive, non-unionized labor and freedom from environmental regulations. In 1990, American companies in Mexico owned over 1,000 *maquiladoras*, assembly-line factories whose workers, mostly young women, earned between $26 and $28 a week, among the lowest factory wages in the world (*Ms.*, 1990: 11). A decade later, 3,500 factories had one million employees earning one-tenth the US minimum wage (Wood, 1999: 3).

The exploitation of developing nations gained international attention in December 1999 with the meeting in Seattle, Washington of the World Trade Organization, a global commercial agency empowered to enforce global commerce rules by imposing economic sanctions on countries that pose barriers to trade and commerce. For several days, both peaceful and disrup-tive protesters took to the streets, demanding redress for a number of ills perpetrated by multinational corporations. These included child labor, environmental destruction, inhumane working conditions, and inade-quate wages. As a result of the demonstrations, public awareness of this issue was greatly heightened. People also became mindful that recent developments such as the 1994 North American Free Trade Agreement and the growing globalization of commerce have actually worsened abuses perpetrated on underdeveloped nations (Ammon, 1999; Casey, 1999; Quinlan, 1999; Deans, 1999; de Borchgrave, 2000).

The United States takes advantage of depressed conditions in South and

Central America on its side of the border as well, hiring undocumented workers for pittance wages to pick fruits and vegetables in southern and western states. Aside from being exploited, these workers have become the focus of citizen anger at the federal government and scapegoats for the country's economic ills. For example, Governor Pete Wilson of California railed at Washington for not controlling illegal immigration. As a result, he claimed, California's public schools were "bursting at the seams" and its public health care centers were "swamped" (Wilson, 1993: 35). Wilson estimated the cost of public services to undocumented immigrants to be $3 billion, and claimed that such people crossed over to the United States specifically to get these benefits. At the same time, he complained that the federal government had abandoned responsibility for these services, leaving the states to pay for them by themselves. Of particular concern to Wilson was the granting of United States citizenship to babies born to undocumented aliens: "Some illegals come to our country simply to have a child born on US soil. That, of course, renders the child eligible for a host of benefits" (Wilson, 1993: 35). These arguments formed the basis of Wilson's re-election campaign in November, 1994. Also voted on in that election was Proposition 187, which would deny undocumented immigrants in California access to public health clinics, social services, and all levels of public education, and would require state employees to report suspected undocumented aliens to the Immigration and Naturalization Service (INS).

Wilson's arguments suffered from a major flaw: California' s own policies in the 1980s actually encouraged illegal immigration. Wilson was a member of the United States Senate at the time Congress was debating the 1986 Immigration Reform and Control Act. This legislation, which eventually passed, included a program for granting legal status to undocumented aliens arriving before 1982 and a provision for penalizing employers of undocumented workers. Wilson's support for the law was conditioned on the inclusion of a provision allowing several hundred thousand "guest workers" into the country on a temporary basis to help harvest crops. Fearing that this would lead to exploitation, several Democrats drafted the Special Agricultural Worker program, under which such workers could apply for legal residence if they had evidence of previous agricultural employment. Wilson acquiesced to this addition. However, while the INS wanted the workers to show such proof before they entered the country, Wilson felt that they should be allowed into the country on their word alone. In a letter to President Reagan, he complained about crops rotting in the fields while the INS carried out burdensome application procedures. Wilson won on this point (Brinkley, 1994).

Eventually, 1.1 million workers acquired legal residence through this program, many with forged documents bought in the United States; this number far exceeded the 350,000 that Wilson had said were needed. These new immigrants then brought over family members who lacked legal status. At the same time, California cities like Los Angeles and San Francisco passed resolutions declaring themselves sanctuaries for illegal aliens from repressive Central American countries, and preventing city officials and police from helping the INS find these refugees. Eventually, state officials acknowledged that the policies implemented in the 1980s helped increase illegal immigration to California. Leslie Goodman, Wilson's deputy chief of staff, said of the state's present problems that "in some ways there have been self-inflicted wounds" (cited in Brinkley, 1994: 1).

From Wilson's point of view, undocumented aliens from the south flee their troubled and overburdened countries only to transport such trouble and burden to the United States. However, the image of the overly-dependent immigrant has been widely challenged. Allan Wernick (1993), a noted immigration attorney, pointed out that undocumented immigrants come to the United States to work, and are ineligible for most public benefits; care for pregnant women is a humanitarian exception. Economists agree that these workers put more into the system than they take out; for example, they pay gas, liquor, and sales taxes, and some pay Social Security and income taxes. Wernick acknowledged the unfairness of leaving the states to pay for services used by immigrants with little support from Washington, since most of the revenues collected from them in the form of taxes go to federal rather than state coffers. This imbalance could be repaired with a more equitable distribution of federal revenues.

In this light, Wilson's nativist rhetoric takes on the appearance of a political ploy. Wernick called Wilson's proposals for denying immigrants maternity care and public education, and for withholding citizenship from children of undocumented aliens born in the United States, "a cynical attempt to divert attention from his state's deepening economic crisis. A 9.8% state unemployment rate is no excuse for scapegoating innocent children and their mothers." According to Wernick, at a time when Wilson's popularity rating was at 15%, these proposals were simply a means of "exploit[ing] the current anti-immigration mood in our country for political gain" (Wernick, 1993: 35). If this was Wilson's strategy, it was a successful one. Wilson won his re-election bid; Proposition 187 passed as well. Soon after the election, a federal judge in Los Angeles temporarily blocked the state from implementing most of the measure's provisions while its constitutionality was investigated. In September 1996, Wilson continued his attack on immigrants by signing an executive order directing state agencies and state-supported colleges and universities to stop offering benefits to undocumented aliens; this measure was also challenged in court (*Immigration Communiqué*, 1996). Eventually, the court declared most of Proposition 187's provisions to be unconstitutional. In August 1999, California Governor Gray Davis dropped the state's appeal of this decision, but the measure's proponents vowed to continue fighting (*Immigration Communiqué*, 1999).

Proposals similar to 187 have appeared in Virginia, Florida, Texas, and New York. In addition, some states with large immigrant populations began petitioning the federal government for help with the expenses of public services. However, in November 1997 the Supreme Court denied the petitions of California and Arizona for such reimbursement. On the federal level, major pieces of legislation placing heavy burdens on immigrants were passed into law in 1996. The Personal Responsibility and Work Opportunity Reconciliation Act and the Illegal Immigration Reform and Immigration Responsibility Act denied public benefits to many legal immigrants. This created an angry response from many organizations as well as numerous court challenges. President Clinton and the Congress, realizing they had overplayed the anti-immigrant sentiment of the public and that they had come to be characterized as lacking compassion and humanity, began to backtrack. In the ensuing three years, additional measures were passed restoring much of the cuts in benefits initiated by the previous laws (*Immigration Communiqué*, 1996–1999). However, some of the harshest provisions of the 1996 legislation remain: low-level officials send refugees back to their persecutors, immigrants who committed minor crimes for which they have paid face deportation, and families are kept from reuniting by arbitrary income requirements on immigrant sponsors (National Immigration Forum, 1999).

Economic Insecurity

As illustrated above, the United States has traditionally relied on new immigrants to do the most menial and lowest-paid work available, the kind of work most Americans would reject if they found themselves jobless. In the 1990s, large numbers of people in California were left without work because of the economic problems of the state and the nation. Governor Wilson, noting the tragedy of ruined crops, did not think to propose that jobless working-class or white-collar Americans turn to employee-starved agricultural work as a means of earning a living. Such work has been the exclusive domain of immigrants from the other side of the border with Mexico, immigrants that many Californians wish to keep out. These same immigrants, however, are considered a source of competition for economic resources.

In the 1980s and early 1990s, Americans across the country and across the socioeconomic spectrum were struggling to make ends meet and were no longer sure about their ability to hold on to employment. As Fishman stated:

> The American economy ... has performed less glamorously than its own mythology and built-in aspirations and expectations had led its

> prior beneficiaries to expect.... This is the first Anglo-American genera-
> tion that has had to face the possibility that it and its children would not
> rise socially to a station in life higher than that of their parents.
> (Fishman, 1988: 133)

In the face of this crisis, Americans were more likely to seek the culprit in factors that were outside their control. A 1994 study of 2,400 workers of various levels of income and skill revealed that employees were reluctant to blame their bosses for their financial insecurity (Uchitelle, 1994). By doing so, they relinquished any responsibility for rectifying their plight. Uchitelle explained:

> If the boss were the target, it would be easier to know what to do:
> people might take action in groups. But public opinion polls show that
> while Americans are increasingly angry about their economic insecu-
> rity, neither business nor the forces that make companies so hard on
> workers are the targets of this anger. It is directed instead at govern-
> ment, immigrants and the poor, among others. (Uchitelle, 1994: 1)

By the end of the 1990s, the economic picture had brightened consider-ably. The Council of Economic Advisors and the Department of Labor reported strong employment gains for all major subgroups of the popula-tion, the creation of 20 million high-paying jobs, wage increases for the entire labor market, a declining poverty rate and declining job displace-ment (US Department of Labor, 1999). However, problems still exist in the growing economic gap between the rich and the non-rich, although experts disagree about the source and extent of the gap (Behr, 2000). And the vola-tility of the stock market has made people aware that the boom may end at any time, sending the economy spiraling down once again (Schlesinger, 2000). The possibility remains that, should the economy worsen and cause people to experience job insecurity once more, immigrants may again become the target of citizen anger and frustration.

In reality, immigrants have hardly anything to do with the economic insecurity of mainstream Americans. A report released by the Urban Insti-tute in the spring of 1994 found that job displacement by immigrants is consistently less than 1% (Fix & Passel, 1994: 49). Immigration contributes only slightly to the decline in work for low-skilled American-born workers; the group most likely to be adversely affected by immigrant workers are the immigrants who preceded them most recently. In fact, it is estimated that were it not for Mexican immigration to Los Angeles County between 1970 and 1980, a number of employers would have moved their operations over-seas, taking with them some 53,000 production jobs, 12,000 non-production jobs, and 25,000 jobs in related industries. In addition, immigrants are just as likely to open their own businesses as non-immigrants: in 1990, 7.2% of immigrants were self-employed, compared with 7.0% of non-immigrants (Fix & Passel, 1994: 53).

In another study, a 1997 panel at the National Academy of Sciences found that immigrants produce substantial benefits to the nation, adding roughly $10 million a year to the country's economic output. Their relatively inexpensive labor helps keep the cost of goods and services down, and the degree to which they displace American workers is negligible. The panel's leader, economist James P. Smith, concluded that "the vast majority of Americans are enjoying a healthier economy as a result of the increased supply of labor and lower prices that result from immigration" (Pear, 1997: 1, 24).

While immigrants at the lower end of the job market pose a minimal challenge to American workers, there is a fear that some industries employing highly-skilled workers pit Americans against foreigners. In 1998, Congress considered raising the quota on foreign nationals coming to the country on the H-1B visa. The employers who hire these workers must prove that they could not find qualified applicants among US citizens. Although foreign nationals are hired for six years, they often receive offers from new employers and can in that way extend their stay. Many go to graduate school in the United States, and they are allowed to apply for a green card, which offers them permanent resident status and the chance to become citizens. By law, they must be paid the prevailing industry salary or the salary that the employer would normally pay the person in that position, to prevent employers from undercutting the wages of US citizens. The fields that make use of these visas include the information technology industry, nursing, and academia.

During the debate over whether to raise the quota of H1-B visas, proponents argued that these workers serve a useful purpose, taking jobs that would otherwise go unfilled and contributing to the economy (Gleckman, 1998; Greengard, 1996). Opponents expressed skepticism that the government could control their salaries, believing that employers would hire them and then pay them less than they would pay Americans. If they do go home, it was argued, the resources put into training them would go to waste. Also, industries that benefit from hiring foreign nationals would be less likely to support educational institutions that train Americans for these jobs (LaPlante, 1998; Marmer Solomon, 1993; Reinert, 1998). Ultimately the cap on the visas nearly doubled, reaching 115,000 per year. However, this number was filled quickly, and lobbyists for high-tech industries continued to push Congress to raise the cap again (Lochhead, 1999).

Thus, in contrast to earlier nativist movements, the present movement is directed not just at poor newcomers, but at immigrants at both ends of the socioeconomic spectrum. Schmid confirms this in her study:

> Within the white working class, fears center on the potential undercutting of established wages and labor standards, as well as increased dependency on already pressed social services and housing. The middle and upper-middle classes feel threatened by immigrants who bring a lot of capital, bid up real-estate values, take over businesses, and succeed in the professions, and whose children will compete for prime white-collar jobs. (Schmid, 1992: 208)

In times of both economic insecurity and economic growth, then, immigrants are in a no-win situation: whether they do well or do poorly, they find themselves the scapegoats for problems they had no role in creating.

Issues of Territoriality and Power

Immigrants who succeed socioeconomically are particularly threatening when they gain control of neighborhoods previously dominated by already-established Americans. We have discussed one example of this phenomenon in Chapter 1, in the case of Monterey Park, California. It was in this city that the official-English movement came into being on the west coast. At about the same time, the movement also showed signs of stirring in a city on the eastern seaboard: Miami, Florida.

While the mostly-white Monterey Park saw its character changed in the 1970s by the influx of investors from Taiwan and Hong Kong, Miami's transformation took place somewhat earlier, as a result of immigrants fleeing Cuba beginning in 1959. The exodus from Cuba, combined with smaller numbers of immigrants from other Spanish-speaking countries, created what sociologist and Miami community organizer Max Castro calls "a lightening Latinization, an enormous cultural change in slightly less than two decades," transforming "the social and cultural climate of the city from one monopolized by dominant North American norms and styles to one in which other traditions and forms competed powerfully for cultural and linguistic space" (Castro, 1992: 181). The imported cultures of Latin America affected all aspects of community life: business, architecture, fashion, and, most irritatingly to English-speakers, the language of the city.

There were of course other American cities with large numbers of Hispanics. But what differentiated Miami from these cities was the economic and political clout of this population. The Cubans who left their homeland were largely middle-class, and quickly established themselves in the business life of the city. If, as we learned above, conservative movements grow out of the struggle of those in power to maintain the status quo, Miami was certainly fertile soil for the official-English movement. The Hispanics in that city didn't fit the expectations that European Americans had for them, and neither did their language. The writer Joan Didion explains:

What was unusual about Spanish in Miami was not that it was so often spoken, but that it was so often heard; in say, Los Angeles, Spanish remained a language only barely registered by the Anglo population, part of the ambient noise, the language spoken by the people who worked in the car wash and came to trim the trees and cleared the tables in restaurants. In Miami Spanish was spoken by the people who ate in the restaurants, the people who owned the cars and the trees, which made, on the socioauditory scale, a considerable difference. (Didion, 1987: 63)

A consequence of the Latinization of Miami and a major source of annoyance for monolingual-English speakers was the need for workers who spoke both Spanish and English. This was a telling sign for mainstream Americans that they no longer had the upper hand; for the first time for many of them, being a monolingual, native English-speaker carried no presumption of advantage in the labor market. In addition, it defied the proverbial melting-pot fantasy; Hispanics in Miami did not have to give up their native identity in order to make it in America.

It is not surprising, then, that in 1980 the citizens of Dade County approved an "anti-bilingual" ordinance, prohibiting funds for projects utilizing any language other than English and promoting any culture other than that of the United States, and insuring that all county governmental meetings, hearings, and publications were in the English language (the ordinance was later amended to exclude emergency medical and other essential services). According to an exit poll by *The Miami Herald*, the measure passed by a vote of 56% to 44%. Statistics on the ethnic backgrounds of the voters parallel those of the 1988 exit polls studied by Schmid (1992): 71% of white non-Hispanics voted for the measure, while more than 80% of Hispanics voted against it. In addition, over half of the non-Hispanic whites who voted in favor said that they would be pleased if the measure made Miami a less attractive place for Spanish-speakers; almost 60% said they would move away from Dade County if it were possible (Tasker, 1980: 16A).

Eventually, the Dade County law did not stand up to federal scrutiny. In March 1993, the Justice Department ruled that the county had violated the Federal Voting Rights Act by failing to distribute voter information in Spanish (*The New York Times*, 1993b). In May of that year, the county commissioners voted to repeal the law (*EPIC*, 1993c). That the ordinance lasted for 13 years is unusual; as we shall see later on, laws designed to restrict the use of languages other than English tend to be quickly challenged. The atmosphere of language intolerance that made the Dade County ordinance possible illustrates the ferocity with which established

Americans react when prospering immigrants challenge their dominant status in their own home town.

While the anti-bilingual movement in Miami failed, its proponents might be comforted by the fact that English prevailed in the city in the following years. Ironically, this has created a problem of another nature for the business community there: While international trade, tourism, and the Spanish-language entertainment industry are booming, there is an increasingly critical lack of bilingual employees in the city's labor pool. A prominent businesswoman, Rosa Sugranes, laments that "we have here 600,000 Hispanics, and we cannot find qualified people to write a letter in Spanish" (Mears, 1997: A2). The city's immigrants are quick to learn English, and their children soon prefer English to their native Spanish. Although 90% of public elementary school children take Spanish class, they tend to stop when they reach middle school, where language instruction is an elective. And, while the Spanish language appears to predominate in public discourse, as Didion describes, many native speakers of the language lack the literacy skills necessary for bilingual positions in the city's businesses. In response to this situation, the Greater Miami Chamber of Commerce mounted a campaign to convince people of the importance for the city's economic development of developing competence in Spanish (Mears, 1997). The lesson here is that, instead of needing legislation to protect and preserve English, what the nation actually needs is greater support for and encouragement of the learning of languages other than the one that already predominates.

US ENGLISH, INC: SPEARHEAD OF THE OFFICIAL-ENGLISH MOVEMENT

The official-English movement owes its birth and its growth to the work of a national organization that has spearheaded legislative efforts at the state and federal levels since the early 1980s. An analysis of US English – its origins, its underlying ideology, and the problems it has faced throughout its existence – strips away the allegedly benign public agenda of the movement to reveal goals which are at their core racist, discriminatory, and undemocratic.

The Origins of US English

As Crawford (1992) describes, US English was the brainchild of an activist ophthalmologist from Michigan, Dr John Tanton. Tanton had a long history of involvement in progressive organizations concerned with social and environmental issues. In the 1960s, he was active in several conservation organizations, including the Sierra Club and the National Audubon Society. His interest in the relationship between demographics and the distribution of resources led him to start a Planned Parenthood chapter in his home state and to become national president of Zero Population Growth in the 1970s. The latter organization was mainly concerned with population issues on an international scale, specifically the uneven distribution of resources between the industrialized and the developing world. Tanton, however, was more concerned with the United States. He argued that immigrants and their children added an undue burden to the population and consequently stymied efforts to distribute the country's resources in an equitable manner. Both Zero Population Growth and the Sierra Club disassociated themselves from this line of thinking.

Tanton reacted by starting his own organization, the Federation for American Immigration Reform (FAIR), in 1979. FAIR focused on the economic and political impact of immigration on Americans, targeting Hispanic immigrants, and undocumented Mexicans in particular, as threats to the general well-being of society. Taking a centrist stance, the organization avoided attacking the Spanish language and eschewed discussion of cultural pluralism and the alleged failure of Hispanics to assimilate.

Once again, Tanton found his views being marginalized. In response, in 1983 he formed US English, enlisting the aid of Senator S.I. Hayakawa. Two years earlier, Hayakawa had proposed an official-English constitutional amendment in Congress (several attempts to legislate English as the official language in this manner have failed). Although FAIR and US English were not officially connected to each other, there were inextricable links: Tanton served as the head of both groups, and they shared an office and a number of employees. Tanton moved away from the immigration issue and concentrated on the language issue. This gave US English the appearance of separating itself from the taint of nativism; it was also a tactical necessity, since Tanton could not argue for assimilation while at the same time supporting limits on immigration. But, as he expressed in an unpublished paper, Tanton believed that immigration and language were "inextricably intertwined" (cited in Crawford, 1992: 153). The connection of US English to immigration concerns would become evident in the ensuing years.

Charges of Racism

In the first years of its existence, US English had a number of triumphs. By 1988, 48 states had considered official-English legislation, and 13 states had laws making English the official language. But the organization's constant strikes against the Spanish language had convinced many Hispanics that they were being targeted. US English attempted to respond to these allegations by choosing Linda Chavez as president in 1987. Chavez was a well-known conservative and a former Reagan official; she was also of Mexican descent, and could be viewed as someone with a special concern for and connection to the Hispanic population. Chavez maintained that official-English laws could only help Hispanics, by encouraging their acquisition of English and their assimilation into mainstream life. She soon learned, however, how real the charges of racism were. After her appointment, a number of members resigned from the organization, and a survey she conducted revealed the anti-Hispanic bias of many regular contributors.

In October, 1988 an article in the *Arizona Republic* justified once and for all the charges of racism. The article cited passages from a memo written by Tanton to a small group of colleagues who met regularly to study matters of language, assimilation, and population. One section reads:

> *Gobernar es poblar* translates "to govern is to populate." In this society where the majority rules, does this hold? Will the present majority peaceably hand over its political power to a group that is simply more fertile? ... Can *homo contraceptivus* compete with *homo progenitiva* if borders aren't controlled? Or is advice to limit one's family simply advice to move over and let someone else with greater reproductive powers occupy the space? ... As Whites see their power and control over their lives declining, will they simply go quietly into the night? Or will there be an explosion? (cited in Crawford, 1992: 151)

This revelation left no doubt about where Tanton stood in regard to immigration. According to Crawford (1992), the other members of the study group, which Tanton selected himself, were of like minds. Among those in the group in 1989 was Garrett Hardin, an ecologist who championed "lifeboat ethics." This policy encourages rich nations to shut out refugees from the developing world in order to save resources and a high standard of living for themselves. Another member was Richard Lamm, a former governor of Colorado, who has said that all South American countries are unsuccessful, and that immigrants from these countries are destined to remain unsuccessful in the United States.

At about the same time as the publication of Tanton's memo, certain financial disclosures regarding US English gave further evidence of its ideological basis. It was revealed that US Inc., the parent corporation of US English, had given tax-deductible contributions to causes such as FAIR, Americans for Border Control, and Californians for Population Stabilization. In addition, it became known that a major contributor to US English was Cordelia Scaife May, an heiress whose favorite causes were organizations dedicated to reducing the population in developing countries or limiting immigration from those countries. In 1983, May's foundation also helped finance the American distribution of an obscure French novel, *The Camp of the Saints*, a futuristic allegory in which starving refugees from the Ganges invade Europe; in the preface, the author warns of the threat of nonwhite immigrants to Western civilization. A major contributor to FAIR also turned out to be the Pioneer Fund, which has a long history of supporting race improvement through eugenics. The first project of its founder, Harry Laughlin, was to distribute films popularizing the Nazi campaign of sterilizing people judged to be of inferior heredity. The Pioneer Fund supported the efforts of Arthur Jensen and William Shockley to prove the intellectual inferiority of blacks. More recently, the 1994 book *The Bell Curve*, by Charles Murray and Richard Herrnstein, cites a number of studies backed by the Pioneer Fund in arguing that intelligence is largely governed by heredity, and that, since African Americans generally get lower scores on standard IQ tests than whites, efforts to improve their intelligence and consequently their socioeconomic status are largely ineffective.

These revelations eventually led to the resignation of both Chavez and Tanton. The noted journalist Walter Cronkite, who had been listed on the organization's letterhead as a member of its advisory board, also stepped down. These defections were part of a series of disclaimers and resignations that had occurred over the years. In 1986, during the campaign for Proposition 63 in California, the author Norman Cousins resigned over the fear that the proposal would cause Latinos and other minorities to be "disadvantaged, denigrated and demeaned" (cited in Trombley, 1986: 3). At the same time, the authors Saul Bellow and Gore Vidal also withdrew their support, although Bellow's name continues to appear on the list of Advisory Board members in the organization's newsletter. In the years immediately following the publication of Tanton's memo, only one more state, Alabama, adopted an official-English law, in 1990.

US English continues to be wary of the stain of racism that has smeared its name. Its most recent chairman is Mauro E. Mujica, a Chilean who came to the United States as a young man to study at Columbia University. Now a prominent businessman, he is a model of the successful, acculturated Hispanic, much in the same way as Linda Chavez was. The organization makes use of his ethnic background in its public relations campaigns. A 1994 advertisement that appeared in several major publications displayed his photograph under the caption "Why a Hispanic Heads An Organization Called US English." In the text, Mujica recalls that, as an immigrant, he knew that adopting English was essential to his future. He describes the mission of the organization as not only preserving English as the common bond of Americans, but also "making sure that every single immigrant has the chance to learn English."

However, US English has not shaken off its anti-Hispanic and anti-immigrant bias. In August 1999, the organization distributed a press release about El Cenizo, a South Texas town on the border with Mexico that had adopted Spanish as its official language, dubbing it "America's first 'Spanish-only city'"(*US English Update*, 1999). Mujica declared this action indicative of the character of recent arrivals: "Unlike earlier generations of immigrants, who understood their responsibility to become Americans, many new immigrants from south of the border refuse to adopt an American identity and refuse to speak our common language." In addition, the press release reported that the city had declared itself a safe haven for illegal immigrants, barring city employees from helping the US Border Patrol apprehend undocumented immigrants.

Media news reports of the city's actions offer a broader picture. With 90% of the residents dominant in Spanish, the city had tried to provide Spanish translation at its open meetings, but many people were still reluctant to participate. When monthly city council meetings were held in Spanish, attendance doubled. According to the new law, while meetings were to be conducted in Spanish, resolutions and ordinances would still be written in English, with translations available on request. An ordinance added to the language measure forbidding city employees from asking residents about their status or helping the Border Patrol identify undocumented people was a response to the Patrol's policy of indiscriminately stopping individuals and asking for proof of their legal status. Finally, the difficulty for new immigrants of finding time to learn English, in light of their heavy work schedules, and not the lack of desire to learn, was cited by one volunteer English teacher as the greatest barrier to their acquisition of the language (Diaz, 1999; Garcia, 1999).

Further Questions About the Nature of US English

US English has had other financial problems, relating to questions about its status as a tax-exempt charitable organization. In order to qualify for this status, only 5–20% of the group's budget may go to lobbying expenses. But it is clear from the organization's activities that its central goal is political: passage of legislation making English the official language and barring other languages from being used by government.

Like other interest groups, US English established two branches, the US English Foundation, a charitable organization through which it raised money, and the US English Legislative Task Force, a lobbying branch through which it carried out political activity. However, unlike other groups, which keep their branches separate, it was revealed that US English had consistently passed large sums of money raised by its charitable arm to its lobbying efforts, sums going beyond the amount allowable by law. In addition, the results of a 1990 audit showed that then-chair and long-time consultant Stanley Diamond had spent large amounts of the group's money for his own benefit. In a letter to the Internal Revenue Service (IRS), which he never sent, Diamond confessed that payments sent to him as consulting fees were actually funneled into political contributions for various state and federal offices, and used to support or oppose state and federal legislation of interest to US English (Crawford, 1992).

In 1993, a report published by the Better Business Bureau's Philanthropic

Advisory Service and the National Charities Information Bureau cited the US English Foundation for non-compliance with four of the standards set by the two organizations. These stipulations were that at least 50% of an organization's income go to programs and activities directly related to the purposes of the organization, that it apply 50% of its public contributions to programs and activities described in solicitations, that fund-raising costs not exceed 35% of related contributions, and that total fund-raising and administrative costs not exceed 50% of the organization's total income. The standards are meant to serve as guidelines for potential donors (*EPIC*, 1993a).

US English subsequently changed its classification to that of a non-profit lobbying organization, and contributions ceased being deductible. However, it officially retained its dual purpose. Each issue of its newsletter *US English Update* explained, "US English is a national, nonprofit, nonpartisan organization founded in 1983 to designate English as the official language of the United States, and to promote opportunities for all people in the United States to learn English." The lobbying arm purportedly took care of the first function; the charitable arm concerned itself with the second. However, there was a huge imbalance in the funds that went towards these goals. In the early 1990s, US English spent between 1% and 7% of its budget providing access to English education (Califa, 1991: 6). The organization periodically reported to its membership on the efforts of the US English Foundation to encourage the learning of English. For example, in 1994 it offered two grants: $5,000 went to Project Citizenship in Arizona, to be used for providing 12 part-time instructors and some teaching materials to prepare 550 immigrants for the citizenship exam; and $2,000, space heaters, and two used computers went to Casa del Pueblo, a Washington, DC group that provides English instruction (*US English Update*, 1994a: 6). The paltriness of these donations pales in contrast to the organization's concurrent activities: lobbying efforts to pass official-English laws on the state and federal level, which certainly involved more substantial sums of money. For example, the organization hired a public relations firm boasting two former state senators to help move legislation in Iowa (*US English Update*, 1994b: 3)

The organization's web site (www.us-english.org) explains that it now consists of two separate organizations: US English, Inc., whose goals are to pass state and federal legislation and to reform bilingual education, and the US English Foundation, Inc., whose goals are to promote opportunities for individuals to learn English and to research language policy issues. The organization has always contended that there is a connection between its two goals. In a book published by US English, de la Peña writes, "Having an official language will require government responsibility for providing more opportunities for immigrants to learn English" (de la Peña, 1991: 120).

However, as we shall see below, the legislation supported by the organization fails to include any provision that requires the government to provide opportunities for learning English. Furthermore, the organization took a stand against such government responsibility. In 1986, US English failed to support an increase in federal funds for adult instruction in English as a second language; the measure passed anyway. The organization's argument that the private sector is better able to deal with this obligation did not prevent it from losing credibility with those who had assumed that US English's main concern was providing educational access to non-English speakers. To save face, in 1987 US English announced its commitment to support private efforts to promote English literacy through a program called Project Golden Door. However, its financial backing did not live up to its initial promises. Its first-year commitment of $650,000 was supposed to rise to $2 million in 1989. Instead, the organization's financial reports showed grants of $42,000 in 1987 and $50,000 in 1988; none were reported in 1989. Furthermore, these funds came from a foundation in Los Angeles and did not draw on public donations (Crawford, 1992: 173–174).

US English continues to claim a role in supporting the language education of immigrants. However, indications are that its efforts are small and require minimal resources. On its 1999 web site, the link to the foundation offered a telephone number for information on the organization's database of ESL classes, for those wanting to take a class or willing to teach one. The site also explained that grants are available to local volunteer organizations that teach English. This was illustrated with a photograph of a passenger van donated to the Villa Maria Center in Erie, Pennsylvania, so that immigrants lacking transportation could attend the center's English classes. While such efforts are helpful, they are likely to reach only small numbers of immigrants, and the focus on volunteer versus professional teachers does not bode well for effective instruction or for classes geared to high-level English-language proficiency.

LANGUAGE RESTRICTIONISM AT THE STATE LEVEL

Official-English advocates have channeled their energies into legislation at both the state and federal levels. State support is considered important in improving the chances for a national law.

The first state law declaring English as the official language was passed in Nebraska in 1920, during the period of virulent anti-German sentiment. In 1923, "American" was made the official language of Illinois; the word was changed to "English" in 1969. All other state actions occurred during the current language-restrictionist period. Virginia declared English the official language in 1981; Indiana, Kentucky, and Tennessee followed in 1984. In 1986, California became the first state to pass an official-English measure by ballot initiative. Official-English laws passed in Arkansas, Mississippi, North Carolina, North Dakota, and South Carolina in 1987. Arizona, Colorado, and Florida passed amendments in 1988; Arizona's law was declared unconstitutional, as we discuss in the next chapter.

Alabama made English its official language in 1990. In 1995, three more states joined the roster: Montana, New Hampshire, and South Dakota. Georgia and Wyoming became official-English states in 1996. In 1998, Missouri passed a law declaring English the common language of the state; the provisions of the bill referred solely to the steps the state would take in offering English-language instruction to non-native speakers, both children and adults, without reference to any specific teaching methodology. In the same year, Alaska passed its official-English law, although several months later this was stayed by an injunction. Finally, an official-English popular initiative won in Utah in November 2000 and was stayed by a temporary restraining order soon after. A ruling by a district court judge declared the law constitutional in March 2001; that ruling was immediately challenged.

In some of these states, particularly those in the South, the law has served merely as a symbolic act; traditionally, states like Mississippi, Kentucky, and Tennessee have not been major destinations for new immigrants. However, as we noted previously, immigrants are no longer drawn just to large urban centers, and their migration across the country has become noticeable. In one instance, in the South, an attempt was made to apply the law to alter a policy affecting non-native speakers of English.

In 1991, Alabama's Department of Public Safety changed its policy of offering the written section of the driver's license exam in languages other than English, citing as justification the state's year-old official-English law. The wording of Alabama's law is of the standard variety, calling on the state to preserve and enhance the role of English as the official language. Alabama had previously offered exams in fifteen languages, but the change was a particular burden on Hispanics, who had migrated to Alabama in significant numbers to work in the poultry plants and fields. A lawsuit, *Sandoval v. Hagan*, challenged this practice, and in 1998 a federal judge declared that the policy violated the 1964 Civil Rights Act provision against national-origin discrimination.

In his decision, the judge noted that the new policy failed to promote the intent of the official-English law, which was to encourage immigrants' use of English and their assimilation into the community. Because public transportation is practically non-existent in Alabama, driving is essential for carrying out everyday tasks, taking children to school, going to work, and responding quickly to medical emergencies. Lack of proficiency in written English was not found to be a problem in driving, since the state utilizes international highway symbols familiar to people who have learned to drive in other countries. The court noted the extra measures that the Department of Public Safety takes to allow the hearing-impaired, the illiterate, and the disabled to fulfill the requirements for obtaining a driver's license. Since individuals in these three categories successfully receive their licenses, become capable drivers, and are able to communicate with law enforcement officials, the court saw no problem with allowing non-English proficient drivers to do so as well (Smith, 1998; *SPLC*, 1998; *Sandoval v. Hagan*, 1998).

While the ruling pertained only to the state's policy regarding the issuing of driver's licenses, US English viewed it as having broader significance. Mauro Mujica characterized the decision as "a blatant violation of the will of the people of Alabama," "a shocking assault on every state's right to make English its Official Language," and "ultimately a threat to the passage of our federal Official English Bill now before Congress" (Mujica, 2000: 1). While playing up the ruling's attack on official English in general, Mujica also tapped into the issue of states' rights, the ability of states to act independently from the federal government. States' rights has been a long-running matter. It has particular resonance in the South, stretching back to the resistance of southern states to the abolition of slavery. In 2000, South Carolina's insistence on flying the Confederate flag above the state capitol, despite its offense to African Americans and others, was considered a states' rights issue.

Calling up these various hot buttons, Mujica looked to the membership to support an appeal of the Alabama case to the Supreme Court. *Alexander v. Sandoval* was heard by the Supreme Court in April 2001. The issue argued was not official English, but the right of citizens to sue a state for non-compliance with federal anti-discrimination law. The Court ruled that private individuals cannot bring discrimination lawsuits regarding state regulations, such as the one issued by Alabama's Department of Public Safety (Greenhouse, 2001). This ruling did not affect the original lawsuit and, in the meantime, Alabama re-instituted the Spanish-language version of its written driving test.

Other states with official-English laws, such as Florida and California, have long been the common destination of immigrants. Florida is a port of entry for Cubans and other Latin Americans; California receives immigrants from the Far East and Mexico; it is also the home of many Americans of Mexican origin. We will see later on that these laws have had a great impact on such residents; it is in these states that major challenges have been raised.

LANGUAGE RESTRICTIONISM AT THE FEDERAL LEVEL

Official-English advocates were successful in presenting a number of language-restrictionist proposals before Congress in the first half of the

1990s. Their success in introducing such legislation was due in large part to a marked increase in support among many citizens and their elected officials for conservative policies, policies that others regarded as unfairly targeting the most vulnerable segments of society, and unlikely to benefit the country's social well-being.

In the fall of 1995, official English gained substantial media attention when it was endorsed by Bob Dole, the majority leader of the US Senate and front-running Republican candidate in the 1996 presidential election. Dole chose to make this announcement in a speech at the national convention of the American Legion, a large, conservative veterans' group founded by World War I servicemen. In his statement, he explained that "with all the divisive forces tearing at our country, we need the glue of language to help hold us together." He denounced bilingual education: "If we want to ensure that all our children have the same opportunities in life, alternative language education should stop" (Broder, 1995: A1). Dole characterized bilingual education "as a means of instilling ethnic pride, or as a therapy for low self-esteem;" he also saw it as a way for intellectuals to rid themselves of "elitist guilt over a culture built on the traditions of the West'" (*The Wall Street Journal*, 1995: A16). In the same speech, on a different but not entirely unrelated topic, he also criticized proposed national standards for teaching American history, on the basis that these standards would destroy American children's belief that "this is the greatest country on the face of the Earth" (Broder, 1995: A1). National chauvinism and egotism are usually at odds with linguistic and cultural pluralism.

The speech generated a variety of reactions. One editorial in *The New York Times* (1995) noted that, while Dole's words were "couched in purest patriotism," his real purpose was to divide the nation; official English is an issue that "reeks of xenophobia and is particularly popular among the conservatives he seems too eager to please." While acknowledging the need for a common language, the editorial rejected the notion that making English the official national language was necessary. Such a law would only serve as "a sign that the society is not so open after all, that people who speak foreign languages are not welcome" (*The New York Times*, 1995: 16).

In another response to Dole's speech, Friedman (1995) stressed the importance of moving children into English: "Students should only be taught in other languages as a bridge to English education. Permanent multilingual education is a road to ruin." However, on a societal level, Friedman acknowledged the need for tolerance of diversity:

> Diversity without a spirit of community leads to tribalism. Community without a spirit of diversity leads to alienation for all minorities.... Unless we give people of diverse ethnic backgrounds a sense of belonging, unless we give them a sense that their identity and heritage

> are valued threads in the tapestry of American society, real community
> is impossible. (Friedman, 1995: 17)

While Friedman took Dole to task for shirking the responsibility of working toward this worthy goal and for using his support of official English to incite divisiveness, he offered no suggestions about how this goal might be achieved. Curiously, he did not consider the possibility that bilingual education might be one avenue leading toward it.

A very different reaction was that of Estrada (1995), who supported the idea of English as the official language but saw the real issue as much broader. Immigrants, he wrote, "understand the importance of learning English and are desirous of doing so." The real problem is the growing number of immigrants and an electorate "frustrated not only with the fraying of the social fabric, but also with being taxed for government assistance to immigrants ... a recipe for ethnic and racial tensions" (Estrada, 1995: M5). Estrada asserted that controlling immigration, and not the language of immigrants, should be the focus of government policy.

Dole's statement brought official English to national attention for the first time; reactions to his statement reveal the complexity of the issue and its association with other related matters. Through it all, the Federal Administration maintained its position in opposition to the legislation. A statement by the Secretary of Education, Richard W. Riley, was released when Congress held its first hearing on an official-English bill on October 18, 1995. The statement read in part:

> It would be sheer folly to deny millions of school children the opportunity to learn English – at a time when the need is greatest. Unfortunately, these efforts to make English the "official" language and to eliminate programs that teach English are more about politics than improving education.... Passing these bills is saying to children, and those who are struggling to learn English, that we don't care if they fall behind and fail. (*NABE*, 1995: 27)

The controversy over official English was further complicated by divisiveness within the minority-language community, specifically over the rights of Native Americans to perpetuate their languages. In late 1995, hearings were held on a Senate version of official English. At one hearing, Senator Daniel Akaka of Hawaii said that he agreed with the general principle of "linguistic unity," but announced his plans to introduce an amendment to reduce the law's impact on Native American languages. Senator Ted Stevens of Alaska, who had convened the hearing as head of the Governmental Affairs Committee, supported such an amendment, noting his earlier support for the Native American Languages Act and the Alaska Native Languages Act. The sponsor of the bill, Richard Shelby of Alabama, was less amenable, arguing that making exceptions for some languages would not solve the problem of the "multilingual demands" on government agencies and programs.

As Crawford (1995) explains, Native Americans may be tempted to believe that their languages, which predated all other languages on American soil, have a prior moral claim that other languages do not, and deserve to be exempted from any official-English law. However, Native Americans are not immune from "the legal and political fallout" (Crawford, 1995: 2) of language-restrictionist legislation. Public schools that make use of the Native American languages of their student populations traditionally relied on grants falling under the purview of the Bilingual Education Act. As mentioned earlier, in an act fulfilling a major goal of the official-English movement, this law was renamed and revised under 2002 education legislation, eliminating any mention of bilingual skills as a desired educational outcome. In addition, Crawford (1995) warns, official-English legislation attacks and legitimizes the denigration of a large, undifferentiated group: all those who insist on speaking a language other than English and who appear to be different from those of mainstream culture. Native Americans cannot avoid falling into that category, and cannot make themselves immune to the heightened stigmatization that official English insures.

In the 2000 presidential election, neither official English nor bilingual education registered to any great extent. Of the four leading candidates (John McCain and George W. Bush vying for the Republican nomination, Bill Bradley and Al Gore competing for the Democratic domination) only one, McCain, registered his opposition to making English the official language; the other three were silent on the issue.

Bilingual education received only slightly more attention. Gore's record consisted of a broad statement made in a speech to an organization of Latino elected officials: "Some will exploit the issue of bilingual education for political gain. I believe we must support bilingual education for educational gain" (Gore, 1999: 4). Explaining his record on education, McCain noted his authorship of a bill in the Senate entitled Educating America's Children for Tomorrow, which "would encourage proficiency in English plus other languages in order to increase our competitiveness in the global market" (McCain, 2000: 2). While not mentioning bilingual education directly, his words appear to lend tacit support to native-language instruction.

Bush's candidacy benefitted from a dramatic improvement in the test scores of Texan children – especially minority children – during his tenure as governor of the state. Bilingual education has been a prominent component of the state's educational system, which serves a large number of Spanish-dominant children; many of its schools are even planning to increase bilingual programs to insure the maintenance and development of

Spanish. Bush was viewed as defying the prevailing Republican stance on ending bilingual education. However, his support lacked much enthusiasm; he was on record as backing bilingual education as long as it was successful in improving English-language proficiency (Bronner, 1999).

George W. Bush eventually received the nomination of the Republican Party at its convention in the summer of 2000. When compared to the Republican platform of 1996, the platform adopted at the 2000 convention revealed a movement from the right to a more centrist stance on a number of issues, including those relevant to language minorities. The 1996 platform called for "the official recognition of English as the nation's common language" and quoted Bob Dole as saying that as "a force for unity," English is "indispensible to the process of transforming untold millions of immigrants from all parts of the globe into citizens of the most open and free society the world has ever seen" (Republican National Committee, 1996: 23). The platform defined the goal of bilingual education to be the teaching of English; it advocated government support for foreign language education and the preservation of Native Alaskan and Native Hawaiian languages and cultures, but described the retention of "heritage languages" to be the province of "homes and cultural institutions" (Republican National Committee, 1996: 23). Among the government's agencies targeted for elimination was the Department of Education, under the principle that "today's government is too large and intrusive and does too many things the people could do better for themselves" (Republican National Committee, 1996: 4). In the name of "a sensible immigration policy" (Republican National Committee, 1996: 22), the platform opposed offering illegal aliens public benefits other than emergency aid, and public aid to and automatic citizenship for children born in the United States of undocumented immigrants.

In contrast, the 2000 Republican Party platform made no mention of either official English or bilingual education. Rather than calling for the elimination of the Department of Education, it maintained that "the federal government must be progressively limited as we return control [of education] to parents, teachers, and local school boards." The platform stressed the need to raise the level of education for all children, quoting Bush: "No child in America should be segregated by low expectations ... imprisoned by illiteracy ... abandoned to frustration and the darkness of self-doubt." In place of previous calls for restricted government aid to undocumented aliens, the platform claimed to offer "a vision of a welcoming society in which all have a place. To all Americans, particularly immigrants and minorities, we send a clear message: this is the party of freedom and progress, and it is your home" (Republican National Party Platform Committee, 2000).

The four days of the convention were notable for the spotlight placed on minorities. Among those called on to give speeches were women, Latinos, blacks, and former Democrats. This was particularly unusual for a party whose leadership is largely male, white and conservative; the best-known long-time Republicans were kept in the background (Toner, 2000; Berke, 2000). Many observers believed that this show of inclusiveness was merely superficial, and that the party's traditional stands on issues such as education had not changed substantially (Staples, 2000; *The New York Times*, 2000). Still, it seemed that the party had learned a lesson: the harsh rhetoric of just a few years earlier, which had targeted those at the bottom rungs of society and charged them with responsibility for the country's problems, had alienated many Americans and made the party's leaders appear mean and lacking in compassion. In a political system dependent on the support and votes of the public, and in a country with a shrinking white, middle-class base, the Republican Party most probably came to realize that continuing in this vein was not in its best interests.

As language-restrictionists observed the presidential campaign, they turned increasingly critical of the widespread use of Spanish, which included a Spanish-language speech given at the Republican Convention and the use of Spanish by both candidates in their stump speeches and web sites. According to US English, this indicated that both Bush and Gore "seem to believe that Hispanics are incapable of understanding any message that is not in Spanish. We believe that this is not only patronizing, but also indicates a tacit acceptance of the notion of a 'bilingual country'" (*US English Update*, undated: 2). It is apparent that the organization had begun noticing a sea change that would make its own work more difficult.

We now turn to an analysis of federal official-English legislation. As mentioned above, a number of proposals have been introduced in Congress. However, the legislation revolves around several major themes, and these themes are described below, along with their supporting and opposing arguments.

The General Role of Government Regarding Language

Language-restrictionist legislation declares English to be the official language of government and makes government responsible for preserving, enhancing, and protecting the language while conducting all business in it. Certain exclusions to the rule are made, for example, when the use of other languages is necessary for protecting public health and safety; for educational purposes, such as foreign-language instruction; for foreign trade, relations, and commerce; and for protecting the rights of criminal victims and defendants.

Language restrictionists argue that making English the official language is necessary to maintain the country's sense of harmony. In a letter to US English members, Mauro Mujica wrote that "preserving our nation's unity ... is one of the top priorities of the American people." In Mujica's view, official English is pitted against the concept of governmental multilingualism.

He continued, "I stand firmly *opposed* to those who are working to make America officially multilingual. On the contrary, I believe that *English* should be the *official language* of the United States. And that the push to divide America's people along language-lines is, in fact, helping *tear our nation apart*" (Mujica,1994c: 2). Members were encouraged to complete an enclosed ballot, in which they were to check one of two statements: "I want Congress to make English the Official Language of the United States" or "I want Congress to make America officially multilingual."

US English's 1999 web site contained a piece by Mujica entitled "Spanish for Bureaucrats?" in which he describes how Buncombe County, North Carolina, whose Hispanic population had doubled in size, had been giving Spanish classes to county prosecutors, emergency dispatchers, firefighters, and emergency medical technicians. While Mujica sees nothing wrong with people learning Spanish, he characterizes the policy as showing "how much the radical multi-culturalists have changed the traditional relationship between immigrants and the United States." Instead of immigrants learning English, he claims, government employees now have to learn Spanish.

Mujica's claim that there is a war between multilingualism and official English is in fact totally false. There is no move by any special interest to make the United States officially multilingual. More important, the idea that multilingualism is incompatible with a common language is unsupportable. English is now the *de facto* official language of the United States. All documents published by government agencies are in English; the fact that the government may at times also publish material in other languages does not affect the status of English as the common language.

Furthermore, the use of other languages in government, far from being divisive, helps smooth the transition of immigrant groups into American society. For those newly-arrived who do not yet speak English, information in their own languages helps them find a place to live, helps them find work and, importantly, helps them find a way to learn English. In addition, considering the time it takes to master a second language, it is important that government employees who are working with the public are able to communicate on a basic level with those who are struggling with English, especially in urgent, life-threatening situations such as fires and medical emergencies. Indeed, official-English advocates have recognized this fact in their legislative proposals by including a long list of exceptions to the exclusive use of English.

The same argument holds for multilingualism or bilingualism at the level of individuals in society. If there are individuals who are multilingual or bilingual, one of the languages spoken is usually the common language of the nation; being multilingual or bilingual cannot possibly prevent communication. Nor does multilingualism cause societal division.

Conflicts among people are usually caused by political, social, and economic factors rather than by the inability to communicate; in a later chapter, we will discuss Switzerland, a multilingual nation with a largely peaceful history. In addition, monolingualism does not guarantee freedom from strife. Civil wars have afflicted most nations, pitting against each other citizens who usually speak the same language.

The Government's Role in Helping Immigrants Learn English

Another theme that runs through federal official-English legislation is the importance to immigrants of learning English. A typical statement explains that knowledge of English empowers immigrants to become successful, responsible citizens. The purpose of the legislation is described as helping immigrants to assimilate and to take advantage of economic and occupational opportunities. However, the bills differ as to how they view the role of government in helping immigrants to learn English. One states that it is the obligation of government to encourage opportunities for individuals to learn English; a companion bill offers a 50% tax credit to employers for expenses incurred in setting up English classes for their employees. Another bill suggests that money saved by the legislation – presumably money not used for multilingual services – be used to provide English-language instruction.

As we have seen, the prominent concern expressed by language restrictionists is that immigrants to America learn English. In their view, the increasing multilingualism of government has discouraged this from happening. In a letter to US English members, Mujica wrote:

> Just a few years ago, immigrants to our shores saw America not as a land of "free services," but as a land of *opportunity*. And they took it as a source of pride and fundamental necessity to learn our language to become successful, contributing citizens. Now, so-called "immigrants' rights" activists insist that foreigners no longer need to learn English *and that the American taxpayer is <u>obligated</u> to pay for translations, teachers and multilingual services for immigrants who don't want to make the effort to learn our language.* (Mujica, July 28, 1995: 2)

In our discussion of US English, we have seen that the organization has actually done very little to further the availability of English-language education for immigrants. It has not supported governmental involvement, nor has it served as a model for private-sector agencies assuming the responsibility of providing immigrants with English-language instruction. Instead, it seems to be relying on the belief that immigrants will automatically learn English if the government does away with multilingual services. In this line of thinking, immigrants need to be motivated to learn English, and this will only happen if the government functions only in English. Once immigrants realize they cannot communicate with the government, they will be convinced of the necessity of learning English, and they will then learn it.

The weakness of this argument is apparent. As we saw in Chapter 2, there is no evidence that today's immigrants are not motivated to learn English. Nor is there a negative correlation between the availability of multilingual services and the demand for English-language classes, as is evident in a state like New York, which has never passed an official-English statute. Also, the mere desire among immigrants to learn English is not enough for them to achieve this goal. The classes have to exist, and that means someone has to underwrite their cost.

The efforts of official-English legislation to make government responsible for offering English-language instruction are extremely feeble. Merely stating that government has this obligation does nothing to help immigrants. Suggesting that money saved by not offering multilingual services be used to fund English classes is another way of doing nothing: if the government is not spending money on multilingual services, it is unlikely that it will track how much money is being saved.

The most substantial proposal is the one that offers a tax rebate to employers who set up English classes for their workers. However, this kind of program would probably not reach the people who are most in need of such instruction: immigrants who are unemployed, and immigrants who are employed in low-wage jobs that don't require any English. Employers of the latter group usually take advantage of the lack of English skills of these workers, knowing that they do not have the ability to fight their unfair treatment. These employees often do not have access to labor unions and as a result are paid below minimum wage, suffer inhumane working conditions, and are denied benefits. Their employers would not be tempted by the tax credit extended to those who offer language classes; indeed, it is because such workers do not know English and are dependent on their bosses that their employers are able to exploit them.

In general, the American workplace today is unlikely to be of help to immigrants who wish to better their English-language proficiency, as Dicker (1998) reveals in a review of business literature on the topic. Until recently, companies have been able to take advantage of the National Workplace Literacy Program, which distributed federal grant money to businesses offering English classes for their employees. In collaboration with outside agencies and universities, some companies used these funds to create multi-level ESL courses as well as courses in math and computers (Stamps, 1998). The restaurant industry found that English classes helped lower the employee turnover rate (Nichols, 1997). However, the program was not renewed by Congress, and those businesses that had taken advantage of the funds are turning to less expensive and less effective means of teaching English, such as peer tutoring and self-paced, computerized instructional packages. Other businesses that employ immigrants in jobs that don't necessitate high-level English skills resort to various methods for communicating with their employees: grouping workers by language, providing graphic instructional charts, using bilingual supervisors, and translating instructional manuals (Thomas & Gregory, 1993/94; Aeppel, 1998; Rimalower, 1992). It appears that neither government nor the private business sector can be counted on to provide newcomers with the English instruction that is necessary for their survival and self-improvement.

Specific Restrictions on the Use of Languages Other Than English

The authors of official-English bills have not considered it sufficient to declare that English be the language in which government conducts all its business. Many of these bills designate specific activities that must be carried out exclusively in English. We will deal with each of these government functions separately.

Naturalization Ceremonies

Some official-English bills call for an amendment to the Immigration and Nationality Act to provide that public ceremonies for admitting new citizens be conducted exclusively in English. Until recently, the language of such ceremonies was not an issue. When US English wrote a letter to the Justice Department protesting a Spanish-language ceremony in Tucson, Arizona that took place in the summer of 1993, the Department answered that this was within the letter of the law. In response, the organization decided to make this practice a focus of its campaign for official English, and succeeded in getting congressional support for legislation to abolish it.

It is easy to see why the organization chose to attack the use of other languages in this particular activity. Citizenship ceremonies mark the official introduction of immigrants into American life. The language used in these ceremonies therefore has great significance. Addressing a congressional subcommittee, Mujica said:

> If the US Government doesn't think English is important enough for immigrants to use in the most important action they will take in their lives, then immigrants can't be blamed for thinking that they can get by without knowing English. The tragedy of this is not symbolic. It has nothing to do with racism or xenophobia as opponents of official English would have you believe. The tragedy lies in the fact that every day an immigrant does not become proficient in English means another day in which that immigrant is "sentenced" to the bottom rung of the economic ladder. (Mujica,1994a)

The legislators who backed this proposal expressed similar sentiments. Senator Lauch Faircloth said:

> It is inconceivable that a person would want to become a citizen of the United States and not have some functional knowledge of the English language. The INS [Immigration and Naturalization Service] is leading [new citizens] to believe they can function in an enclave that speaks only their own language. It is undermining the common thread that binds us together and makes us all Americans. (*US English Update*, 1994c)

Representative Bill Emerson claimed that the INS was sending a message to immigrants that "legally, you are one of us. Linguistically, you are not." Representative Ron Packard expressed it this way: "For us to set a pattern by swearing them into this country and not using the language that they will use in this country is ludicrous, quite frankly" (both cited in *US English Update*, 1994c: 4).

Clearly, US English exaggerates the effect of citizenship ceremonies conducted in languages other than English. The ceremony takes less than an hour; as soon as it's over, the new citizens go out into the world facing the same challenges that they faced before the ceremony. In Chapter 2 we gave evidence of the great demand for adult ESL classes and of the enthusiasm for these classes expressed by those able to find such instruction. It is unlikely that non-English citizenship ceremonies will erase immigrants' need, or dampen their enthusiasm for learning English.

Representative Emerson contends that foreign-language citizenship ceremonies give new Americans the message that using their language separates them from other Americans. This is an example of the pressure society places on immigrants to assimilate, telling them that by giving up their nativeness they can become the same as everyone else. However, not all immigrants want to be the same as everyone else. This pressure to assimilate also conflicts with US English's purported support for the use of native languages in private situations. According to Mujica, "It is not the purpose of US English to ban Spanish or any other language from being spoken. I myself speak Spanish at home and in some of my business dealings" (Mujica, 1995: 3). However, if immigrants buy into the necessity of total assimilation, might they believe that speaking their mother tongue at home is a sign of being un-American?

Mujica is on target when he states that immigrants who don't learn English are relegated to the margins of society. However, he does not prove that there is any connection between non-English citizenship ceremonies and the failure to learn English. Nor does he attempt to prove that insuring English-language citizenship ceremonies will increase enthusiasm for or the availability of English-language instruction.

Income Tax Documents

Another element of official-English legislation is the stipulation that the Internal Revenue Service (IRS) publish tax forms and related documents only in English. This provision was also the result of a US English campaign.

In early 1994, US English learned that the IRS, in a test program, was about to send out half a million tax return forms and instruction booklets written in Spanish. This would be the first time in its 131-year history that the IRS would use a language other than English. Mujica sent a letter to IRS Commissioner Margaret Richardson, stating that he was "troubled by the message this sends to taxpayers that it is not necessary to learn the English language." He expressed concern that the IRS was "establishing a dangerous and costly precedent without adequate input from the general public and their elected representatives" (cited in *US English Update*, 1994d: 1). Representative Ron Packard also wrote to Richardson, invoking the need for "a channel of communication common to all the diverse people of America. By publishing official documents in Spanish, I believe the IRS undermines this important common link" (cited in *US English Update*, 1994d: 2).

In a letter to US English members, Mujica warned that "multi-language forces" had wide support in the Clinton Administration, and that it was necessary to let the government know how many Americans were opposed to "wasting huge amounts" on the publishing of documents in languages other than English (Mujica, 1994b: 1). He urged members to tell elected officials that they "resent the fact that a major government agency has taken steps to promote multilingualism – which fosters divisiveness and promotes the idea that citizens do not have to learn the English language to be productive members of our society" (enclosure with Mujica, 1994b). The letter also warned that, with over 300 languages spoken in the country, soon speakers of all these languages, including French, Chinese, Italian, and Croatian, would expect to receive tax forms in their languages.

Once again, US English largely exaggerates the effect of governmental use of languages other than English. There is little danger that Spanish-speakers receiving forms in their language will conclude that they don't need to learn English, or that such a practice will undermine the prominence of English as the common language. In addition, it is unreasonable to expect the government to seek approval from citizens and legislators for all its decisions. In fact, there is a long history of government offering services and publishing documents in the languages of new immigrants without such approval.

Instead of fostering divisiveness, the IRS was actually motivated by a desire to bring Spanish-speaking residents closer into mainstream American life. Mujica quotes the IRS as explaining that the use of the Spanish tax forms was meant to "educate taxpayers about their responsibilities and improve compliance" (Mujica, 1994b: 1). Mujica also states that the IRS was planning to send out forms in other languages, such as Vietnamese. The danger of the IRS printing forms in 300 languages is absurd. In all probability, the IRS made its decision based on its identification of language groups with large numbers of immigrants who have not yet acquired English proficiency. It is also probable that, if the IRS continues the practice in the future, it will change the languages in which it prints tax forms as immigration patterns and demographic factors dictate.

The expense of printing documents in other languages is a point that language restrictionists continually bring up in their campaigns. Clearly, the IRS would not incur such expense if it did not expect the benefits of increased tax revenues to make the cost worthwhile. The same argument can be applied to any service in a non-English language. For instance, printing voting materials in other languages involves spending money, but results in increased participation in the electoral process, a highly-sought goal in a democracy. Also, the extent to which the government publishes documents in other languages has been greatly exaggerated by official-English advocates. In a study by the US General Accounting Office of 400,000 titles, representing about half of all documents put out by the federal government between 1990 and 1994, found that only 265 had been translated into one or more foreign languages (*Hispanic Link Weekly Report*, 1995: 1). Despite an on-going campaign by US English, government agencies such as the IRS continue to use languages other than English to communicate with the public.

Bilingual Education
Some official-English legislation explicitly abolishes bilingual education. These proposals call for the repeal of Title VII of the Elementary and Secondary Education Act of 1965 and the termination of the Office of Bilingual Education and Minority Languages. One piece of legislation allows the government to assist educators in the transition of students from bilingual programs to special alternative instruction that does not make use of their native languages.

We have seen throughout this book that bilingual education has been attacked vehemently by language restrictionists. Spanish-dominant children who are placed into bilingual programs are viewed as "victims of federal, state and local policies that promote teaching Hispanic children in their native language at the expense of teaching them English" (Chavez, 1991b: 59). As a result of these policies, it is claimed, these children "will end up denied the American Dream their parents came seeking" (Chavez, 1991b: 60). The administration created to institute native-language instruction is depicted as "fighting to maintain its primacy and prerogatives unchallenged, even though bilingual programs have, in the majority of cases, proven unsuccessful" (Porter, 1990: 6).

Bilingual education received its most serious attack in California. A state with a large number of foreign-born, the presence of anti-immigrant sentiment has been evident for several decades, as borne out by the passage of an official-English law in 1986 and the 1994 Proposition 187. The latter, a popular initiative added to the regular election by the gathering of a sufficient number of citizen signatures, would have denied public services and education to undocumented aliens; it never went into effect. The former, making English the official language of the state, was targeted mainly at eliminating bilingual education, but because bilingual education was protected by federal statute, it remained intact. It took a millionaire software entrepreneur, Ron Unz, to revive the fight in 1998, with his drive for the so-called English Language Education for Children in the Public Schools Initiative, or Proposition 227. Like the anti-immigrant proposition before it, a successful campaign allowed the proposal to be placed on the 1998 election ballot.

Unz was hardly an expert on bilingual education; he had never visited a bilingual classroom, had no professional background in education, and didn't have any children. He did, however, have aspirations for public office, and is described by Crawford (1998) as espousing a neo-conservative agenda to reposition the Republican Party as pro-immigrant but pro-assimilation. The text of his proposal, also known as the Unz Initiative, owed much of its rhetoric to the official-English movement. It referred to English as "the national public language of the United States of America and the state of California." It also reminded the government of its duty "to provide all of California's children ... with the skills necessary to become productive members of our society, and of these skills, literacy in the English language is among the most important." Characterizing as a failure the state's record of educating immigrant children, the initiative required that all children who are not native speakers of English be placed in "sheltered English immersion" or "structured English immersion" programs, in which "nearly all classroom instruction is in English," for no more than one year before being transferred to mainstream classes. Waivers could be requested by parents to allow their children to receive native-language instruction. Finally, $50 million was to be allocated for English-language classes for adults, who would then pledge to provide English-language tutoring to the children in their communities (Unz & Tuchman, 1998).

Unz's rationales for the initiative were easily challenged by the experts. While Unz called bilingual education a total failure for California's 1.4 million limited-English-proficient children, only 30% of these children were actually in bilingual programs; if they were failing, it was not due to bilingual education. Similarly, he cited the statistic that 95% of limited-

English-proficient children per year fail to be redesignated as fluent English-proficient students. However, this figure included all non-native speakers of English, most of whom were not in bilingual programs. Unz also blamed bilingual education for the high rate of drop-outs from public high schools, ignoring the data showing that the drop-out rate for Latinos had decreased since bilingual education was authorized in 1967 (Lyons, 1998).

The initiative had other serious flaws. There was little evidence that the program described for limited-English proficient children – one year of English immersion – is an effective one. Rather, the literature shows immersion to be inferior to native-language instruction. It also shows that the acquisition of academic English is a lengthy process; one year is hardly sufficient. Finally, it is unlikely that the adults in minority-language communities, many of whom are poorly educated themselves, would be able to acquire the academic-level English they would need to tutor their children adequately.

With a low voter turnout, the initiative passed. Crawford (1998), a former journalist himself, blames the press for facilitating the success of the measure. Ignoring the wealth of research on the positive results of bilingual education, the falseness of Unz's statistics, and the implications of the measure, the media was far more interested in reporting Unz's progress in amassing support. Even though it was not true, the press was attracted to the idea that Latinos were largely in favor of the initiative. Reporters portrayed Unz as a selfless millionaire fighting for poor immigrants, while bilingual educators were characterized as self-serving and corrupt. The media treated everyone's opinion on bilingual education equally; Unz's unsupported assertions were considered as valid as the explanations of research data offered by Stephen Krashen, a respected professor at the University of Southern California. A false story about Hispanic parents unable to get their children out of bilingual classes was widely reported, while the true stories of frustrated parents trying to get their children into bilingual classes never made the newspapers. As we have seen in previous discussions about the media, bilingual education is not treated with the objectivity it deserves, allowing opponents to use the tactics described by Cummins (1994) to influence educational policy for their own political ends.

Immediately after the result of the vote was announced, minority-rights advocates filed suit in the Federal District Court of San Francisco to prevent the implementation of the law, citing violations of the Constitution's promise of equal protection and federal education and civil rights statutes (Bronner, 1998). Richard Riley, US Secretary of Education, issued his opinion that "adoption of the Unz Amendment will lead to fewer children learning English and many children falling further behind in their studies" (Riley, 1998: 2). However, California's education officials were allowed to begin dismantling bilingual programs and replacing them with one-year immersion classes. Meanwhile, bilingual educators went into high gear to protect their programs. They organized efforts to get the parents of the children in bilingual education to sign the waivers needed to keep their children in the programs (García, 1999). Some districts took advantage of the vagueness of the proposal in calling for "nearly all"' instruction in English, claiming that the 60% or 49% of English instruction they were using was in compliance (*Riverside Press-Enterprise*, 1998). Others requested permission to set up alternative, magnet, or charter schools that do not have to follow state education codes and regulations (*Associated Press*, 1998).

The ultimate impact of Proposition 227 is under debate. Eugene García, Dean of the Graduate School of Education at the University of California, Berkeley, predicts little change; he believes that educators who use English-language instruction will only have their beliefs confirmed by the initiative, while those who advocate bilingual instruction will defy the new law (García, 1999). Stephen Krashen, meanwhile, is more pessimistic, and points to reports of the alleged successes of the newly-implemented immersion programs (Krashen, 1999). And there is substantial confusion surrounding the results to date. One year after the approval of the initiative, the state issued test data showing that the proposal had done little to improve the academic achievement of limited-English proficient children. However, Unz was able to combine the numbers in a way that allowed him to claim an "unprecedented" increase in the test scores of these students (Asimov & May, 1999).

In the meantime, the English for the Children campaign moved on. An initiative stricter than the one in California was proposed for Arizona's 1999 election. Opposed by the Navajo Nation Council (Shebala, 1999), among others, the measure passed by a two-to-one ratio (Steinberg, 2000). Unz traveled to New York City, where he claimed that polls showed strong support in both the city and state (Tierney, 1999); the city's education officials, however, announced that there were no plans to scale back bilingual education (Bronner, 1998). Elsewhere in the country, bilingual programs were also under attack. Denver, Colorado and Albuquerque, New Mexico were cited by the Department of Education's Office for Civil Rights for failing to properly staff, fund, and evaluate bilingual programs, causing controversies over whether to fix bilingual education or discard it (Sahagun, 1998; Sandlin & Franck, 1999). In Bethlehem, Pennsylvania, when a district superintendent found out that it took several years for Hispanic children in bilingual programs to be mainstreamed, he spearheaded a successful effort to abolish the programs and replace them with all-English instruction (Miller, 1996).

Finally, as mentioned previously, the 2002 revision of the Bilingual Education Act dealt a powerful blow to federal support for native-language instruction. It was part of a larger measure of school reform that the Bush administration called "No Child Left Behind." All mention of bilingualism was expunged. The Bilingual Education Act became the English Language Acquisition Act; the Office of Bilingual Education and Minority Language Affairs (OBEMLA) was renamed the Office of English Language Acquisition, Language Enhancement, and Academic Achievement for Limited-English-Proficient Students (OELALEAALEPS). In place of a program of competitive grants, funds were to be distributed to states based on enrollment of English language learners and immigrant students. States would have greater power than previously in directing the use of the money, including the ability to impose specific pedagogy. This new means of funding distribution also meant that money would most likely become scarcer, since it would be spread out over more states and more students. While the law stipulated that federal programs be grounded in "scientifically based research," this was left often to broad interpretation. Finally, the success of such programs would be measured by English language proficiency alone, which was expected to discourage programs using native-language instruction (Crawford, 2002). So, while federal official-English legislation has never managed to see the light, one of its major goals – the dismantling of bilingual education – took a giant step towards being realized with the passage of this education law.

A dangerous trend seems to be emerging. When fixable problems in bilingual programs are publicized, when policy makers and the public fail to receive proper information about how the programs work and what their successes are, the decision is often made to throw out native-language instruction altogether. However, from our thorough discussion of bilingual instruction, it should be clear that a blanket condemnation is hardly called for. American educators know what works and what doesn't; what is needed is a re-evaluation of the criteria by which native-language instruction is governed.

In the process, many toes will be stepped on. After all, it is only with the compliance of the federal government and some members of minority-language groups that poor bilingual programs have been allowed to function. Politics often get in the way of good education, and the basis for much governmental policy is tolerance and support for social inequity and the protection of the status quo. As we learned from Del Valle (1998), despite the efforts of grass-roots organizations to realize their vision of bilingual education as encompassing many languages and cultures and addressing the educational needs of a broad range of children, the government consistently responds by reducing it to a remedy for eliminating the English-language deficiencies of minority children. We may also be guided here by the words of the linguist Lily Wong Fillmore:

Bilingual education is seen by the public, and by too many of the educators charged with implementing it, not as giving [limited-English proficient] students a fighting chance to function in an otherwise all-English environment, but as freeing them from the obligation of immediate and absolute assimilation. This has been at the heart of the controversy for the past 20 years. Because bilingual education recognizes the educational validity of languages other than English and cultures other than "American," it is regarded with suspicion and treated accordingly. Only when we have eliminated this prejudice – that to be united, Americans must give up the very things that make them interesting – only then will good bilingual programs outnumber the bad. (Wong Fillmore, 1992: 376)

Bilingual Voting Information and Ballots

Another specific target of official-English legislation is the elimination of voting information and ballots in non-English languages. The 1965 Voting Rights Act, with amendments added in 1975, mandates bilingual elections in districts where a minority-language group constitutes more than 5% of the total population and has high illiteracy and low voter-registration rates. Some official-English bills rescind this provision.

Language restrictionists consider bilingual elections to be another roadblock to the acquisition of English by language minorities. Representative Norman Shumway explains:

We are fostering policies which discourage language minorities from learning English, and we are sending conflicting and confusing signals to those language minorities. For example, we expect all those under the age of 50 seeking naturalization to demonstrate competence in English as a condition of citizenship. However, in 375 jurisdictions in 21 states, the federal government still requires that ballots be printed in languages other than English. How can we require English knowledge on the one hand, then turn around and encourage dependency on other languages with the other? (Shumway, 1988: 123)

As with all other non-English governmental services, bilingual elections are unlikely to discourage language minorities from learning English. Instead, they encourage citizens who may be reluctant to vote because of the language barrier to go to the polls, and greater voter turnout is something that should be valued in a democracy. In 1982, the Mexican American Legal Defense and Education Fund commissioned a study of bilingual elections. Approximately one-third of the Hispanics studied said they would be less likely to vote without Spanish-language help. The study also found that those most likely to use Spanish-language aids were people over 65, people with a low level of education, and people with low incomes (Avila, 1983: 10).

The need for bilingual voting grew out of the experiences of many minority-language citizens who were treated poorly at voting sites and were often flatly denied their lawful right to vote. Their experiences mirrored those of many African Americans who were discouraged from voting by literacy-test requirements, poll taxes, and other tactics of intimidation. Policies of this type were aimed at preventing vulnerable segments of society from gaining the power of the vote and thereby undermining the control that the more advantaged classes had over them. With the current attack on bilingual elections, these tactics continue.

Shumway points to the apparent contradiction between asking immigrants to demonstrate competence in English as a part of acquiring citizenship and allowing them to vote in their native languages. However, the written test for citizenship requires a third-to-fifth-grade level of English proficiency (people who are at least 50 years old and have been legal residents for at least 20 years are exempt from the test). Ballots are often written in more complex language than an elementary-school child could handle. It makes sense, then, to allow voters with a limited grasp of English to get the information they need in the language that is most accessible to them.

Some may argue for raising the proficiency level of English needed for acquiring citizenship. But this would result in an unfair, elitist selection process. Many people who have not had the advantages of an adequate education are law-abiding and contributing members of society. Society recognizes high-level literacy as important for full social participation and the full realization of personal goals, and efforts should be made to help all Americans attain such literacy. But it is not an appropriate qualification for citizenship.

Finally, the cost of bilingual services is a common complaint of language restrictionists. Avila gives an interesting perspective on the expenses incurred for bilingual elections:

> In November 1980, San Francisco spent over $58,000 to send English-language pamphlets to San Franciscans who never voted. Bilingual elections, by contrast, cost from $25,000 to $40,000 per election. With Asians and Hispanics forming about one-third of this city, we can be sure their taxes cover those costs. (Avila, 1983: 11)

Government's Role in Regulating the Private Language of Citizens

Most official-English legislation is aimed at the language used by government. However, one bill goes beyond declaring English the official language of government. It designates English as the preferred language of communication among American citizens, and assigns to government the role of promoting and supporting the use of English by the public.

The supporters of more mainstream legislation have distanced themselves from legislation of this type. Representative Bill Emerson, in an interview with *US English Update*, explained that the legislation he sponsored

> is a well-written, focused bill that sets clear, common-sense parameters for making English the language of our government.... Other bills ... stray from this intent, and address other areas like the total abolition of bilingual education or the use of English in the private sector. This is an extreme approach that dooms the other bills to legislative failure. (*US English Update*, 1995: 3)

Mujica also asserts his organization's defense of private speech, stating, "We are not opposed to anyone speaking languages other than English and strongly support the right of everyone to use their language of choice in their homes, churches and private lives." What US English objects to, he continues, is "government at all levels being expected to accommodate languages other than English in cases other than those covering urgent services related to health, safety and administration of justice" (Mujica, 1994a).

There are several problems with this position. One is the failure to recognize that many immigrants do not possess the level of English proficiency that would allow them to communicate with government in that language. If they must deal with government agencies in situations other than what Mujica categorizes as "urgent," what are they to do? Immigrants who have not fully acquired English have no recourse but to use their native languages.

The second problem has to do with the extent to which government is involved in the private lives of its citizens. Mujica assumes that there is a clear-cut boundary between citizens' personal lives and their dealings with government. However, government often plays a significant role in citizens' lives beyond routine interactions such as paying taxes and filling out census forms. Some of the most important steps an individual takes may occur under governmental jurisdiction.

For immigrants, becoming a citizen is one such step. One could argue that taking an oath of allegiance to one's adopted country is an extremely personal act, one that marks a pivotal moment in the life of an individual. Yet US English would deny people the right to take this oath in their native language. How would Mujica defend governmental intrusion into this aspect of private life? The same could be said for other acts that take place under the aegis of government: a bride and groom reciting their marriage vows in a civil ceremony, or a newly-graduated police officer being sworn into service. The line between public and private is not as clear as Mujica would have us believe.

Furthermore, the government often sets the tone for how the public deals with societal issues. State official-English laws have encouraged a general lack of tolerance for non-English languages that often goes beyond the intent of the legislation. For example, after Florida passed its law, many citizens interpreted it to mean that foreign languages were outlawed in the public arena. A telephone operator refused to let a collect call go through because the caller spoke in Spanish. A woman trying to place a phone order to a department store in Spanish received a recitation of the ordinance by a store clerk, who then hung up on her (Ingwerson, 1988). Feelings of antagonism toward language minorities are at a dangerous level in American society; any law that can be interpreted as sanctioning such antagonism only exacerbates the problems of human interaction that now exist.

Finally, it is important to point out that every proposal that US English supports would have the effect of diminishing the presence of non-English languages in the private sector. Making government monolingual is seen as a way of coercing immigrants to speak English rather than their native languages. Newcomers are given the message that being "linguistically different" will make it harder for them to be accepted into society. Under official-English law, the preservation of immigrant languages, through cultural activities such as publications, concerts, and theater presentations, would be the sole responsibility of the private sector. Without the support of government, it would be difficult for ethnic groups to keep these languages alive. Finally, the elimination of long-term bilingual programs would make it harder for minority-language parents to pass down their languages to the next generation. Their children would quickly learn that English is more valuable than their heritage language, and the transition from bilingualism to English monolingualism would be more rapid than it is now. In light of this, Mujica's stance that US English defends the private use of languages other than English can only be interpreted as disingenuous.

US English may shy away from the blatancy of the provision calling English the "preferred" language of citizens, but this position describes rather accurately the core philosophy of the organization.

CONCLUSION

The current official-English movement did not spring into existence by surprise. It is instead the reappearance of a conservative dogma of nativism, specifically targeting immigrant languages, that has woven itself into the fabric of American life. In this chapter, we traced the history of attitudes towards non-English languages, a history marked by alternating periods of tolerance, promotion, and restriction of such languages. We focused on the climate of nativism that sowed the seeds for the present language-restrictionist movement. Our attention then turned to US English, the organization that has led the call for making English the official language of government. In doing this, we stripped away the organization's facade of concern for newcomers to the United States, and revealed the anti-immigrant sentiments at the heart of the organization's work, sentiments that are little different from those underlying the bouts of immigrant scapegoating that have marked American history from its beginning.

We then looked at current language-restrictionist legislation, beginning with the status of state laws and moving to a description of federal bills. We discussed the stand in favor of official-English taken by Bob Dole, a major contender in the 1996 presidential election, and followed the issues of official English and bilingual education into the 2000 presidential campaign. We described the major elements of federal legislation: the general role of government regarding language, its obligation to help immigrants learn English, specific restrictions on the use of languages other than English, and the government's role in regulating the private language of citizens. From this analysis, we conclude that such legislation would do little to help immigrants learn English or adjust to life in their new country. Instead, it would only make the already challenging lives of minority-language speakers more difficult and devoid of dignity.

This discussion perhaps paints a too-dismal picture. While language restrictionism has made significant strides into American life, it has also found substantial resistance. Language pluralism is an important part of American society, and in the face of the official-English movement it has found a strong defense among many citizens. In the next chapter, we will examine resistance to language restrictionism in greater detail.

CHAPTER 6

Challenges to Language Restrictionism

INTRODUCTION

Despite the gains made by language restrictionism in the 1980s and 90s, it has faced significant challenges as well. These challenges are the focus of the present chapter. We will see that resistance to official English has at times been successful and at other times has failed. The defense of language pluralism, however, is a continuing process.

An often overlooked fact is that one state in the nation, Hawaii, has two official languages; other states, such as Louisiana, New Mexico, and Texas, have laws providing for the use of English and additional languages. We will describe the ways in which the governments of these states make use of non-English languages, and review the history of multilingualism in these states. We will then look at the particular situation of Puerto Rico, a United States commonwealth whose population is largely Spanish-dominant. US English has tried to sell the idea of official English to Puerto Rico as a prerequisite for statehood, with little success.

The official-English movement has prompted a counter movement in defense of language pluralism. Although there is no national counterpart to US English, existing organizations that consider language pluralism to be compatible with their larger goals have been moved to act; we will describe their work. We will then look at how activist groups around the country have mobilized efforts against official English both nationally and in particular states.

There has been one successful effort to overturn a state official-English law, *Yniguez v. Mofford*. Two state employees argued that the law interfered

216

with their First Amendment rights. We will examine the circumstances of the case and the reasons for the court's decision.

A major battleground for language freedom has been the workplace. With the growing population of non-English-speaking residents has come both a growing need to accommodate this population's language needs and a greater opportunity for interactions between people with different native languages. Issues concerning the role of language in power politics, the meaning of bilingualism, and the place of private language in the public arena are the consequences of a linguistically-heterogeneous public life. In the last part of the chapter, we will discuss two legal cases, *Gutierrez v. Municipal Court of the Southeast Judicial District, County of Los Angeles* and *Garcia v. Spun Steak*, which deal with these issues in their challenge to language restrictions in the workplace. We will then discuss the current status of English-only rules and the impact of official-English laws on minority-language workers.

MULTILINGUALISM IN THE STATES

Hawaii is the only state that has two official languages. However, other states have legal provisions for the use of languages in addition to English; Louisiana, New Mexico, and Texas will be discussed here. The laws of these states recognize the significance of the languages of native peoples as well as those of the Europeans who settled there.

Hawaii

Interestingly, US English counts Hawaii as an official-English state. In reality, the Hawaiian state constitution designates both English and Hawaiian as official languages, with Hawaiian required for public acts and transactions as provided by law. The constitution includes a Hawaiian-language state motto; it was felt that an English-language version would not be able to convey the beauty and symbolism expressed in Hawaiian (Lee, 1993). Hawaiian statutory law also designates Hawaiian and English as official languages.

Officers of the state are advised that Hawaiian is not to be regarded as a foreign language, but one of which courts and judges must take notice. Another statute names Hawaiian as the native language of the state and notes that it may be used on all emblems and symbols representing Hawaii and all its agencies and subdivisions. The official "popular" name of the state is "The *Aloha* State," and its citizens are described as being guided by the "*Aloha* Spirit": "the working philosophy of native Hawaiians.... 'Aloha' means mutual regard and affection and extends warmth in caring with no obligation in return" (*Hawaii Statutes*, 1995: 30). The traits of character that express this spirit are given in both languages: kindness ("*akahai*"), unity ("*lokahi*"), agreeable ("*oluolu*"), humility ("*haahaa*"), and patience ("*ahonui*"). The state motto is also written in both languages.

The state's official recognition of two languages belies a much more complex linguistic history, involving languages in addition to English and Hawaiian, and the phenomenon of language mixing. As explained by Bickerton (1998), the location of the island made it the principal port of call for trading vessels beginning in the latter eighteenth century, putting Hawaiians in contact with English-speaking Europeans and resulting in the mixing of the two languages into pidgin English. Another form of speech, pidgin Hawaiian, developed with the establishment of the plantation economy; this was the language of communication between overseers and Hawaiian workers. The linguistic form stabilized in the mid-nineteenth century, as it was used by Hawaiians, Europeans, and the first immigrants to the island. The plantation owners began importing workers in larger numbers, first from China and Portugal, then Japan and Korea, and finally Puerto Rico and the Philippines. These newcomers added to the new language; there was word-borrowing by both Hawaiians and immigrants.

As we mentioned briefly in Chapter 1, a pidgin develops and stabilizes in the second generation, when it becomes the mother tongue of the children of those who first created it. This is the case with pidgin Hawaiian, which acquired uniformity and grammatical structure in its second generation, becoming known as Hawaiian Creole English. Having become a full-fledged language, it was no longer confined to the plantation, and was used in every aspect of life.

Pure Hawaiian was also going through changes. As Reinecke (1969) explains, the Protestant missionaries in the 1820s had a significant role in the development of the language. The missionaries taught English to natives with high status, but saw Hawaiian as the language of universal education for the rest of the population. They created a written form of the language, taught it first to adults and then children, translated the Bible into Hawaiian, and preached in that language. It became the language of high literature and religious publications.

However, by the end of the century, the language had fallen into decline. The Hawaiian monarchy toppled, the native population declined in proportion to other ethnic groups, and English gained in status. While European children were taught at elite English-language schools, others went to inferior schools using Hawaiian as the language of instruction. As Bickerton (1998) explains, from 1882 on, all children were taught in English; however, non-European children, whose teachers were not proficient in the language, generally didn't learn English well. Hawaiian English Creole remained the language of the common people, derided by academics and excluded from the schools. Only in the 1970s was Hawaiian English Creole deemed a legitimate language by the educational establishment.

First-generation immigrants continued to speak their native languages. For the Chinese and Japanese, whose numbers were large, the native languages were kept alive through social groups, language schools for the young, and publications. Creole rather than English served immigrants well as a second language, since contact with English-speakers was minimal. Creole was useful not only with Hawaiians and other immigrants, but also with children of the same nationality group. These children moved among several languages, learning a form of standardized English at school and using a mixture of their ethnic language and Creole with the older generation. The ruling class was largely tolerant of this language diversity, save for a brief period after World War I, when there was an attempt to close Japanese language schools. In the face of strong opposition from the Japanese, the schools remained open. This was, according to Reinecke, "the only instance in Hawaiian history of a conflict having difference of language as its ostensible cause" (Reinecke, 1969: 128).

Hawaiian English Creole is used less often today, in the face of increased migration from mainland United States and pressures from government and business. In a well-publicized 1989 case, *Kakahua et al. v. Friday*, a meteorologist with the National Weather Service in Honolulu was denied promotion to a position which involved, as a minor function, orally recording the weather forecast; his standard Hawaiian Creole accent was noted as the deciding factor. The job went instead to a male Anglo applicant with no college degree or background in meteorology. In court, a speech consultant rated the Anglo's speech superior to Kakahua's in broadcasting skill, and it was determined that the Weather Service had not discriminated on the basis of Kahakua's accent (Sklarewitz, 1992). While the mainstream continues to devalue Creole, however, young working-class locals prize it as a mark that distinguishes them from European Americans, and there is greater tolerance for Creole use in schools. It is not likely to go away in the near future.

Efforts to revitalize Hawaiian are also bearing fruit. In 1983 the Native Hawaiian community opened three preschool Punana Leo Language Immersion Programs, based on the "language nest" programs for Maori children in New Zealand. The schools were begun as private, non-profit institutions, with Native Hawaiian teachers using only the Hawaiian language for ten hours of instruction, five days a week. Courses in the language were also offered to parents, who were required to use the language at home. In 1987, as a result of lobbying by the schools' organizers and parents, the Hawaiian state education department granted the preschools state funding, allowing the teachers exemptions from the usual requirements for academic training and certification.

As successful as the schools were, they were not enough to stem the loss of the language; besides the children in Punana Leo preschools, the only speakers of the language were the elderly, who were quickly dying off. To fill the demographic gap, immersion programs began expanding into the upper grades, and community activists urged the state education department to mandate the teaching of Hawaiian in the upper grades and college (Zepeda & Hill, 1992). By the end of the 1990s, nearly two thousand children statewide were in Hawaiian immersion programs; these children usually perform well academically and attain high English-language proficiency in addition to their proficiency in Hawaiian (Wilson, 1999).

Immigrant languages continue to have a place in Hawaiian society. According to Bickerton (1998), interest in Japanese is maintained by the constant influx of Japanese tourists to the island as well as by the immigrant population; Hawaii has two television stations that broadcast mostly in Japanese. For residents from Central America and Mexico, the public access channel broadcasts Spanish-language programs several hours a week. Bickerton believes that the language situation in Hawaii, probably the country's most linguistically diverse and racially tolerant state, "argues strongly against the validity of the increasingly popular 'English-only' position, which holds that social and cultural integration cannot proceed unless all languages but the dominant one are ruthlessly suppressed. Indeed, efforts to impose monolingualism failed completely" (Bickerton, 1998: 53). This makes US English's designation of Hawaii as an official-English state all the more ironic.

Louisiana

US English also claims Louisiana as an official-English state, attaching the date 1811 to its inception. This refers to the passage of the Louisiana Enabling Act by Congress in that year, requiring that English be the language of all official proceedings in the territory of Orleans as a requirement for statehood (Mujica, 1997a). Such requirements were also placed on other territories in the Southwest; their relevance to modern times is questionable, since all state governments now function in English whether or not they have an official-English declaration. In addition, an 1855 law states that "it is sufficient in all the parishes of the state to publish advertisements, judicial and otherwise, notices, and publications required by law, in the English language only" (West's, 1987: 30). This statute falls short of making English the official language; it may, however, be one of first uses of the phrase, eventually adopted by US English, "English only."

Given the influence of the French language and culture in the history of this state, it is not surprising that subsequent laws revised those mentioned above to make provisions for the use of French. One states that advertisements "shall be made in the English language and may in addition be duplicated in the French language;" state and local officials and public institutions "are reconfirmed in the traditional right to publish documents in the French language in addition to English" (*West's*, 1982b: 62). Another statute requires that the French language, history, and culture be taught in public elementary and high schools (*West's*, 1982a: 591–593).

Louisiana legislators apparently recognized the role of multilingualism in the economic well-being of the state. They authorized the governor to establish the Council for the Development of French in Louisiana (CODOFIL), which was empowered "to do any and all things necessary to accomplish the development, utilization and preservation of the French language as found in the state of Louisiana for the cultural, economic and tourist benefit of the state" (*West's*, 1989: 296). Another agency, the Council for the Development of Spanish in Louisiana, had a similar goal for that language; it was directed to "utilize the resources provided by the significant Spanish-language population of Louisiana" to foster tourism and trade (*West's*, 1989: 300).

In 1987 two Louisianans in Congress proposed a Cultural Rights Amendment, although it was never enacted. The lawmakers were apparently inspired by their state's own laws. Article 12 of Louisiana's 1974 Constitution includes the statement that "the right of the people to preserve, foster, and promote their respective historic linguistic and cultural origins is recognized" (*West's*, 1977: 874).

As in the case of Hawaii, Louisiana's history involves a greater degree of linguistic diversity than is indicated in its laws. As Garner (1997) explains, the French settled the area in 1682, establishing their language as the main conduit of communication. The importation of slaves from Africa and the Caribbean colonies of France, Spanish control of the colony in the last half of the eighteenth century, and the influx of French-speaking immigrants expelled from British Canada (briefly mentioned in Chapter 2) and elsewhere complicated the linguistic situation. Louisiana French developed into different variants: colonial French, which has died out and which was the closest approximation to standard French; Acadian or Cajun French, a variety spoken by the descendants of Canadian immigrants and the Native Americans and other immigrants absorbed into the group; and Black French, or Creole French, influenced by the languages of African slaves. Rather than being different languages, these variations form a continuum, with standard French at one end, Creole French at the other, and Cajun French in between. English has had an influence on all three varieties.

According to Marshall (1997), social relations between ethnic groups were historically very fluid. Free people of color had contact with everyone – colonists, Indians, and slaves. Because farms and plantations were small, white owners and their families had direct contact with their slaves. Slaves from different parts of Africa mixed with each other, and poor whites and immigrants mixed with slaves. As a result, residents learned a range of variants of French. This remains true today. Blyth explains that "it's typical for multilingual speakers in Louisiana to move back and forth along the continuum to suit communicative needs, frequently mixing varieties in the process" (Blyth, 1997: 27).

However, there exists a definite hierarchical structure in the relationship of these varieties to each other and to English. Valdman (1997) explains that English stands at the apex of the structure, followed by standard French, Cajun French, and finally Louisiana Creole. Creole is the most stigmatized variety owing to its association with slavery; even though some whites speak it, they are reluctant to use it in front of strangers, and often deny knowing it altogether.

This hierarchy did not occur without a struggle. Even before Louisiana was absorbed into the United States, English began to dominate French. The state constitutions written between 1812 and 1879 varied in their recognition of French as an official language alongside English. In 1921, English became the sole language of instruction, formalizing the unequal status of the two languages. Cajun communities began to lose their isolation along with the construction of modern roads, the assimilation of young men into the armed forces, and the migration between Texas and Louisiana sparked by the oil boom. French, in all its variants, lost a great deal of ground (Blyth, 1997).

This loss was not officially recognized until the 1960s, when the statutes allowing the use of French began to appear. For defenders of the French language, however, these laws, and Article 12 of the 1974 Constitution, fell short of the goal of raising the status of French to match that of English. In addition, when CODOFIL, established in 1978, began a movement to restore the French language in the state through education, radio and television programming, and publications, the variant chosen was standard French. Native speakers of French in the state were never consulted; representatives from France, however, did play a role. It became clear that the goals of CODOFIL were based more on the economic needs of the state rather than the revival of the state's heritage culture; there were no concrete plans to help foster Cajun French.

In reaction to this, in the 1980s a popular counter-movement was instituted by the Cajun intellectual and artistic community. A written norm for Cajun French was established. Interest in Cajun music grew, there was a resurgence of Cajun literature, and people began to document Cajun history and the contemporary challenges of Cajun ethnicity. Cajun culture became so popular that, to an extent, it was co-opted by the larger society; it has sparked a resurgence in tourism, and the descriptor "Cajun" is now attached to many elements of Louisiana culture that have no real connection to Cajun culture (Henry, 1997).

A smaller counter-movement occurred for French Creole. In the 1990s an African-Louisianan middle-class group, Creole, Inc., created the English-language monthly *Creole Magazine*, which included lessons in Creole and a column on Creole linguistics. The magazine, however, was short-lived (Valdman, 1997).

The efforts of the Louisiana government to restore competence in French were not wholly successful. French-language periodicals and television and radio programs did not survive. In the schools, funds were insufficient and local educators varied in their enthusiasm for French-language instruction. Cajun French families refused to use standard French at home, and objected to the importing of French language teachers from France. Many felt that the status of Cajun French was being further eroded by the absence of the language variety in education. Educational efforts failed to create a significant number of French/English bilingual youth, despite the fact that Louisiana requires more foreign-language classes in elementary school than any other state (*Times-Picayune*, 1998). CODOFIL did act as a stimulant to the revival and definition of Cajun language and culture. However, it is doubtful whether Cajun French will survive beyond the year 2010, when it is predicted that there will be no dominant speakers of the language left. Blyth writes, "Educators and activists envision a future for 'French as a functional second language in the state.'... Exactly what form this functional second language will take is the sociolinguistic question of the future" (Blyth, 1997: 43).

Louisiana thus presents another example of what happens when a language power structure is imposed on a population, as official-English advocates are attempting to do. The domination of English over French nearly wiped out the French language, at which point the state began attempts to revive it. The decisions to restore standard French over the popular varieties, without consultation with those who spoke the language and cared most about it, and to import teachers from France are reminiscent of the assimilationist vs. pluralist bilingual education policies regarding Spanish that Rolf Kjolseth found in the Southwest, as discussed in Chapter 4. As a result of these policies, French became merely a "foreign language," and history has shown that Americans do badly at learning foreign languages. Neither standard French nor the variants that are an inherent part of the state's culture and history are faring well.

The Southwest: New Mexico and Texas

The presence of Spanish and Native American languages in the Southwest has influenced the laws of New Mexico and Texas. When New Mexico's constitution was written, it provided for the publication of all laws in English and Spanish for the first twenty years of the state's existence, after which the legislature was empowered to use Spanish as it saw fit. The constitution established provisions for the training of teachers in both languages in order to serve Spanish-speaking pupils better. It also made it illegal to deny children of Spanish descent the right to attend school, and, to ensure that they would receive an equal education, prohibited the separation of these children from others.

Statutory and constitutional laws call for the use of Spanish in a wide range of governmental activities, including elections, the publication of proceedings of the meetings of local entities (such as school boards and county commissions), the posting of legal notices, and bilingual/multicultural education. In addition, there is both an English-language and Spanish-language state song and salute to the state flag (*New Mexico*, 1978; *Constitution of the State of New Mexico*, 1978).

New Mexico also has a sizable population of Native Americans; a 1990 US Census Report, based on a sample, estimated 76,738 persons speaking Native American languages at home (Reddy, 1995). State law provides for oral assistance in the voting process "when a minority language is historically unwritten" (*New Mexico*, 1978: 11), a reference to certain Native American languages. Oral assistance is also mandated for "minority language voters who cannot read sufficiently well to exercise the elective franchise" (*New Mexico*, 1978: 18), which applies to both Native Americans and Hispanics.

As in New Mexico, Texas law recognizes that many of its citizens are dominant in the Spanish language. The state's laws provide for Spanish-language voter registration applications, regular and absentee voting ballots, and voting instruction posters. Interpreters are required if a voter cannot understand the language of a ballot, or if there is a need for a non-English dominant voter to communicate with an election officer who knows only English (*Vernon's*, 1986). In counties that are on the border with Mexico, judges are instructed to hire qualified Spanish–English court interpreters if they determine a need for them (*Vernon's*, 1997b). In counties with at least 2,000 Spanish-dominant residents, public utilities are required to create plans for giving such residents access to their services and programs (*Texas*, 1999). Finally, as the law recognizes English as "the basic language" of the state (*Vernon's*, 1997a: 369), bilingual education and special education are provided to non-English-dominant children "to ensure students' reasonable proficiency in the English language and ability to achieve academic success" (*Vernon's*, 1997a: 347).

Multilingualism has been a predominant element in the history of the Southwest. When the Spanish arrived in the so-called New World, their Castilian language became a part of a larger linguistic landscape; they encouraged the use of Native American languages as well as the learning of Spanish. As we noted in Chapter 2, Native Americans of mixed ancestry, *mestizos*, were most likely to learn Spanish. Many Native Americans knew one or more indigenous language in addition to their own; Nahuatl served as a lingua franca among the natives until Spanish took over this function. When English entered the scene as a result of land purchase, conquest, and annexation, it contributed to the various forms of language use:

monolingualism, bilingualism, and multilingualism in Native American languages, Spanish, and English (Ferguson & Heath, 1981).

Of course, English eventually became dominant. New Mexico was ceded to the United States in 1848, but English-speakers remained a minority until after 1900; both English and Spanish were used in schools and in legal and governmental proceedings. The government refused to grant statehood until 1912, when the number of English-speaking residents exceeded the number of Spanish-speakers, and the territory was sufficiently "Americanized." From then on, Spanish declined precipitously, until it was no longer used in public life (Conklin & Lourie, 1983). The annexation of Texas in 1848 resulted in sweeping changes: conversion to a capitalist, agrarian-based economy; the transformation of the growing Mexican population into a landless, labor-dependent, racially-segregated class; the introduction of Mexican children into the United States school system and the decline of Spanish-language schools; and the growing hegemony of United States popular culture through the mass media. The Spanish language and Mexican culture became increasingly stigmatized as the English language and United States culture rose in prestige (Limón, 1982).

Because of the extensive contact between language groups in this area, language borrowing and combining was common. The appearance of Aztec loanwords in US Southwest Spanish and Native American languages today suggests that this contact began in prehistoric times. Combinations such as American Indian Pidgin English, Indian–Spanish–English Pidgin, Chinese Pidgin English and Chinese English have all been identified (Brandt, 1982). A southwestern Texas community with a mixed Native American and African background speaks a language sometimes referred to as Seminole or Texas Seminole; it exhibits similarities to the Gullah language of African Americans in South Carolina (Nichols, 1981).

Native American children vary in their linguistic repertoire when they begin school. They may be monolingual in their native tongue (Navajo, for example), bilingual in their native language and English, or monolingual in Indian English, a variant that is often stigmatized by educators. Native American languages have been codified and are taught in community literacy classes, university language classes, and bilingual programs (Brandt, 1982).

The Spanish heard today in the Southwest (Chicano Spanish) has a number of variants, both geographical and social. According to Conklin and Lourie (1983), regional differences are not as great as the social ones. There are four social dialects: Northern Mexican Spanish, Popular Spanish, Mixed Spanish (also called Tex-Mex or Spanglish), and a slang known as *caló*. Chicanos often speak more than one dialect, shifting from one to the other depending on the topic or the conversation partner; English is used with those who do not know any of the Spanish variants. The linguistic virtuosity of the Chicanos is reflected in the comments of a young man from East Austin, Texas:

> If you're gonna make anything, you know, or do anything, you have to know how to communicate and you're never gonna have the same group. You may be talking to an Anglo, so you have to learn to speak English. You may be talking to the poor white, then you talk the slang or hippie; then you talk to the mexicano professional *que avienta puras palabras grandes* (who spouts only big words), you have to speak that way, *los viejitos de otra manera y de aí a la gente de tu edad, mexicanos, el estilo de nosotros y aí está* (with old people another way and then with people your own age, mexicanos, our way of talking [*caló*] and there it is). (Elías-Olivares, 1979: 132–13; cited in Conklin & Lourie, 1983: 187)

Despite the stigmatization of Spanish in modern times, the language gained political and social capital during the 1960s and 70s. Inspired by the black civil rights and anti-war movements, Chicano students at the University of Texas organized to fight for the rights of those Mexican Americans who had less opportunity for success in the wider society than they did. The students who came from large urban enclaves or border communities found that using Spanish was a useful rhetorical tool in connecting with their compatriots outside the university and in shaping the university group's ideology. Monolingual English-speaking Chicano students were moved to acquire the language. According to Limón, in this period of social change and upheaval, Spanish became a means of "calling forth of a political self;" use of the language "may well have evoked a socially and linguistically repressed ancestral lineage and political sentiment" and "was a powerful impetus in moving people to political action on behalf of the present-day community" (Limón, 1982: 328–329).

Finally, it is important to remember the immigrant languages that contributed to the multilingual culture of the Southwest. As they did in many other states, the Germans had a significant presence in Texas. Today, there are Texas cities with names derived from the German language, and German is still spoken by the descendants of nineteenth-century immigrants (Conklin & Lourie, 1983; Gilbert, 1981). Despite the contention of official-English advocates that multilingualism causes disunity, the language diversity of the Southwest has never caused dissension; without an official status, English dominates and other languages, in all their rich variation, flourish alongside it.

THE LANGUAGE ISSUE IN PUERTO RICO

While the states fight over whether or not to make English the official language, a much more complex situation faces Puerto Rico. An island with a rich heritage and strong allegiance to the Spanish language, it is a part of the United States without the physical and cultural connections that hold the states together.

The language issue has long plagued Puerto Rico. When the United States established a military government on the island in 1898, it set out to Americanize its citizens. The Spanish spoken by the citizens of Puerto Rico was considered of little value within the military establishment, which foresaw the transformation of the population into one that spoke exclusively in English.

The question of the language of instruction in the schools became a major source of contention. The United States sought to make English the language of education, but resistance to this plan made its realization impossible. Different combinations of Spanish and English use were attempted. By the 1940s, the United States conceded to the use of Spanish as the means of instruction, with English as a priority academic subject. Still, the schools have never been very successful in making Puerto Ricans proficient in the English language (Language Policy Task Force, 1978).

Puerto Ricans have long debated whether the introduction of English into the island's life has damaged or helped Puerto Rico. Vélez (1986) traces the debate among Puerto Rican intellectuals and identifies three periods in which this debate reached its greatest intensity. These are the 1940s, when the question of the language of school instruction was at issue; the 1960s, when parochial schools fought to continue using English as the language of instruction; and the 1980s, when the language issue became entangled in the larger issue of political status. Reviewing journals from the 1940s and the 1960s, Vélez (1986) synthesizes the opposing arguments.

On one side of the debate was the argument that learning a second language is a neutral, non-political endeavor. Those who supported this view felt that English did not interfere with Puerto Rican Spanish or lead to its deterioration; rather, they believed there was a significant commercial value in knowing English. On the other side of the debate was the argument that the intrusion of English had the potential for damaging Puerto Rico as a separate identity, and that English was actually destroying the Spanish language (despite evidence to the contrary gathered by sociolinguists). Supporters of this viewpoint held that the Spanish language was also endangered by a number of societal factors: the desire of new members of the middle class to separate themselves from the poverty of their past, the influence of the mass media, the penetration of North American companies into the island, and the need for a working knowledge of English as a prerequisite for employment. Those who held this opinion saw conserving Spanish as the salvation of the island. These writers felt that there was a need for government policies to protect Spanish against the erosion of Puerto Rica's cultural heritage and against its political dependency on the

United States. Vélez concludes, "Many members of the Puerto Rican intelligentsia saw their country undergoing a process of cultural transformation that could cause irreparable damage to its national integrity.... The ambivalence of Puerto Ricans with reference to English is a result of their perception of themselves as a culture under siege" (Vélez, 1986: 10).

This quote is as relevant today as it was in the 1940s and the 1960s. The question of the status of English and Spanish is closely tied to the question of the island's political status, a matter of much contention in present-day Puerto Rico. Those who support statehood want to see English strengthened; those who favor maintaining commonwealth status or declaring independence from the United States insist on making Spanish the official language. As the political fortunes of parties with different views on the island's future change, so does the relative status of English and Spanish.

The debate over political and linguistic status came to a head in the 1990s. The Languages Act, passed early in the century and making both English and Spanish official languages, was replaced in 1991 by a Spanish-only law, under the leadership of the Popular Democratic Party, which supports commonwealth status. Then, in January 1993, recently-elected Governor Pedro Rosselló of the New Progressive Party signed a law making both English and Spanish official languages of the island once again. Rosselló regarded this action as a major step toward Puerto Rico becoming the fifty-first state (*EPIC*, 1993b).

There was strong opposition to this move. Many Puerto Ricans considered the law to be further evidence of the Americanization of Puerto Rico. When the bill was signed, the Independence Party drew 80,000 to 100,000 people to a protest demonstration in San Juan, with participants shouting "Inglés, no!" (*The New York Times*, 1993a: A12). The following November, a plebiscite on the status of the island resulted in a rejection of statehood by a slight margin; 48% voted for continued commonwealth status, 46% for statehood, and 4% for independence (Rohter, 1993: A1). One of the arguments for continued commonwealth status was that statehood would force Puerto Rico to give up its linguistic and cultural identity. However, it was generally understood that the people desired a change in the status quo. Governor Rosselló and other leaders were expected to negotiate with the United States for an "enhanced" commonwealth status, one that would have less of a colonial nature.

Official-English proponents on the continent were not idle during all of this. Articles on the language situation of Puerto Rico began to appear in US English literature in 1987. In the fall of 1988, US English launched a mail campaign in Puerto Rico, sending a letter by former Senator Hayakawa to several thousand islanders. The letter spoke of the undesirability of preserving Spanish at the expense of English and referred to the dangers of bilingualism present on the mainland, giving as an example the predominance of Spanish in Miami. It invited Puerto Ricans to join the organization and to send in contributions. On July 14, 1989, Luis Acle of US English appeared before the Senate Committee on Energy and Natural Resources, regarding a request by Puerto Rican leaders to decide the issue of the island's status with a legally-binding plebiscite. In his testimony, Acle said:

> Now, during these historical debates, we feel it would be badly misleading for the people of Puerto Rico to vote in the plebiscite thinking that any language, other than English, can be the official language of a state in the Union. English is the common language of the people of the United States, and one day will be recognized as the official language of government in this country. At that time, we believe that Puerto Rico, as all other states, will follow the laws of the land and accept English as the official language of government. (cited in Rúa, 1992: 86–87)

Acle prodded the Senate to include the language issue in the plebiscite: "I would urge you to consider the negative effect of leaving the matter of language in a cloud of ambiguity. Any hesitation to openly address the issue of the language of government could be interpreted as a lack of sincerity and responsibility on the part of the Congress" (cited in Rúa, 1992: 87). In the end, however, the committee failed to approve the plebiscite, and it never took place (García Passalacqua, 1994).

Shortly after Acle's testimony, there was a marked increase in US English's involvement in Puerto Rico's language issue. The late-1989 and early-1990 issues of *US English Update* included several articles concerning the commonwealth. These articles were circulated widely among prominent members of federal and state governments. In early 1990, executive director Kathryn Bricker took a trip to the island, meeting with the leaders of various political parties and establishing connections with sympathizers there, whom she claimed numbered 100. Bricker stated publicly that it would take years to pass a constitutional amendment making English the official language, and that while the organization worked toward that goal, it was also concentrating on passing official-English laws at the state level. This explained the organization's interest in the possibility of Puerto Rico becoming a state.

At this time, articles began to appear in the press in Puerto Rico and on the mainland expressing support for making English the official language of Puerto Rico. Spanish-language instruction was viewed as holding the island back from technological progress and high-quality education. Puerto Rico was compared to Quebec, with the insinuation that Puerto Rico's bilingualism would lead to political unrest. In mainland United States, essays propagated warnings of what would happen if the United

States continued to maintain close ties with, or accepted as a state, an island whose major language was Spanish.

However, portents of what the opposite scenario, an official-English Puerto Rico, would be like were already in evidence. In 1988, employees at the Base Militar Borinquen Station in Aguadilla were prohibited from using Spanish. The workers went to the press, forcing the United States military to reconsider the policy and to appoint a new director for the base. Two years later, a similar incident occurred at the National Park Service in San Juan, which was run by a North American director. When workers there were told to speak only English, they also contacted the press, calling the rule *"un acto de discriminación, racismo y hostilidad"* ("an act of discrimination, racism, and hostility") (cited in Rúa, 1992: 89). The director claimed that union negotiations were always conducted in English, but that employees were never forced to use English among themselves.

The issue of Puerto Rico's status resurfaced in the late 1990s with a new plebiscite proposal. H.R. 856, the United States – Puerto Rico Political Status Act, called for a referendum by the end of 1998 offering the Puerto Rican population three choices: continued commonwealth status, independence or free association, or statehood. It went further than previous proposals in requiring a ten-year transition plan with specifications for each of the possible outcomes; if statehood was favored, the proposal called for plans to promote the learning and use of English (http:// thomas.loc.gov).

In testimony before the House Committee on Resources, Mauro Mujica of US English renewed the call for a discussion of the language issue. He questioned how a Spanish-dominant population could integrate into an English-dominant society, warned of a separatist movement similar to that of Quebec, and reminded legislators of the language conditions imposed on the territories of Louisiana, Oklahoma, New Mexico, and Arizona before they could be admitted into the union (Mujica, 1997a). However, an "English-only" amendment proposed a year later by Republican Gerald Solomon of New York was defeated. On March 4, 1998, the original piece of legislation, thought by language restrictionists to have inadequate English-language provisions, passed by a vote of 209 to 208. Twenty percent of Republican legislators voted for the bill, a significant figure given the party's traditional lack of concern for Hispanic issues. Many saw the vote, and the failure to pass Solomon's amendment, as a sign that Republicans were trying to rehabilitate their party in the eyes of the growing Hispanic population (Mujica, 1998; Hitt, 1998; Gugliotta, 1998).

In July 1998, the Senate Energy and Natural Resources Committee held hearings on H.R. 856, but the full Senate never voted on it. Instead, the Puerto Rican legislature put together its own referendum, with five choices: statehood, independence, free association, commonwealth, and "none of the above." Statehood received 46.5% of the vote and "none of the above" received 50.2% Reasons for choosing "none of the above" were mixed; some voters reported that they favored commonwealth status but with conditions not spelled out on the ballot, while others said they were voting against Rosselló. In all, the outcome was considered ambiguous (Branigin, 1998).

At the same time, the language issue continued to be fought out in the public schools. In 1997 the Puerto Rico Department of Education announced a new policy called *Proyecto Para Formar un Ciudadano Bilingüe* (Project for Developing a Bilingual Citizen). The policy would intensify the study of English by introducing English-language textbooks in academic courses, extending the length of English-language classes, and giving priority to reading and writing in English, beginning in the first grade. Based on the 1993 law making English and Spanish co-official languages, it was seen as one more tactic in the long-running attempt to Americanize the island and in support of Governor Rosselló's plans for statehood. Teachers' organizations complained that the already under-funded schools had neither the resources nor the personnel to institute the changes, and that the policy would further exacerbate the problem of low academic achievement, which included falling scores on tests of the Spanish language. Many teachers vowed to defy the rule and continue teaching in Spanish (Navarro, 1997). The Academia Puertorriqueña de la Lengua Española, made up of professionals representing various disciplines, argued that the policy was based on research in bilingual education inapplicable to the situation of children in Puerto Rico, since the research dealt with minority-language children living in a majority-language culture. It warned that the policy would lead to inadequate learning of both languages and would hamper the intellectual development of Puerto Rican children (Academia Puertorriqueña, 1998).

At the end of the century, then, the future status of Puerto Rico remained uncertain. However, whatever destiny awaits Puerto Rico, it is clear that the official-English movement in mainland United States will try to influence the language question on the island. While US English claims that official-English status is essential for Puerto Rican statehood, it cannot contest the fact that most states do not have such status. In addition, the existence of an officially bilingual state, Hawaii, argues against the insistence that a Puerto Rican state should claim only English as its official language.

In the future, if multilingualism becomes more acceptable to the American people, and more states adopt official bilingualism, statehood might gain popularity among those living on the island. If, on the other hand, a federal official-English law is passed, statehood may appear less desirable. However, there are other factors involved. The island's present status has mixed blessings: Puerto Ricans pay no federal taxes but receive social security and other benefits; they don't vote in federal elections but are subject to the military draft. The language issue will be one important factor among others as the debate on the island's future continues. Whatever happens, though, it is improbable that Puerto Ricans will give up their deeply-rooted ties to the Spanish language.

THE MOVEMENT AGAINST OFFICIAL ENGLISH

Unlike proponents of official English, those on the opposite side of the issue have not united to form a national organization devoted solely to preventing passage of such legislation, one that would be the counterpart of US English. However, existing organizations have worked by themselves and in combination with each other to fight the official-English movement. In this section we review the actions these groups have taken to affirm their communities' commitment to diversity and to respond to the introduction of official-English legislation in their states.

The Reaction of Existing Organizations

The rise of the current language-restrictionist movement alarmed many organizations that supported the goal of language freedom. In the wake of the 1986 passage of California's Proposition 63, a number of these organizations came together to form a coalition under the title English Plus Information Clearinghouse (EPIC). The group's statement of purpose declared its goal as supporting the concept of "English Plus": full access to English-language education for non-native speakers and the mastery of second or multiple languages for everyone. Forty-nine organizations signed the statement initially. These included teachers' associations (such as the American Council on the Teaching of Foreign Languages, the Conference on College Composition and Communication, and Teachers of English to Speakers of Other Languages), ethnic advocacy groups (such as the American Jewish Committee, Chinese for Affirmative Action, and the Haitian American Anti-Defamation League), and civil rights groups (such as the American Civil Liberties Union). Staffed by the National Immigration, Refugee and Citizenship Forum and the Joint National Committee for Languages, EPIC created an archive of information relevant to the official-English movement to aid the individual advocacy efforts of its member organizations. It also put out a bimonthly newsletter, *EPIC Events*, tracking activities around the country. The newsletter was published from spring 1988 to fall 1993.

Individual organizations also passed internal resolutions protesting the official-English movement. Professional groups which declared themselves opposed to official English include the National Council of Teachers of English, the American Psychological Association, the Linguistic Society of America, the Modern Language Association, and the National Association for Bilingual Education. Ethnic advocacy groups which declared their opposition include the American Arab Anti-Discrimination Committee, the Cuban American National Council, and the League of United Latin American Citizens (*EPIC*, 1988a).

The work of civil rights groups has been essential to the movement to quell official English. A number of these organizations have taken on the defense of language rights in specific legal cases, such as the Mexican American Legal Defense and Education Fund, the Puerto Rican Legal Defense and Education Fund, and the American Civil Liberties Union. In the previous chapter, we mentioned the 1998 lawsuit in Alabama that overturned the state's policy of administering the written driver's test in English only. That case, *Sandoval v. Hagan*, was brought by both the American Civil Liberties Union and the Southern Poverty Law Center. The latter organization also filed a successful lawsuit against an Alabama tax assessor found to be depriving limited-English-speaking immigrants of tax exemptions that they lawfully deserved. The Center found that the tax assessor, known for his anti-immigrant sentiments, asked only limited-English-speaking home owners to take a brief oath before their exemption applications could be filed; since these home owners were not able to take the oath in English, they were denied the exemption (*SPLC*, 2000). Such organizations have also helped to educate the public. For example, the Asian Pacific American Legal Center of Southern California's Language Rights Project, begun in 1989, distributes information to employers and employees regarding language rights in the workplace, a common site in the battle over language use, as we will see below.

Activities Against Official English

While some states have moved to declare English the official language, restricting government functions to the use of one language, a few states have gone in the opposite direction. Four states have passed resolutions endorsing the policy of "English Plus," as described above. New Mexico was the first, in 1989, followed by Washington and Oregon; Rhode Island did the same in 1992.

Measures endorsing cultural pluralism have also been introduced at the Congressional level, although to little effect. As mentioned earlier in the chapter, in 1987 Senator John Breaux and Representative Jimmy Hayes, both of Louisiana, proposed a Cultural Rights Amendment, which would recognize "the right of the people to preserve, foster, and promote their respective historic, linguistic, and cultural origins." No action was taken by Congress at that time (Draper & Jiménez, 1990). In 1995, José Serrano of New York introduced the English-Plus Resolution in the House of Representatives. This document calls for the conservation and development of the nation's linguistic resources and the continued provision of governmental services in languages other than English (Yang & López, 1995). However, as a resolution, it does not carry the weight of law. If passed, it could not be enforced.

Local communities have also seen fit to reaffirm their commitment to diversity, by passing resolutions declaring themselves multicultural, multilingual, bilingual, or multiracial. Resolutions of this nature were passed in Atlanta, Georgia and Osceola County, Florida in 1986; Dallas and San Antonio, Texas, Tucson and South Tucson, Arizona, and Washington, DC in 1987; and Cleveland and Lorain, Ohio and Pima County, Arizona in 1988 (*EPIC Events*, 1988a).

In some places, opposition to the official-English movement has taken on more active forms. Massachusetts English Plus, for example, is a coalition of educators and activists dedicated to educating the community about the importance of maintaining language and cultural diversity. In November 1991, the coalition organized an entire month of projects. These projects included a bilingual art/writing contest, public displays of writing by adult ESL students at various sites in Boston and Cambridge, forums on bilingual education and official English, and a multicultural festival (Louie, 1992). The Language Rights Coalition of New York, another umbrella group for ethnic, civil rights, and educational associations, organized an alternative celebration for Columbus Day, 1990. While this holiday generally focuses on the "discovery" of America and turns a blind eye to the glorification of colonization in American history, National Language Rights Day was an affirmation of diversity, with a combination of speeches and multicultural presentations held on the steps of the Capitol in Washington, DC (Ramos, 1990).

Reactions to State Official-English Measures

Much of the public work against the official-English movement has been reactive, with people coming together at the same time as, or immediately after, language-restrictionist measures are proposed. In Arizona, for instance, a US-English-backed organization called Arizonans for Official English put together Proposition 106, an extremely restrictive constitutional amendment, for the 1988 ballot. Meanwhile, a group of community leaders, educators, and elected officials formed Arizona English, which proposed an amendment of its own encouraging English proficiency while guaranteeing the right to learn and use other languages. Arizona English failed to get its proposal on the ballot, but Arizonans for Official English succeeded.

Opponents reorganized into a group called No on 106 Committee/ Arizonans Against Constitutional Tampering, enlisting the support of prominent state leaders (O'Donnell, 1988). The official-English amendment passed. As we will see below, its constitutionality was successfully challenged.

Similar efforts took place in other states. Opponents of official English in Colorado formed Coloradoans for Language Freedom and Colorado Unity, garnering support from the governor, the lieutenant governor, the Greater Chamber of Commerce and many religious and civil fights organizations (*EPIC*, 1988b). In Florida, opponents of the English Language Amendment, which was voted on in November, 1988, formed the Orlando English Plus Group, Tampa Opponents of Amendment 11, Dade County-English Plus, and Speak Up Now (SUN) for Florida (Castro, 1988). As in Arizona, these efforts were not sufficient to stop passage of the measures. However, in New York a number of organizations helped defeat an official-English bill in the State Assembly's education subcommittee in 1987.

During the 1986 electoral campaign in California, opposition to the state's official-English proposition was expressed by major politicians, newspapers, and a number of organizations. However, it failed to inhibit widespread public support for the measure, which passed easily. After the election, Californians United formed to monitor its effects, tracking incidents of discrimination, proposing legislation to offset the consequences, looking for challenges to the law's legality, and waging a public education campaign. It also sponsored a national conference examining language issues in the summer of 1988 (*EPIC*, 1988c). Ultimately, the official-English law had little effect. Its main target, bilingual education, remained protected by federal legislation. Opponents of this pedagogical practice eventually turned their energies to the campaign for the 1998 English Language Education for Children in the Public Schools Initiative, or Proposition 227, discussed in the previous chapter.

Throughout the 1990s and into the new century, language restrictionists continued to target states that had not yet passed official-English laws. In some instances, they were able to succeed. Georgia's law, which restricts the publication of state records and the provision of state services to English, took three years to be realized. Each year it pushed further through the political process, and in 1996 the governor signed the law he had vetoed the previous year. In doing so, official-English advocates managed to rout persistent allegations of bigotry and xenophobia brought by organizations such as the Latin American Association (Soto, 1995; McCarthy, 1996).

The outcome of the campaign in Alaska was more problematic for official-English advocates. The issue was particularly sensitive to the state, given the precarious nature of Native American languages and cultures there. Only two of the state's Native American languages are being learned in the traditional way: by parents speaking the language to their children (Krauss, 1995). Language-revival efforts are stymied by native speakers' sentiments towards their own languages, feelings of shame and embarrassment absorbed through years of negative messages imparted by government and public schools. Many bilingual programs in Alaska are assimilationist in nature; educators demonstrate ambivalence toward Native American languages, often devaluing them while urging the learning of other languages with historical roots in the state, such as French, Spanish, Russian, and Japanese (Dauenhauer & Dauenhauer, 1998).

Of particular concern to those opposed to official English was the effect that it would have on the Native American population. The American Civil Liberties Union of Alaska (AkCLU) pointed to the fact that Native American languages were being used in many local government bodies, such as village councils, fish and game advisory boards, and school boards. In addition, the renewed interest among the younger generation in learning languages in danger of extinction, such as that of Siberian Yup'ik, a language spoken on St Lawrence Island in the Bering Strait, would be threatened by the devaluation of native languages that would result from designating English as the official language.

Ironically, while official-English advocates generally play on anti-immigrant sentiments, Alaskans for a Common Language acknowledged that the state does not have a problem with immigrants who lack English-language skills. In fact, Alaska is quite proud of its international atmosphere. Nevertheless, the group was successful in getting the measure on the November 1998 ballot, and it passed with 70% of the vote. AkCLU, in conjunction with the Native American Rights Fund and the North Slope Borough, filed a lawsuit, *Alakayak, et al. v. State of Alaska*, on behalf of over two dozen plaintiffs. The lawsuit claimed that those named (including public officials, Spanish-speakers, Inupiaq-speakers and Yup'ik-speakers; teachers, parents and administrators) would be denied their constitutional rights to free speech and expression, to have access to their government and to petition it for redress of grievances, and to equal protection under the law. In response, a Superior Court judge issued an injunction on March 4, 1999, one day before the law was to go into effect (*ACLU Newswire*, 1998, 1999a, 1999b).

Utah was another state waging a war against official English at the end of the century. In 1996, an ultra-conservative freshman state legislator, Tammy Rowan, was urged to take up a cause, and she decided on official English. From 1996 to 1999, a succession of official-English bills were introduced, each of which was defeated. Shortly after the introduction of the first piece of legislation, groups and individuals opposed to official English formed Utah Common Voices, held rallies, attended hearings, and debated Rowan while US English mounted its own publicity campaign.

A very conservative state and the home of the Latter-Day Saints Church, or Mormons, Utah was perhaps an inevitable target; in addition, a vibrant economy was attracting a growing Hispanic migration, making the state vulnerable to language restrictionists' ability to tap anti-immigrant feelings. However, multilingualism is considered one of the state's great assets; Church missionaries work throughout the world, and many converts emigrate to the state. Utah Common Voices was successful in turning back official English partly by appealing to the population's conservative values (for example, a belief in the authoritative role of parents in the family structure), and partly by appealing to the state's history of assimilating people from different cultures and its respect for diversity. By 1999, Tammy Rowan was losing support from her colleagues, and she herself voted against an official-English bill in February of that year (Eggington, 2000).

At the same time, however, US English turned its efforts to collecting signatures for a ballot initiative for the fall 2000 election. US English claimed that at least 75% of Utahns supported the measure, while Mata Finau, head of Utah Common Voices, maintained that pro-official-English lawmakers were "bureaucrats ... trying to impose their legislative ideals on the populace of Utah" (Wolfson, 2000). The proposal required government to conduct business in English, with exceptions for tourism, health, law enforcement and court proceedings, and in schools, universities, and libraries. It passed in all but one county (May & Fahys, 2000). A lawsuit was filed, stating that the law would impede the ability of government officials to communicate with or design programs for non-native English speakers. The plaintiffs claimed the law was in violation of the First Amendment, including the clause guaranteeing the right of constituents to petition the government, and the Fourteenth Amendment, which guarantees equal protection. The suit led to a temporary restraining order (*Salt Lake Tribune*, 2000).

During hearings conducted at the end of January 2001, speakers argued over the wording of the law. Critics, including the state's assistant attorney general, interpreted the designation of English as the "sole" and "official" language as precluding any government activity in languages other than English. Utahns for Official English maintained that the two words could be removed, and that the law didn't prohibit such activity. However, once an initiative is passed into law, it cannot be changed. In addition, it was unclear why the law would be necessary at all if the words were removed (Khashan, 2001). A district judge ultimately declared the law constitutional, since it allowed for "unofficial" communications between government and the public in any language (*Associated Press*, 2001).

A final example of a state battling official English is Iowa, in the heartland of the nation. Like many states throughout the South and Midwest, in the 1990s the burgeoning poultry industry, offering grueling but plentiful work, began to lure immigrants from all over, principally Hispanics but also Bosnians, Ukrainians, Nigerians, Czechs, Vietnamese, and Pacific Islanders. As usual, these newcomers were willing to take the kinds of jobs that white Americans, already dwindling in number in Iowa, would not touch. In one tiny farm town, Postville, an entrepreneur opened a kosher slaughterhouse; as a consequence, the town acquired a substantial community of Orthodox Jews. In addition to the poultry farms, Iowa began participating in the growing global economy, and some immigrants came to take high-paying, skilled positions in manufacturing.

In a state that was 95% white, the change in demographics was dramatic, and elicited different reactions. Some Iowans welcomed the change, basking in the opportunity to experience different cultures, especially as immigrants began opening ethnic restaurants and food stores. They also saw their children being introduced to the world through their new classmates. Others, however, retained the traditional sense of wariness and distrust of outsiders that is characteristic of an isolated population. They tended to attribute the state's ills – increased educational and welfare costs, gang activity, and drug abuse – to these outsiders.

This situation was fertile ground for the seed of official English. Language restrictionists began working at the local level; several counties voted down official-English measures. As had happened before, Hispanics took the brunt of anti-immigrant animosity and were the specific target of official-English advocates. The sponsor of a state official-English proposal, Representative Mike Cormack, reported hearing from constituents that they feared their town, Fort Dodge, would soon be inundated with Latino immigrants, as had happened in neighboring towns. In preparation for Iowa's presidential caucus on January 24, 2000, a series of anti-immigrant ads were placed in the Des Moines Register, sponsored by a group of organizations including the American Immigration Control Foundation (Marks, 1998; Simon, 1999; Puente, 2000; Edsall, 2000; Herman, 2000; Rounds, 2000).

In Iowa, as elsewhere in the country, the language battle seems destined to continue into the new century. However, this battle appears to be expanding beyond the traditional means of lawmaking. More and more often, as we have seen above, language issues such as official English and bilingual education are becoming the substance of so-called popular or ballot initiatives at the state or local level. As the political reporter David Broder (2000) explains, initiatives were originally championed as a way to bypass monied special-interest groups that unduly influenced legislators and stymied the passage of progressive laws. Today, however, they are in the hands of the special-interest groups themselves. Broder reports that putting a measure on a ballot and mounting a public-relations campaign for its passage cost millions of dollars; it has become, in essence, a new type of business enterprise. The job of those involved in this business is not to explain the proposal, but to get people to vote for it; the campaigns, on both sides, end up distorting the issues.

According to Broder's analysis, the ballot-initiative process has several other inherent dangers. It flouts the tenets of representative democracy by putting important issues in the hands of the small percentage of individuals who go to the polls, and who generally vote in their own personal interests rather than those of the larger community. In addition, there is no account-ability involved. In the regular law-making process, elected officials know their constituents pay attention to how they vote on issues and base their continued support for the officials on their actions, but in the ballot-initia-tive process, no one is held accountable. It is not surprising, then, that anti-bilingual education and official-English proposals increasingly end up on election-day ballots; lawmakers who hope to get re-elected or to run for higher office often shy away from supporting such proposals in their legis-latures for fear of offending the growing number of minority-language voters. The result is that the fate of language policies ends up in the hands of citizens lacking the knowledge and objectivity to make fair and reasoned decisions about them.

THE REVERSAL OF THE OFFICIAL-ENGLISH LAW IN ARIZONA

To date, there has been only one successful legal challenge to a state offi-cial-English law. *Yniguez v. Mofford* (1990) brought to the courts the question of whether government employees could be denied the right to speak in a language other than English.

Arizona's official-English amendment, passed in 1988, made English the language of the ballot, the public schools, and all government functions and actions. Shortly after passage of the law, a suit was filed on behalf of Maria-Kelly F. Yniguez, with Jaime P. Gutierrez, against the state. Yniguez was an insurance-claims manager working for the state Risk Management Division. Before the law was passed, she often used Spanish in dealing with clients, but stopped this practice for fear of breaking the law. Gutierrez was a state senator from Tucson who habitually used Spanish to communicate with constituents. Gutierrez did not stop doing this after the amendment was passed, but was concerned that if he continued to speak Spanish, he might be breaking the law. The defendants claimed that the law interfered with their First Amendment right to free speech.

In February 1990, US District Judge Paul Rosenblatt ruled in favor of the defendants and declared the English language amendment unconstitu-tional. Rosenblatt insisted that states may not require their officers or employees to relinquish rights guaranteed them by the First Amendment. He cited examples of instances in which state officers or employees often use other languages: legislators speaking to their constituents, employees com-menting on matters of public concern, and judges performing marriage ceremonies. The official-English amendment would force these officials to either violate their oaths to obey the state constitution, subjecting themselves to possible sanctions or law suits, or to curtail their right to free speech.

Arizona's Attorney General, Bob Corbin, expressed the state's position that the law did not prevent people like Yniguez and Gutierrez from using Spanish, because it applied only to official state acts of government entities and not to the day-to-day operations of government. However, the amendment covered, in the actual phrasing, "all governmental officials and employees during the performance of governmental business" (*Yniguez v. Mofford*, 1990: 316), with exceptions made for education, public health and safety, and the protection of the rights of criminals and crime victims. Rosenblatt believed that the state's interpretation of the law did not coincide with the wording of the law, causing a great deal of ambiguity for those trying to understand and abide by the law.

A consequence of this ambiguity, stated Rosenblatt, was that people would steer far clearer of the bounds of the law than was necessary. This is precisely what Yniguez did when she decided to stop using Spanish when dealing with clients. The amendment therefore had the "potential for chilling First Amendment rights." Rosenblatt concluded that "a law which reasonably results in such restrictions is substantially overbroad" (*Yniguez v. Mofford*, 1990: 315), and he voided the amendment.

Arizona's governor, Rose Mofford, who had opposed the amendment all along, did not appeal Rosenblatt's decision. However, an appeal filed by Arizonans for Official English was granted in July 1991. The case languished for several years. At the end of 1994, the Ninth Court of Appeals upheld Rosenblatt's ruling (Contín, 1994).

Arizonans for Official English managed to bring the case to the US Supreme Court's attention in 1997. Without ruling on the merits of the case, this court set aside the previous ruling based on two factors: Yniguez had already left her state job at the time the appeals court started hearing the case, and Arizona's Supreme Court should have been allowed to rule on the case first. This court was soon to have its turn anyway, as a second challenge to the official-English law, *Ruiz v. Symington*, whose plaintiffs included elected officials, state employees, and a public school teacher, was already making its way through the state judicial system. When it reached the Arizona Supreme Court in the spring of 1998, the law was again declared unconstitutional. A final effort to revive official English in Arizona failed in January 1999, when the US Supreme Court, again declining to rule on the merits of the case, let the state's Supreme Court decision stand. Admitting defeat, the architect of the original proposal, Bob Park, announced that he would turn his attention to a new ballot initiative to restrict bilingual education (Crawford, 1997; Greenhouse, 1997, 1999; Fisher, 1999). As mentioned previously, that initiative passed, and became law in November of the following year (Steinberg, 2000).

Yniguez v. Mofford demonstrates the tenuousness of the rationale for official-English laws. Proponents claim concern for the well-being of non-native speakers of English and a desire to help them adjust to life in the United States. Declaring English as the official language is supposed to be both a symbolic act for everyone and an aid to immigrants in their acculturation process. However, when it comes to implementing such an act, proponents are forced to make exceptions in those areas that make them seem insensitive to immigrants' needs (besides being subject to legal challenge), for example, in education, public health and safety, and the legal system.

In the same way, the impulse to force all government activities to be carried out in English must be balanced by a show of compassion for those who have not mastered English, including the people who are most likely to be marginalized by society. Arizona's Attorney General tried to forge a position which both supported official English and allowed for a compassionate stance: English would be the official language of the state, but its exclusive use in governmental business was not necessary. It is understandable why this position was considered ambiguous. Interpreted in this manner, the law would change little with regard to the use of languages by government, thereby casting doubt on the need for an official-English law at all.

LEGAL CHALLENGES TO LANGUAGE RESTRICTIONISM IN THE WORKPLACE

Workplace Bilingualism

Yniguez v. Mofford demonstrates that the multilingual nature of the American population compels the government to make some use of languages other than English. The strong presence of language minorities also means that the public workplace is bound to be multilingual as well.

As McGroarty (1990) explains, bilingualism is a prominent feature of the American workplace. Immigrants, many of whom fall into a subordinate social category, are generally under pressure to conform to the language demands of the superordinate class, native speakers of English. However, English is not a necessity for entry into the workforce. Large immigrant groups tend to cluster in a few major metropolitan areas, such as New York and Los Angeles. In these ethnic communities, the newly-arrived are able to get jobs where their compatriots already work, and where the native language is the major means of communication. Some immigrant communities acquire a coordinate social status, with enough economic and political resources to promote the use of native languages in occupational settings; the Cuban population in Miami is an example. These communities are especially accessible to limited-English-speaking job seekers.

This doesn't mean that English is not valuable. For those who want to improve their job situation in the industry to which they have been introduced, or who aspire to a different means of employment, learning English is a necessity. Business owners in coordinate-status enclaves who learn English are better able to expand both their pool of employees and their consumer base. For these reasons, most immigrants acquire some degree of proficiency in English, and consequently become bilingual.

This resulting bilingualism gives immigrants a marketable skill. For immigrants who continue to work in their ethnic communities, their language abilities allow them to serve as intermediaries between their enclaves and the English-speaking world. For example, a bilingual supervisor is able to bridge the communication gap between an English-speaking boss and minority-language workers. Or a bilingual member of an ethnic enclave can serve as the contact between the community and those outside who have products and services to offer. For those who leave their communities, proficiency in English is obviously a must. However, acquiring English does not mean that the native language must be sacrificed. McGroarty speculates that native-language loss might not only limit employment possibilities, but might also result in the loss of "a source of social strength and distinctiveness that might contribute indirectly to economic success" (McGroarty, 1990: 175).

The language-restrictionist movement therefore attempts to thwart a natural state of affairs in American society. It has become clear that many people do not see official-English laws as merely symbolic; rather, they interpret such laws as license to force non-English-dominant people to speak English, and to prevent them from speaking their native languages. This has become a particular source of contention in the workplace, where people of different languages are forced into contact with each other. Attempts to restrict language use on the job not only go against the grain of the American immigrant experience, they may also constitute illegal discrimination. Complicating the situation is the coming together of two conflicting forces: the pressure to make everyone speak English, and the common business exigency of using languages other than English.

We now focus on two legal cases in which English-only rules were challenged by minority-language employees. These two have been chosen because the different court decisions illustrate the arguments for and against implementing English-only rules in the workplace, and point out the difficulties that American society faces regarding language use in public. Each case will be described briefly; then the major issues involved will be analyzed.

The Cases

Gutierrez v. Municipal Court of the Southeast Judicial District, County of Los Angeles

In March 1985, eight months before Proposition 63, declaring English the official language of California, became law, Alva Gutierrez filed suit against her employers, three judges at a municipal court in Los Angeles. Gutierrez was a bilingual deputy court clerk, one of whose duties was to translate for the Spanish-speaking public. Earlier that year, her employers had instituted a personnel rule requiring all workers to speak in English except when translating or during breaks and lunchtime. The impetus for this rule was an incident in which an African American employee tripped and, unable to understand Spanish, interpreted the banter of several Hispanic employees nearby as joking at her expense. The rule was intended to improve racial harmony and assuage the discomfort that English-dominant workers felt in the presence of Spanish-language conversation. Gutierrez argued that the rule constituted racial and national-origin discrimination; Title VII of the 1964 Civil Rights Act prohibits discrimination in employment, including rules that have a disparate impact on a protected class of workers.

A district judge halted the enforcement of the rule, and Gutierrez's employers appealed. Judge Stephen Reinhardt ruled in favor of Gutierrez in January 1988, upholding the lower court's injunction against the rule (*Gutierrez*, 1988a). After Reinhardt's ruling, a judicial panel rejected a petition for rehearing and a petition to rehear the case as a full court. Three judges disagreed with the denial of a full-court rehearing; their opinion was represented in a statement by Judge Alex Kozinski (*Gutierrez*, 1988b). A year later, the Supreme Court dismissed the case on the grounds that the lawsuit was moot; Gutierrez had quit her job and accepted a monetary settlement (Crawford, 1992).

Garcia v. Spun Steak Company, San Francisco

Priscilla Garcia and Maricela Buitrago were bilingual assembly-line workers at the Spun Steak Company, a producer of poultry and meat products. Among the 33 employees at the company, 24 were Spanish-speaking, most of them Hispanics; two had little English mastery, and the rest were bilinguals with varying degrees of proficiency in English. Until 1990, Spanish was spoken freely in the factory. However, the company began to receive complaints that some workers were using Spanish to harass and insult other workers. Specifically, Garcia and Buitrago were accused of making derogatory, racist remarks in Spanish about two workers, one African American and the other Chinese American.

In light of these complaints, the company president implemented an English-only rule. He cited three reasons for the rule. The first was to promote racial harmony. The second was to enhance worker safety, since some English-speakers said that hearing Spanish distracted them while they operated machinery. The third was to enhance product quality; the plant's United States Department of Agriculture (USDA) inspector spoke no Spanish and couldn't understand product-related concerns expressed in that language. The rule stated that only English was to be spoken in connection with work, and that Spanish was allowed only during lunch, breaks, and employees' free time. Workers were urged not to use Spanish in ways that led others to suffer humiliation. A second rule forbade offensive racial, sexual, or personal remarks of any kind.

Enforcement of the rule was not strict; some workers continued to use Spanish without incident. Exceptions to the rule were made for the clean-up crew and for certain workers who were able to speak Spanish to their foreman at his discretion. Of the two workers who spoke no English at all, one was exempt from the rule because he was on the clean-up crew. The second, an assembly-line worker, was also exempt; however, the rule did not bother her, because she preferred to eschew small talk while working.

In November 1990, Garcia and Buitrago received warning letters concerning their use of Spanish, and were separated on the assembly line for two months. Their union, Local 115 of the Commercial Workers International Union, AFL-CIO, filed a complaint, to no effect. In May 1991, Garcia and Buitrago filed charges of discrimination against Spun Steak with the Equal Employment Opportunity Commission (EEOC), which determined that there was reasonable cause to believe the company had violated Title VII of the Civil Rights Act. In September of that year, the two workers and their local union filed suit on behalf of all the Spanish-speaking employees.

A district court decided in their favor, finding that the English-only rule denied them a privilege of employment that the English-speaking workers enjoyed. Also, the court ruled that Spun Steak had failed to show a business justification for the rule. Spun Steak appealed (*Garcia*, 1993), with the EEOC participating in oral arguments. The appeals panel, whose decision was written by Judge O'Scannlain, found that Spun Steak had not violated Title VII in adopting the English-only rule, and reversed the decision.

The Business-Necessity Guideline

One of the major issues in these cases was how English-only rules fit into the legal system. There are in fact no laws regarding such a policy. However, there is a set of guidelines on language restrictions written by the EEOC. One guideline makes it incumbent on the employer to show that there is a business necessity for such a policy. Recognizing that the native language of an individual is often an essential national-origin characteristic, the EEOC established the guidelines to prevent English-only rules from creating an atmosphere of intimidation. However, guidelines are not legally enforceable, and the two judges in these cases weighed in with different opinions.

In *Gutierrez*, Reinhardt, supporting the guidelines, pointed out that there was no business justification for an English-only rule. He argued that in this case the language employees chose to use with each other did not interfere with their duties. He also pointed out that the clerks were already required to use Spanish when dealing with limited-English-speaking Hispanics having business with the court, and that their additional use of Spanish with each other would make little difference in the work atmosphere. Reinhardt also believed that the rule unfairly disadvantaged Hispanics because their identity was closely linked to the Spanish language. He wrote, "Although an individual may learn English and become assimilated into American society, his primary language remains an important link to his ethnic culture and identity." This language may also be the means by which established Americans identify those of foreign origin. "Because language and accents are identifying characteristics, rules which have a negative effect on bilinguals, individuals with accents, or non-English speakers, may be mere pretexts for intentional national origin discrimination" (*Gutierrez*, 1988a: 1039).

In *Garcia*, O'Scanlainn rejected the business-necessity guideline. He insisted that English-only rules do not always produce an atmosphere of intimidation. In this case, he wrote, "the bilingual employees are able to comply with the rule, and there is no evidence to show that the atmosphere at Spun Steak in general is infused with hostility toward Hispanic workers" (*Garcia*, 1993: 1489). O'Scannlain also invoked the tradition of Congress of resisting federal regulation of private business, of striking a balance between preventing discrimination and preserving the independence of the employer. He stated that the EEOC guidelines contravene that tradition by presuming that an English-only policy has a negative effect on a particular class of employees.

It is apparent that the two judges had different ideological orientations with regard to language minorities and English-only rules. Reinhardt was sensitive to the negative effect that language restriction has on those who are not native speakers of English. O'Scannlain was largely unsympathetic to the situation of language minorities, giving more weight to the rights of the employer than to the potential discrimination of employees. Kozinski, who argued against Reinhardt's decision, fell in closely with O'Scannlain. This ideological rift continues to be evident in the issues discussed below.

Employer Justifications for English-Only Rules

In both of these cases, the employers offered reasons for implementing an English-only rule. We examine these reasons below.

Racial Harmony

Racial harmony was a major justification for the policy in both cases. In *Gutierrez*, the employers, several Los Angeles municipal court judges, claimed that Spanish was being used to convey discriminatory and insulting remarks directed at non-Spanish-speaking clerks, and to undermine supervision. However, Reinhardt found no evidence of the inappropriate use of Spanish. Three supervisors admitted in affidavits that hearing Spanish made them feel uncomfortable, but conceded that since they didn't speak Spanish, they could not tell whether the employees' Spanish remarks were discriminatory or insubordinate. In addition, there was evidence that non-Spanish-speaking clerks had made racially-discriminatory remarks about Hispanic workers, and the rule had actually increased racial tension because its effect was to belittle Hispanics. The employer argued that the rule was necessary to assuage non-Spanish-speaking workers' suspicions that the Spanish-speakers were concealing derogatory remarks about them. However, Reinhardt pointed out that there was only one complaint of this nature filed, it did not constitute a business necessity, and it was insufficient justification for a rule that resulted in an adverse effect on a specific group of people.

The employer in *Garcia*, Spun Steak, also pointed to the need for racial harmony as justification for the English-only rule. O'Scannlain supported this justification. The rule had been instituted in response to the complaints of non-Spanish-speaking employees about alleged Spanish-language insults by Hispanic workers. According to O'Scannlain, the rule was necessary to prevent bilingual workers from using Spanish to intimidate others.

These two decisions demonstrate the differences between the judges with regard to their concern for and trust in the employees on the basis of their linguistic orientation. In *Gutierrez*, Reinhardt pointed out the lack of evidence that Spanish had been used in ways that would have created disharmony in the workplace, while adding that there was proof of derogatory remarks in the other direction, from English-speakers to Spanish-speakers. Also, he did not consider the suspicions of English-speakers about the use of Spanish sufficient justification for the English-only policy. In *Garcia*, O'Scannlain found no proof of discrimination against the bilingual workers. However, the only evidence that derogatory Spanish-language remarks had been directed against other workers was the word of the alleged targets of these remarks, and O'Scannlain took this word as the truth. In situations of this type, corroborating evidence seems necessary; it is reasonable to suspect that these workers might be lying. Without such evidence, the source of disharmony – whether the Spanish-speakers, the English-speakers, or both – cannot be ascertained.

Worker Safety and Product Quality

Spun Steak noted two additional reasons for instituting an English-only rule. O'Scannlain did not comment on these reasons. However, we will address the weaknesses in these arguments.

According to Spun Steak, the English-only policy was necessary to insure worker safety. The company explained that some English-speakers became distracted when they heard Spanish being spoken, and this affected their ability to operate machinery in a safe manner. Like O'Scannlain, the company demonstrated more concern for the English-speakers than for the Spanish-speakers, as well as a tendency to validate the perceptions of the former group. It is not surprising that the English-speakers reacted this way to hearing Spanish, since they appeared to harbor a certain amount of suspicion of and dislike for those who speak it. However, instead of making the English-speakers confront these feelings, Spun Steak placed the burden on the Spanish-speakers to curtail their use of their native language. It is doubtful that such a measure would have an effect on the racial disharmony that the rule was meant to eradicate.

Lastly, the English-only policy was considered necessary for protecting product quality. The company explained that the plant's USDA inspector routinely interviewed workers on the assembly line. The inspector did not speak Spanish, and therefore could not understand product-related concerns expressed in that language. However, this argument ignores the fact that most of the Spanish-speaking workers were also capable of speaking English. They could easily switch from Spanish to English when they needed to speak to the inspector; those with weak English skills could turn to their co-workers to translate for them. As has often happened, the meaning of bilingualism is misidentified here as the exclusive use of a non-English language. We will see in continuing our analysis of these cases that much of the support for an English-only policy is based on misunderstandings of the nature of bilingualism.

Were the English-Only Rules Successful?

Given the purported goals of the English-only rules instituted at the work sites described here, it is reasonable to ask whether the rules resulted in a better environment for the workers. O'Scannlain never mentioned whether worker safety or product quality were enhanced by the language policy. However, we do know that racial harmony was not an outcome of the English-only rules. In *Gutierrez*, Reinhardt noted that racial hostility had increased since the rule was implemented because it caused Hispanics to feel belittled. There was also evidence of racially discriminatory remarks by English-speaking workers directed at Hispanic employees after the rule went into effect. As for *Garcia*, it is difficult to believe that the animosity between the bilingual and English-speaking workers was assuaged in any significant way by the English-only rule. The existence of the case itself points to the hostility that the rule generated.

The Meaning of Bilingualism

As mentioned above, after Reinhardt's ruling in *Gutierrez*, the case was appealed. The petition to rehear the case was denied, but a minority opinion on this decision was written by Judge Alex Kozinski. One of Kozinski's arguments was that the English-only rule did not have a discriminatory impact. He reasoned that language was not an immutable characteristic, like race or national origin. Gutierrez was perfectly capable of speaking English; her decision to speak Spanish was not out of necessity, but out of choice.

This may have been true for Gutierrez and her colleagues, since their job involved dealing with both English- and Spanish-speakers. However, this may not be the case for all employees whose native languages are not English. Individual bilingualism falls somewhere along a continuum; bilinguals reach some degree of competence in their second language, but their first language is usually the stronger one. For many, speaking in a second language involves a great degree of effort, and does place a significant burden on them.

In addition, just because Gutierrez was able to speak English competently, there is considerable doubt as to whether she should have been compelled to speak it when it was not necessary for her job performance. Kozinski failed to address this point; he seemed to assume that anyone who knows how to speak English would consequently want to speak it exclusively. He appeared to give little importance to the connection, acknowledged by Reinhardt, between native language and cultural identity.

At the core of negative attitudes toward, and misunderstanding of, bilingualism is an inherent distrust of those who speak a language other than English. Kozinski supported the opinion of the English-speaking employees that the rule was not racially motivated, but was merely a means of creating a more harmonious atmosphere. He cited a letter signed by eight of these employees, who complained that the matter "has now been turned into an issue of ethnic background and civil rights. In reality the only issue is common courtesy" (*Gutierrez*, 1988b: 1192). He also noted that one employee had tried to explain to Gutierrez her discomfort at hearing Spanish, with little result. Kozinski quoted the employee as saying, "I couldn't make her see how bad it feels when you know the people around you are purposely talking so that you cannot understand" (*Gutierrez*, 1988b: 1193, footnote 13).

Kozinski reinforced, without question or challenge, the English-speaking employees' perceptions of their Hispanic co-workers. To them, the use of Spanish was solely a means of expressing malice toward those who were not Hispanic. The Spanish language itself had become a symbol of this alleged malice, and hearing it inevitably evoked distrust and suspicion. It therefore had to be eradicated. However, a more impartial observer can see that barring Spanish would do little to solve the inter-group antagonism that plagued this workplace.

Finally, Kozinski contended that, without the English-only work rule, the cause of equal opportunity in the workplace was endangered. Workers would have to be divided into two tracks, one for English-speakers and another for speakers of the non-English language, with different supervisors for each track. Here, Kozinski lost sight of the meaning of bilingualism. A bilingual employee is one who is able to move between two languages as the need arises. Those who are capable of speaking both English and Spanish do not choose to use Spanish all the time. Rather, they want to be able to speak Spanish when communicating with others who speak the language at times when it doesn't interfere with their work, and when monolingual English-speakers are not involved in the conversation. Having bilingual speakers in a workplace does not necessitate separating employees according to language.

In *Garcia*, O'Scannlain's interpretation of bilingualism mirrored that of Kozinski. O'Scannlain pointed out that employees who had only minimal English proficiency were exempt from the rule; all the others were capable of speaking English. The rule therefore had no significant impact on them, and was not discriminatory. Like Kozinski, O'Scannlain believed that anyone who knows English is not burdened by having to speak it exclusively, even if that person knows another language. He allowed that bilingual workers may slip into Spanish at times, and that this language-switching may not be totally volitional. However,

> the fact that a bilingual employee may, on occasion, unconsciously substitute a Spanish word in place of an English one does not override our conclusion that the bilingual employee can easily comply with the rule. In short, we conclude that a bilingual employee is not denied a privilege of employment by the English-only rule. (*Garcia*, 1993: 1488)

What he is denied, however, is his bilingualism.

In this line of thinking, English is the preferred language; Spanish is the language to be avoided. The basis of support for the English-only rule is that, unless they are forced to speak English all the time, the bilingual workers will speak only Spanish. This explains Spun Steak's product-quality justification for the policy, which we touched on above: the USDA inspector, who regularly interviewed workers regarding their concerns, knew only English. Why this justified making the employees speak English at all other times is difficult to fathom. It is obvious that O'Scannlain missed the point of bilingualism altogether.

Like Kozinski, O'Scannlain reinforced the negative attitudes towards Spanish and Spanish-speakers that brought about the English-only rule and the lawsuit. He wrote, "There is substantial evidence in the record demonstrating that the policy was enacted to prevent the employees from intentionally using their fluency in Spanish to isolate and to intimidate members of other ethnic groups" (*Garcia*, 1993: 1489). This misinterpretation of the use of a non-English language creates an atmosphere in which bilingualism cannot survive.

It should be pointed out that there is no mention made of the extent to which the bilingual workers spoke Spanish over English during the course of the workday. Given the inter-group antagonism that existed, it is likely that the workers divided themselves by linguistic preference when it was in their power to do so, for example, on the assembly line or during lunch breaks. If this was the case, the language divisions reflected the hostile atmosphere between the two groups; given more harmonious relations, the bilingual workers would have made use of both languages as they interacted with a wider range of friends. However, O'Scannlain totally ignored the group dynamics in this case, preferring instead to place the blame for the hostility on the use of an unfairly maligned language.

Private Speech in Public Spaces

In the previous chapter, we noted that official-English legislation would allow government control over private speech and behavior. These two cases also deal with the issue of language privacy.

In *Gutierrez*, Reinhardt argued that when employees are working with each other and not dealing with the public, they should be able to converse in the language of their choice. Kozinski took a different view, stating,

> A nation of immigrants, we have been willing to embrace English as our public language, preserving native tongues and dialects for private and family occasions.... When employees bring their private language into a public workplace, this creates a difficult and sensitive problem for those around them who do not speak the language. (*Gutierrez*, 1988b: 1193)

Employers are justified in establishing English-only rules when the use of another language "seriously undermine[s] workplace morale." In this case, such a rule was justified by the "legitimate complaint by a black employee about what she believed were insulting comments made in a language she could not understand" (*Gutierrez*, 1988b: 1193)

Kozinski's wording acknowledges that the actual nature of the Spanish remarks made in this incident could not be verified. However, the fact that the black clerk believed the remarks were derogatory and directed at her was enough to legitimize her perception. In Kozinski's view, everyone must understand what everyone else is saying so that no one will say anything that might be construed as malicious.

One problem with this argument is that, even when everyone is speaking the same language, there is no guarantee that what is said will be properly heard and interpreted. In this particular example, recall that the complaining employee thought she heard insulting Spanish-language remarks when she tripped. However, the same thing could have happened if everyone had been speaking English. The clerk may have tripped some distance away from the bilingual workers and may not have been able to hear their English-language comments clearly. If they had laughed at a joke one of them told, the clerk may have thought the laughter was at her expense. It is likely that language was not the overriding factor here. Given the existing atmosphere of hostility between the English-speaking and the bilingual clerks, the misinterpretation of remarks may have occurred regardless of the language in which they were expressed.

The more serious problem with this argument, however, is its implied restrictions on private speech. Private conversations are an intrinsic part of workplace interactions. Two people may go into an office and close the door in order to converse. An employee may call a relative or friend on the phone and speak about a private matter in her native language. The participants in a conversation should not be forced to use a language comprehensible to those not involved in the exchange; in the workplace, as in any other public place, inclusiveness is not required. If those who are excluded feel uncomfortable, their discomfort most likely stems from their own insecurities or prejudices. While such discomfort must be acknowledged and dealt with, it doesn't justify curtailing private speech.

The issue of language privacy also came up in *Garcia*. *Garcia* contended that the English-only rule denied the bilingual employees a privilege of employment enjoyed by the English-speakers: the ability to converse on the job in the language with which they felt most comfortable. O'Scannlain replied that a privilege is given at the discretion of the employer, who has the right to define its contours. He gave these examples: "An employer may allow employees to converse on the job, but only during certain times of the day or during the performance of certain tasks. The employer may proscribe certain topics as inappropriate during working hours or may even forbid the use of certain words, such as profanity" (*Garcia*, 1993: 1487). In this case, O'Scannlain claimed, Spun Steak exercised its prerogative to define the privilege of conversing as limited to the English language.

As we noted previously, O'Scannlain tended to place the rights of the employer over those of the employee. Under objective analysis, some of his examples of privilege limitations seem more reasonable than others. What separates these examples is the extent to which they may be justified as necessary for conducting business. In a workplace where delicate tasks require a high level of concentration, one can imagine an employer specifying when and where employees may engage in free conversation. The proscription of certain topics of conversation, the banning of profanity, and the restriction of conversation to a particular language are linked much more loosely to business necessity, and seem to have more to do with the personal preferences of the employer. In these instances, it might be argued that the employer is stepping over a crucial boundary. We recall that O'Scannlain rejected the business-necessity guideline. However, without some restrictions on their ability to define the workplace atmosphere, employers may feel free to tell their workers what to say, think, or believe in, infringing on rights guaranteed under United States law.

Power Politics

An important aspect of *Gutierrez* was the linguistic distinction between those in power and their subordinates: the supervisors were all monolingual English-speakers, while a number of clerks were bilingual. This was the source of a certain amount of discomfort on the part of the supervisors, resulting from the loss of control they felt when Spanish was being spoken. More importantly, the extent to which this linguistic and national-origin division was entrenched is revealed in one of the reasons that Gutierrez's employers gave for the English-only rule: supervisors could not evaluate the work of employees using Spanish.

Reinhardt saw the absurdity of this argument. Part of the clerks' job was to deal with the Spanish-speaking public. Consequently, this part of their work needed to be evaluated. Reinhardt suggested assigning Spanish-speaking supervisors to evaluate clerks when they dealt with the Hispanic public. The fact that this was not being done suggests that the employers may have been unconcerned about the quality of service being offered to this population.

Kozinski rejected Reinhardt's solution as facile, claiming that it would lead to another problem:

> By deciding to speak another language during working hours, employees can limit who may qualify for supervisorial positions. If fluency in a second language is the *sine qua non* of supervisorial status, employees who are not bilingual, including other people of color, will be effectively eliminated from consideration for these coveted positions. (*Gutierrez*, 1988b: 1194)

This statement illustrates the fear that bilingualism engenders among those who are monolingual and have always assumed their right to power. But the fear is, essentially, baseless. It is unlikely that in any workplace monolingual speakers will be completely replaced by bilingual speakers; the power status quo does not undergo such drastic change. In this particular case, bilingualism would not be a prerequisite for the position of supervisor. There would have to be some supervisors capable of evaluating the work of clerks dealing with the Spanish-speaking public; monolingual English-speakers would have to yield their complete domination of this position. Also, if clerks are allowed to speak Spanish when not dealing with the public – that is, when engaged in routine chores such as filing papers –

there is no reason why their supervisors need to understand what they are saying. If there is an atmosphere of trust between supervisors and subordinates, if the language of workers is not automatically assumed to be of a suspicious nature, private conversations would remain just that: private.

The Alleged Divisiveness of Multilingualism

As we have seen before, a common theme of language restrictionists is the destructiveness and divisiveness of multilingualism. Nations that have both linguistically diverse populations and sociopolitical strife are cited as examples. Kozinski resorted to these same arguments in explaining his support for English-only work rules.

According to Kozinski, "as sad experience elsewhere has shown, language can be a potent source of racial and ethnic discrimination, exacerbating geographic, cultural, religious, ethnic and class divisions." One example is "the long-standing division between the French-speaking Walloons and the Flemish-speaking population of Belgium" (*Gutierrez*, 1988b: 1192). However, as with the other nations he mentions, this particular example does not hold up. Ironically, a footnote in Kosinski's text actually argues against the primacy of language in the conflict between French-speaking Belgians and Flemish-speaking Dutch.

Kozinski cited a Belgian writer, Pierre van den Berghe, who described how French-speakers looked down on the Flemish language as being uncultured and inferior. Van den Berghe recalled his physician grandfather, who "segregated his patients by class" (*Gutierrez*, 1988b: 1193, footnote 9). A maid was instructed to judge prospective patients through a basement window; those dressed modestly were directed to a sparse waiting room reserved for working-class patients, while those of better means were directed to the plush family parlor. As it turned out, the working-class patients were all speakers of Flemish, while the better-dressed were speakers of French. Kozinski explained, "Bigotry and class consciousness, manifestations of what [van den Berghe] termed this invidious bilingualism, bore great resemblance to attitudes reflected in the demeaning Jim Crow laws"(*Gutierrez*, 1988b: 1192, footnote 9), referring to past policies in the southern part of the United States that kept African Americans segregated from and in inferior status to whites.

But Kozinski seems to have it the wrong way around: invidious comparisons between the French and Flemish languages grew out of, rather than were the source of, bigotry and class consciousness. The doctor's maid judged people on their dress which, in this case, was a characteristic of class, as was language. Language is symbolic of the group of people who speak it; if that group is stigmatized by society, then its language is stigmatized by association. The use of more than one language in a society does not in itself cause divisiveness, just as the use of more than one language in a workplace does not automatically create disharmony.

Workplace Language Restrictions and the Law

These cases raise questions that are bound to be asked again and again in our increasingly multilingual society. What, if anything, justifies the implementation of English-only rules? Do such rules promote racial harmony or exacerbate existing racial tensions? If employers have the right to regulate the language use of their employees, how far can they go in controlling workers' private speech? The increased need for bilingual employees raises further issues. One is the feasibility of controlling when and where each of the languages may be used. A second, receiving increased attention lately, is whether and how to compensate those workers whose native languages are called on in their work (Fritsch, 1996; Fiagome, 1996).

In his decision, O'Scannlain pointed out that at present the law offers no discussion of English-only policies and whether or not they are presumed to be discriminatory. Also missing from the law is an understanding of what bilingualism is and what it is not. This is an area that the judicial system needs to define more clearly. Whether the EEOC guidelines are eventually encoded into law, or whether other laws are written, remains to be seen. It is likely that more of these cases will come to the attention of the public and the judicial system, and a more explicit picture of where the law stands will emerge.

In the meantime, it has become clear that official-English legislation is having an effect on the workplace, as described in Dicker (1998). Sklarewitz (1992) and D'O'Brian (1991) point to state official-English laws as influential in employers' decisions to implement English-only work rules, even though the laws do not legitimize such rules. According to Parliman and Shoeman, decisions that favor language restrictions suggest that "the courts are buying into the underlying premise of the English-only movement" (Parliman & Shoeman, 1994: 559). In analyzing the state of legal cases involving English-only rules, these authors see the English-only movement prevailing in the "trend toward greater judicial recognition of both employer prerogative and the rights of native English speakers and a corresponding diminished support for the claims of non-English-speaking employees" (Parliman & Shoeman, 1994: 564).

For its part, US English has responded by attempting to set private business in an adversarial position to the federal government and its powers of regulation. Mujica writes that "it is outrageous for 'Big Brother' Government to send federal agents out to dictate to small private businesses the languages in which their employees should operate." Finding in this situation another source of attack for official-English advocacy, he labels the EEOC's guidelines on English-only rules as a further example of "Federal bureaucrats ... actively using Americans' tax dollars to promote official multilingualism" (Mujica, 1997b: 1). However, since the EEOC is merely an advisory agency, there is no action that US English can take against it.

Evidence now exists that official-English laws are detrimental to workers who are not native speakers of English. Zavodny (1998) used data from the 1980 and 1990 Censuses to determine if state official-English laws have an effect on the income of men with limited-English proficiency. Comparing 14 states that passed such laws between 1980 and 1988 with the 35 states without such laws, she found that men in this category living in official-English states had lower annual earnings relative to their counter-parts in non-official-English states and relative to English-proficient workers in official-English states. These results were obtained while controlling for other factors, such as an increase in the number of limited-English proficient workers, out-migration from official-English states, prejudice towards minorities, and changes in the economic climate of the states. Zavodny (1998) points to the need for further investigation into the causes of the findings – for example, whether official-English states are more likely to have workplace English-only rules, and whether it is these rules that directly cause income disparity. Clearly, there is a need to monitor official-English laws in this way; evidence such as Zavodny's is a powerful weapon in proving the discriminatory effect of language restrictionism.

CONCLUSION

In this chapter we discussed the forces in the United States working against language restrictionism. We saw how Hawaii, Louisiana, New Mexico and Texas make official use of languages in addition to English. We described the challenge to official English presented by the commonwealth of Puerto Rico, a part of the United States with a largely monolingual-Spanish population. We reviewed the activities of groups around the country that have mobilized against official English. One successful legal challenge to state official English was described. Finally, we detailed the issues in two cases challenging English-only rules in the workplace, and discussed the link between employment difficulties facing language minorities and the passage of state official-English laws.

At this point in our discussion, it has become clear that, at many levels of American society, from the ordinary citizen to its elected representatives to the judges who interpret its laws, there is a profound lack of understanding of what language diversity is and what it can be. Americans tend to be rather inward-looking. They often fancy themselves superior to everyone else, the upholders of democratic ideals in the midst of a world that is often cruel and tyrannical; if this were not the case, why would so many leave their homes for America, often at great risk their own lives? But it may serve

Americans greatly if they did look beyond their borders to see how people in other nations live and, specifically, how they deal with language diversity in a positive and fulfilling manner. In doing so, they may be able to learn some valuable lessons, since it is probable that the United States will continue to be a society with many different languages for a long time to come.

CHAPTER 7

Lessons in Multilingualism Beyond the United States

INTRODUCTION

Most Americans accept the idea of the United States as a monolingual nation. There is some recognition of the presence of languages other than English, but English reigns as the one *de facto* official language. When we look outside the United States, however, we see that multilingualism is the more common linguistic condition.

Tove Skutnabb-Kangas writes that "the large majority of the world's states are *de facto* multilingual in the sense that several languages, native to the area, are spoken inside their borders" (Skutnabb-Kangas, 1990: 6). In Europe, only five states – Iceland, Liechtenstein, Monaco, Portugal, and San Marino – can be said to be monolingual. Roughly 6,700 oral languages are spoken today, divided among political states that number between 170 and 230 (Skutnabb-Kangas, 2000). This means that some countries have speakers of a great variety of languages; Nigeria, for instance, has over 500.

However, a small number of languages have prominent status in the world's nation states. In some cases one language functions as the *de facto* official language. In other cases, the government recognizes one or more languages as having a certain status. Recognition as an official language confers the highest status; recognition as a national language usually confers a somewhat lesser status; countries may also recognize regional languages. As Skutnabb-Kangas (1990) explains, in the multilingual countries of sub-Saharan Africa, official status is given to European languages, while indigenous languages are sometimes recognized as national languages. Skutnabb-Kangas (2000) calculates that English is an official language in over 70 countries, French in 25, Spanish in 18, Arabic in 19,

Portuguese and German in 6, and Malay, Chinese, and Tamil in 3. Languages that are given status by the government are those that are widely used in institutions and widely taught in schools. The extent to which the speakers of other languages are aided in using and disseminating their languages and teaching them to their children varies widely; lack of such support may exacerbate internal political and social conflicts.

In this chapter, we will examine how several countries deal with multilingualism. First we will look at two examples of nations that designate more than one official language: Canada and Switzerland. Then, we will consider the revival of regional languages in Western Europe and the case of language diversity in India. In doing so, we will be able to respond to the frequent argument of the official-English movement that bilingualism or multilingualism is destructive to the functioning of a nation. Instead, our examination will show how the fostering of more than one language leads to greater national harmony. This analysis of multilingualism in other countries holds lessons for the United States in its own struggle to address the needs of language minorities.

THE QUESTION OF LANGUAGE IN CANADA

Perhaps because of its proximity to the United States, Canada is often cited by American language restrictionists as an example of the dangers of bilingualism. The late S.I. Hayakawa, a US senator and leader of the modern official-English movement, wrote the following, referring to the French-Canadian independence movement in Quebec:

> For the first time in our history, our nation is faced with the possibility of the kind of linguistic division that has torn apart Canada in recent years.... Political differences become hardened and made immeasurably more difficult to resolve when they are accompanied by differences of language – and therefore conflicts of ethnic pride. (Hayakawa, 1985: 99–100)

Linda Chavez, former president of US English, writes:

> The real fear of many Americans is that Hispanics will one day be a group large and powerful enough to insist that the United States adopt a bilingual policy. That fear is not so far-fetched, as Canada's example demonstrates. French-Canadians make up only about one-quarter of the Canadian population, but they have succeeded in forcing the entire country to recognize and use French as an official language.... Will something similar happen with Spanish, when nearly one-third of the US population is Hispanic? The mere possibility drives some Americans to make sure that day does not come. (Chavez, 1991a: 88–89)

Hayakawa errs in his assessment of the secessionist movement in Quebec. Language is an important issue, but not in the way he suggests. It is not linguistic diversity that has contributed to the movement, but disregard for the linguistic rights of French-speaking people. Hayakawa insinuates that were it not for linguistic and ethnic differences, political differences would be easier to resolve. However, such differences cannot be wished away. In Quebec, ethnicity and language have been the characteristics that determine who has access to power and status and who does not. Diversity does not automatically cause divisiveness, but differences within a population may be used to create and maintain political inequity.

The kind of fear that Chavez seeks to inflame with her statement is unwarranted. In reality, French Canadians did not force bilingualism on their English-speaking compatriots. Canada was created as a bilingual/ bicultural state. Despite this designation, the federal government and its agencies outside Quebec are still largely monolingual in English. The analogy between French Canadians and Hispanics in the United States is therefore spurious. Chavez is blatantly feeding on anti-Hispanic sentiments that have intensified with the growth of this population in American society. She portrays the official-English movement as a means of neutralizing the threat that Hispanics pose to those who now hold power.

Statements such as the ones above, seeking superficial and emotional analogies to the current situation in the United States, defy the complexity behind the language question in Canada. In the following pages we will explore the issue in greater depth, so that we can gain some insight into how Canada has attempted to deal with language diversity.

The History of Pluralism in Canada

Like the United States, Canada is a country long populated by outsiders, as described by Kilbourn (1989). Its original inhabitants fought a losing war for survival against incoming waves of Europeans. The first of these were Norsemen, who settled Newfoundland around 1000. In the fifteenth century, Basque and Portuguese fisherman who worked the Great Banks decided to set down roots. French and Italian explorers landed in Canada in the 1500s, eventually establishing permanent settlements such as Quebec in the early 1600s. Acadians, Germans, and Highlanders established isolated ethnic communities on the Atlantic Coast. Canada tended to attract persecuted people: from the colonies to the south, Pennsylvania Dutch, poor farmers and Indians; from the British Isles, exiles driven out by poverty. American slaves escaping via the Underground Railroad often sought refuge in Canada as well.

This tradition continued into the twentieth century, with Eastern European Jews, Ukrainians, Armenians, Hungarians, Czechs, Ugandans, Vietnamese, Sikhs, Tamils, and Latin Americans seeking a better life in

Canada. In the latter part of the century, the largest number of immigrants tended to be from the poorer regions of Italy, Greece, Portugal, and the West Indies. But more prosperous immigrants came as well: from Great Britain, the United States, northern Europe, Hong Kong, Taiwan, and India.

Because of the vastness of Canada, early settlers could live among people of their own language and culture with no need to communicate with others of a different heritage. Kilbourn writes:

> To a seventeenth- or even an early nineteenth-century observer, it would have seemed preposterous that someday Canada's separated and largely uninhabited sea coasts, river valleys, lake shores, forests, and plains would become a single geographical expression, let alone one political entity. Even after it was all nominally organized under one government between 1867 and 1873, with the high arctic islands and Newfoundland added later, this second largest country on earth was still not a nation in either the European or the American sense of the word. (Kilbourn, 1989: 8)

This geographical fact, along with the heterogeneous nature of Canada's population, has made it difficult to define what it means to be Canadian. Kilbourn continues:

> Its people are not of one predominant race or culture, or identifiable by a common history, language or ideology. One may speak almost any tongue with any accent and belong to any race, and still plausibly be Canadian. The Canadian passport was for many years the one international racketeers and spies favored most for forgery. There could have been no such thing as an Un-Canadian Activities Committee. (Kilbourn, 1989: 8)

Graubard concurs:

> As the country has become increasingly multiethnic and multiracial, there has been little propensity to shed certain of these identities, to value them less. The melting-pot process, if it remains salient for the United States – a disputable proposition to some – has little relevance to Canada, where ethnicity remains a formidable social force. (Graubard, 1989: vii)

According to Kilbourn (1989), the early history of the nation laid the basis for the establishment of a multinational state characterized by social and political equality. The creation of the confederacy, mentioned above in Kilbourn's quote, was not an easy one. Retired British regiments had settled along the shores of the St Lawrence and eastern Lake Ontario according to their cultural groups and in isolation from each other: Gaelic-speaking Catholic Highlanders, Presbyterian Scots, Lowlanders, German Lutherans, and German Catholics. The provinces on the Atlantic each had distinctive characteristics: Newfoundland's settlers were largely from Ireland and the English West Country; Nova Scotia's people came from Scotland and New England. In addition, the Atlantic provinces differed from the interior provinces of Quebec and Ontario. None of these colonies were much in favor of confederation. The impetus for confederation, however, came from leaders in Toronto and Montreal, who needed a powerful central government in order to compete economically with the United States. Also, the British government was eager to rid itself of the burden of colonial administration and defense.

Kilbourn (1989) notes that it has taken a long time for Canada to acquire the attributes of a nation. Its constitution was sent from the British Parliament only in 1982. However, the document has a unique characteristic that illustrates the country's dedication to multinational liberal democracy: along with insuring individual rights, it also established the collective rights of its two founding peoples – the British and the French – to special linguistic and cultural status. Also acknowledged are the rights of native peoples, women, and the disabled, and the multicultural aspect of Canadian society.

Acknowledgment of Canada's native peoples, or Aboriginals, was a decidedly belated step. Like the United States, the original inhabitants of Canada were a large and varied population; over sixty languages and eleven language families have been identified. As Fettes (1998) explains, the federal government instituted the Indian Act to control all aspects of Aboriginal life. Beginning in the mid-nineteenth century, Aboriginal languages were excluded from Canadian schools and public life. As in the United States, children were separated from their parents and put into boarding schools, where they were forced to learn English. This practice was abandoned in the 1960s, but the effect on language loss was extensive. An attempt to turn around the precipitous decline of Aboriginal languages and cultures came with the Trudeau government of the late 1960s and early 1970s, which framed its policy as "multiculturalism in a bilingual framework." This began a period of experimentation with bilingual and bicultural education, which was met with varying degrees of success for the wide range of Aboriginal languages.

As we can see, dealing with linguistic diversity has not been easy for Canada. We now turn to the struggle that has engaged the province of Quebec. We will see that, despite the insistence of language-restrictionist proponents in the United States, efforts to protect the French-Canadian language and culture have not led to divisiveness. Instead, it has been the erosion of French-Canadian identity and the inability of the group to secure for itself a valued status in Quebec society that led some Québécois to demand separation from Canada.

The Independence Movement in Quebec

Coleman (1984) identifies the roots of Quebec's independence movement in the transfer of the colony of New France from the French to the British in 1763. Under French rule, French Canadians had dominated the fur trade and held important positions in the colony's government. Under British rule, they were stripped of both economic and political power and, turning to the poorly-compensated vocation of agriculture, fell into a position of dependency on British North America. This dependent status continued as Quebec's economy was integrated into that of industrialized North America, leading to an erosion of the French Canadian identity and a sense of disempowerment that have persisted.

Coleman (1984) insists that to understand how Quebec arrived at this state, it is important to understand the structure of traditional, agricultural Quebec society; once this is explained, one can see how the institutions that dominated this society no longer served those in the growing industrial sector. The dominant influence in agricultural Quebec was the Roman Catholic Church. In rural French Canada, Catholicism was closely identified with being French Canadian. Traditional intellectuals believed that religion gave a culture shape, that it was the inspiration behind the rules of everyday life. The Church controlled all aspects of life. One of its roles was to make sure that people had food and shelter; without these basics, the faithful could not receive the grace of God. So, the Church controlled all social-welfare institutions, such as charities, hospitals, and orphanages. To some extent, as the Québécois moved into the industrial sector, the Church also encouraged activities to improve their living and working conditions, such as the formation of unions and housing cooperatives.

A second role of the Church was to teach the truth. All education was under its supervision, and all subject matter was presented from a Christian viewpoint. The Church believed that advanced education was necessary only for the social elite. The children of this class entered what were called "classical colleges," which offered a very traditional curriculum and were the main access route to university.

Third, the Church considered itself the final arbiter of what was good and what was evil in society. It intervened often in matters not only religious but political and literary as well. The Church saw itself as the upholder of the French-Canadian values of communalism and spiritualism.

Fourth, in controlling all aspects of French-Canadian life, the Church was also the repository and defender of the French-Canadian language. Through the use of the language in religious services, in education, and in all the institutions people turned to for sustenance, the Church preserved the language through which French-Canadian culture was expressed, and which would become the defining characteristic of the people.

As Coleman (1984) describes, by the 1940s, large numbers of people in Quebec had turned to industrial jobs in mining and manufacturing, more lucrative areas of work than farming. The circumstances of life in urban Quebec differed greatly from those in the rural regions; the traditional structure of French-Canadian society was unsuited for this new way of life. Urban existence created health and social problems that the Church could not deal with. The education system, with its traditional, religious perspective, and its restriction of higher learning to the elite, was not suited to prepare large numbers of workers for skilled, technical jobs. Those in the industrial sector were indoctrinated into a set of values emphasizing individualism and materialism, in contrast to the communalist, spiritualist values upheld by the Church. In the industrial workplace, French was the language of those at the bottom; English was the medium of communication between worker and management and among those in managerial positions, and it was the language of the new technology. English dominated in government as well. As a result, French was a language of decreasing value in the new, modern society, and those who did not know English had little hope of upward socioeconomic mobility. In addition, post-World War II refugees settling in Quebec decreased the proportion of native Francophones in the province. These refugees, recognizing the socioeconomic importance of English, often preferred to place their children in English schools rather than in French schools.

The Québécois agreed that a change was in order. In 1960, the *Parti libéral* was voted into power, backed by organized labor, the Francophone business class, and some members of the middle-class intelligentsia, three groups that had forged together a new vision of Quebec. Writes Coleman, "'The atmosphere in Quebec's Francophone community in the early 1960s, the feeling that a Quiet Revolution was taking place, rested on a consensus on how to proceed in economic, educational, social, and cultural policy" (Coleman, 1984: 215). However, despite the high hopes of its designers, the Quiet Revolution ended in disappointment, for the reasons discussed below.

First, the government failed to carry out a systematic plan that would lead to an independent Francophone economy. It was hoped that the state would take actions to gain control of Quebec's natural resources and create a Quebec-centered industry for processing these materials, to replace the existing practice of shipping raw materials out of the province; this was never carried out. While the state did help the Francophone business class to expand, the benefits of this expansion did not reach the community as a whole; the economy continued to be unstable, and workers were subjected to layoffs and uncertain job prospects. Francophone businesses were never able to compete with larger Canadian and United States corporations; government intervention helped them join into partnerships with these corporations, but the larger firms maintained their economic power and control.

This uneven balance of power made it more difficult for Quebec to sustain its distinct culture. Francophone businesses that prospered looked outside Quebec for an expanded market, losing interest in an exclusively French-Canadian consumer market. Likewise, workers seeking to improve their job status in North American-led companies found it helpful to adopt the values of North American culture. Middle-class French Canadians (journalists, academics, teachers, technical professionals) found themselves using more English than French in their work; French remained a second-class language, and Francophones were blocked from career advancement.

Second, changes in education added to rather than alleviated this trend. The state took over all aspects of education except religious instruction, which was left in the hands of the Church. The government was concerned largely with educating skilled manpower for the new capitalist economy, giving little thought to the effect of this orientation on Francophone culture. Schooling beyond the elementary level was opened up to everyone. New secondary schools offered a general education program for all students and two special tracks: an academic stream for those preparing to go to college, and a commercial and vocational stream for others. Post-secondary institutes provided further instruction, also in two tracks: a technical and general education track for pre-university students, and an advanced technical track for others. The *Université du Québec* was established, with campuses in outlying regions.

These changes brought education in Quebec more in line with other Canadian and United States schools. It also heightened a feeling of anxiety that had been growing among the middle class. Coleman describes this feeling as "a sense of loss ... a sense that old cultural values had been discarded and that no new values unique to French-Canadian society and derived from its history had been put in their place" (Coleman, 1984: 181). In addition, the new system did little to change Quebec's social structure. The lower class was largely tracked into vocational fields, while the middle and upper classes were prepared for university; private schools continued to be the province of the elite and were subsidized by the state. Organized labor complained that Quebec's educational reforms failed to support their concept of a pluralistic society with the Francophone community at its head.

Third, in the 1940s and 50s, the inability of Catholic health and social services agencies to address the needs of Quebec's growing population of industrial workers, and the desire of national leaders to create a greater sense of Canadian unity, led to a gradual takeover of these areas by the federal government. The Québécois were thus integrated into a system that offered social security benefits, a national health program, old age security, and unemployment assistance. The federal government left to the provinces those areas of social welfare thought not to be necessary for the regulation of the national economy, such as the administration of hospitals, asylums, and orphanages. Quebec created uniform standards and supervisory bodies to administer these institutions, and the resulting system differed little from those in North America in general. It lacked the distinct philosophical and cultural ethos of French Canada which had marked social service agencies when they were under the aegis of the Church.

Fourth, in the 1960s, the French language was elevated as the primary characteristic of the French-Canadian identity. The Quebec government initiated a number of policies meant to revive the floundering status of the language. All private companies and local and provincial government agencies were required to institute francization programs that would make French the language of communication at all levels of employment. Efforts were made to bring the Quebec variety of French closer to the international standard of French, and to expand the economic and technical lexicons that would allow French to be the language of business- and industry-related communication. These steps were intended to remove the linguistic barriers that had prevented French Canadians from pursuing high-level jobs. Educational policy made it imperative for all children to learn French, whether they attended English-language or French-language schools. Quebec was made to look in all respects like a monolingual province: all government and business activity, even in English-speaking communities, was carried on in French; an advertising campaign extolled the francization process and tried to convince all Québécois of the inevitability of monolingualism. Nationally, the federal government passed the Official Languages Act in 1969, giving English and French equal status and encouraging government agencies to offer bilingual services.

The effect of these policies was the opposite of what their planners had intended. Coleman points out that, while "policies designed to reinforce the use of [the French] language might ... strengthen a distinctive culture" and help counter the effects of the economic, social, and educational reforms we have described, they were in actuality "adjuncts to the policies of economic development ... facilitating greater integration of Quebec's Francophone community into the North American economy and culture" (Coleman, 1984: 184). As a result of these language policies, the Francophone business class was allowed to grow, but it grew by becoming a part of rather than by competing with the larger, Anglophone capitalist class of the United States and the rest of Canada. With all businesses in Quebec operating in the French language, the line between foreign-controlled and Francophone-controlled enterprises was blurred, weakening the nationalist struggle against foreign-business domination.

As all residents of Quebec, regardless of their heritage, were educated similarly, worked together in French, and were served by the same institutions, the distinctiveness of the French-Canadian culture weakened, and the question of who was and who was not French Canadian intensified. The standardization and modernization of French led to a growing chasm between the new, formal language and the older, informal language of tradition, further diminishing the role of French in preserving a distinctive French-Canadian culture. In addition, despite the Official Languages Act, French gained little status nationally; while federal agencies operating in the province became bilingual, such services were rarer outside Quebec.

The move in the direction of French monolingualism also left a great deal of bitterness among native speakers of English. This population had to fight harder than ever for the right to educate its children in English. The people also saw their ability to function publicly in their native language severely curtailed.

Thus, the reforms that had promised the creation of an independent and culturally intact Francophone society had failed, and the three sectors of society that had supported these reforms – organized labor, the Francophone business class, and members of the middle-class intelligentsia – were greatly disappointed. Disillusioned voices from these three camps gave birth to the independence movement in the late 1960s and sustained its growth in the 1970s. The policies of Quebec's government in the succeeding decades continued to move the province toward integration into the North American economy, and even the leading independence party backed away from its demands for a combined political and economic independence. What continues to fuel the independence movement, according to Coleman, is the loss of "that inner quality of what it means to be a Québécois ... a gnawing fear that this feeling, this sense of self, might soon no longer be passed on to the young because the institutional framework within which the young live will contradict and undermine that inner spirit" (Coleman, 1984: 227).

The Language Issue Today

In many respects, Quebec is a less conflicted place than it used to be. Popular support for secession is at 39%, a new low, and the French language appears to be firmly entrenched as 83% of the population (six million people) speak French (Brooke, 2000). The robust status of French in Quebec has encouraged foreign-language educators to send students there to study French at university language immersion programs and summer language camps, as a more convenient and affordable alternative to France. The American Association of Teachers of French now alternates its annual meetings between France and Quebec (Brooke, 1999). However, French nationalists insist that the linguistic gains made in the province are fragile, and that English still looms as a significant threat. The native French-speaking population has been eroded by a decreasing birth rate, and

Quebec's weight in Canada's total population has slipped from one-third at the time of confederation to one-quarter. To shore up the population, provincial leaders proposed expanding the number of immigrants from French-speaking nations by almost 50% from 2000 to 2003 (Brooke, 2000).

Quebec's leaders continue to be vigilant in their efforts to bolster the economic, political, and social status of the French language. In the winter of 2000, they announced their support for a proposal to make Ottawa, the nation's capital in the province of Ontario, a bilingual city under a consolidation plan to take effect in January 2001. Ontario's premier, Mike Harris, rejected the proposal. Although this angered the Québécois, they eventually let go of their opposition to Harris' decision. Despite their fervor, they no doubt knew that, if Ottawa, with a French-speaking population of 15%, were to be made bilingual, Canadians outside Quebec could then insist that Montreal, with an English-speaking population of 17%, follow suit (Brooke, 2000).

To a large extent, Quebec has remained economically dependent on an Anglophone economy. The dealings in the early 1990s between the province and a US chain of superstores, Wal-Mart, serve as an apt example. Wal-Mart made its first blunder when its stores in New York mailed English-language circulars to residents of Quebec. Then the chain sent an English-language memo from its Toronto headquarters to 750 Quebec-based managers, requiring them to work 12 extra hours a week without a salary increase. Wal-Mart apologized for its lack of cultural sensitivity, but the president of Quebec's trade-union federation called the chain "the model of savage capitalism." A former Member of Parliament criticized this statement, denouncing its militant rhetoric from the 1970s, and asked, "Is this any way to welcome foreign investors to Quebec?" (Chipello, 1994: B9). One can easily see that what happened was much more than an example of cultural ignorance. The language insult was the more overt one. The more subtle insult was the fact that Quebec workers were still under the thumb of a non-Francophone enterprise. The incident underscores Quebec's failure to achieve economic independence.

In a further challenge to Anglophone corporate domination, Quebec has battled non-Canadian companies that sell their products in the province. In 1999, Quebec threatened to pull Nintendo and Sony video games from store shelves for failing to comply with the Charter of the French Language, which stipulates that all game products should have French-language packaging and include French-language warranties and instructions. In January 2000, an agreement was reached in which the companies agreed to put French-language manuals and warranties in all games sold in the province (Dillich, 2000). At that time, Quebec also succeeded in putting French-language Pokémon cards in the hands of its Francophone children (Brooke, 2000).

The provincial government remains vigilant in its monitoring of Quebec-based businesses, but has at times been forced to ease up on its imposition of French monolingualism. One issue that gained wide attention was that of the language of shop signs. In 1977, a bill was passed banning all publicly-placed signs that were in languages other than French. Eleven years later, the Canadian Supreme Court found the law unconstitutional. However, the Quebec government found a loophole, allowing it to demand that external signs be in French; signs inside establishments could be in other languages, but the French signs had to be larger. This law enraged non-Francophones. As in the issue of Ottawa's bilingualism, they asked why the rest of Canada should be held to function bilingually, while Quebec remained monolingual (Walsh, 1992). One angry Anglophone took the issue to the United Nations Commission on Human Rights, which ruled that the law violated its International Covenant on Civil and Political Rights (*The New York Times*, 1993c). In response, a new bill was introduced allowing stores to display non-French signs, as long as larger, French signs were displayed alongside them. There was little opposition to this bill, with most Francophones agreeing that the compromise was necessary for the sake of social cohesion (*The Economist*, 1993).

Another example of a case in which in the provincial government appeared to lack sufficient restraint involved an Internet web site created by the *Office de la langue française*. The web site contains a blacklist of all the companies not in compliance with the law requiring all businesses with at least 50 employees to obtain a certificate attesting to the use of French in the workplace. In early 2000, the agency was accused of being overzealous, since some of the businesses listed were in the process of acquiring the certificate, and some did not know that they had been listed. Many decried the unnecessary public humiliation that these businesses suffered (Peritz, 2000).

Quebec's fervent pursuit of protecting the French language overreached once again in the spring of 2000. When Air France announced a new policy requiring its pilots to speak English with air traffic controllers at Charles de Gaulle Airport in Paris, in the interests of more accurate communication, French nationalist leaders in Quebec registered their disapproval. Louise Beaudoin, the *Parti québécois'* international relations minister, said, "The imperialism of the English language has to have its limits somewhere. If France surrenders, well, just imagine us" (cited in Fotheringham, 2000). She also noted the growing use of English in France, and suggested that France join forces with Quebec in stemming the domination of English over French (Johnson, 2000).

These comments were met with some derision. As Fotheringham (2000) explains, while Ottawa's airport allows pilots to communicate either in English or French, it is a relatively small operation and cannot be compared to the airport in Paris, which must deal with airlines from all over the world. For the sake of convenience and efficiency, it is not surprising that English has become the lingua franca of international air traffic control. Fotheringham responds wth skepticism to Beaudoin's comments about the need to fight English imperialism; "Coca-colonization," he contends, "is unstoppable." Johnson (2000) points out that, given the differences between the French spoken in Quebec and the French spoken in France, French men and women would find the idea of Québécois helping them preserve the purity of French rather laughable. Johnson (2000) also points out that many Asian countries are sending their young people to Canada to acquaint them with the English language and North American tastes; when they return, they will be able to help Asian businesses market their products to the US and Canada. As the economic well-being of Quebec rests on its ability to sell its products to English-speakers in Canada and elsewhere, Johnson (2000) recommends that the Québécois spend less time and effort worrying about French and more of the same learning English. While these comments seem to be devoid of any sensitivity to the situation Québécois that face in trying to protect their language against the all-powerful English, they do have some validity.

In addition to the criticism that French nationalists receive from outside, they must also contend with criticism from within. The move toward French monolingualism has created a kind of resistance that, ironically, once came from the Francophone community itself: those whose native languages are not French must fight for the right to use them. For English-speakers, this resistance has historical roots, but its activists have not been able to rest, continuing the fight for the right to English-language education, libraries, and health services (Allen, 1991).

Polls have shown that many Anglophones are uncertain whether they will stay in Quebec, regardless of the political status of the province. Because the Francophone community has a stake in keeping English-speakers in Quebec, they have made efforts to make them feel more welcome. One program was initiated to hire more Anglophones in civil-service positions; in the early 1990s, Anglophones held less than 1% of these jobs at the same time that they constituted 12% of the population (Came, 1991b: 11). Just as language was not the only issue for Francophones in the 1940s and 50s, language is not the only issue for Anglophones today.

Other voices that have joined the protest against French monolingualism come from the one out of five residents of Quebec who are "allophones," native speakers of some 35 languages that are neither English nor French. These residents accept the need to learn and use French, but possess a sense of loyalty to a united Canada that aligns them more closely to Anglophones than to Francophones. Even so, allophones have come to realize the need to defend their own interests. While, like many English-speakers, they are opposed to separatism, they have formed a political coalition to prevent the debate from becoming a polarized, Francophone–Anglophone issue. The groups that have banded together include the Hellenic Congress of Quebec, and the Quebec wings of both the Canadian Jewish Congress and the National Congress of Italian-Canadians (Came, 1991a).

In other parts of the country that also have Francophone communities, the language question is just as complex. Heller's (1994) description of the language situation of Franco-Ontarians shows that this Francophone community faces issues that are both similar to and different from those of the Québécois. The nationalist movement in Quebec affected the rest of Canada by raising the status of French in the eyes of the entire society. Both federal and provincial governments have been obligated to recruit greater numbers of bilingual civil servants, and non-Francophones – including Anglophones, immigrants, and Native Americans – have become more interested in acquiring French. According to Heller (1994), for the Franco-Ontarians, this has created a problem similar to that faced by the Québécois: how to define who belongs and who doesn't belong to the community of Francophones. In addition, bilingualism was historically the terrain of Francophones, their path to power. Now, with more people becoming bilingual, the advantages gained from bilingualism are available to a wider population. As Heller puts it, French and English are "forms of symbolic capital" (Heller, 1994: 12) whose relative value has shifted with the increased prestige of French; now, knowledge of both languages can be exchanged for coveted jobs, status, and power.

This can be seen in particular in the Ontario educational system. Heller (1994) explains that Franco-Ontarian parents are no longer the only ones interested in putting their children into French-language schools. Aside from speakers of other languages, the student population now includes immigrant children from countries where French is a second official language, the language of instruction, or the language of wide communication, as well as Francophone children from other parts of Canada. Since the Franco-Ontarian community has traditionally viewed control of these schools as an important source of empowerment, the presence of these other groups is not always welcome. It also creates an atmosphere in which a number of languages and a number of varieties of French compete for attention and status. The teachers and the administration control which variety of French is the conduit of knowledge; the students use their choice of language or language variety to include or exclude classmates from their friendship networks.

In several very important ways, however, Franco-Ontarians differ from Francophone Québécois. Heller (1994) points out that Franco-Ontarians have never had, nor expect to have, dominant political or economic control; they are dependent on Anglophone institutions. While the Québécois invested themselves in French monolingualism, Franco-Ontarians have acknowledged the necessity of being bilingual. They pursue different avenues in adjusting to their minority status: activism for the Francophone cause, in the style of Québécois nationalism; acceptance of Anglophone domination while quietly pushing for Francophone rights in specific situations; or total assimilation. But generally they all recognize bilingualism as the route to "full and free entry into provincial, national and indeed international economic and political networks" (Heller, 1994: 22).

In addition, Franco-Ontarians have developed their own, unique form of the language. As Moss (2000) explains, during the Quiet Revolution, French nationalists in Quebec literally turned their backs on their French compatriots outside the province, leading to the creation of separate, subnational ethnolinguistic identities among these groups. In Ontario, English is the language of work, English and standard French are the languages of education and official bilingualism, and the Franco-Ontarian dialect serves as the means of expression of the Franco-Ontarian identity. This identity is one of secondary status and inferiority, as seen from both outside and inside the group; it is an identity in which "the collective sense of dispossession, exile, or deracination is constant" (Moss, 2000: 589). As Franco-Ontarians attempt to hold on to their cultural identity in the face of the constant threat of Anglo assimilation, the voices coming from fiction and drama are often described as angry, impotent, violent, blasphemous, scatological, and antisocial.

According to Moss, the Franco-Ontarian dialect itself, as it is manifested in art, reflects the nature of a group caught between two cultures and languages. The points at which it differs from other varieties of French are often the result of the transfer of English grammar and syntax. Code-switching between French and English is common, and English trade names often pop up as reminders of Anglo economic domination. Profanity and vulgarity, however, are usually expressed in French. Common themes found in Franco-Ontarian theater are poverty, family dysfunction, alienation and insecurity. In these dramas, characters sometimes express frustration at their inability to express themselves in either standard English or standard French.

Thus, while bilingualism is the only way that Francophones outside Quebec can survive, it presents problems of identity for the community. Because the community is marginalized, its language, which combines English and French, is marginalized as well. It has come to represent people who are downtrodden and second-class; as Moss explains, educated Francophones often hyper-correct their French in order to distinguish it from Franco-Ontarian. In the past three decades, Franco-Ontarian drama, a reflection of the community, "has often been an expression of collective dispossession and linguistic minorization combined with a protest against social, economic, political, and intellectual elites" (Moss, 2000: 611).

Meanwhile, official bilingualism in Ontario, as in other parts of Anglophone Canada, is limited. Francophones have the right to ask for services in French; in actuality, these services are minimal, and English is the dominant language of public interaction. As a consequence, Franco-Ontarians continue to struggle with the problem of how to participate fully in an Anglophone-controlled society while maintaining their Francophone identity and their ability to define and accomplish their own goals. As Heller walks the multilingual streets of Toronto, she notes that "somewhere in this maze of languages, French is trying to find its place" (Heller, 1994: 223)

In many parts of Canada, there has been a decline in support for federally sanctioned bilingualism. Two reasons cited are the costs of implementing the law and the contradictory monolingual policy of Quebec. The third is the growing political voice of those whose mother tongues are neither English nor French, which has posed a formidable challenge to the concept of a bicultural Canada. There is disagreement as to whether bilingualism would survive in the provinces without a federal mandate. Minority-group members tend to think that it wouldn't. A long-time advocate for English-language services in Quebec insists, "Losing bilingualism would be devastating to us" (cited in Allen, 1991: 16). New Brunswick, where one-third of the population consists of French-speaking Acadians, is Canada's only officially bilingual province; this status has insured Acadian control over French-language education and access to a wide range of government services in French. Notes one Acadian resident, "Without bilingualism, our culture will not survive" (cited in DeMont, 1991: 19).

One battle that minority-French populations have been fighting, and in some cases winning, is the right to French-language education for their children. Canada's 1982 Charter of Rights and Freedoms declares that English-speaking and French-speaking children have a constitutional right to be educated in their own language in communities "where numbers warrant." While this is an inherently ambiguous statement, Francophone communities have pushed the government to recognize this right in spite of their small size. In 1997, the 600 French-speaking citizens of St Claude in Manitoba decided to create their own French-language school. Initially, teachers worked for free, but the community soon sued to have the province recognize its school as part of the French School Division and to get appropriate funding. In January 2000, the Supreme Court of Canada ordered Prince Edward Island to build a French-language school for its Francophone community of Summerside. Recognizing the forces of Anglophone assimilation that the small community faced, the Court declared that "the school is the single most important institution for the survival of the official language minority" (Walker, 2000).

Despite the somewhat flagging national interest in official bilingualism, the government has maintained its support of English–French bilingualism through education. In 1999, Ottawa increased its annual budget for official-language education by $50 million, to $219 million. It now requires all provinces to develop formal action plans for official-language education, and aims by 2010 to have half of all teenagers graduating from high school effectively bilingual. In April 2000, the government sponsored a "French for the Future" conference, a multi-city event promoting the career advantages of bilingualism (Schofield, 2000).

French immersion programs now compete with other options, as some school districts offer instruction in a number of different languages. Interest in immersion has slumped in some provinces, but is growing in others. In the provinces where it is popular, it has gained a reputation for offering a superior overall education in addition to the promise of better employment that is attached to knowing French. In New Brunswick, which has the highest percentage of students in French immersion outside Quebec, immersion students consistently score higher on standardized tests than students in other programs. Some Canadians complain that immersion draws the best and wealthiest students away from English-language schools, even though immersion is usually federally funded, and that it has created an extensive academic divide in the nation. However, others contend that immersion instruction should be praised rather than criticized for its success (Schofield, 2000).

In the meantime, the struggle between English and French in Canada has distracted the country from dealing with the issue of Aboriginal languages and, according to Fettes (1998), has constrained the development of a more comprehensive approach to language issues. Norris (1998) reports that Aboriginal languages are now the most endangered in the world. Reviving and ensuring the continued development of these languages is fraught with challenges. Fettes (1998) points to the wide variation in these languages in linguistic aspects, size, distribution, vitality, and degree of literacy. For example, the three largest language families represent 93% of people claiming Aboriginal mother tongues, while the eight others represent 7%. In the former category, 147,000 people claim mother tongue languages in the Algonquian family; in the latter category, 145 speakers claim Tlingit family languages. There are also individual languages outside any of the 11 families; Malecite has 660 speakers (Norris, 1998). The question of whether to "modernize" the languages in order to make them translatable into English is difficult to resolve. Also, distributing resources where they are needed is a challenging task, given the fact that a language may be robust in one area but in danger of extinction in another (Fettes, 1998).

Recent statistics show the extent of language loss, but also offer some hope. In general, the number of people speaking Aboriginal languages at home is decreasing, and the age of these speakers is increasing. As young people leave their reservations, they tend to assimilate to English and lose their Aboriginal languages. However, in some small mother-tongue language populations, members of the younger generation are learning their ancestral Aboriginal languages in school as second languages. Fettes (1998) reports that, of the one million Canadians of Aboriginal descent, more than half of them express feelings of attachment to their ancestral language, even if they don't speak it. Also, the 1991 Aboriginal Peoples' Survey found a high level of interest among adults in either re-learning the mother tongues they have lost or learning their mother tongues as a second language (Norris, 1998).

Years of federal policies regarding the revival of Aboriginal languages have yielded mixed results, but do point to some tactics that are more successful than others. Fettes (1998) contrasts the policies in two different parts of the country. Under the Official Languages Act for the Northwest Territories, passed in 1984, Aboriginal languages were to be taught as second languages in the first three years of school, with no instruction required after the second grade; more inclusive use of native languages was introduced later. While public services in the native languages are supposed to be offered, many services are not publicized and the government often fails to spend all the funds allotted for this purpose. Services are based on the model of official language policy for French and English, with a focus on written standard language; Aboriginal languages with no or limited written form are at a disadvantage. Finally, implementation of programs have remained federally controlled; the promise of the creation of regional advisory councils has not been met.

In contrast to this top-down approach, Aboriginal language policy in the Yukon is a model of local control. Each First Nation is responsible for its own language program, with the goal of long-term sustainability. School instruction is not considered sufficient to attain this goal; home and community use of the language is essential. In the Yukon, local communities engage in activities to preserve the oral and written forms of their languages. Oral histories, songs, legends, and music are recorded. The communities produce language promotion materials such as calendars and genealogy booklets, as well as radio and television programs to promote pride in language and culture. Although this policy tends to lack political clout and its projects are often susceptible to government cuts, this approach to language revitalization seems to be the more successful one. It fits in with the recent federal decision to dismantle the Indian Act and transfer control over issues of governance, education, and culture to Aboriginal political institutions, control that is sometimes shared with provincial governments. As First Nations move toward self-government, it remains to be seen how their language rights issues will be played out on the national scene. Fettes maintains that Canada needs to question "the assumptions behind the present linguistic regime ... with its implicit imposition of functional monolingualism on the greater part of the population" (Fettes, 1998: 147). Restating the old Trudeau policy, Fettes believes that it is necessary for the country to move toward a policy of "multiculturalism in a multilingual framework" (Fettes, 1998: 147). Such a framework would have to include not only Aboriginal Canadians, but also Canadian immigrants whose languages are neither English nor French.

Lessons for the United States

As neighbors, Canada and the United States have some experiences in common; Schmidt (1998), however, sees these as mere surface similarities. The original territories were settled by competing colonial powers (Britain and France in Canada, Britain and Spain in the United States) that left different cultural, social, and political legacies. The subordinated communities experienced conquest by the dominant groups as a central historical reality, and this subordination resulted in nationalist movements in the 1960s, the key goals of which were linguistic and cultural preservation. National debates centered on official language policy, education policy for minority-language children, and linguistic access to political and civil rights. At both the federal and local levels of government, the key issue became how to achieve equality for all groups while maintaining a sense of national unity.

According to Schmidt (1998), the differences between Canada and the United States are much deeper than the similarities. The two countries took very different routes in dealing with heterogeneous populations (with the exception of their policies towards Native Americans; both supported the destruction of these cultures and only came around to championing their cause when they were near extinction). Canada settled on a pluralist approach, considered to be a moderate solution, while rejecting assimilation as an extreme and politically suicidal alternative. The United States chose assimilation as its preferred policy; pluralism has been viewed by many in this country as potentially dangerous, and those espousing pluralism have been consistently put on the defensive. Distinct histories underlie these decisions. The development of nationalization and nationalist sentiment began early in the United States, and was bolstered by the War of Independence, the War of 1812, westward expansion, and the Civil War. Canada began its nation-building a full century after the United States, in 1867. As Schmidt (1998) points out, it is not surprising that the US nativist movement, with its demands for cultural and linguistic conformity, has no parallel in Canadian history.

In addition, the two subordinated groups (the French in Canada, the Mexicans and, later on, other Latin Americans in the United States) are distinct in character as well as historical experience. France was a colonial power equal to the British, while Mexico was always economically and politically dwarfed by the United States. Anglo-Canadian accommodation to Francophones was motivated by a fear of US encroachment; no parallel motivation existed for Anglo-US accommodation to Mexicans. When the French in Quebec came under British rule, the only occupation open to them was farming, an endeavor in which they were not in competition with Anglo society; with two centuries devoid of out-migration, they created a cohesive, insular, self-conscious ethnic group with a distinctive identity. When Mexicans came under US domination, they were transformed from a pastoral people into a landless proletariat, treated as racially inferior and subjected to assimilationist pressures. With the permeability of national borders and the influx of other Latin Americans, it was more difficult for them to achieve consensus on a distinct group identity.

The French had a numerical advantage in Canada; only in the mid-nineteenth century did the British outnumber them. In Quebec, where the French have always been the majority, this advantage was used to gain control of the province's economic and political destiny. Mexicans in the southwestern part of the United States were early on outnumbered by Anglos; as we learned in the last chapter, New Mexico was not allowed to join the nation until the Anglo population was greater than the Mexican one. Latinos have never been a majority in any one state and, while demographic predictions point to a smaller Anglo population and a larger minority population in the future, no one minority group is expected to predominate. Having gained political control over Quebec, the Francophones were able to establish their own provincial language and education policies because of the decentralized nature of the Canadian political structure. States in the United States are less autonomous, and their policies are kept in check by federal statutory and constitutional law. Canada has a well-developed, sub-national welfare state, which allowed the Québécois to remedy the uneven distribution of economic power between Anglophones and Francophones beginning in the 1960s. In the United States, there is a less-developed local welfare state, and Latinos lack the numerical and political clout to effect significant change in the distribution of resources.

Finally, as Brym (1998) argues, the French Québécois possess a high degree of what Breton (1964) calls *institutional completeness*, measured by the amount and complexity of community organizations serving the members' religious, educational, political, recreational, national, and professional needs. Institutional completeness increases the effect of ethnic-group membership on socioeconomic standing in the larger society and motivates greater identification with the ethnolinguistic group.

Latinos in the United States, in contrast, with less extensive formal organizations and "fewer 'public spaces' in which to interact and reinforce their own language" (Schmidt, 1998: 66) (that is, without negative reactions from Anglos), have less incentive to identify themselves in ethnolinguistic terms.

These factors have led the French in Canada and the Latinos in the United States to acquire different political aspirations. The Québécois demanded a *confederal* resolution to ethnic diversity, which required a recognition that French-speakers and English-speakers have equal status. US Latinos have sought a *pluralistic* approach, which recognizes English as the dominant language and requires governmental use of and support for other languages. In light of these factors, Schmidt sees little possibility of Latinos mounting an independence movement parallel to that of the Québécois. As if in response to Chavez (1991a), he writes, "It seems apparent that Latinos have had a surer grasp of their political reality than have the assimilationist pundits seeking to generate widespread alarm over the separatist implications of pluralistic language policy proposals" (Schmidt, 1998: 67).

The two countries' different philosophies with regard to their heterogeneous populations have translated into different legal strategies. As Ricento (1998a, 1998b) explains, Canada makes use of legislation to protect the collective rights of minority groups with the goal of maintaining cultural and linguistic pluralism. In the United States, there is no legal protection for pluralism or the collective rights of minorities. Instead, bilingualism and bilingual services are means by which the fundamental rights of individuals are protected and enforced. The Bilingual Education Act was implemented to remedy the inadequate education of minority-language children; bilingual instruction was seen as a way to ease the assimilation process for these children. Ricento (1998a) reminds us that this law imparted no value judgment on social bilingualism, and did not challenge the basic assumption of the dominance of the English language. Instead, its goal was to right a societal wrong.

In previous chapters, we have seen how this works with regard to language restrictionism outside the field of education. State official-English laws have been passed in the absence of any national or state language policy. They remain unchallenged until or unless they are seen as abrogating existing laws. Thus, Arizona's law fell because it defied the constitutional right to free speech, Alaska's law is being challenged on several constitutional grounds, and Alabama's decision to drop its non-English written driver's test was successfully struck down under civil rights law prohibiting discrimination on the basis of national origin. English-only work rules have come under the scrutiny of the Equal Employment Opportunity Commission for their potential for abrogating the civil rights of national-origin groups.

However, in any area of US life dealing with language minorities, their rights remain vulnerable. First, the protection of their rights is necessarily a reaction to a proposed or existing policy or law, and depends on the existence of an individual or group willing to file a lawsuit, and an individual or group willing and able to mount a legal defense. Second, the legal system allows wide room for interpretation of the constitutional and statutory laws that are called on to protect language minorities. In the case of English-only work rules, we saw that judges differ on the question of whether having a mother tongue other than English constitutes being a member of a protected national-origin group and also differ in their opinions of the EEOC's guidelines for English-only rules. Finally, the remedies instituted to right social wrongs may or may not be adequate. A long-standing debate has existed over whether the educational programs, bilingual or otherwise, that were supposed to make up for the deficient education of minority-language children have been adequate to this goal.

What divides Canada and the United States, then, at its deepest level, is the value they place on pluralism and their willingness to commit public support for it. It is here that Schmidt sees a warning for the United States:

> Unprepared for a pluralist understanding of their national identity, some Anglos may also continue to perceive state support for bilingualism and biculturalism as an important threat to their personal identity as Americans as well. To the degree that anxiety finds political expression, it is possible that there will be increased Anglo support for a relatively aggressive and restrictive policy of assimilation. This development, in turn, could very well trigger a backlash of ethnic political cohesion in the now much larger minority populations of the country.... Ironically, then, the most important lesson that may be derived from this analysis is that an aggressive policy of linguistic assimilation in the United States may be more likely to push Latinos in the direction of increased separatism than any desire on their part to emulate the example of the Québécois in Canada. (Schmidt, 1998: 67)

By the same token, it can be argued that Quebec has overreached in its efforts to implement linguistic assimilation. The following US editorial, while failing to point out that the threat to French from English is much more of a reality than the threat to English from Spanish, makes this point as it compares the linguistic situations of the two countries:

> The pity is that the Quebec language war caricatures a serious debate. French-speakers are fearful of being overwhelmed by English-speakers, as the latter are by Spanish-speakers in Florida. These worries are scarcely new.... In fact, monolingual America has gone so far the other way that it trails virtually all industrial countries in language skills.

A confident majority accepts and welcomes minority cultures. Given the pervasiveness of English in America, the majority tongue needs no legal protection. One wonders how English-speakers in Miami who charge that Hispanic immigrants have created "another Cuba" can be indifferent to the vitality that bilingualism brings to their city.

That's also true of Montreal. It is a human perversity that linguistic diversity should be seen as a curse. (*The New York Times*, 1993c: A20)

OFFICIAL MULTILINGUALISM IN SWITZERLAND

An often-used argument of the official-English movement is that the common acceptance of one language is necessary for the smooth functioning of a nation of diverse peoples. Consider the following words of former Senator Walter Huddleston, explaining his decision to sponsor an English Language Amendment:

Almost alone among the world's very large and populous nations, the United States enjoys the blessings of one primary language, spoken and understood by most of its citizens. The previously unquestioned acceptance of this language by immigrants from every linguistic and cultural background has enabled us to come together as one people. It has allowed us to discuss our differences, to argue about our problems, and to compromise on solutions. It has allowed us to develop a stable and cohesive society that is the envy of many fractured ones. (Huddleston, 1983: 114)

Huddleston implies that without the common acceptance of one language, the United States would not be the well-functioning and harmonious country it is today. Some may think Huddleston's characterization of the nation is somewhat idealized. However, if we accept the fact that the United States does function reasonably well as a democracy, what is questionable is the degree to which this can be attributed to the fact that all its citizens agree to use one language. First, it may be argued that while many citizens speak English for formal purposes (in acquiring an education, in their professional lives, in dealing with government agencies) they also speak their native languages on informal, personal occasions. Second, if we look outside the United States, we find one very strong example of a nation known for its social stability and cohesiveness that has maintained a continuous commitment to multilingualism. This country is Switzerland.

According to McRae, Switzerland's linguistic pluralism has seldom caused serious conflict in the country's history. His analysis of Swiss society demonstrates how the successful coexistence of its various linguistic groups "has been built upon an intricate combination of historical, structural, attitudinal, and institutional factors skillfully and patiently woven into a reinforcing pattern by human effort and statesmanship" (McRae, 1983: 240). The salient points of this analysis are presented below.

The History

As McRae (1983) explains, Switzerland gained its multilingual nature through a process of expansion. The Swiss state began in 1291 as an alliance between three German-speaking cantons against outside invaders. The next four centuries saw the accretion of ten more cantons, also comprised mostly of German-speakers. The cantons remained politically separate, but through their alliance emerged a common Swiss outlook, including a commitment to neutrality in the conflicts surrounding them. German was the official language of the Confederation until the end of the eighteenth century. One of the original cantons, Fribourg, had a significant population of French-speakers, but a policy of Germanization was instituted by the ruling aristocracy there.

Beginning in the sixteenth century, the Confederation extended its influence to surrounding regions where French, Italian, and Romansh were spoken. These regions were linked to Switzerland through treaties, or were ruled as subject territories by the cantons. In either case, their local autonomy and linguistic diversity were respected.

The Confederation collapsed in 1798 under the influence of the French Revolution and the invading French army. A new government, the Helvetic Republic, was instituted from Paris. It called for a centralized democratic state, with eight new cantons formed from associated territories. Laws were to be published in German, French, and Italian, and the speakers of all three languages were to be treated on an equal basis. This government did not last long, and in 1815 power was restored to the old cantonal aristocracies; German again became the official language.

But the idea of official multilingualism had been implanted in Swiss thought. The wave of liberalism and revolutions that swept through Europe in the nineteenth century brought renewed calls for reform in Switzerland. In 1847, after a 25-day war pitting the more liberal Protestants against the more conservative Catholics, a new constitution was signed, forming a democracy with three national languages: German, French, and Italian. Revisions to the constitution ensued, but the language clause remained unchanged.

The world conflicts of the twentieth century had the effect of drawing the Swiss closer together. The rise of the German Empire evoked increasing admiration from the German Swiss. Germany's invasion of Belgium in 1914 worsened the rift that had been growing between German and French Swiss. In response, deliberate efforts were made to rally all Swiss around a set of independent values and a commitment to neutrality.

The growing power of Italy led to the protection of Switzerland's most vulnerable language, Romansh. Linguists believe that Romansh is derived from the vernacular Latin, with Celtic, Illyrian, and Etruscan roots, and has been heavily influenced over the centuries by Italian and German dialects. Romansh exists in the form of five groups of language varieties spoken in isolated populations in the Graubunden canton. Shortly after World War I, Italian philologists began expounding pseudo-scientific theories alleging the Romansh dialects to be varieties of Italian. Italy used these theories to claim the Romansh-speaking area of Switzerland as its own. In response to the threat of Fascist incursion, Switzerland formally recognized Romansh as its fourth national language in 1938, while declaring the other three to be official languages (McRae, 1983; Stephens, 1978).

McRae (1983) points out that most of the conflicts in Switzerland's history were caused by nonlinguistic factors. In its early years, differences between forest cantons and urban confederations and between town and countryside within urban cantons were the major sources of tension. From the time of the Reformation on, religious differences were the primary cause of divisiveness, and led to armed conflicts in 1531, 1656, 1712, and 1847. In the nineteenth century, religious division was transformed into a struggle between liberalism and conservatism; in the twentieth century, religion and social class were the main determinants of the Swiss party system. In addition, when conflicts over language or class have occurred, most of the time they have been resolved through peaceful techniques dating from the days of the original Confederation: arbitration, mediation, and friendly compromise.

Social Structure and Linguistic Diversity

As McRae (1983) explains, the four languages of Switzerland are generally found in distinct regions of the country. These regions do not coincide with cantonal divisions; as a result, more than one language group may live in the same canton, and cantons may have more than one official language. Of the 26 cantons and half-cantons, German is the official language of seventeen cantons; German and French of three cantons; French of four cantons; Italian of one canton; and German, Italian, and Romansh of one canton.

The linguistic regions are largely homogeneous, but some Swiss do move to regions in which a language other than their own predominates. Impressionistic evidence suggests a certain degree of variation with regard to how these migrants adapt to the language of their new home. German-speakers tend to adopt the French language when they move to French-speaking regions, but French-speakers hold on to their language in German Switzerland. Italian- and Romansh-speakers switch rapidly to German and French when they move, while German-speakers in Italian and Romansh regions tend to maintain their German.

Because these preferences do not result in any significant linguistic tensions, there is little research to explain why language groups adapt differently in this way. However, German and French are clearly the dominant languages of the nation, and the preferences of migrants illustrate this. Those who are not native speakers of these languages acknowledge the importance of learning them; German-speakers are willing to adapt to French, but are less eager to switch to Italian or Romansh.

There is also a plausible reason why French-speakers are reluctant to cede their language when they migrate to German Switzerland. German-speakers are the numerically dominant population of Switzerland, but the French language has a status that allows it to compete with German. French has always been associated with royalty; it was the language of the ruling aristocracies in several German-speaking cantons beginning in the seventeenth centruy. Also, it has had a long history as the language of international diplomacy. McRae (1983) points to impressionistic evidence that, when German-speakers and French-speakers communicate, orally or in writing, French is their language of preference.

The language diversity of Switzerland is not limited to the existence of four languages; dialect diversity must also be taken into account. Among German-speakers, the standard variety of the language coexists with a number of local dialects. The local varieties preserve people's connection to their roots and help define their Swiss identity; competence in standard German provides access to the literary and scientific cultures of the German-speaking world outside Switzerland. The various French patois that existed before the Reformation have long since died out. Standard French was the language of religion and written texts brought over from France; during the French Revolution, patois were considered to be symbols of feudalism. However, some evidence of Franco-Provençal still exists in the language. In Italian Switzerland, regional varieties of the language are used in informal situations, while standard Italian is the language of education, government, religion, and tourism.

As mentioned above, Romansh has existed as five dialect clusters rather than one language. There has never been a central urban area where a standard variety could develop and, in contrast to the three other languages, there is no Romansh outside Switzerland that might serve as a model for standardization. It was only in 1982 that Romansh linguists began to put together a standardized form of the language, setting spelling rules and making up words for terms that do not exist in the dialects (*The Economist*, 1988).

McRae (1983) describes a number of characteristics besides language that differentiate the Swiss, and these characteristics often cut across language divisions. Religion, the most important source of tension in Swiss history, is one. While the Italian Swiss are mostly Roman Catholic, the three other language groups are comprised of significant populations of Roman

Catholics and Protestants. Since religious affiliation is a major determinant of Swiss political-party affiliation, it supersedes linguistic identity in importance in the political arena.

Several factors other than language are significant determinants of socioeconomic status. The existence of urban centers is indicative of greater economic opportunity; they are also magnets that draw people from rural regions. German Switzerland has three large metropolitan centers, French Switzerland has two, Italian Switzerland has three small cities, and Romansh Switzerland has none. The type of terrain in the linguistic regions also determines economic viability; mountainous regions have problems of depopulation and difficulty of access that do not plague the plateaux, and they are in most need of federal development projects. The Romansh region is the only one that is predominantly mountainous. In terms of occupational status, the four language regions are relatively similar; but the Romansh region is more heavily represented by traditional, family-oriented types of employment, such as agricultural work. McRae explains: "From the perspective of a century or more, it is the mountain and rural cantons that have been most obviously bypassed by prosperity and economic development, and the exodus of population from these less favored areas has been a continuing process throughout the period" (McRae, 1983: 92). Given the above factors, it is not surprising that the German and French regions are the more prosperous ones.

Group Images, Attitudes, and a Common Political Culture

Research shows that the language groups have positive images of themselves and positive attitudes toward each other. Each group sees itself as different from, and somewhat superior to, the others. But while they ascribe to other groups different traits than those that they ascribe to themselves, they still see others in a positive light. There is also a great deal of concurrence between the way groups view themselves and the way others view them. For example, in one study the French and German Swiss both described the French Swiss as polished, active, young, rounded, gay, handsome, lively, and liberal. The two groups described the German Swiss as strong, rough, active, healthy, noisy, courageous, and constant (Fischer, 1961; Fischer & Weidmann 1961; Fischer & Trier, 1962; cited in McRae, 1983: 95). Such positive attitudes make for healthy inter-group relations.

The three major language groups offer similar support to all three of the main Swiss political parties. Some issues polarize voters along linguistic lines, such as foreign relations, military defense, women's suffrage, and the extension of federal powers. This polarization has historical roots in the ideological differences between the language groups; the French Swiss have traditionally been antimilitant, liberal, individualistic, and impatient with authority, and the French and Italian cantons have tended to resist the increasing powers of the central government. However, there is still a strong common political culture that bonds the Swiss together.

At the heart of this culture is a dedication to diversity in a variety of forms: linguistic, religious, ideological, and economic. Tolerance for diversity is transmitted through the process of socialization. For example, a study of school history textbooks in French and German Switzerland found tendencies to emphasize themes that unite the subcultures, stress consensus, give both sides of disputes and underline the importance of mediation (Schmid, 1978; Schmid, 1981; cited in McRae, 1983: 103).

The political structure of the government puts these values into action. The legislative process relies on a consensual, consultative, and inclusive style of decision-making. This allows the government to resolve problems stemming from its diverse population in a peaceful way. For example, Jura, a French-speaking territory in the German canton of Bern, was the site of a separatist movement in the 1950s, a reaction to the territory's longstanding religious, linguistic, economic, and political marginalization. With help from the federal government, Bern engaged its citizens in a lengthy search for a political solution to the problem, the result being the establishment of Jura as a new canton in 1978. The process exemplified the Swiss practice of recognizing new divisions in its society and adjusting its political system to accommodate them.

To put the issue of linguistic differences into further perspective, anecdotal evidence indicates that the Swiss feel closer ties to each other, regardless of their linguistic affiliation, than to foreigners with whom they share a linguistic bond. One German Swiss came to realize that "we have a concept of nationality that does not coincide with the speech community" when he noted the difference between his experience speaking German to a French-speaking Swiss and speaking it to a German-speaker from Germany: "The French Swiss and I used different words for the same concepts, but we understood one another. The Viennese and I used the same words for different concepts, and so understood each other not at all" (Schürch, 1943; cited in McRae, 1983: 103).

Multilingualism in Government and Institutions

As McRae (1983) further explains, Swiss federal law is based on three principles that insure linguistic freedom. The first is the principle of the *absolute equality* of the four Swiss languages and language groups. The second is the *linguistic sovereignty* of the cantons, giving language groups the autonomy to pursue their separate cultural goals. The third is the principle of *territoriality*, the right of each canton or linguistic region to preserve and defend, with federal help if needed, its linguistic character against outside forces that attempt to alter or endanger it. Migrants are expected to acquire knowledge of the local language. Federal authorities are obliged to deal with the cantons in their official language or languages; individuals may deal with federal offices in the official language of their choice. This principle has become more difficult to uphold since World War II, in light of increased mobility and the influx of foreign workers to Switzerland, but it remains unchallenged.

Switzerland has a parliamentary system, and through its system of cantonal elections and its process of choosing committee members, each language group is fairly represented in all legislative proceedings. The federal government publishes its laws in the three official languages – French, German, and Italian – and representatives are free to speak in any of these languages. However, meetings are generally conducted in French and German. Italian-speaking and Romansh-speaking representatives are generally fluent in one of these languages.

Recognition of the multilingual nature of Switzerland is inherent in all Swiss institutions. In filling civil service jobs, the government attempts to have all language groups fairly represented. Knowledge of two official languages is necessary for these positions, with higher levels of proficiency needed for career advancement; courses in the official languages and English are part of federal in-service training programs. In the army, soldiers and officers are addressed and instructed in one of the three official languages. However, commands are given in German, since they require instant response and translation takes too much time. Army personnel are encouraged to improve their knowledge of the languages of the localities to which they are assigned.

Educational matters are controlled largely by the cantons. The language of instruction follows the principle of territoriality; however, children whose native languages are not the regional language are allowed instruction in their native languages for a number of years determined by the canton, after which they are instructed in the regional language. All cantons require the learning of a second official language, either French or German, at the secondary level. It is compulsory for schools to offer a third language on an optional basis; English is a popular choice.

In Graubunden, the trilingual canton, educational policy departs somewhat from the territoriality principle. In the German region, French is learned as a second language; in the Italian and Romansh regions, German is introduced in the fourth or fifth grade and French is taught as a third language beginning in the seventh grade. In Romansh regions, German becomes the language of instruction after the fourth grade, and Romansh is then taught as a subject. German is so important for Italian-speaking and Romansh-speaking children because cantonal education beyond the level of compulsory schooling is available to them only in German.

Beyond high school, Switzerland has seven universities. In three, classes are conducted in German, another three offer instruction in French, and one is bilingual German–French. Two federal institutes of technology offer equivalent standards and degrees; one is German-speaking, the other French-speaking.

The federal government actively supports and encourages cultural maintenance. Fundamental to its policies is the recognition that, because of the small size of their populations, the Italian- and Romansh-speaking regions need greater resources for linguistic and cultural maintenance than those regions inhabited by German- and French-speakers. Aid to these regions includes funds for television and radio broadcasting, subsidies to elementary schools for projects such as the development of textbooks, and support for theatrical, musical, artistic, and literary endeavors. The federal government subsidizes an on-going multi-volume dictionary of Swiss dialects. It also supports the Pro Helvetia Foundation, whose goals are to build on the linguistic and cultural diversity of the different regions, facilitate cultural exchanges, and disseminate Swiss thought and culture abroad.

Linguistic Frictions

While the Swiss Constitution proclaims the state's commitment to multi-lingualism and to the equality of all language groups, some language tensions do exist. According to Andres, the country's reputation for economic prosperity, political stability and good relationships between social and linguistic groups is built partly on truth and partly on myth. German-speaking Swiss comprise the largest linguistic group and command greater political and economic power than the other three groups, giving the German language a position of superiority and leading, in part, to "the subliminal uneasiness of the non-German-speaking Swiss toward the dominant population group" (Andres, 1990: 16). German cantons are the home bases of most of the country's large firms, resulting in what is called "the economic colonization of the Swiss Romande whose businessmen take the early morning flights from Geneva to Zurich to get their orders" (Church, 2000: 105). In addition, Swiss Germans generally oppose the country's participation in political activities with other nations, such as the European Union and Francophone summits. Such participation, according to Church, "is not just a matter of foreign policy in the abstract because Union membership would strengthen Swiss ties with a mainly French-speaking institution, allowing Brussels to balance the power of Zurich" (Church, 2000: 105–106). Political power and language power are thus inextricably linked.

The French, Italian, and Romansh Swiss have had to work hard to counteract the importance of the German language. According to Andres (1990), the French Swiss identify strongly with their native language and with the French-speaking community outside Switzerland, partially as a hedge against potential feelings of inferiority. This has led to their rather militant attitude toward fair representation of French-speakers in the government, and to their strong interest in seeing French taught as the second language for the other linguistic groups.

Meanwhile, English has become a widely preferred second language for many Swiss. The French Swiss themselves are more attracted to the English language than to German. While standard German is taught in the schools, the German-speaking community makes use of both standard German and Swiss German; learning standard German does not guarantee an easy entrée into that community. According to Church (2000), Swiss German has become standardized and thus more comprehensible among Germans, coming into its own as a separate language; at the same time, it stands as a barrier to communication with speakers of other languages. On the other hand, as Andres (1990) explains, English, a politically, economically, and scientifically important language, holds out the promise of better job prospects without the complications posed by the two varieties of German. In addition, among German Swiss, English is becoming a more popular second language than French. The French face the probability that, as English gains in importance in Switzerland, the French language will fall in status. This is compounded by the shifting influence of English and French on the world stage. While French was once the preferred language of the European upper and middle classes and has a history as the language of international diplomacy, it has lost in prestige to English, now the predominant language of worldwide communication.

An example of the incursion of English into Swiss life, and the conflict it engenders, is the decision of Switzerland's largest German-speaking canton, Zurich, to make English instruction compulsory for grade-school children in the fall of 1998. Nearby French cantons swiftly responded by complaining that the policy would threaten the status of French and undermine political unity. Fear was expressed that English would become the country's principal means of communication between French and German Swiss. A former French culture minister urged the Swiss to reject this form of "linguistic McDonaldization." However, it appears likely that the Swiss will not follow this advice. A 1997 poll found that the majority of Swiss want their children to learn English as a second language. Lugano, an Italian-speaking canton, followed Zurich's lead, and a Swiss education commission has recommended that English be compulsory in primary schools (Olson, 1998). The stance of the French Swiss is somewhat conflicted: they are attracted more to English than to German, but don't want English to threaten their own language.

The Italian Swiss have always been a linguistically and economically marginal group in Switzerland. They have a significant attachment to their own variety of Italian, one which they do not share with other language groups, who learn standard Italian as a second language. In fact, many Italian Swiss have difficulty using standard Italian orally. For most Italian

Swiss, the need to learn French or German is imperative, whether or not they leave their own linguistic region. For these reasons, the continued marginalization of the Italian language is of concern to the Italian Swiss.

The most vulnerable linguistic group among the native Swiss are the Romansh, who face continued marginalization for a variety of reasons. The Romansh population is the smallest of the linguistic groups, and the only one that regularly decreased numerically throughout the twentieth century. In the Swiss census of 1990, 36,632 people declared Romansh to be the language they spoke best, compared to 51,128 in the 1980 census. In March 1996, voters approved an amendment to bolster federal spending for the promotion of the language. The measure was part of a government plan also designed to check the growing use of English and to foster the speaking of Italian (*Houston Chronicle*, 1996).

Despite the continuing process of language standardization, the status of Romansh as a national language but not an official language puts it in particular peril. The Romansh cannot use their language in communicating with the federal government. In addition, the language is not legally protected at the local level; if German-speaking Swiss become numerically dominant in a particular community, the community can officially become German-speaking. The dominance of German in the region's schools has further marginalized the Romansh language.

Andres (1990) points out that, despite the multilingualism of the Swiss government, individual bilingualism is not universal. Bilingualism develops most strongly in areas where there is language contact between the linguistic groups, such as along the borders of language regions. More particularly, those who become bilingual in these regions tend to be the language minorities. Bilingualism is a necessity for the marginalized language groups, the Italians and the Romansh and, to some extent, the French. For the German Swiss, bilingualism is prestigious but not a necessity. The teaching of Italian and Romansh as a second language is limited; courses in Italian meet a few hours a week, and Romansh courses are not often offered, owing to the lack of teachers and the low demand. The Swiss census does not collect data on bilingualism, asking only for the respondents' mother tongues. In sum, writes Andres, "there is a constitutional commitment by the Confederation to multilingualism but ... no policy exists to make it a reality for individuals" (Andres, 1990: 39).

As Switzerland faces a new century, it is also contending with significant economic, political, and social changes threatening its precarious cultural and linguistic balance. These include increased business competition from the European Union, fears of unemployment, a need to reassess the nation's historical neutrality on the international political stage, a growing lack of confidence in government, and a growing style of competitiveness in the political system. Demographic changes have created an increasingly elderly population and one that is increasingly dependent on foreigners (Church, 2000). Of the 7 million Swiss, 1.4 million (20%) are from other countries. Many were recruited from Italy, Portugal, Spain, and the former Yugoslavia during the labor shortages of the 1960s and 70s (Olson, 2000). These newcomers have tipped the linguistic balance of the cantons. In addition, more people live in the major cities, which have experienced rising rates of crime, illegal drug use, poverty, divorce, and suicide. According to Church (2000), the Swiss political structure is ill-equipped to handle these new pressures, a situation which has led to the rise of the right-wing, anti-immigrant Swiss People's Party. In the parliamentary elections of October 1999, the party received 23% of the votes, threatening the balance of regional interests and language groups which the governing coalition of the four major political parties had maintained since 1959 (Olson, 1999).

The anti-immigrant sentiment embodied by the Swiss People's Party was evident in one local election. At the turn of the century, many of the country's immigrants, having completed the required twelve years of residence, began applying for citizenship. In March 2000, voters in the town of Emmen in the canton of Lucerne participated in a first-time event: deciding which of the 56 family and individual applications for citizenship would be granted. The voters reviewed booklets with photographs and personal information on the applicants and approved only four families, all of Italian origin; many of the rejected were Yugoslavian. In other large Swiss cities, such as Zurich and Bern, local branches of the Swiss People's Party have proposed similar elections (Olson, 2000).

Church (2000) points out that traditional forms of cultural management are not set up to bestow stable and equal social rights on the Swiss immigrant population. In addition, just as the French–English power struggle in Canada diverted attention away from the language issues of Aboriginal and immigrant Canadians, the Swiss media's focus on the power struggle between French- and German-speakers has prevented it from paying attention to Switzerland's other language problems. The most notable of these is "the need to adapt multiculturalism to accommodate new arrivals in the country" (Church, 2000: 112). Still, Church believes that the nation will find a way to do this, noting that the new constitution, passed in 1999, "does enshrine [clear] commitments to mutual respect and comprehension" (Church, 2000: 110).

Lessons for the United States

Like Canada, Switzerland took a different path in response to linguistic and cultural pluralism than the United States did. Both nations underwent expansions that drew new communities into the fold, but in very different ways. In Switzerland, the German cantons incorporated French-, Italian-, and Romansh-speaking regions. Under the influence of European liberalism, principles of autonomy and tolerance for diversity were established, and the cultural and linguistic uniqueness of each canton was respected. This structure bears a similarity to that of Canada, which allows its provinces considerable autonomy as well. In contrast, the United States advanced its territorial expansion in a more imperialistic way. A variety of cultures marked each of the territories: Native American and Spanish in the Southwest; French, Spanish, African, and Native American in Louisiana; and Hawaiian and various immigrant cultures in Hawaii. The United States' belief in its superiority and the consequent Americanization of these territories resulted in the decline of this cultural and linguistic diversity; by the time the territories became states, English generally ruled. Only years later, when mainstream America was willing to face its ill-conceived self-centeredness, were attempts begun to revive the nation's historic but dying cultures and languages.

This perspective puts the current situation of Puerto Rico into focus. Puerto Rico shares some characteristics with the former territories of the United States. Like the territories, it became a part of the United States, but basically as a poor second cousin. Its culture and language are different from those of the mainstream United States, and for the past century it has been subjected to attempts at Americanization. However, unlike the territories, Puerto Rico has held on to its own identity, refusing to give up its language and culture, aided by the homogeneity of the island's population and its physical separateness from the United States. Unlike Switzerland, the United States will not accept a new addition unless it first conforms to mainstream norms. This is why the prospect of Puerto Rican statehood is so contentious.

Another major difference between the Swiss and the Americans is in the composition of their populations. The four major linguistic groups in Switzerland (the French, the German, the Italians, and the Romansh) are all of European origin. Despite the internal wars that have marked European history, the proximity of the nations has encouraged extensive contact through travel and migration. As a result, Europeans share many common bonds. The positive intergroup attitudes mentioned above attest to these bonds. Likewise, in Canada the two founding peoples were European: the British and the French.

In contrast, the United States is made up of groups of people who consider themselves very different from each other. They differ in how and why they find themselves part of the nation: Native Americans were the earliest inhabitants; Europeans arrived first as explorers and later as immigrants fleeing political or religious persecution or economic distress; Africans were forced to migrate as slaves; Mexicans automatically became residents as a result of border wars; newcomers from Asia, Africa, and Latin America continue the immigrant dream of self-renewal. European Americans have historically considered themselves superior (in language, culture, and race) to all the other groups, resulting in the creation of an inherently stratified society. It is not surprising, then, that the principles of linguistic and cultural pluralism and equality that underlie the political culture of Switzerland are absent from American culture.

On the level of individual multilingualism, the two countries are also diametrically opposed. The Swiss are expected to learn two or three languages at school, and often know more than one variety of their native language. Children whose native tongues are different from the languages of their regions are guaranteed native-language instruction for the first few years of their education. The system is not perfect; some languages are considered more important than others, and in reality individual bilingualism is not universal. However, the struggle of marginalized language groups to keep their languages viable is respected. In contrast, Americans pay lip service to the importance of learning a second language, but are rarely successful at it. Foreign-language programs have only limited success, and are often the first ones cut when budgets need to be curtailed. To many Americans, programs allowing immigrant children to develop their native languages while learning English are considered a waste of time and money, an unnecessary concession to minority groups. Both countries have multilingual populations, but while the Swiss use this diversity to their advantage, Americans persist in disregarding the potential benefits that language pluralism offers.

Changing times have revealed that Switzerland is far from immune to internal conflict. Immigration has challenged the nation's concept of diversity. The Emmen election shows that not all newcomers are considered part of the Swiss family, even if they do come from Europe. It remains to be seen whether language groups other than the four recognized nationally will come to receive the same rights and protections. Likewise, the United States finds itself with large groups of people of different cultures and languages demanding the equality promised them in the country's guiding documents. The nation's leaders should heed the lessons of Switzerland: political, economic, and linguistic power are closely tied, and conflicts can be averted if these forms of power are shared in an equitable manner.

MULTILINGUALISM IN COUNTRIES DOMINATED BY ONE LANGUAGE

In many countries that are historically multilingual, one language, which may or may not be indigenous, dominates. No matter how strong the hold of this language, other languages spoken in the country are not easily suppressed. In this section, we will examine the recent language revival in Western Europe, an example of renewed recognition of the benefits of linguistic diversity. By way of contrast, we will also look at a non-European country, India, and its ongoing struggle against the imposition of a single national language.

Language Revival in Western Europe

As explained by Spring (1998), the post-World War II period in Europe was marked by activity meant to bring the countries into cooperation with each other. With help from the United States' Marshall Plan, Western European nations formed the European Community (EU), whose goal was to create a regional trading block within the larger global economy. While economic growth is the basis of the organization, efforts at unity also involve fostering a common political, educational, and cultural identity. Because the United States has cornered the global market on popular culture, the EU focuses on high culture, creating continent-wide classical music orchestras and sponsoring activities around themes of European history and literature. Since European literature is written in different languages, provisions are made for translations of contemporary literary works. The EU recognizes fifteen official languages, and funds translation projects and educational exchange programs for foreign-language instruction; in 1996 a position paper on education and training proposed the goal of proficiency in three European languages for all students. Thus, the EU has attempted to resolve the inherent tensions between a common European identity and distinct national ties with the philosophy of "diversity within unity" (Spring, 1998: 100).

As Spring suggests, however, efforts to sustain European languages by recognizing their equality and supporting multilingualism in them must face the formidable obstacle of the global domination of English. Evidence is strong that English has pervaded many areas of European life. Previously, we discussed how English has surpassed French as the preferred second language in Switzerland. Tagliabue (1998) notes that in many European countries the use of English words in commercial advertising is thought to impart an "international flavor." A German phone company now sends out bills with the categories "City-Calls" and "German-Calls," a policy protested by the Institute for the German Language. A large-appliance maker in Italy has made English the company language, owing to the recruitment of managers from France, Britain, the Netherlands, and Portugal. And while in the past Europeans from small countries, such as Finland and Denmark, often used English, today young adults from large countries such as Italy, Germany and France, having lived, studied and worked abroad, are comfortable with English and use it widely.

Incursions of English into European life have not gone uncontested. In 1994 the French culture minister attempted to promote a law requiring that 3,000 commonly used English words be replaced by their French equivalents. However, while government officials are required to follow the new language rules, France's Constitutional Council ruled that the policy could not be applied to ordinary citizens, since it violated the right to free expression guaranteed by the 1789 Declaration of the Rights of Man (Tagliabue, 1998). Thus, France shares with the United States a constitutional guarantee that prevents government from curbing the speech of its citizens, allowing individuals to use the language or languages of their choice.

In addition to the Americanization of Europe, many fear that modernization and the creation of a European identity threaten the local cultures that mark each nation. Simons (1993) notes that the peace and tranquillity of the Provence countryside have been sullied by the introduction of high-technology industries and the sale of entire villages to outsiders for vacation spots. In addition, the local culture is rarely represented on television. Throughout Western Europe, similar concerns have been raised. As Europe moves toward unification, local projects to preserve languages and cultures have blossomed.

What began as a grass-roots movement of regionalism is now embraced by official agencies. The EU established the European Bureau for Lesser Used Languages in 1982. In the 1990s, its $4.2 million annual budget helped finance projects such as computer software development in Gaelic in Ireland, courses in Friulian in northern Italy, and an information center for Frisian in the Netherlands. In November, 1993, eleven members of the 26-state Council of Europe, which promotes democracy and human rights, signed a charter pledging to encourage the use of indigenous languages in schools and in public life (Simons, 1993).

In France, the government announced a plan in January 1993 to promote bilingual education in indigenous languages. It also called for local governments to set up councils to promote regional language and culture through publications, theater, music, and film. In doing this, the government was responding to a grass-roots movement that has been under way for some time. In 1983, private groups formed an organization to rescue Provençal. It now operates 17 private bilingual schools. With government help, radio stations in Toulouse and Marseilles broadcast short news programs in Occitan, the family of dialects of which Provençal is a part (and the term preferred by some specialists). The University of Montpellier now awards degrees in Occitan. A professor of the dialect explains its growing popularity: "It is appealing because the language offers people a sense of identity that is not hostile to others, that is not exclusive. Anyone can join in" (cited in Simons, 1993: A8). Other languages being revived in France are Corsican, Breton, and Basque.

In many cases, the revival of regional languages represents a turnaround of political policies of linguistic repression. As Simons (1993) explains, for centuries French authorities considered provincial languages to be vulgar and backward, and fought to impose standardized French in an attempt to solidify national unity. Likewise, during Francisco Franco's forty-year dictatorship of Spain, citizens were pressured into speaking Castilian Spanish over regional languages such as Catalan and Basque. Franco rescinded laws recognizing local dialects that had been passed by the previous Republican government. After Franco's death, Spain's democratic constitution gave Castilian status as the country's official language, but recognized others as well, leaving regional parliaments to decide the balance (Gooch, 1998).

In Catalonia, legislation passed in the 1980s under the leadership of Premier Jordi Pujol had the goal of making the region bilingual, through education in both languages and the mandatory use of Catalan in regional government offices. Most Catalonians went along with these policies; approximately 95% of the population, including the large minority not of Catalan descent, now understands Catalan. However, with the passage of the 1998 Catalan Language Law, there was the sense among many people that Pujol had gone too far. Along with the promotion of Catalan in the workplace and the Catalan labeling of products, the law required 50% of new films in movie theaters and at least 25% of songs played on music stations to be in Catalan. The artistic and business communities balked at the restrictions, which would limit their clientele. Film companies complained of the extra costs of dubbing, and the region's film distributors challenged the law. The Babel Forum, a pressure group of Catalan writers and artists, argued that the government had gone too far and had created a divisive, discriminatory system favoring native speakers of Catalan over native speakers of Castilian. The language issue was considered a serious threat to Pujol's tenure as premier (Gooch, 1998; *The Economist*, 1999). In many respects, the Catalan situation mirrors that of Quebec: defenders of a language long repressed, now holding power, are being accused of unduly repressing the more powerful language with which it must compete.

Despite the struggles and obstacles that attend language revival, the status of language pluralism in Europe is generally positive. A report by the Bureau for Lesser Used Languages, published in Brussels in January 1997, stated that the revival of more than forty minority languages, along with the spread of English as a lingua franca, is transforming Europe's linguistic environment (Palmer, 1997). New technology is helping preserve some minority languages, as exemplified by a Scots Gaelic web site (http://www.smo.uhi.ac.uk/saoghal/mion-chanain). Although some minority languages are struggling to survive in the new information age, or are under threat from a dominant national language, the Bureau claims that their extinction is no longer inevitable. The report states that English appears to be a greater threat to national languages such as French than it is to minority and regional languages. In fact, the integration of Europe seems to be safeguarding and encouraging minority languages, since both the

European Union and the Council of Europe have vowed to make respect for linguistic diversity a fundamental human right (Palmer, 1997). In comparison to Europe on this point, the United States appears woefully unprogressive.

Minority Languages in India

As Wolfson (1989) explains, before the arrival of Europeans Asia and Africa were linguistically and ethnically complex. During the era of colonialism, ethnic and tribal language rivalries were kept in check while European languages were imposed. With the fall of colonialism came the task of deciding whether to depose the widely used official European languages and replace them with native languages.

At the time of India's independence in 1947, English was entrenched as the language of administration, formal education, law, commerce, and journalism, and an elite sector of Indian society was trained in English to assume the best jobs. India's new constitution recognized Hindi as the official language and English as the associated official language, to be phased out after a limited number of years. Fifteen regional languages were designated as official state languages (Southworth, 1985). In addition, 418 languages are "listed" in the constitution, and many are used as vehicles of cultural transmission. All-India Radio broadcasts in 24 languages and 146 dialects, newspapers are published in at least 34 languages, primary education is conducted in 67 languages, and literary work is done in 80. The constitution guarantees all citizens the right to conserve their languages, and all religious and linguistic minorities have the right to establish and administer educational institutions of their choice (Choudhry, 200).

However, the official stamp of multilingualism did not solve India's linguistic and socioeconomic inequities. English was never phased out as a major language of national government. As Southworth (1985) points out, the variety of Hindi chosen to be the official language of the Hindi-speaking region and of the nation was used exclusively by the local Hindi elite and was largely incomprehensible to most Hindi-speakers, allowing the Hindi elite to maintain its power and status. The same occurred with other regional languages. These regional languages now largely serve as the media of instruction through college, with English being available in some urban areas. However, neither the standardized forms of regional languages nor English are readily accessible to most Indians.

An indication that India is becoming more democratic and expansive in its leadership was the election of H.D. Deve Gowda as prime minister in 1996. Gowda was the first Indian leader to be neither a Brahmin nor a member of the upper caste. He was the son of a humble farmer, had a modest education, and spoke only one language, Kannada. Since several members of his cabinet spoke only Hindi, Gowda had to rely on translators at the start of his tenure, at the same time vowing to become proficient in Hindi within three months (Goldenberg, 1996).

While many of India's minority languages are employed in government and education, Pattanayak (1985) points out that the official use of these languages in these capacities came about only when minority-language groups generated sufficient pressure, not as a result of deliberate policy planning. In addition, Dua (1985) notes that support for minority languages is not uniform. For example, some states provide primary schooling in minority languages; others don't. The type of literature published in minority languages depends on the funds available through national, state, and local governments, and on the values of the minority groups; some groups concentrate on religious material and school textbooks, while others put their resources into adult literature. According to Choudhry (2000), some state officials hope that minority languages within their jurisdictions will die out before they even get a chance to be vehicles of education. Thus, many factors are at play in determining whether minority languages are given the chance to grow and accommodate the contemporary needs of the communities where they are spoken.

Similarly, Dua (1985) points out that the development of and support for these languages is based to a large extent on the attitudes of both majority-language and minority-language groups in a particular region. Does the majority group expect the minority to assimilate? Does the minority group view its language as a symbol of second-class status, or as a medium for education and cultural transmission? To the extent that the minority group is able to control the use of its language, it must find a balance between emphasizing its language, and thereby risking the alienation of members who see value in learning the majority language, and emphasizing the majority language, thereby risking total assimilation and loss of its distinct identity.

Preservation of language diversity in India is also an emotional issue, especially after so many years of fighting the dominance of English. Raghu Vira, a leader of the movement for language freedom, wrote of the "heartless smothering of Indian languages" (Vira, 1965: 265), and explained: "Every language is proud of its achievements and will not yield to any other in point of beauty and force. Moreover, the loyalty to one's language is natural and deep-rooted" (Vira, 1965: 2). A contemporary Indian novel, *In Custody*, tells of a declining Urdu poet who is interviewed by a college lecturer. The poet is resigned to the loss of his language, while the lecturer is committed to its preservation. The film producer Ismail Merchant describes why he bought the rights to the novel: "It's very sad to see beautiful things go and be unable to stop it. Even if it is only a drop in the ocean, it is important that you have a voice" (cited in Kythreotis, 1993: H23).

However, it is evident that English is valued in India in a way that India's indigenous languages are not. Aside from being a neutral language for wider communication, the symbolic social status attached to English has resulted in an "Anglomania ... detrimental not only to the growth of Indian languages but also to the 'normal' development of Indian society" (Choudhry, 2000). Even politicians who denounce the use of English send their children to English-medium schools. As the language of advancement and modernity, English also dominates the latest forms of communication. A leading India media company joined San Francisco-based ZDNet to create ZDNet India, an English-language web service, to accommodate the exponentially expanding subscriber base of Internet users in India (*PR Newswire*, 2000). Even when the Information Age reaches rural India, it is likely to arrive speaking English, the dominant language of the Worldwide Web. Non-profit groups and local governments have launched small experiments bringing computers to isolated areas of the country. While some programs distribute specific information in the local language, operation of the computers is usually in the hands of the most educated, English-speaking members of the community (Dugger, 2000).

India must also contend with the persistent ideology of English-language superiority. In the introduction to an anthology of fifty years of Indian writing in English, the renowned author Salman Rushdie writes,

> The prose writing – both fiction and non-fiction – created in this period by Indian writers working in English, is proving to be a stronger and more important body of work than most of what has been produced in the 16 "official languages" of India, the so-called "vernacular languages," during the same time. ... This new, and still burgeoning, "Indo-Anglian" literature represents perhaps the most valuable contribution that India has yet made to the world of books. (Rushdie & West, 1997: viii)

One critic takes Rushdie to task:

> This remark must surely be an oversight, for he cannot mean that what he is promoting is superior to the *Mahabharata*, the *Ramayana*, the plays of Kalidasa, the Tamil classics, etc. And how can he so gratuitously put down the 16 "official languages" of India when he admits that he cannot read any of these languages? (Amirthanayagam, 1997) [The number of official languages changes with each new constitution.]

In a dispute over the academic curriculum at Duke University which also involved the status of Indian languages, the campus newspaper published the opinions of two students who opposed a petition to elevate Hindi from a collection of courses to a full major. One wrote that Hindi should not be taught because it "is a language spoken in a Third World country overwrought with disease and poverty." The other averred that "the values of the West – the power of reason, the sanctity of individual rights and the unfettered pursuit of happiness – are superior to the values of a primitive, impoverished country like India" (Mishra, 1999; *The Wall Street Journal*, 1999).

As India struggles with these issues, what is clear is that the answer does not lie in narrowing down the choices of languages to be used. When this happens, it only exacerbates socioeconomic inequity. During colonial times, only the elite were able to learn English, thereby reassuring the continuation of their privileged status. Little has changed today; even for those who have access to English-language education, most have no opportunity to practice it in their communities. Standardized Hindi is also inaccessible to most Indians. Pattanayak aptly summarizes the situation of India; his words have significance for all multilingual nations:

> From a predominantly monolingual point of view many languages are a nuisance as their acquisition is considered a load; they are uneconomical and politically untenable.... In the case of multilingual countries, the reverse is the case. For them, restrictions in the choice of languages they use is a nuisance, and one language is not only uneconomical, but it is politically and socially absurd. The enormity of resources spent to produce the four percent of English-knowing persons in India over the past 200 years would prove the absurdity of the efforts to replace many languages by one under democratic planning. The cultural deprivation and sociopolitical inequality introduced by the approach of monolingual control of a multilingual polity makes nonsense of any talk of such economic benefit. (Pattanayak, 1985: 402)

CONCLUSION

In this chapter, we examined how countries other than the United States cope with language diversity. We discovered that official multilingual policy promotes harmony and inter-group relations. The history of Canada shows that when government fails to support the principle of multilingualism, causing language minorities to suffer diminished status, discontent results; when minority languages are protected, and minority-group members find greater avenues for socioeconomic mobility, divisiveness is averted. The case of Switzerland suggests that the official use of more than one language is compatible with a secure and equitable society. While the German Swiss and their language tend to be dominant, respect is given to the efforts of the other linguistic groups to keep their languages viable.

For countries in which only one language is officially recognized, the other languages that exist in the population are not easily suppressed. In Western Europe, where political and economic ties between nations are being secured by the creation of the European Community, and where modernization and Americanization have led to a more homogeneous culture, there has been a movement for the revival of regional languages as a way of reaffirming the distinctiveness of each nation. In India, resistance to the institutionalization of English has found shape in a call for the language rights of those who speak the many local languages.

And what of the United States? There are those who understand the absurdity of Americans' dependence on a single language. Former Senator Paul Simon calls Americans "linguistically malnourished" (Simon, 1992: 5); Hayden disparagingly characterizes the United States as "the land of the monolingual" (Hayden, 1979: 93). Many Americans seem unaware of the advantages attached to multilingualism: it gives individuals a sense of identity; it creates a more equitable society; it promotes harmonious relations among linguistic groups; it adds richness to the shared culture; it allows for better foreign relations. In the next and final chapter, we will contemplate what America might look like if Americans were able to rid themselves of their attachment to monolingualism.

CHAPTER 8

The Possibilities of a Pluralistic, Multilingual America

INTRODUCTION

Diversity is a force of nature that is not easily suppressed. The concept of a "melting-pot" America, a work-in-progress that will eventually yield a population of homogeneous citizens, is nothing more than an illusion. Once Americans accept this, they need to engage in a new discussion. At the crux of this discussion is the question: how can diversity be successfully embraced and put to use to create a more harmonious, equitable society? This will be the focus of the present chapter.

First, we will discuss the various forms of multicultural education and two antecedents, ethnic studies and intercultural education. We will hear from critics, including advocates of anti-racial education, who evaluate multicultural education as it exists today and see little significant development from its early genesis. The concept of multiculturalism is also challenged by an alternative vision of society called cosmopolitanism.

Essential to a cosmopolitan, pluralistic view of society is the existence of opportunities for groups to know and understand one another. A project of the National Immigration Forum (Quiroz, 1995) offers an example of how this is working today. The Forum studied successful efforts to organize immigrant and non-immigrant groups around a common community problem. One of the challenges confronting these projects has been the task of overcoming the barriers between the groups, barriers erected by language and cultural differences and by the negative stereotypes that the groups have of each other. Generally, the focus of activity on the common problem has tended to push these issues to the background.

The fostering of a common language is an essential part of bringing people together. In the previous chapter, we learned that forcing everyone to use a single language is not practical. A better approach would be to foster universal bilingualism. We will discuss how elements of multiculturalism, cosmopolitanism, and bilingualism may be joined to create a model pluralistic society. We will then explore ways to encourage bilingualism, for children and for adults, both immigrant and American-born. Finally, we will contemplate the effect that universal bilingualism would have on life in America.

MULTICULTURALISM AND ITS CRITICS

While many of today's thinkers and educators acknowledge that the United States is a heterogeneous society (Schlesinger, 1992; Myers, 1994; Carnevale, 1995; Arthur & Shapiro, 1995; Eoyang, 1995; Bernstein, 1994), they do not always agree on the roles that different cultures should have in American life. The concept of multiculturalism, in particular, encompasses several viewpoints in this respect, especially with regard to education.

In reviewing the literature on multicultural education, Sleeter and Grant (1987) categorize five approaches:

- *Teaching the Culturally Different* seeks to foster, within existing programs, positive group identity among children of color with the goal of assimilating them into the cultural mainstream and the existing social structure.
- The *Human Relations* approach focuses on teaching students how to get along with each other better.
- The *Single Group Studies* method offers courses about distinct ethnic, gender, and social-class groups.
- *Multicultural Education* promotes cultural pluralism and social equality by reforming school programs so that they reflect the diversity of the population.
- The *Education that is Multicultural and Social Reconstructionist* approach gets students to challenge the inequity of the current social structure and to promote cultural diversity through academic research and community projects.

Sleeter and Grant (1987) find significant limitations in these approaches. They aspire to different goals, while sharing a very general commitment to enact "changes in education that are supposed to benefit people of color" (Sleeter and Grant, 1987: 436). The Teaching the Culturally Different approach places all the obligation on minority students to fit into the mainstream. The first four approaches focus on changes at the classroom level rather than on instituting school-wide reform. Merely learning about other groups, such as their languages, cultures, holidays, and customs, does little to help actual intergroup relations. The authors note the lack of commitment to change in the arenas where the power to control education resides: the community, school administrators, government policy makers, and teacher educators. Nor do they find much discussion of the problems that underlie the unequal treatment of groups, such as racism and social stratification. Only the last approach, argue Sleeter and Grant, comes close to dealing with the roots of social inequity, and that approach is the least developed.

Banks (1995) agrees that multicultural education has yet to evolve into a significant form. He traces the movement back to earlier reform efforts. The idea of studying particular ethnic groups came from late nineteenth-century black scholars, who realized the need to integrate knowledge about African Americans into school and college curricula. This activity was developed more intensely with the black studies movement of the 1960s and 70s, during which scholars pursued a deep knowledge of black history and culture with the goal of empowering and enhancing the African American community. As advocates demanded and won black studies programs at schools and universities, other groups (Puerto Ricans, Mexican Americans, Native Americans, and Asian Americans) followed suit.

A second reform effort was the intergroup or intercultural education movement. This movement was a response to the mass migration of ethnic and racial groups to the north after World War II, and sought to defuse ethnic tensions, reduce prejudice, and create interracial understanding among students. It emphasized democratic living and interracial cooperation within mainstream society and the sharing of a common culture. However, Olneck (1990) claims, the attitude of intercultural educators toward cultural diversity was essentially ambiguous. They sought to portray cultural differences among people as variants of universal practices. Displays of ethnicity were to become part of a repository of American culture while losing their connection to group identity. The perpetuation of distinct ethnic groups was not a desired outcome.

As Banks (1995) explains, these two reform efforts were not compatible. The leaders of the ethnic studies movement were people of color, largely outside of mainstream institutions. They advocated the creation of parallel ethnic institutions for the survival of separate ethnic groups. The leaders of the intergroup education movement were largely white liberals. Paying little attention to issues of power and structural inequality, they envisioned a nation in which ethnic and racial differences were minimized, and ethnic groups were easily assimilated into mainstream culture and institutions.

The intergroup education movement died out in the 1960s and 70s, a weak voice during a period in which ethnic groups were demanding recognition of their existence and their fair share of power. However, its goal of assimilating various groups into mainstream society without challenging the existing social structure is reflected in the weak forms of multicultural education that now exist. Troyna (1992) labels multiculturalism as the most liberal variety of the assimilationist perspective. Banks (1995) is critical of the fact that the most prevalent form of multicultural education is what he terms *content integration*, which involves putting information about ethnic groups into existing curricula. More work is needed in the other areas of multicultural education:

- the *knowledge construction process*, getting students to look at information as a reflection of the writer's purpose and viewpoint and to formulate their own interpretations of reality;
- *prejudice reduction*, developing more democratic attitudes, values, and behaviors;
- *equity pedagogy*, improving the academic achievement of low-income students;
- *empowering school culture and social structure*, changing the structure of the school system at its core.

A true multicultural school experience includes "content, examples, and realistic images of diverse racial and ethnic groups," learning activities in which "students from diverse groups work to attain shared goals," "simulated images of ethnic groups that present them in positive and realistic ways," and adults who "model the attitudes and behaviors they are trying to teach" (Banks, 1995: 19).

Throughout the literature on multicultural education is an acknowledgment of the need to deal with racism and prejudice. Multicultural educators propose programs under the rubrics *human relations* and *prejudice reduction*. According to Rattansi (1992), advocates of another approach, antiracist education, contend that the assumptions behind these programs are false. Multiculturalists argue that at the root of intolerance and prejudice is ignorance, which can be attacked by teaching groups of students about each other. This assumes that individuals hold prejudices in a systematic and non-contradictory manner, and that prejudice can be cured with a particular pedagogy. However, Rattansi (1992) points to the research on racist discourse, which shows that views about a particular group vary with context and audience, and that people may support anti-discriminatory policies in one context but not another. For example, African Americans are often viewed as lazy and willing to live off welfare, but also as superb athletes who honor their sports teams, their hometowns, and their nation. Alliances between students of different ethnic groups may form in a particular classroom, but may be unrecognized in the cafeteria or outside school grounds. Sexuality may also complicate racial encounters; men of one ethnicity are often socialized to protect their neighborhoods against incursions from men of another ethnicity. Considering the complexity of inter-ethnic relations, it is not surprising that there is little research on the effectiveness of teaching about cultures in the fight against prejudice.

Anti-racist educators also take multiculturalists to task for ignoring the role that institutions play in fostering prejudice. In this respect, their criticism of multicultural education parallels those of Sleeter and Grant (1987) and Banks (1995). The racism of the wider society, they argue, is inherently imbedded in the educational system. It appears not only in sanctioned policies, such as those that track students into academically demanding or academically simplified programs, but in everyday encounters and the actions and words of principals, teachers, and school personnel. Even in their recognition of the need to find "positive images" of different ethnic groups, multicultural educators assume that there is one, objective representation of reality, and that if they look hard enough, these educators will recognize it. In addition, "'positive images' tend to privilege middle-class, heterosexual, familial respectability" (Rattansi, 1992: 34); that is, they show minority groups in the forms that most resemble those of mainstream society. Anti-racist educators pursue a more democratic objective: "the search for mechanisms for giving voice to a range of representations, and for encouraging critical dialogue and interrogation of all intellectual and political frameworks" (Rattansi, 1992: 34).

While multicultural educators acknowledge the diverse bases of cultural differentiation, such as ethnicity, class, and gender, Rattansi points to the lack of focus on differentiation within minority communities, such as economic and sexual distinctions. Also, little attention is paid to the ways in which the boundaries are drawn and redrawn in encounters within minority groups and in relation to majority groups. Consideration of these changing boundaries casts doubt on the "simple additive model of ... cultural diversity" (Rattansi, 1992: 39) in the discourse of multiculturalism. It calls for a re-thinking of the definition of "culture" and the ways in which educators can be said to teach about "other cultures."

Olneck contends that multicultural education has remained undeveloped because "the tolerable limits of pluralism in American education remain quite narrow." He points to the fact that all movements that have the goal of redressing inequities in status and power must contend with "the ideological and material resources of opposing dominant groups and institutions." In addition, multiculturalism must deal with "anxieties over the potential for division and conflict that public recognition and endorsement of ethnicity are perceived by some to engender" (Olneck, 1990: 166).

The focus of the American ethos is on the individual rather than on the group. We have seen this in our previous discussion of language policy, in

Chapter 7. Ricento (1998b) points out that the United States offers no legal protection of minority-language groups; instead, efforts to fight language discrimination must be framed as protecting the rights of individuals. The message that society relays to young people and to newcomers is that in America everyone is the same, and that through hard work and perseverance, anyone can succeed. When the realities of racism and discrimination are brought forward, this message is challenged by another: If you are black or Latino, you might not succeed; the deck is stacked against you. This challenging message leads to greater group identification and calls for collective rights and empowerment, an orientation diametrically opposed to that of individual struggle and success.

This explains to some extent why multiculturalists avoid an examination of how deeply different minority groups are, and how different their lives are from those in mainstream society. It also explains why some Americans seek to downplay ethnicity altogether, insisting that people look to other types of affiliation with which to identify. Hollinger (1995), for example, criticizes the "ethno-racial pentagon," the five classifications often used by the government to track societal inequity and discrimination: European American, African American, Latino, Asian American, and Native American. Individuals are at times forced to identify with one of the blocs; until recently, this was a problem for respondents filling out the Census who claimed membership in more than one bloc. However, Hollinger argues, some people are more free to disassociate themselves from their blocs than others. A person of Polish ancestry may or may not choose to identify with her Polishness; it is one that is not forced on her by society, and she may prefer a non-descent community as her major affiliation, say, the community of attorneys. However, someone of African American ancestry cannot decide to disassociate herself as an African American, even if she also has strains of European and Native American blood in her make-up. Furthermore, if she chooses not to participate in African American culture, she may be shunned by others who share her heritage. The ethno-racial pentagon, according to Hollinger, "is a framework for politics and culture ... It is a statement that certain affiliations matter more than others" (Hollinger, 1995: 24).

Because of the limitations of the ethno-racial pentagon, Hollinger (1995) sees a need to move beyond multiculturalism. Multiculturalism, he argues, puts too much emphasis on descent-based affiliations, and ignores other communities to which individuals may belong. Multiculturalists get bogged down in debating whether particular groups are trying to assert their superiority; they are overly concerned with defining the differences and similarities among the groups. Furthermore, writes Hollinger (1995), by acknowledging that some ethno-racial groups have more privileges than others, and focusing on the boundaries between these groups, multiculturalism does little to advance equality. The educator Henry Louis Gates, Jr, agrees that multiculturalism has become too entangled with what he calls "identity politics": "The invocation of 'multiculturalism' is quite often a ruse, used to provide respectable cover for political enlistment of racial and ethnic solidarity. Increasingly uneasy with talk of descent-based identities – race, ethnicity – we seek to redeem them in the shiny currency of 'culture'" (Gates, 1993: 116).

Hollinger offers as an alternate framework the idea of *cosmopolitanism*. Historically, cosmopolitanism is associated with the Enlightenment of the eighteenth century and its "impulse toward worldly breadth;" it is also identified with individuals who travel widely and are considered "citizens of the world" (Hollinger, 1995: 5). While such people have also been considered rootless, Hollinger proposes a cosmopolitanism with sensitivity to the importance of roots. The roots to which he refers, however, are not proscribed by heredity alone. The cosmopolitan perspective recognizes that people may identify with several different communities at once, both descent-based and non-descent-based. Individuals should also be free to choose the extent to which they identify with each community, and the relative importance of these communities to them. While people can't change their parentage, they can decide whether and how much to participate in their descent-based community, just as many people do with regard to the religious affiliation of their parentage.

Cosmopolitanism recognizes that people of different ethnic and racial backgrounds tend to connect with each other and form new communities around common needs and interests. These new communities break down the boundaries set up by the ethno-racial pentagon; Hollinger (1995) gives as an example a Punjabi-Mexican community in rural California. The notion that affiliations are created in many ways recalls Rattansi's point about the "shifting boundaries and alliances" that form within and among communities, and his rejection of a simple, additive model of cultural diversity. Angela Davis, the noted African American political activist, adds her voice to this discussion:

> I ... think that race has become an increasingly obsolete way of constructing community because it is based on unchangeable, immutable biological facts in a very pseudo-scientific way ... I'm interested in communities that aren't static in that way ... I'm not suggesting that we do not anchor ourselves in our communities. But I think, to use a metaphor, the rope attached to that anchor should be large enough to allow us to move into other communities. (Davis, 1992: 11)

While Hollinger contributes an important perspective to the discussion, there are weaknesses in his vision of a pluralistic society. Individuals may choose the degree of strength of their ties to an ethnic collectivity; however, in order for that ethnic collectivity to survive, it needs the strong participation of many members. Without such participation, the ethnic displays that individuals carry will be regarded as merely part of the American culture, an expected outcome of the early intercultural education movement much criticized by its evaluators. In addition, cosmopolitanism may not have equal appeal to all minority groups, especially those that are culturally and/or religiously conservative. The low rate of inter-marriage between Chinese Americans and other ethnic groups was mentioned in Chapter 2. In some American communities, conflicts among Jews who follow different practices threaten their ability to live together peacefully (Freedman, 2000).

While Hollinger argues that people are too closely identified with ethno-racial groups of unequal power, and criticizes multiculturalism for failing to solve this inequity, cosmopolitanism does little to eliminate it either. An African American physician who chooses to identify more strongly with her professional colleagues than with fellow African Americans does not help to alleviate racial prejudice; by downplaying her ethnicity, she allows her colleagues to ignore it and any bigotry that they may harbor. The "ethno-racial pentagon" helps the government track the under-representation of minority groups in various professions; even as the physician chooses not to bring attention to herself as an African American, it is possible that she may see few African American colleagues around her. Finally, downplaying ethnic differences does not eliminate other existing forms of inequity. Socioeconomic status will still be determined by one's means of earning a living; professionals will still be on the top rung, and manual laborers on the bottom. If racism and discrimination are ignored, ethno-racial minorities will continue to be under-represented at the top rung and over-represented at the bottom.

Still, Hollinger does contribute an important perspective to the vision of a pluralist society. His call for the "recognition, acceptance, and eager exploration of diversity," and his suggestion that "each individual and collective unit ... absorb as much varied experience as it can" (Hollinger, 1995: 84) are welcome. Another important aspect of his work is that it brings the discussion of pluralism out of the school context. The work of Freeman (1998), discussed in Chapter 4, shows that even successful school reform has a limited effect on the larger society. And as writers mentioned in this chapter explain, learning "about" other cultures in school cannot substitute for real and complex interactions among diverse groups of people. In America today, there are isolated examples of communities trying to embrace diversity and create new associations. When groups transcend traditional boundaries, tensions and problems will inevitably arise. In the next section, we will look at some of these communities, examining how they came together and what roadblocks they encountered along the way.

THE COMMUNITY INNOVATIONS PROJECT OF THE NATIONAL IMMIGRATION FORUM

The National Immigration Forum is a confederation of some 200 organizations that focuses on federal immigration and refugee policy issues. In 1992, it decided to take a slightly different direction by examining the role of immigrants and refugees in American communities. The Community Innovations Project, launched in 1993, looked for examples of newcomers and established residents, of different racial and ethnic backgrounds, coming together to solve a common problem. The project targeted four cities with large immigrant populations and with histories of problems related to racial and ethnic differences: Chicago, Los Angeles, New York, and Washington, DC. The results of the project are described in Quiroz (1995).

These projects illustrate what Hollinger (1995) refers to as cosmopolitanism. They involve people moving beyond the boundaries of the labels that society has placed on them to form new, voluntary associations. They do not reject their descent-based affiliations; instead, they add an additional affiliation to their identities.

It is important to understand how the coming together of these groups differs from integration. Integration, as we discussed in Chapter 1, is enforced by government; it does not spring from the needs of the community. Often, government integration policy results in the further separation of groups rather than their coming together. For example, in neighborhoods where the government moves in a minority group, whites frequently move out. The projects described by Quiroz (1995) are inherently different: a common problem draws people together, the initiative to solve the problem comes from the community itself, and there is little opportunity for either of the groups to move away. Also, in Chapter 1, we examined the argument of those opposed to language pluralism that integration inevitably erases the differences between people. However, even in the projects described here, in which people come together voluntarily, there is no "melting-pot" effect. Differences between the groups do not disappear, but they do need to be addressed.

Three themes arising from these projects are relevant to our discussion. These are the tendency of people in power to use the differences between groups to their advantage, the need for the groups to transcend negative attitudes and perceptions, and the need to deal with the language barrier.

Using Diversity to Divide

Diversity in itself is not a problem. However, it becomes a problem when those with power use it to set less powerful groups against each other. The result benefits those in power and helps maintain the social status quo.

In Washington, DC, a community-organizing project, Washington Inner

City Self-Help (WISH), helps tenants in apartment buildings to form resident associations. WISH was established in the late 1970s to assist mostly African American tenants to fight rent hikes and evictions, actions taken by landlords to encourage tenants to move out so that their apartments could be rented to people with higher incomes. In the 1980s, Central American immigrants began moving into neighborhoods that had previously been largely African American. WISH noticed that landlords, knowing that they could get the Latinos to pay higher rents, were setting the new Latino tenants against the African Americans so that the African Americans would move out. WISH now makes sure that resident associations involve representatives from all the ethnic groups living in a building, encouraging the groups to work together against the landlords.

Latinos and African Americans have also been set against each other in employment situations. In Washington, DC, for example, most of the janitors who work for privately-owned buildings are Latinos, while government janitors are African American. Latino janitors are more easily taken advantage of, since their lack of English and immigrant status make them less likely to challenge questionable employer practices. Private companies that offer janitorial services to building owners often deny employees the right to organize unions and violate health and safety laws. Even when African Americans are employed in commercial buildings, they are separated from their Latino counterparts. What emerged from this situation was the formation of two unions: Local 82, a predominantly African American government janitors union, and Justice for Janitors, a largely Latino commercial janitors union. In 1991, however, the two unions joined to advocate for workplace improvements for all janitors. For example, they targeted a local janitorial service company that refused to hire African Americans. Government and commercial janitors held demonstrations against the company, which led to an investigation by the Equal Employment Opportunity Commission.

These examples illustrate the negative consequences of defining people solely by their membership in the ethno-racial pentagon. Because some of the categories in this pentagon (African American and Latino American) are socially stigmatized, mainstream society finds it easy to pit members of these groups against each other, with the result that both groups suffer. But when African Americans and Latino Americans define themselves in other ways (as tenants and janitors) they find common links with each other. In creating new affiliations, as Hollinger (1995) suggests, they acquire newfound sources of strength and power.

Transcending Negative Attitudes and Perceptions

In the course of working together, immigrants and established residents have to face the negative attitudes that the groups often hold about each other. WISH' s efforts to form resident organizations, mentioned above, have run into this problem. African American residents complain about the lack of cleanliness of their Salvadoran neighbors, while the Salvadorans complain about the criminal activity among African Americans. However, there is little time and money to address these issues; the focus of the organization is on improving the living environment.

The pressures of surviving in a difficult situation often set off feelings of suspicion among groups. A tenants' support group in Northern Virginia, near Washington, DC, includes whites, African Americans, and Central Americans. Many of the African Americans, who have battled for many years for decent housing, resent the newly arrived Central Americans, often feeling that more is being done for the immigrants and that they are taking over. In Chicago, parents and community leaders from adjacent African American and Mexican neighborhoods formed a coalition to deal with inter-group tensions. At its first meeting, several African Americans charged the Mexicans with racism, prompting an open discussion of the biases and prejudices existing in both groups. While the coalition has helped improve communication and has initiated several successful projects, the sense of competition between the groups is still present. At a housing development for female-headed families of different ethnic backgrounds in Los Angeles, interpersonal tensions arose between some Mexican and Central American women, erupting over such small matters as what kind of food to serve during council meetings. A conflict-resolution expert was hired to train resident facilitators from each of the ethnic groups to intervene when disputes arose.

From these cases we can see that a truly pluralistic society is not easy to create. Americans are socialized from an early age to see themselves and others in terms of race and ethnicity. They have absorbed the bigotry and prejudice that has permeated American society throughout its history. Even those who are themselves the objects of bigotry have adopted the bigoted views that mainstream society holds toward other marginalized groups. This suggests that the creation of new affiliations that cross descent-based identifications can only come about when people cease to view each other in the biased manner to which they have been conditioned.

Dealing with Language Differences

When immigrants and established residents come together, the lack of a common language is bound to be an issue. If meetings are held in one language, the members of the group who don't speak that language are isolated. In the projects described by Quiroz (1995), the issue is resolved largely through the use of translation. The tenant associations organized by WISH hold their meetings in each language spoken by the residents. The tenant support group in Northern Virginia holds bilingual Spanish–

English meetings and publishes a bilingual newsletter. However, meetings are conducted mostly in Spanish; the person who facilitates the meetings is also the simultaneous translator. The Los Angeles housing development has a bilingual/bicultural child care center. Resident council meetings are held in Spanish, with volunteers providing English and Korean translation.

Translation is undoubtedly the most efficient means of transcending the language barrier in circumstances such as those faced by these projects, when time is limited and the focus is on improving the quality of life of the groups involved. However, it puts constraints on the kind of one-on-one interaction that would bring people from these groups to a deeper understanding and appreciation of one another. One hint of this kind of interaction is documented by Quiroz (1995). In Chicago, several refugee-run mutual assistance associations joined a local community development organization to launch a home-ownership project in a section of the city where both immigrants and established residents live. When the townhouses were completed and their new owners had moved in, an African American resident happened to meet a young boy who spoke only Spanish. The African American called over his two daughters, who were enrolled in a bilingual elementary school. When the girls started speaking to their new neighbor in Spanish, the boy was overcome with emotion. Said the father, "It meant so much to have an American child speak to him. It was good for us and for him to know that his culture is important to us" (cited in Quiroz, 1995: 33).

Quiroz concludes that "interaction between newcomers and established residents broadens the perspective of people in both groups, allows each to learn from the expertise and skills of the other, and increases the odds of improving the quality of life for all" (Quiroz, 1995: 81). Broadening one's experience and advancing one's status are exactly the aims of Hollinger's (1995) conception of cosmopolitanism. Beyond the projects described by Quiroz (1995), an essential part of learning about and learning from others is knowing their language.

THE ROLE OF BILINGUALISM IN A PLURALISTIC SOCIETY

In constructing an equitable, pluralistic society, we would be helped by combining some of the ideas mentioned in our discussion of multiculturalism and cosmopolitanism. From the former, we take the notion that the perpetuation of ethno-racial groups is of great importance. From the latter, we take the idea that alliances between ethno-racial groups are beneficial in seeking the socioeconomic advancement of all those who are marginalized. Bilingualism helps to serve both these ends.

A cosmopolitan society must be built on the ability of individuals to transcend their usual social spheres and make contact with people who are different from them. Native language may be one characteristic that sets people apart. As we have seen in Quiroz (1995), translation offers one way in which people with the same concerns but different languages can communicate. However, the need for an intermediary sets constraints on the relationship that develops between members of different language groups. When people come together around a common issue to work against a common adversary, they need to learn to trust each other. Trust grows through intimate contact, through connections on a very personal level. This level of contact cannot happen through a translator. How can people communicate about personal topics – family, food, friendships, emotions – without a common language?

The affiliations discussed by Quiroz (1995) are limited, not only by their lack of a common language but also by the stereotypes the groups have of each other. The antagonism that has developed is the exact problem that the intercultural education movement sought to eradicate; it is also reminiscent of the hostilities described in the legal cases concerning language restrictionism that we discussed in Chapter 6. All these instances point to the need for the groups to understand each other better, and the need for a common means of communication. Two questions then arise: whether there must be only one common language, and whether that language has to be English. Some of the judges whose rulings we have discussed would undoubtedly say yes to both questions. However, the insistence that everyone speaks the native language of one group immediately creates a situation in which the groups are not equally valued; in this way, the status quo of unequal empowerment is maintained. If the individuals in both groups learn the language of the other group, greater understanding and intimacy ensue, with no threat to the balance of power between the groups.

A society that was bilingual but not cosmopolitan would also be diminished. In such a society, individuals would identify primarily and most strongly with those of the same heritage. Opportunities to forge new relationships across ethno-racial lines would be limited, in turn limiting opportunities to break down the stereotypes that minority groups have of each other and that mainstream society has of minority groups. People would know both English and their heritage language, but English would serve a very narrow, utilitarian purpose, as a mere tool necessary for getting by in the larger, multi-ethnic society, rather than as a means of broadening professional and social contacts. As we discussed in Chapter 3, this would be an example of what Schumann (1978) refers to as instrumental rather than integrative language-learning motivation. People who hold this attitude toward English might encounter limits to their ability to improve their socioeconomic status.

Multiculturalism calls for a vigorous and sustained effort to perpetuate ethnic sub-groups within society. At the same time, such groups need to advocate for themselves, for their socioeconomic advancement, and for acceptance as equals to mainstream Americans at all levels of participation in society. This involves advocating for greater acceptance of their languages, for an adjustment in the unequal balance of power between English and the minority languages represented across the nation. Without this redistribution of linguistic power, American society may experience the type of fragmentation that critics of cultural pluralism, such as Schlesinger (1992) and Porter (1990), warn against: a society that fosters rather than mitigates hostility, prejudice, and negative stereotyping.

In this way, we come to the conclusion that the goal of a democratic, pluralistic society is best met by combining elements of multiculturalism and cosmopolitanism with bilingualism. Bilingualism can never be a bad thing, but it must be balanced. Those who speak English as a first language have the advantage over those who are born into a different tongue and must struggle to master the dominant language. Aside from the uneven distribution of power and resources that result from this situation, it hampers true communication and understanding across social, economic, and linguistic barriers. English-dominant Americans who know only a few words of Spanish cannot really relate to Hispanic Americans; Hispanic Americans who acquire only a rudimentary level of English cannot hope to dispel the stereotypes that established Americans may harbor about them. When people of diverse backgrounds need to come together around a common purpose, the linguistic barriers between them must be torn down in a way that avoids valuing one group over the other. Universal bilingualism is the way that this can be accomplished. In the next section, we will explore ways to encourage such bilingualism.

FOSTERING BILINGUALISM

Hollinger (1995) prods Americans to look beyond the associations that currently shape their identities, to seek new associations that will broaden their world view and improve their quality of life. When people decide to do this, the lines that separate one group from another become more porous; the differences between "us" and "them" lessen. Under these circumstances, second-language learning should be facilitated, based on what we know about the process. As we discussed in Chapter 3, the social and psychological distance between learners and speakers of the target language has a powerful effect on the learning process. If this distance can be shortened, language learning becomes easier. Motivation is also a strong factor. If the learners sincerely want to join the community of those who speak the target language (and believe that they will be welcomed), they have a decided advantage. We also discussed the effect on second-language acquisition of ego permeability, the ability to let down one's guard on one's identity and allow the language and behavioral characteristics of the target language to enter.

In an ideal pluralistic society, the desire to learn a second language is two-way: established residents are as eager to learn one or more immigrant languages as immigrants are to learn English. Group membership is not hierarchical; all affiliations are equally valuable, all languages worthy of acquiring. The Anglo-conformity model of immigrant adaptation described in Chapter 2 (in which immigrants shed their native identities and take on all the trappings of being "American") is antithetical to this type of society. People are allowed to be different from each other, but they are also encouraged to share with others aspects of their native identity, language being one of them.

This type of society is not easily created. However, fostering bilingualism can help move people closer to this goal. Breaking down the language barriers between groups helps them learn more about each other and dispels existing prejudices they may have toward each other. The contact that ensues from the removal of these barriers may make people realize what they have in common. This may foster the creation of new affiliations. Thus, bilingualism may be viewed as both a product of cosmopolitan society and a catalyst for its development. We will now examine ways of encouraging bilingualism, among children and adults.

Encouraging Bilingualism Among Children

In dealing with the education of both majority-language and minority-language children, it is important to keep in mind that no single approach or method works for every situation. Pauley writes, "To be successful, education policies must be designed with the diverse needs and problems of real classrooms in mind; all too often, universal mandates fail this simple test" (Pauley, 1992: 489). He points out that a policy that works with one teacher in one school may be disastrous in another setting, that "the productive core of schooling is the individual classroom" (Pauley, 1992: 490). With regard to the instruction of minority-language children, Pauley suggests that "local school officials consult with teachers, students, and families to determine which classrooms, teachers, and children are well-suited to participate in bilingual instruction, and which classrooms, teachers, and children are suited for other approaches" (Pauley, 1992: 489).

This argument for local control of education is one we have encountered before. In Chapter 4, we discussed the work of Rolf Kjolseth (1973), who, examining bilingual programs in the Southwest in the 1960s, found that the majority of these programs were created and controlled by the federal educational establishment. With little knowledge of the needs of Mexican American children and their parents, educators had fashioned a kind of program that was not bilingual at all. Rather, it was designed to wean children away from their native language and toward monolingualism in English, guided by "a kind of cultural and linguistic 'counterinsurgency' policy" (Kjolseth, 1973: 16). In contrast, programs that were nurtured at the local level and involved the parents and community were few and far between. The miles of distance between these two kinds of programs can be compared to the distance between governmental integration policies and projects such as those described by Quiroz (1995) above.

The needs and characteristics of a particular community should guide its leaders in deciding what kind of education is most effective in promoting bilingualism. Schools serving a community dominated by speakers of one particular minority language are best suited for what we have previously called maintenance bilingual programs. These programs provide instruction in the minority language until a sufficient degree of literacy has been achieved, followed by instruction in the English language and the addition of English as a medium of instruction. Where there are sufficient numbers of native speakers of English and native speakers of a minority language in the same community, equal numbers from each of these groups could be chosen for a school that offers a dual-language program, in which each group learns the other's language. Both languages would be offered as subjects of study and both languages would be used as media of instruction.

Some communities have a more linguistically heterogeneous population, with speakers of English and speakers of a variety of other languages. In this case, English may be chosen as the language of instruction. However, there should be opportunities for students of the same native language to work together, with those more advanced in English helping those less advanced. Students might also work on projects written or presented in their own languages and in English, as a means of helping develop both languages. A linguistically heterogeneous student population also offers the opportunity for a number of experimental programs geared toward bilingualism for everyone. The school might provide a certain number of academic courses given in a minority language, both for English-speakers who are taking instruction in that language and for native speakers of the language. The study of other countries might be linked to the study of the languages spoken there, with students who are natives of these countries serving as information sources. The school might also pair up English-speakers with minority-language speakers so that they could exchange tutoring sessions in each of the languages.

Some communities may not have speakers of a minority language; their schools may serve English-speakers only. In this case, the traditional paradigm of teaching second languages in dry, exercise-driven classes meted out two or three times a week should be set aside for more innovative and successful methods. Partial immersion programs, in which students study one or two academic subjects taught in a second language, are one possibility. But even if there are few language minorities in the immediate community, schools can establish links with other neighborhoods to take advantage of the linguistic wealth that exists in many cities. Face-to-face encounters between English-dominant and minority-language students would stimulate language learning for both groups. Also, with the increasing presence of computers in schools, communication through electronic mail could also be enlisted to stimulate language acquisition as well as the exchange of cultural and historical information; case studies of global networking projects are described in Cummins and Sayers (1995). Any means of bringing together children who are isolated from each other socially, economically, and geographically can only benefit the future of American society in the long run.

Encouraging Bilingualism Among Adults

While children are learning in an atmosphere that places value on cultural and linguistic pluralism, it is important for the adults in their communities to embrace these values as well. As with education, the social needs and the make-up of communities differ greatly. The suggestions that follow are offered as general guidelines for encouraging diversity and cosmopolitanism at the local level.

People come to adulthood through very different life experiences. Along the way, the accumulated experiences of some adults lead them to a natural tolerance for newcomers and an appreciation of their struggles; others reach a different state of mind in this regard. In particular, some people have a great deal of impatience with immigrants who have difficulty adjusting to the language and culture of their new home. Local groups, such as civic or religious organizations, might promote discussion of such issues. Speakers who might be capable of opening minds include Americans who have lived abroad and who can talk about the adjustment difficulties they faced, immigrants who have successfully adapted to American life, and professionals who deal regularly with immigrants. Immigrants and non-immigrants would benefit from discussing incidents in which cultural misunderstandings have fomented feelings of mutual hostility. Before people can cross the boundaries that traditionally define them and create new associations, they need to know each other more fully and rid themselves of existing prejudices and stereotypes.

One of the best ways to understand how difficult it is to adjust to a new language is to go through the experience oneself. We cannot transplant Americans to another country and tell them that this strange place is now their new home. But we can give them the chance to learn a new language. This is a particularly ripe opportunity for bringing people together. Immigrants could serve as teachers of a second language to Americans; in exchange, Americans could offer instruction in English to immigrants.

Community centers or libraries might offer the space for this activity. In this way, today's adult Americans might acquire the bilingualism that they failed to acquire when they were in school.

Both immigrants and non-immigrants would benefit from the strong presence of non-English languages and cultures in the community. Residents could encourage public and school libraries to buy books in the languages of their local minority groups. Local groups could sponsor multilingual/multicultural festivals, featuring the food, art, music, theater, and literature of all the nationality groups represented in a particular neighborhood. Citizens could ask their city or state officials to declare their jurisdictions officially multilingual, multi-ethnic, and/or multicultural. They would then have some leverage in asking their governments to provide funds for activities that encourage cross-cultural understanding and foster bilingualism in immigrants and non-immigrants.

THE BENEFITS OF A BILINGUAL SOCIETY

In an ideal, bilingual America, every resident would speak English and another language; cultural and linguistic diversity would be considered assets. Such a society would have enormous advantages for everyone.

Immigrants, for their part, would have a much less difficult time adjusting to their new life. A government staffed by workers knowing a variety of languages could communicate easily with newcomers, giving them information about how to find jobs, places to live, and English classes. Newcomers might be less likely to confine their lives to their isolated ethnic ghettos; knowing that there are Americans who speak their language would encourage them to participate more fully in the city beyond their neighborhood. Contact between immigrants and established Americans would be more frequent, which might mitigate the production of stereotypes and prejudices that often brew in both groups. It would also encourage the creation of new associations that characterize a cosmopolitan society as described by Hollinger (1995). These new associations might open up job opportunities to immigrants that might otherwise not exist; immigrants might also discover that their knowledge of their native language is a marketable skill. Greater access to the wider society and to job opportunities might reduce immigrant dependence on governmental assistance.

Adult immigrants might learn English more easily, as a result of greater contact with English-speakers and the knowledge that they are not expected to substitute their new language for their own. Immigrant children would find a welcoming atmosphere in their schools. Like their parents, they too would be relieved to find that the language and culture of school need not replace their own language and culture. The rift between immigrant children and parents, which often results when children are pressured to acculturate to American ways, would be avoided. Parents could be more extensively involved in their children's education, which would benefit the entire family.

Established Americans would benefit also. The enjoyment of the cultural expression of different ethnic groups would no longer be limited to the groups themselves. Ethnic neighborhoods would not be as daunting and impenetrable to Americans who spoke the language of those neighborhoods. An American learning Chinese could make great strides by spending time in his city's Chinatown, speaking to vendors, ordering food in the restaurants, going to Chinese-language movies. Aside from acquiring the language, this American would also pick up the kind of first-hand cultural knowledge that is not available in language textbooks. Considering the variety of nationalities represented in the United States, an entire world would be opened up to Americans, especially to those who have never had the opportunity to travel abroad.

Of course, immigrants and established residents do presently come into contact with each other in a variety of situations. But the types of contacts described above differ on a very fundamental level from the interactions that are now common. Today, immigrants are more often than not in a subordinate position to established residents. They are the employees, the servers, the seekers of information, permission, or approval. The new kind of contacts would be different: immigrants would be viewed as having something valuable to give to established residents; they would become the givers rather than the receivers. Or, in some cases, both immigrant and established resident would have something valuable to give to the other. It would be difficult to totally eliminate interactions in which immigrants are subordinate; historically, first-generation immigrants start near the bottom of the social ladder and pave the way for a better status for their children. But the opportunity to interact with citizens on a more equal footing would help make immigrants feel welcomed, would ease their integration into American society, and would further the causes of equality and democracy that the country claims as its foundation.

Established Americans would benefit from bilingualism on many levels. Personally, their ability to form friendships and social contacts with people from other cultures would broaden their knowledge of the world and generally enrich their lives. When they traveled abroad, they would be able to interact with people on a one-to-one basis, making the travel experience far more memorable. Professionally, they would be able to take advantage of opportunities that might not be available to them otherwise. They might, for example, work in a foreign country for a period of time, collaborate with foreign colleagues in the United States, or read professional journals published abroad. Bilingual employees are often more valuable to their bosses than monolingual employees, and may be able to acquire coveted positions at high salaries.

The bilingualism of all American residents, citizens and the newly-arrived, would benefit the nation in many ways. Diplomatic missions abroad would have an easier time finding employees fluent in the languages and knowledgeable about the cultures of the countries where they are stationed. Communication with foreign governments would be more accurate; the United States would avoid the kind of errors in translations that often have dire consequences for its relationship with these governments. For private enterprises, having employees knowledgeable in other languages would help open up foreign markets that entrepreneurs might not have dreamed of otherwise.

This picture of a bilingual America is somewhat optimistic. While knowing more than one language certainly enhances a person's life, not everyone can easily be convinced that this is something that he or she should pursue. For Americans who grow up speaking the language of greatest power and use in the world, bilingualism may be viewed as an attractive but unnecessary asset. Those who are not drawn to professions in international business or foreign diplomacy will probably not be instrumentally motivated to learn another language, and Americans travel the world without having to know the languages of the countries they visit. Since society places so little value and status on the languages of immigrants, English-speaking Americans of low socioeconomic status are particularly unlikely to see any benefits from learning them. In addition, learning a second language is a lengthy, arduous process, and many people have little time or aptitude for it. Still, given what we have learned about the lack of encouragement and resources for achieving bilingualism that are available to Americans at present, it becomes clear that society could do a lot more for those who might be convinced to learn another language. In doing so, society might see significant advantages.

CONCLUSION

In this chapter, we examined multicultural education in its various forms, antiracist education, and a view of America called cosmopolitanism. From multiculturalism we learned of the importance of maintaining ethno-racial identity and working towards a society in which inequities based on these group divisions are eliminated. From cosmopolitanism, we took the idea that groups can reach beyond their boundaries to form new alliances. We saw some real-life examples of this in the associations formed by immigrant and non-immigrant groups who came together to overcome common problems. We learned that one of the barriers they faced was linguistic, which led to a discussion of how elements of bilingualism, multiculturalism, and cosmopolitanism can be mutually beneficial. We then discussed how bilingualism might be encouraged among children and adults. Finally, we painted a picture of what an America that embraced cultural and linguistic diversity would be like. If Americans allowed themselves to be guided by this "impulse toward worldly breadth" (Hollinger, 1995: 5), there would probably be many advantages for individuals and for American society as a whole.

Epilogue

This has been a book about languages in America. But it has also been a book about a lot more than languages. If there is one thing that this author wishes her readers to learn from this book, it is that language issues are never just language issues. They tell us a lot about the essence of a society.

As we have learned, most nations in the world have populations that are both ethnically and linguistically diverse. The language policies of these nations say a lot about how those in power value and treat people who are considered to be ethnic and/or linguistic minorities. If the majority language is the sole means of communication used by the government, and if the government supports cultural activity in that language alone, it transmits the message that the majority language is superior to all others. This means that people who speak this language are also superior; language minorities are relegated to second-class status. Minority languages may be tolerated, especially when used in minority communities, but the ability to speak the languages is not a valuable asset outside these communities and may actually hinder upward mobility and access to power. In addition, educational opportunities for language minorities may be limited, making it difficult for them to learn the majority language well. This insures that they remain in second-class status, and that those who speak the majority language maintain their hold on wealth and power.

In the opposite scenario, a government that communicates and fosters cultural activity in a variety of languages transmits the message that all people are valued equally. Knowledge of minority languages is considered an asset and can enhance employment opportunities. Everyone is encouraged to become bilingual or multilingual. Language minorities develop their own languages and also learn the majority language, while those who speak the majority language learn one or more minority languages. Non-standard varieties of the majority language are also valued, and the government supports their maintenance. Educational opportunities are likely to be more equitable across the society. The quality of a child's education is less dependent on the ethnicity or language of his or her family, how much that family earns, or where it lives. Power and wealth are likely to be more evenly distributed; this is a society that truly puts the principles of democracy into practice.

The United States is struggling to decide what kind of society it wants to be. There are those who are committed to maintaining the status quo, with a small layer of the American population – mostly European American – holding on to its presumption of power. These are the people who insist on the supremacy of English, and who fight to repress other languages. Their adversaries have a different vision of the nation. In this vision, power and wealth are distributed among everyone. English remains the major language of communication, but it is not what links Americans to each other. The real link is the belief that all Americans, no matter what they look like, where they come from, or what their home language is, make a contribution to society; each person's uniqueness deserves to be treated with dignity and respect.

Language is power. Controlling a people's language is one way that those in power maintain control over others. As we watch the development of language policy in the United States, we are also watching the future of the nation.

References

Academia Puertorriqueña (1998) *La Enseñanza del Español y del Inglés en Puerto Rico: Una Polémica de Cien Años*. San Juan: Academia Puertorriqueña de la Lengua Española.

ACLU Newswire (1998) Alaskans debate English as official language. September 15. On WWW at http://www.aclu.org/news/w091598a.html.

ACLU Newswire (1999a) ACLU: Native American and community groups seek to block Alaska's "English Only" law. February 12. On WWW at http://www.aclu.org/news/1999/n021299b.html.

ACLU Newswire (1999b) Court halts enforcement of Alaska's English-Only initiative. March 3. On WWW at http://www.aclu.org/1999/n030399b.html.

Adger, C.T. (1997) Language policy and public knowledge. Center for Applied Linguistics, January. On WWW at http://www.cal.org/ebonics/eboped.html.

Aeppel, T. (1998) A 3Com factory hires a lot of immigrants, gets mix of languages. *The Wall Street Journal*, March 30, pp. A1, A11.

Aikman, D. (1992) Is that correct? *Time*, April 20, p. 81.

Allen, G. (1991) Bilingualism under fire. *Maclean's*, April 22, pp. 16–17.

Altman, I. (1991) A New World in the old: Local society and Spanish emigration to the Indies. In I. Altman and J. Horn (eds) *"To Make America": European Emigration in the Early Modern Period* (pp. 30–58). Berkeley and Los Angeles: University of California Press.

Altman, I. and Horn, J. (1991) Introduction. In I. Altman and J. Horn (eds) *"To Make America": European Emigration in the Early Modern Period* (pp. 1–29). Berkeley and Los Angeles: University of California Press.

Amirthanayagam, G. (1997) Writing after midnight. *The Washington Post* (Book World), September 7, p.10.

Ammon, C.V. (1999) WTO protests reflect concern for globalization. *Times Union*, December 29, p. A10.

Andersson, T. (1971) Bilingual education: The American experience. Paper presented at a conference sponsored by the Ontario Institute for Studies in Education, Toronto, Canada.

Andres, F. (1990) Language relations in multilingual Switzerland. *Multilingua* 9 (1), 11–45.

Armbruster, W. (1992) Chamber report says US competitiveness lagging. *The Journal of Commerce*, January 30, p. 3A.

Arthur, B., Farrar, D. and Bradford, G. (1974) Evaluation reactions of college students to dialect differences in the English of Mexican-Americans. *Language and Science* 17, 255–270.

Arthur, J. and Shapiro, A. (eds) (1995) *Campus Wars: Multiculturalism and the Politics of Difference.* Boulder, CO: Westview Press.

Asher, J.J. (1969) The total physical response approach to second language learning. *Modern Language Journal* 53 (1), 3–17.

Asher, J.J. and García, R. (1969) The optimal age to learn a foreign language. *Modern Language Journal* 53 (5), 334–341.

Asher, J.J., Kusudo, J.A. and de la Torre, R. (1974) Learning a second language through commands: The second field test. *Modern Language Journal* 58 (1–2), 24–32.

Asimov, N. and May, M. (1999) Fluent English a big factor in student scores: Statewide school tests show achievement gap. *San Francisco Chronicle,* July 23, p. A1.

Associated Press (1998) Bilingual education schools may sneak past Prop. 227. July 29. On WWW at http://www2.humnet.ucla.edu/people//macswan/AP15.htm.

Associated Press (2001) Judge set to release ruling on case challenging initiative. March 5.

Atchison, R.M (1894) Retention of immigrants' native language harms America. In T. O'Neill (ed.) *Immigration: Opposing Viewpoints* (1992, pp. 93–96). San Diego: Greenhaven Press.

Avila, J.G. (1983) The case for bilingual ballots. *San Francisco Sunday Examiner & Chronicle,* October 16, pp. 9–11.

Bailyn, B. (1986) *Voyagers to the West: A Passage in the Peopling of America on the Eve of the Revolution.* New York: Knopf (distributed by Random House).

Bain, B.C. and Yu, A. (1978) Toward an integration of Piaget and Vygotsky: A cross-cultural replication (France, Germany, Canada) concerning cognitive consequences of bilinguality. In M. Paradis (ed.) *Aspects of Bilingualism* (pp. 113–126). Columbia, SC: Hornbeam Press.

Baker, C. (1993) *Foundations of Bilingual Education and Bilingualism.* Clevedon: Multilingual Matters.

Baker, K.A. and de Kanter, A.A. (1991) *Effectiveness of Bilingual Education: A Review of the Literature.* Washington, DC: Office of Planning, Budget and Evaluation, Department of Education.

Banas, C. (1997) Naperville schools add language instruction: No specifics on how to fit in new classes. *Chicago Tribune,* June 4, p. 2D.

Banks, J.A. (1995) Multicultural education: Historical development, dimensions, and practice. In J.A. Banks and C.A. McGee Banks (eds) *Handbook of Research on Multicultural Education* (pp. 3–24). New York: MacMillan Publishing USA.

Barasch, R.M. and James, C.V. (1993) *Beyond the Monitor Model: Comments on Current Theory and Practice in Second Language Acquisition.* Boston: Heinle & Heinle Publishers.

Barnes, J.E. (2000) From Russia with news: TV station may be bought. *The New York Times,* January 9, Sec. 14, p. 9.

Behr, P. (2000) By the numbers: The rich, still different from most: 2 surveys show a wider gap, but the conclusions are at odds. *The Washington Post,* January 24, p. F13.

Berger, Jerry (1999) Magazine for Balkan immigrants makes a splash. *St Louis Post-Dispatch,* November 21, p. A2.

Berger, Joseph (1989) Unorthodox path to language teaches schoolchildren to live it. *The New York Times,* March 29, pp. A1, B8.

Berger, Joseph (1993) School programs assailed as bilingual bureaucracy. *The New York Times,* January 4, pp. A1, B4.

Berke, R.L. (2000) Powell calls for inclusion of minorities. *The New York Times*, August 1, pp. A1, A14.

Bernstein, R. (1994) *Dictatorship of Virtue: Multiculturalism and the Battle for America's Future*. New York: A.A. Knopf.

Bickerton, D. (1998) Language and language contact. In M. Haas (ed.) *Multicultural Hawai'i: The Fabric of a Multiethnic Society* (pp. 53–66). New York: Garland Publishing, Inc.

Bixler, M. (1999) Immigrants fostering own media: Outlets produced for, by foreign-born residents rise as culture voids are filled. *The Atlanta Journal-Constitution*, November 23, p. D1.

Black Scholar (1997) Text of the Oakland School Board Resolution on Ebonics. *The Black Scholar* 27 (1), 4.

Blakeslee, S. (1997) When an adult adds a language, it's one brain, two systems. *The New York Times*, July 15, p. C4.

Blyth, C. (1997) The sociolinguistic situation of Cajun French: The effects of language shift and language loss. In A. Valdman (ed.) *French and Creole in Louisiana* (pp. 25–46). New York: Plenum Press.

de Borchgrave, A. (2000) WTO protests portend grave new world. *Insight on the News*, January 10–17, pp. 44–45.

Borrell, J. (1987) In the zone: The end of an American enclave. *Time*, July 20, pp. 8–9.

Brandt, E.A. (1982) A research agenda for Native American languages. In F. Barkin, E.A. Brandt and J. Ornstein-Galicia (eds) *Bilingualism and Language Contact: Spanish, English and Native American Languages* (pp. 26–47). New York: Teachers College Press.

Branigan, W. (1998) Puerto Rico leader vows to press for statehood; Governor says vote showed desire for change even though his side trailed. *The Washington Post*, December 15, p. A10.

Breton, R. (1964) Institutional completeness of ethnic communities and the personal relations of immigrants. *The American Journal of Sociology* 70 (2), 193–205.

Brinkley, J. (1994) California's woes on aliens appear largely self-inflicted. *The New York Times*, October 15, pp. A1, A10.

Brod, R. and Huber, B.J. (1991–92) Foreign language enrollments in United States institutes of higher education, Fall 1990. *Association of Departments of Foreign Languages Bulletin* 23 (3).

Broder, D.S. (1995) Dole backs official English. *The New York Times*, September 5, pp. A1, A5.

Broder, D.S. (2000) *Democracy Derailed: Initiative Campaigns and the Power of Money*. New York: Harcourt, Inc.

Bronner, E. (1998) Defeat of bilingual education is challenged in federal court. *The New York Times*, June 4, p. A25.

Bronner, E. (1999) Turnaround in Texas schools looks good for Bush in 2000. *The New York Times*, May 26, pp. A1, A20.

Brooke, J. (1999) Quebec gains as a language lab. *The New York Times*, October 16, p. A16.

Brooke, J. (2000) Pokémon wins a battle but not the language war. *The New York Times*, March 15, p. A4.

Brovsky, C. (1998) Study touts English classes: Aurora council claims teaching isn't the city's job. *Denver Post*, March 5, p. B2.

Brym, R.J. with Fox, B.J. (1989) *From Culture to Power: The Sociology of English Canada*. New York: Oxford University Press.

Burstall, C. (1975) Primary French in the balance. *Educational Research* 17, 193–198.

Calvo, D. (1999) As the channels turn: Soaps draw viewers to Telemundo; Soap operas boost no. 2 Spanish-language TV station. *The Washington Post*, December 25, p. C2.

Califa, A.J. (1989) Declaring English the official language: Prejudice spoken here. *Harvard Civil Rights-Civil Liberties Law Review* 24, 293–348.

Califa, A.J. (1991) The attack on minority speakers in the United States. *EPIC Events* IV (5), 6–7.

Came, B. (1991a) The fear in the middle. *Maclean's*, April 22, p. 20.

Came, B. (1991b) A growing fury. *Maclean's*, June 3, pp. 10–11.

Carnevale, A.P. (1995) *The American Mosaic: An In-Depth Report on the Future of Diversity at Work*. New York: McGraw-Hill.

Carringer, D.C. (1974) Creative thinking abilities of Mexican youth: The relationship of bilingualism. *Journal of Cross-Cultural Psychology* 5, 492–504.

Carter, R. (1998) School watch: Words of the world going international; Beginning this fall, all elementary students in the Atlanta public schools will be taught a foreign language. *The Atlanta Journal-Constitution*, June 18, p. JD8.

Casey, M. (1999) Free trade is costly to workers' lives. *Times Union*, November 29, p. A7.

Castillo, R. (1992) Miami immigrants' aspirations include "accent reduction." *The Washington Post*, May 28, p. A3.

Castro, M. (1988) Florida wages battle. *EPIC Events* I (4), 1, 4.

Castro, M. (1992) On the curious question of language in Miami. In J. Crawford (ed.) *Language Loyalties: A Source Book on the Official English Controversy* (pp. 178–186). Chicago: The University of Chicago Press.

Cazden, C.B. (1992) *Language Minority Education in the United States: Implications of the Ramirez Report*. Santa Cruz: National Center for Research on Cultural Diversity and Second Language Learning.

Century 23 (1881–82) Russian Jews and Gentiles from a Russian point of view.

Chan, S. (1991) *Asian Americans: An Interpretive History*. Boston: Twyane.

Chavez, L. (1991a) *Out of the Barrio: Toward a New Politics of Hispanic Assimilation*. New York: Basic Books, Inc.

Chavez, L. (1991b) Why bilingual education fails Hispanic children. *McCall's*, March, 118, 59–60.

Chickering, J. (1848) *Immigration into the United States*. Boston: Charles C. Little and James Brown.

Chipello, C.J. (1994) Strictly speaking, Wal-Mart may need lessons in French. *The Wall Street Journal*, April 13, p. B9.

Choquette, L. (1991) Recruitment of French emigrants to Canada, 1600–1760. In I. Altman and J. Horn (eds) *"To Make America": European Emigration in the Early Modern Period* (pp. 131–171). Berkeley and Los Angeles: University of California Press.

Choudhry, A. (2000) India: Bursting at the linguistic seams. *The Unesco Courier* 53 (4), 33–34.

Christian, D. and Mahrer, C. (1991–1992) *Two-Way Bilingual Programs in the United States*. Santa Cruz: The National Center for Research on Cultural Diversity and Second Language Learning.

Christian, D. and Mahrer, C. (1992–1993) *Supplement of Two-Way Bilingual Programs in the United States*. Santa Cruz: The National Center for Research on Cultural Diversity and Second Language Learning.

Church, C.H. (2000) Switzerland: A paradigm in evolution. *Parliamentary Affairs* 53 (1), 96–113.

Clark, E.J. (1995) "How did you learn to write in English when you haven't been taught in English?" The language experience approach in a dual language program. *Bilingual Research Journal* 19 (3 & 4), 611–627.

Clément, R., Dörnyei, Z. and Noels, K.A. (1994) Motivation, self-confidence, and group cohesion in the foreign language classroom. *Language Learning* 44 (3), 417–448.

Coleman, W.D. (1984) *The Independence Movement in Quebec 1945–1980*. Toronto: The University of Toronto Press.

Collier, V. (1989) How long? A synthesis of research on academic achievement in a second language. *TESOL Quarterly* 23 (3), 509–531.

Collins, C. (1994) To help a child become bilingual. *The New York Times*, September 29, pp. C1, C10.

Conklin, N.F. and Lourie, M.A. (1983) *A Host of Tongues: Language Communities in the United States*. New York: The Free Press.

Constitution of the State of New Mexico (1978) 1992 Replacement Pamphlet. Charlottesville, VA: The Michie Company.

Contín, M. (1994) 9th Circuit court overturns Arizona English only. *Hispanic Link Weekly Report*, December 19, p. 1.

Cook, A. (undated) US English membership letter.

Cooper, K.J. (1991) Reinterpreting bilingual classes. *The Washington Post*, February 12, p. A17.

Cordasco, F. (1976) The children of immigrants in the schools: Historical analogues of educational deprivation. In F. Cordasco (ed.) *Bilingual Schooling in the United States: A Sourcebook for Educational Personnel* (pp. 27–36). New York: McGraw-Hill Book Company.

Crawford, J. (1992) *Hold Your Tongue: Bilingualism and the Politics of "English Only."* Reading: Addison-Wesley Publishing Company.

Crawford, J. (1995) English-Only bill may exempt Native Americans. December 7. On WWW at http://ourworld.compuserve.com/homepages/jcrawford/NAHJ.htm.

Crawford, J. (1997) *Best Evidence: Research Foundations of the Bilingual Education Act*. Washington, DC: National Clearinghouse for Bilingual Education. On WWW at http://www.ncbe.gwu.edu/ncbepubs/reports/bestevidence/research.htm.

Crawford, J. (1998) The bilingual education story: Why can't the news media get it right? Presentation to the National Association of Hispanic Journalists, Miami, June 26. On WWW at http://ourword.compuserve.com/homepages/jwcrawford/NAHJ.htm

Crawford, J. (1999) *Bilingual Education: History, Politics, Theory and Practice*. Los Angeles: Bilingual Educational Services, Inc.

Crawford, J. (2002) Obituary: The Bilingual Education Act 1968–2002. On WWW at http://ourworld.compuserve.com/homepages/JWCRAWFORD/T7obit.htm.

de Crevecoeur, M-G-J. (1904) *Letters from an American Farmer*. New York: Fox, Duffield & Co.

Cubberly, E.P. (1909) *Changing Conceptions of Education*. Boston: Houghton Miffllin Company.

Cummins, J. (1979) Linguistic interdependence and the educational development of bilingual children. *Review of Educational Research* 49, 222–251.

Cummins, J. (1983) *Heritage Language Education. A Literature Review*. Ontario: Ministry of Education.

Cummins, J. (1987) Bilingual education and politics. *Education Digest* 53 (3), 30–33.

Cummins, J. (1994) The discourse of disinformation: The debate on bilingual education and language rights in the United States. In T. Skutnabb-Kangas and R. Phillipson (eds) *Linguistic Human Rights: Overcoming Linguistic Discrimination* (pp. 159–177). Berlin: Mouton de Gruyter.

Cummins, J. and Gulutsan, M. (1974) Some effects of bilingualism on cognitive functioning. In S. Carey (ed.) *Bilingualism, Biculturalism and Education*. Edmonton, Canada: The University of Alberta Press.

Cummins, J. and Sayers, D. (1995) *Brave New Schools: Challenging Cultural Illiteracy through Global Learning Networks*. New York: St. Martin's Press.

Curran, C.A. (1972) *Counseling-Learning: A Whole-Person Model for Education*. New York: Grune and Stratton.

Daniels, R. (1991) *Coming to America: A History of Immigration and Ethnicity in American Life*. New York: HarperPerennial.

Dauenhauer, N.M. and Dauenhauer, R. (1998) Technical, emotional, and ideological issues in reversing language shift: Examples from Southeast Alaska. In L.A. Grenoble and L.J. Whaley (eds) *Endangered Languages: Language Loss and Community Response* (pp. 57–98). Cambridge: Cambridge University Press.

Davis, A. (1992) Rope. *The New York Times*, May 24, Sec. 4, p. 11.

Deans, B. (1999) Seattle cops, crowds clash again: Clinton signs a largely symbolic ban on child labor as the WTO meets; In the streets, protesters make their feelings known. *The Atlanta Constitution-Journal*, December 3, p. A3.

Del Valle, S. (1998) Bilingual education for Puerto Ricans in New York City: From hope to compromise. *Harvard Educational Review* 68 (2), 193–217.

DeMont, J. (1991) For the love of language. *Maclean's*, April 22, p. 19.

Diaz, M.B. (1999) Across America: Texas city speaks with a foreign accent: El Cenizo votes to make Spanish its official language. *Detroit News*, September 13, p. A2.

Dicker, S.J. (1993) The universal second language requirement: An inadequate substitute for bilingual education (A reply to Aaron Wildavsky). *Journal of Policy Analysis and Management* 12 (4), 779–785.

Dicker, S.J. (1998) Adaptation and assimilation: US business responses to linguistic diversity in the workplace. *Journal of Multilingual and Multicultural Development* 19 (4), 282–302.

Didion, J. (1987) *Miami*. New York: Simon & Schuster.

Dillich, S. (2000) Sony, Nintendo comply with French language charter. *Computer Dealer News*, March 10, p. 42.

Dine, P. (2000) Buchanan's call for debate on immigration likely will go unheeded. *St Louis Dispatch*, January 23, p. A8.

D'O'Brian, J. (1991) Only English speakers need apply. *Management Review* 80 (1), 41–45.

Dolson, D.P. and Mayer, J. (1992) Longitudinal study of three program models for language-minority students. *Bilingual Research Journal* 16 (1 & 2), 105–157.

Dörnyei, Z. (1994) Motivation and motivating in the foreign language classroom. *The Modern Language Journal* 78 (3), 273–284.

Draper, J.B. and Jiménez, M. (1990) Language debates in the United States: A decade in review. *EPIC Events* II (5), 1, 4, 7.

Dua, H.R. (1985) Sociolinguistic inequality and language problems of linguistic minorities in India. In N. Wolfson and J. Manes (eds) *Language of Inequality* (pp. 355–372). Berlin: Mouton Publishers.

Dugger, C.W. (2000) Connecting rural India to the world. *The New York Times*, May 28, pp. 1, 10.

Dulay, H., Burt, M. and Krashen, S. (1982) *Language Two*. New York: Oxford University Press.

Dunn, A. (1995) Greeted at nation's front door, many visitors stay on illegally. *The New York Times*, January 3, pp. A1, B2.

The Economist (1988). Quarta lingua. February 27, p. 42.

The Economist (1993) English is fine if French is bigger. May 15, pp. 46, 50.

The Economist (1999) Europe: Catalans versus Hollywood. March 6, p. 51.

Edsall, T.B. (2000) Facing the changing face of Iowa: Primary hopefuls stomp amid new economic, cultural landscape. *The Washington Post*, January 15, p. A6.

Edwards, W.F. (1991) Linguistic relations between Black English and Caribbean Creoles. In W.F. Edwards and D. Winford (eds) *Verb Phrase Patterns in Black English and Creole* (pp. 15–24). Detroit: Wayne State University Press.

Eggington, W. (2000) The so-far successful resistance to Official English in Utah. Paper presented at the American Association for Applied Linguistics Annual Conference, Vancouver, BC, Canada, March 13.

Eisenstein, M. (1982) A study of social variation in adult second language acquisition. *Language Learning* 32 (2), 367–391.

Eisenstein, M. (1986) Target language variation and second-language acquisition: Learning English in New York City. *World Englishes* 5 (1), 31–46.

Eisenstein, M. and Verdi, G. (1985) The intelligibility of social dialects for working-class adult learners of English. *Language Learning* 35 (2), 287–298.

Elías-Olivares, L. (1979) Language use in a Chicano community: A sociolinguistic approach. In J.B. Pride (ed.) *Sociolinguistic Aspects of Language Learning and Teaching* (pp. 120–134). Oxford: Oxford University Press.

Elson, R. (1964) *Guardians of Tradition*. Lincoln: University of Nebraska Press.

Ensz, K.Y. (1982) French attitudes toward typical speech errors of American speakers of French. *Modern Language Journal* 66, 133–139.

Eoyang, E.C. (1995) *Coat of Many Colors: Reflections on Diversity by a Minority of One*. Boston: Beacon Press.

EPIC (1988a) Resolutions celebrating ethnic diversity and cultural pluralism. *EPIC Events* I (2), 6.

EPIC (1988b) Fate of Colorado initiative unknown. *EPIC Events* I (4), 1, 6.

EPIC (1988c) English Plus advocates discuss plans for future. *EPIC Events* I (5), 1, 5.

EPIC (1993a) US English out of compliance with philanthropic standards. *EPIC Events* V (5), 3.

EPIC (1993b) English and Spanish granted co-equal status in Puerto Rico. *EPIC Events* V (5) 1, 5.

EPIC (1993c) English Only law repealed in Dade County. *EPIC Events* VI (1), 1, 3.

Erdrich, L. (2000) Two languages in mind, but just one in the heart. *The New York Times*, May 22, pp. E1–2.

Ervin-Tripp, S.M. (1974) Is second language learning like the first? *TESOL Quarterly* 8 (2), 111–127.

Estrada, R. (1995) Dole is half-right on "English-only." *The Los Angeles Times*, September 10, p. M5.

Fairgrieve, J. and Young, E. (1925) *The New World and the Old*. New York: Appleton and Co.

Farrell, E. (1997) Chinese Golden Venture refugees freed from jail. *Christianity Today*, April 28, p. 81.

Fasold, R.W. (1972) *Tense Marking in Black English: A Linguistic and Social Analysis*. Washington, DC: Center for Applied Linguistics.

Fathman, A. (1975) The relationship between age and second language productive ability. *Language Learning* 25 (2), 245–253.

Federal Register (2000) Executive Order 13166 of August 11, 2000: Improving access to services for people with limited English proficiency. *Federal Register* 65 (159), August 16, 50121–50122.

Feinberg, L. (1981) Reagan denounces Carter's proposed rules on bilingual education. *The Washington Post*, March 1, p. C5.

Ferguson, C.A. and Heath, S.B. (1981) Languages before English. In C.A. Ferguson and S.B. Heath (eds) *Languages in the USA* (pp. 111–115). Cambridge: Cambridge University Press.

Fettes, M. (1998) Life on the edge: Canada's Aboriginal languages under official bilingualism. In T. Ricento and B. Burnaby (eds) *Language and Politics in the United States and Canada: Myths and Realities* (pp. 117–149). Mahwah, NJ: Lawrence Erlbaum Associates.

Fiagome, C. (1996) Bilingual job, higher pay. *The Christian Science Monitor*, January 26, p. 3.

Fischer, H. (1961). Ce que la méthode des "semantic differentials" apporte au probleme des images des peuples. *Revue de psychologie des peuples* 16, 306–318.

Fischer, H. and Trier, U.P. (1962). *Das Verhåltnis zwischen Deutschschweizer und Westchweizer: Eine Sozialpsychologische Untersuchung.* Bern: Huber.

Fischer, H. and Weidmann, H. (1961) Deutsche, Franzosen, Italiener und Österreicher in der Sichtjunger Schweizer. *Schweizerische Zeitschrift für Volkswirtschaft un Statistik* 97, 435–54.

Fisher, H. (1999) English Only amendment hits "end of road." *Arizona Daily Star*, January 12.

Fishman, J.A. (1966) Planned reinforcement of language maintenance in the United States: Suggestions for the conservation of a neglected national resource. In J.A. Fishman (ed.) *Language Loyalty in the United States: The Maintenance and Perpetuation of Non-English Mother Tongues by American Ethnic and Religious Groups* (pp. 369–391). The Hague: Mouton.

Fishman, J.A. (1988) "English Only": Its ghosts, myths, and dangers. *The International Journal of the Sociology of Language* 74, 125–140.

Fishman, J.A. (1991) *Reversing Language Shift*. Clevedon: Multilingual Matters.

Fishman, J.A., Gertner, M. and Lowy, E. (1980) The non-English language resources of the United States: A preliminary reconnaissance. Report to the US Department of Education.

Fix, M. and Passel, J.S. (1994) *Immigration and Immigrants: Setting the Record Straight.* Washington, DC: The Urban Institute.

Fong, T.P. (1994) *The First Suburban Chinatown: The Remaking of Monterey Park, California.* Philadelpia: Temple University Press.

Fotheringham, A. (2000) Losing the language battle. *McClean's*, April 10, p. 88.

Fox, M. (1999) Dialects: The good, the bad and the ugly: They're all myths. *The New York Times Magazine*, September 12, pp. 40, 42.

Franklin, J.L. (1998) English joins immigrants' core curriculum: Waiting list grows as newer arrivals, firms seek classes. *Boston Globe*, Oct. 11, p. 1.

Freedberg, L. and McLeod, R.G. (1998) The other side of the law: Despite all US efforts to curb it, immigration is rising. *San Francisco Chronicle*, Oct. 13, p. A1.

Freedman, S.G. (2000) *Jew vs. Jew: The Struggle for the Soul of American Jewry.* New York: Simon & Schuster.

Freeman, R.D. (1996) Dual-language planning at Oyster Bilingual School: "It's much more than language." *TESOL Quarterly* 30 (3), 557–582.

Freeman, R.D. (1998) *Bilingual Education and Social Change*. Clevedon: Multilingual Matters.

Friedman, T.L. (1995) My fellow immigrants. *The New York Times*, September 10, Sect. 4, p. 17.

Fritsch, P. (1996) Bilingual employees are seeking more pay, and many now get it. *The Wall Street Journal*, November 13, pp. A1, A15.

Frye, A.E. (1895) *Grammar School Geography* (Reprinted 1902). Boston: Ginn and Co.

Frye, A.E. (1898) *Elements of Geography*. Boston: Ginn and Co.

Gaarder, A.B. (1967) Organization of the bilingual school. *Journal of Social Issues* 23 (2), 110–120.

Gaarder, A.B. (1970) The first seventy-six bilingual education projects. In "Bilingualism and Language Contact: Anthropological, Linguistic, Psychological and Sociological Aspects." J.E. Alatis (ed.) *Georgetown Monograph Series on Languages and Linguistics*, No. 23. Washington, D.C.: Georgetown University Press.

Gallup, G. Jr. and Castelli, J. (1989) *The People's Religion: American Faith in the 90s*. New York: MacMillan Publishing Co.

García, E. (1999) The impact of Proposition 227 on the use of native languages in California schools. Presentation at Bilingualism and Biliteracy Through Schooling: An International Symposium, Long Island University, Brooklyn, NY, July 15.

Garcia, G.X. (1999) Across America: Texas city draws unwanted attention: El Cenizo's switch to Spanish angers the white minority. *Detroit News*, December 19, p. A2.

García, O. (1985) Bilingualism in the United States: Present attitudes in the light of past policies. In S. Greenbaum (ed.) *The English Language Today* (pp. 147–158). Oxford: Pergamon Institute of English.

García, O. (1992) For it is in giving that we receive: A history of language policy in the United States. Paper presented at a conference on American Pluralism: Toward a History of the Discussion, State University of New York, Stonybrook, June 7.

Garcia (1993) *Garcia v. Spun Steak* 998 F2d 1480 (9th Cir).

García Passalacqua, J.M. (1994) The 1993 plebiscite in Puerto Rico: A first step to decolonization? *Current History*, March, pp. 103–107.

Gardner, R.C. and Lambert, W.E. (1972) *Attitudes and Motivation in Second Language Learning*. Rowley, MA: Newbury House Publishers.

Gardner, R.C. and MacIntyre, P.D. (1991) An instrumental motivation in language study: Who says it isn't effective? *Studies in Second Language Acquisition* 13, 57–72.

Gardner, R.W., Robie, B. and Smith, P.C. (1985) Asian Americans: Growth, change, and diversity. *Population Bulletin* 40 (4).

Garner, K.J. (1997) Louisiana Creole. Universal survey of languages. On WWW at http://www.teleport.com/~napoleon/louisianafrenchcreole/intro.html.

Gary, J.O. (1975) Delayed oral practice in initial stages of second language learning. In M.K. Burt and H.C. Dulay (eds) *New Directions in Second Language Teaching, Learning and Bilingual Education*. Washington, DC: TESOL.

Gates, H.L. Jr. (1993) The weaning of America. *The New Yorker*, April 19, pp. 113–117.

Gerken, L.A. and McIntosh, B.J. (1993) Interplay of function morphemes and prosody in early language. *Developmental Psychology* 29 (3), 448–457.

Gemery, H.A. (1980) Emigration from the British Isles to the New World, 1630–1700: Inferences from colonial populations. *Research in Economic History* 5, 179–231.

Genesee, F. (1981) A comparison of early and late second language learning. *Canadian Journal of Behavioral Science* 13 (2), 115–128.

Gilbert, G.G. (1981) French and German: A comparative study. In C.A. Ferguson and S.B. Heath (eds) *Language in the USA* (pp. 257–272). Cambridge: Cambridge University Press.

Gleckman, J. (1998) High-tech talent: Don't bolt the golden door. *Business Week*, March 16, p. 30.

Goldenberg, S. (1996) Simple son of the soil set to dirty hands for India. *The Guardian*, June 13, p. 16.

Gonzalez, G. (1977) Teaching bilingual children. In *Bilingual Education: Current Perspectives* (Vol. 2, pp. 53–59). Arlington, VA: Center for Applied Linguistics.

Gooch, A. (1998) Catalan quotas spark fear of Babel. *The Guardian*, July 9, p. 20.

Gordon, M.M. (1964) *Assimilation in American Life: The Role of Race, Religion, and National Origin*. New York: Oxford University Press.

Gore, A. (1999) Remarks as prepared for delivery by Vice President Al Gore. NALEO 16th Annual Conference, June 19. On WWW at http://www.algore2000.com/speeches/speeches_naleo_061999.html.

Graubard, S.R. (ed.) (1989) *In Search of Canada*. New Brunswick: Transaction Publishers.

Greenbaum, W. (1974) America in search of a new ideal: An essay on the rise of pluralism. *Harvard Educational Review* 44 (3), 411–440.

Greengard, S. (1996) Gain the edge in the knowledge race. *Personnel Journal*, August, pp. 52–54.

Greenhouse, L. (1997) Justices set aside reversal of "English Only" measure. *The New York Times*, March 4, p. A17.

Greenhouse, L. (1999) Appeal to save English-Only rule fails. *The New York Times*, January 12, p. A16.

Greenhouse, L. (2001) Supreme Court limits scope of a main civil rights law. *The New York Times*, April 25, p. A14.

Greer, C. (1972) *The Great School Legend: A Revisionist Interpretation of American Public Education*. New York: Basic Books, Inc.

Grenier, G. (1984) Shifts to English as usual language by Americans of Spanish mother tongue. *Social Science Quarterly* 65, 537–550.

Gross, J. (2000) For Latino laborers, dual lives: Welcomed at work, but shunned at home in suburbs. *The New York Times*, January 5, pp. B1, B4.

Gross, T. (1995) "Fresh Air." National Public Radio, September 19.

Gugliotta, G. (1998) Phone battle mirrors Puerto Rico's identity crisis. *The Washington Post*, July 9, p. A1.

Guiora, A.Z., Beit-Hallahmi, B., Brannon, R.C.L., Dull, C.Y. and Scovel, T. (1972) The effects of experimentally induced changes in ego status on pronunciation ability in a second language: An exploratory study. *Comprehensive Psychiatry* 13, 421–428.

Gutierrez (1998a) *Gutierrez v. Municipal Court of the Southeast Judicial District, Los Angeles* 838 F2d 1031 (9th Cir).

Gutierrez (1988b) *Gutierrez v. Municipal Court of the Southeast Judicial District, Los Angeles* 861 F2d 1187 (9th Cir).

Harvey, C. (1976) General descriptions of bilingual programs that meet students' needs. In F. Cordasco (ed.) *Bilingual Schooling in the United States: A Sourcebook for Educational Personnel* (pp. 226–232). New York: McGraw-Hill Book Company.

Haugen, E. (1956) *Bilingualism in the Americas: A Bibliography and Research Guide* (publication of the American Dialect Society No. 26). Alabama: University of Alabama Press.

Hawaii Statutes (1995) *Hawaii Revised Statutes Annotated* (Vol. 1). Charlottesville, VA: The Michie Company.

Hayakawa, S.I. (1985) The case for official English. In J. Crawford (ed.) *Language Loyalties: A Source Book on the Official English Controversy* (1992, pp. 94–100). Chicago: The University of Chicago Press.

Hayden, R.L. (1979) Toward a national foreign language policy. *Journal of Communication* 29 (2), 93–101.

Heller, M. (1994) *Crosswords: Language, Education and Ethnicity in French Ontario.* New York: Mouton de Gruyter.

Henry, J. (1997) The Louisiana French movement: Actors and actions in social change. In A. Valdman (ed.) *French and Creole in Louisiana* (pp. 183–213). New York: Plenum Press.

Herman, D.M. (2000) "Official English" legislation in Iowa: Public attitudes and reasoning in a monolingual English state. Paper presented at the American Association of Applied Linguistics Annual Conference, Vancouver, BC, Canada, March 13.

Herskovits, M.J. (1949) *Man and his Works.* New York: Alfred A. Knopf.

Higham, J. (1955) *Strangers in the Land.* New Brunswick: Rutgers University Press.

Hispanic Link Weekly Report (1995) 99.94% of documents are printed in English. October 2, p. 1.

Hitt, G. (1998) "English Only" amendment to House bill on Puerto Rico exposes GOP fissures. *The Wall Street Journal,* March 5, p. A24.

Hoffman, E. (1989) *Lost in Translation: A Life in a New Language.* New York: E.P. Dutton.

Hollinger, D.A. (1995) *Postethnic America: Beyond Multiculturalism.* New York: Basic Books.

Holm, A. and Holm, W. (1990) Rock Point, a Navajo way to go to school: A valediction. *The Annals of the American Academy of Political and Social Science* 508, 170–184.

Holman, J.R. (1998) Learning a language. *Better Homes and Gardens,* January, pp. 40, 42.

Holzman, M. (1997) *The Language of Children: Evolution and Development of Secondary Consciousness and Language.* Cambridge, MA: Blackwell Publishers Inc.

Horn, J. (1991) "To parts beyond the seas": Free emigration to the Chesapeake in the seventeenth century. In I. Altman and J. Horn (eds) *"To Make America": European Emigration in the Early Modern Period* (pp. 85–130). Berkeley and Los Angeles: University of Los Angeles Press.

Hornberger, N. (1989) Continua of biliteracy. *Review of Educational Research* 59 (3), 271–296.

Houston Chronicle (1996) World briefs: Swiss back language. March 11, p. 12.

Howe, I. (1976) *World of Our Fathers.* New York: Harcourt Brace Jovanovich.

Howe, M. (1990) Immigrants swell languages classes. *The New York Times,* January 7, p. 26L.

Huang, J. and Hatch, E. (1978) A Chinese child's acquisition of English. In E.M. Hatch (ed.) *Second Language Acquisition: A Book of Readings* (pp. 118–131). Rowley: Newbury House Publishers.

Huddleston, W. (1983) The misdirected policy of bilingualism. In J. Crawford (ed.) *Language Loyalties: A Source Book on the Official English Controversy* (1992, pp. 114–118). Chicago: The University of Chicago Press.

Hughes, J. (1998) INS nabs 26 illegal workers: 12 East Europeans may signal new network. *Denver Post,* August 29, p. B5.

Hutchinson, E.O. (1997) The fallacy of Ebonics. *The Black Scholar* 27 (1), 36–37.

Imhoff, G. (1990) The position of US English on bilingual education. *The Annals of the American Academy of Political and Social Science* 508, 48–61.

INS (1993) *Statistical Yearbook of the Immigration and Naturalization Service.* Washington, DC: Government Printing Office.

Immigration Communiqué (1996–1999) On WWW at http://www.fedpub.com/fedpub/immigrat. Weekly.

Ingam, C. (1986) Prop. 63 backers aim at bilingual education. *The Los Angeles Times,* November 24, pp. 3, 16.

Ingwerson, M. (1988) English-only laws: How broad? *Christian Science Monitor,* Nov. 29, pp. 3, 4.

Isser, N. and Schwartz, L.L. (1985) *The American School and the Melting-pot: Minority Self-Esteem and Public Education.* Bristol: Windom Hall Press.

Jackson, B. (1998) Volunteers tend residents' needs. *Times Union,* April 28, p. B5.

Jarvis, A.C., Lebredo, R. and Mena-Ayllón, F. (1991) *¡Continuemos!* Lexington: D.C. Heath Company.

John, V.P. and Homer, V.M. (1971) *Early Childhood Bilingual Education.* New York: The Modern Language Association of America.

Johnson, A. (2000) Just say non. *Canadian Business,* April 17, p. 6.

Jones, F.R. (1994) The lone language learners: A diary study. *System* 22, 441–454.

Jones, F.R. (1998) Self-instruction and success: A learner-profile study. *Applied Linguistics* 19 (3), 378–406.

Kallen, H.H. (1924) *Culture and Democracy in the United States: Studies in the Group Psychology of the American Peoples.* New York: Boni & Liveright, Inc.

Kang,, K.C. (1997) The Times poll: Chinese in the Southland; A changing picture. *The Los Angeles Times,* June 29, p. A1.

Kaplan, D.A. (1993) Dumber than we thought. *Newsweek,* September 20, pp. 44–45.

Kennedy, R.J.R. (1944) Single or triple melting-pot? Intermarriage trends in New Haven, 1870–1940. *American Journal of Sociology* 49 (4), 331–339.

Keyser, L. (1986) English: From sea to shining sea. *Insight,* October 20, 51–53.

Khashan, N. (2001) Judge: English-Only may be benign. *Salt Lake Tribune,* February 1.

Kilbourn, W. (1989) The peaceable kingdom still. In S.R. Graubard (ed.) *In Search of Canada* (pp. 1–29). New Brunswick: Transaction Publishers.

Kim, K.H.S., Relkin, N.R., Lee, K-M. and Hirsch, J. (1997) Distinct cortical areas associated with native and second languages. *Nature* 388, July 10, 171–174.

Kjolseth, R. (1973) Bilingual education programs in the United States: For assimilation or pluralism? In P.R. Turner (ed.) *Bilingualism in the Southwest* (pp. 3–27). Tucson: The University of Arizona Press.

Kloss, H. (1977) *The American Bilingual Tradition.* Rowley, MA: Newbury House Publishers.

Kossoudji, S.A. (1988) English language ability and the labor market opportunities of Hispanic and East Asian immigrant men. *Journal of Labor Economic* 6 (2), 205–228.

Krashen, S.D. (1982) *Principles and Practice in Second Language Acquisition.* New York: Pergamon Press.

Krashen, S.D. (1999) Bilingual education in the United States. Presentation at Bilingualism and Biliteracy Through Schooling: An International Symposium, Long Island University, Brooklyn, NY, July 16.

Krashen, S.D. and Terrell, T.D. (1983) *The Natural Approach: Language Acquisition in the Classroom.* Oxford: Pergamon Press; San Francisco: Alemany Press.

Krauss, M. (1995) Language loss in Alaska, the United States, and the world. *Frame of Reference* 6 (1), 3–5.

Kristof, N.D. (1991) Chinese relations. *The New York Times Magazine*, August 18, pp. 8, 10.

Kurylo, E. (1998) Language of learning: Metro Atlanta libraries are serving the growing immigrant population with resources for people trying to learn English. *The Atlanta Journal-Constitution*, June 6, p. D1.

Kythreotis, A. (1993) Ismail Merchant tries a different job: Director. *The New York Times*, May 9, Sect. 2, p. H23.

Labov, W. (1966) *The Social Stratification of English in New York City*. Washington, DC: The Center for Applied Linguistics.

Labov, W. (1972) *Language in the Inner City: Studies in Black English Vernacular*. Philadelphia: University of Pennsylvania Press.

Labov, W. (1997) Testimony on Ebonics given before the Subcommittee on Labor, Health and Human Services and Education of the Senate Appropriations Committee, January 23. University of Pennsylvania. On WWW at http://www.ling.upenn.edu/~labov/L102/Ebonics_test.html.

Lambert, R.D. (1987) The improvement of foreign language competency in the United States. *The Annals of the American Association of Political and Social Science* 490, pp. 9–19.

Lambert, W.E., Anisfeld, M. and Yeni-Komshian, G. (1965) Evaluational reactions of Jewish and Arab adolescents to dialect and language variations. *Journal of Personality and Social Psychology* 2 (1), 84–90.

Lambert, W.E., Gardner, R.C., Olton, R. and Tunstall, K. (1970) A study of the roles of attitudes and motivation in second-language learning. In J.A. Fishman (ed.) *Readings in the Sociology of Language*. The Hague: Mouton.

Lambert, W.E., Hodgson, R.C., Gardner, R.C. and Fillenbaum, S. (1960) Evaluational reactions to spoken languages. *Journal of Abnormal and Social Psychology* 60 (1), 44–51.

Lambert, W.E. and Tucker, G.R. (1972) *Bilingual Education of Children: The St Lambert Experiment*. Rowley: Newbury House Publishers, Inc.

Landry, R.G. (1974) A comparison of second language learners and monolinguals on divergent thinking tasks at the elementary school level. *Modern Language Journal* 58, 10–15.

Lange, D.L. (1987) The language teaching curriculum and a national agenda. *The Annals of the American Academy of Political and Social Science* 490, 70–96.

Language Policy Task Force (1978) Language policy and the Puerto Rican community. *The Bilingual Review/La Revista Bilingüe* 5 (1 & 2), 1–33.

Lapkin, S., Swain, M., Kanin, J. and Hanna, G. (1980) *Report on the 1979 Evaluation of the Peel County Late French Immersion Program, Grades 8, 9, 10, 11 and 12*. Toronto: Ontario Institute for Studies in Education.

LaPlante, A. (1998) Border war. *Computerworld*, March 9, p. 92–93.

Lardner, G. Jr. (1991) Language education for national security: $180 million program proposed in Senate. *The Washington Post*, July 19, p. B8.

Larsen, D.N. and Smalley, W.A. (1972) *Becoming Bilingual, A Guide to Language Learning*. New Canaan, CT: Practical Anthropology.

Larsen-Freeman, D. (1987) Recent innovations in language teaching methodology. *The Annals of the American Academy of Political and Social Science* 490, 51–69.

Lee, A.F. (1993) *The Hawaii State Constitution: A Reference Guide*. Westport: Greenwood Press.

Leftwich, J. (1956) *Israel Zangwill*. London: James Clarke & Co. Limited.

Legarreta, D. (1979) The effects of program models on language acquisition by Spanish speaking children. *TESOL Quarterly* 13 (4), 521–534.

Leibowitz, A.H. (1978) Language policy in the United States. In H. LaFontaine, B. Persky and L. Golubchick (eds) *Bilingual Education*. Wayne, NJ: Avery Publishing Group Inc.

Lenneberg, E.H. (1967) *Biological Foundations of Language*. New York: Wiley.

Leopold, W.F. (1939–1949) *Speech Development of a Bilingual Child: A Linguist's Record*. Evanston: Northwestern University Press.

Leuck, T. (1991) New York ranks high in housing bias. *The New York Times*, November 3, pp. 1R, 12R.

Li, W.L. (1982) The language shift of Chinese-Americans. *International Journal of Social Language* 38, 109–124.

Limón, José E. (1982) El meeting: History, folk Spanish, and ethnic nationalism in a Chicano student community. In J. Amastae and L. Elías-Olivares (eds) *Spanish in the United States: Sociolinguistic Aspects* (pp. 301–332). Cambridge: Cambridge University Press.

Linguistic Society of America (1997) LSA resolution on the Oakland "Ebonics" issue. January. On WWW at http://www.lsadc.org/ebonics.html.

Linton, R. (1940) The processes of culture transfer. In R. Linton (ed.) *Acculturation in Seven American Indian Tribes* (pp. 483–500). New York: D. Appleton-Century Company, Inc.

Lo, C.Y.H. (1982) Countermovements and conservative movements in the contemporary US. *Annual Review of Sociology*, 107–134.

Lochhead, C. (1999) High-tech leaders beg reluctant senators for more work visas. *San Francisco Chronicle*, October 23, p. A5.

Long, M. (1983) Does second language instruction make a difference? A review of research. *TESOL Quarterly* 17 (3), 359–382.

Louie, T. (1992) English Plus at work in Massachusetts. *EPIC Events* IV (6), 1, 2.

Lyons, L. (1998) Unztruthfulness of the California "English for the Children" campaign. *NABE News* 21 (4), 1, 6.

Macías, R.F. (1979) Language choice and human rights in the United States. In J.E. Alatis and G.R. Tucker (eds) *Georgetown University Round Table on Languages and Linguistics*. Washington, DC: Georgetown University Press.

MacIntyre, P.D., Noels, K.A. and Clément, R. (1997) Biases in self-ratings of second language proficiency: The role of language anxiety. *Language Learning* 47 (2), 265–287.

Mägiste, E. (1984) Further evidence for the optimal age hypothesis in second language learning. In J.P. Lantolf and A. Labarca (eds) *Research in Second Language Learning: Focus on the Classroom* (pp. 51–57). Norwood, NJ: Ablex Publishing Corporation.

Marks, A. (1998) Small-town America as Ellis Island. *Christian Science Monitor*, June 30, 1.

Marmer Solomon, C. (1993) Two weaknesses in the U.S. immigration system. *Personnel Journal*, February, pp. 60–61.

Marriott, M. (1992) Lollipops and languages. *The New York Times* (Education Life Section), January 5, pp. 44–45.

Marshall, M.M. (1997) The origin and development of Louisiana Creole French. In A. Valdman (ed.) *French and Creole in Louisiana* (pp. 333–347). New York: Plenum Press.

Masny, D. (1984) The role of language and cognition in second language metalinguistic awareness. In J.P. Lantolf and A. Labarca (eds) *Research in Second Language Learning: Focus on the Classroom* (pp. 59–73). Norwood, NJ: Ablex Publishing Corporation.

Massey, D.S. (1995) The new immigration and ethnicity in the United States. *Population and Development Review* 21 (3), 631–652.

May, H. and Fahys, J. (2000) It's official: English Only. *Salt Lake Tribune*, November 8. On WWW at http://ourworld.compuserve.com/homepages/JWCRAWFORD/SLT8.htm.

McCain, J. (2000) Education: The cornerstone of our nation's future. On WWW at http://www.mccain2000.com/issues/education.html.

McCarthy, R. (1996) Governor refuses to block landfill, OKs official English, car rental tax. *The Atlanta Journal-Constitution*, April 26, p. C3.

McGroarty, M.E. (1990) Bilingualism in the workplace. *The Annals of the American Academy of Political and Social Science* 511, 159–179.

McLaughlin, B. (1978) *Second-Language Acquisition in Childhood*. Hillsdale: Laurence Erlbaum Associates.

McMurry, F.M. and Tarr, R. (1908) *An Advanced Geography*. New York: MacMillan Co.

McRae, K.D. (1983) *Conflict and Compromise in Multilingual Societies: Switzerland* (Vol. 1). Waterloo: Wilfred Laurier University Press.

Mears, T. (1997) Miami Hispanics losing their Spanish: Impact on Latin American trade feared. *Boston Globe*, October 5, p. A2.

Meyer, M.M. and Finenberg, S.E. (eds) (1992) *The Case of Bilingual Education Strategies*. Washington, DC: National Academy Press.

Miller, J.J. (1996) Bilingual education's abolitionists. *The Wall Street Journal*, April 10, A6.

Miller, S.C. (1969) *The Unwelcome Immigrant*. Berkeley: University of California Press.

Mishra, D. (1999) Letters to the Editor: Opponents of Hindi wrote racist letters. *The Wall Street Journal*, May 21, p. A13.

Modiano, N. (1968) National or mother tongue language in beginning reading. *Research in the Teaching of English* 2, 32–43.

Morison, S. H. (1990) A Spanish-English dual-language program in New York City. *The Annals of the American Academy of Political and Social Science* 508, 160–169.

Morris, C. (1909) *Home Life in all Lands, How the World Lives*. Philadelphia: J.B. Lippincott and Co.

Moss, J. (2000) Le Théâtre franco-ontarien: Dramatic spectacles of linguistic otherness. *University of Toronto Quarterly* 69 (2), 587–614.

Murray, C. and Herrnstein, R. (1994) *The Bell Curve*. New York: The Free Press.

Ms. (1990) Mexico: Made in "maquiladoras," November/December, p. 11.

Mujica, M.E. (1994a) Statement before the Subcommittee on Commerce, Justice, State, the Judiciary and Related Agencies of the House Appropriations Committee, April 26. Washington, DC: US English, Inc.

Mujica, M.E. (1994b) US English membership letter, September 12.

Mujica, M.E. (1994c) US English membership letter, November 9.

Mujica, M.E. (1995) US English membership letter, July 28.

Mujica, M.E. (1997a) Testimony before the House Committee on Resources regarding H.R. 856 "The United States-Puerto Rico Political Status Act," March 19. On WWW at http://www.us-english.org/testimony/htm.

Mujica, M.E. (1997b) US English membership letter, April 21.

Mujica, M.E. (1998) House passes PR status bill. On WWW at http://www.us-english.org/prpasses.htm.

Mujica, M.E. (2000) US English membership letter, May 3.

Myers, E.R. (ed.) (1994) *Challenges of a Changing America: Perspectives on Immigration and Multiculturalism in the United States*. San Francisco: Austin & Winfield.

NABE (1993) Census reports sharp increase in number of non-English language speaking Americans. *NABE News* 16 (6), 1, 25.

NABE (1995) Statement from Secretary Riley about "Official Language Act." *NABE News* 19 (2), 27.

Nakamura, D. (1998) In melting pot, English a hot commodity. *The Washington Post*, May 7, p. V1.

National Immigration Forum (1999) Fix '96: Restore America's tradition as a nation of immigrants and a nation of just laws. On WWW at http://www.immigrationforum.org/fix96/whatisfix'96.htm.

National Review (1990) The new apartheid. *National Review*, July 23, pp. 14–16.

Navarro, M. (1997) Puerto Rico teachers resist teaching in English. *The New York Times*, May 19, p. A12.

New Mexico (1978) *New Mexico Statutes Annotated* (Vol. 1). Charlottesville, VA: The Michie Company.

New York City Board of Education (1991–92) *Dropout Reduction Through Education, Achievement, and Motivation (Project DREAM), Transitional Bilingual Education Grant T003A90063: Final Evaluation Profile*. New York City Board of Education.

The New York Times (1981) In plain English. October 10, p. 24.

The New York Times (1989) US English advertisement. July 25, p. A7.

The New York Times (1991) Immigrants protest veto in English classes. November 11, p. A12.

The New York Times (1993a) "Inglés, No!" Puerto Ricans shout as language bill nears approval. January 25, p. A12.

The New York Times (1993b) "English Only" law fails rights test. March 19, p. B16.

The New York Times (1993c) Turning loopy over language. May 18, p. A20.

The New York Times (1993d) A legislative infant, needing care. October 2, p. A22.

The New York Times (1995) Campaign English from Senator Dole. September 10, Sect. 4, p. 16.

The New York Times (1999) By the numbers: Choosing the right language. November 24, p. B11.

The New York Times (2000) Image and reality on education. August 1, p. A20.

Newman, M. (2001a) "I represent me": Identity construction in a teenage rap crew. In K. Henning, N. Netherton and L. Peterson (eds) *Proceedings of the 9th Annual Symposium about Language and Society: Austin*. Austin, TX: University of Texas, Department of Linguistics.

Newman, M. (2001b) "Not dogmatically: It's all about me": Ideological conflict in a high school rap crew. *Taboo: The Journal of Culture and Education* 5 (2), 51–58.

Ng, F. (1998) *The Taiwanese Americans*. Westport, CT: Greenwood Press.

Nichols, D. (1997) Speaking well of language lessons. *Restaurant Business*, April 1, p. 126.

Nichols, P.C. (1981) Creoles of the USA. In C.A. Ferguson and S.B. Heath (eds) *Languages in the USA* (pp. 69–91). Cambridge: Cambridge University Press.

Norris, M.J. (1998) Canada's Aboriginal languages. *Canadian Social Trends* 51 (Winter), 8–16.

Norton, M. (1999) Boat carrying Haitians sinks near Bahamas. *Boston Globe*, March 25, p. A27.

O'Donnell, K. (1988) Arizona groups prepare for November. *EPIC Events* I (4), 1, 5.

O'Hanlon, A. (1998) Area schools make the grade on state report card: Improvements shown in most categories. *The Washington Post*, March 29, p. V1.

Ojito, M. (1999) To talk like a New Yorker, sign up for Spanish lessons. *The New York Times*, October 18, pp. A1, B4.

Olneck, M.R. (1990) The recurring dream: Symbolism and ideology in intercultural and multicultural education. *American Journal of Education* 98 (2), 147–174.

Olson, E. (1998) Switzerland bandies words over "linguistic McDonaldization." *The Christian Science Monitor*, November 16, p. 8.

Olson, E. (1999) Right-wing political party leads in Swiss elections, endangering 40-year coalition. *The New York Times*, October 25, p. A16.

Olson, E. (2000) Who's Swiss? City votes against most foreigners. *The Globe and Mail*, March 13, pp. A1, A18.

O'Neill, T. (ed.) (1992) *Immigration: Opposing Viewpoints*. San Diego: Greenhaven Press.

Palmer, J. (1997) EU welcomes language barriers: A report shows that minorities are rediscovering their own voice despite the spread of English. *The Guardian*, January 23, p. 1.

Pan, P.P. (1999) Demonstration presses for immigration rule change: 5,000 urge Congress to grant new amnesty. *The Washington Post*, October 17, p. C5.

Pan, S. (1997) Chinese in New York. In O. García and J.A. Fishman (eds) *The Multilingual Apple: Languages in New York City* (pp. 231–255). Berlin: Mouton de Gruyter.

Panetta, L.E. (1999) Foreign language education: If "scandalous" in the 20th century, what will it be in the 21st century? Paper presented at the Stanford Language Center, Stanford University, May 7. On WWW at http:// language.stanford.edu/about/conferencepapers/panettapaper.html.

Park, R.E. and Burgess, E.W. (1921) *Introduction to the Science of Sociology*. Chicago: The University of Chicago Press.

Parliman, G.C. and Shoeman, R.J. (1994) National origin discrimination or employer prerogative? An analysis of language rights in the workplace. *Employee Relations Law Journal* 19 (4), 551–565.

Pattanayak, D.P. (1985) Diversity in communication and languages: Predicament of a multilingual nation state: India, a case study. In N. Wolfson and J. Manes (eds) *Language of Inequality* (pp. 399–407). Berlin: Mouton Publishers.

Pauley, E. (1992) The trouble with universalistic solutions: Does one size fit all? *Journal of Policy Analysis and Management* 11 (3), 487–491.

Pear, R. (1997) Academy's report says immigration benefits the US. *The New York Times*, May 18, p. 1, 24.

de la Peña, F. (1991) *Democracy or Babel? The Case for Official English*. Washington, DC: US English.

Penner, S.G. (1987) Parental responses to grammatical and ungrammatical child utterances. *Child Development* 58, 376–384.

Peritz, I. (2000) Language cops pillory violators on Web. *The Globe and Mail*, March 16, p. A7.

Perry, T. and Delpit, L. (eds) (1998) *The Real Ebonics Debate: Power, Language, and the Education of African-American Children*. Boston: Beacon Press.

Plissner, M. (2001) Learning to love language in a bilingual school. *The New York Times*, June 23, p. A13.

Politzer, R.L. and Weiss, L. (1969) Developmental aspects of auditory discrimination, echo response and recall. *Modern Language Journal* 53, 75–85.

Porter, R.P. (1990) *Forked Tongue: The Politics of Bilingual Education*. New York: Basic Books, Inc.

The Post-Standard (1998) Ebonics update: The withering ridicule and misperceptions of Oakland's teaching strategy have come and gone. Now comes word and evidence that this language program may actually work. June 18, p. A16.

Potovsky, V.A. (1974) Effects of delay in oral practice at the beginning of second language learning. *Modern Language Journal* 58 (5–6), 229–239.

PR Newswire (2000) ZDNet and Jasubhai Interactive launch ZDNet India. April 18, p. 1.

Puente, T. (2000) Wave of Hispanic immigrants alters demographics in the heartland. *Chicago Tribune*, January 16, p. 3.

Quinlan, M. (1999) Protest in Seattle highlights serious problems with WTO. *Buffalo News*, December 18, p. 2.

Quinn, L.D. (1967) Chink, Chink, Chinaman. *Pacific Northwest Quarterly* 57 (2).

Quiroz, J.T. (1995) *Together in Our Differences: How Newcomers and Established Residents are Rebuilding American Communities*. Washington, DC: The National Immigration Forum.

Ramirez, A.G. and Politzer, R.L. (1976) The acquisition of English and maintenance of Spanish in a bilingual program. In J.E. Alatis and K. Twaddell (eds) *English as a Second Language in Bilingual Education* (pp. 186–196). Washington, DC: TESOL.

Ramirez, D.J., Yuen, S.D. and Ramey, D.R. (1991) *Longitudinal Study of Structured Immersion Strategy, Early-Exit and Late-Exit Transitional Bilingual Education Programs for Language-Minority Children*. San Mateo: Aguirre International.

Ramos, S. (1990) National Language Rights Day: Speaking out against official English legislation. *EPIC Events* III (5), 1.

Rattansi, A. (1992) Changing the subject? Racism, culture and education. In J. Donald and A. Rattansi (eds) *"Race," Culture and Difference* (pp. 11–48). London: Sage Publications.

Redfield, R., Linton, R. and Herskovits, M.J. (1936) A memorandum for the study of acculturation. *American Anthropologist* 38, 149–152.

Reddy, M.A. (1995) American Indian languages spoken at home, by region and state, 1990. *Statistical Record of Native North Americans*. New York: Gale Research Inc.

Redway, J.W. (1902) *The New Basis of Geography* (reprinted 1914). New York: Macmillan Co.

Reinecke, J.E. (1969) *Language and Dialect in Hawaii*. Honolulu: University of Hawaii Press.

Reinert, J.R. (1998) More visas? A windfall for lawyers. *Computerworld*, April 20, p. 37.

Reitman, V. (1994) Tots do swimmingly in language-immersion programs. *The Wall Street Journal*, February 15, pp. B1, B10.

Republican National Committee (1996) *The Republican Platform*. Prentice Hall Documents Library. August 12. On WWW at http://hcl.chass.ncsu.edu/garson/dye/docs/rplat96.htm.

Republican National Platform Committee (2000) 2000 GOP platform: Renewing America's purpose. Together. On WWW at http://www.gopconvention.com/platform/platform.html.

Ricento, T. (1998a) National language policy in the United States. In T. Ricento and B. Burnaby (eds) *Language and Politics in the United States and Canada: Myths and Realities* (pp. 85–112). Mahwah, NJ: Lawrence Erlbaum Associates.

Ricento, T. (1998b) Partitioning by language: Whose rights are threatened? In T. Ricento and B. Burnaby (eds) *Language and Politics in the United States and Canada: Myths and Realities* (pp. 317–330). Mahwah, NJ: Lawrence Erlbaum Associates.

Rickford, J.R. and Rickford, A.E. (1995) Dialect readers revisited. *Linguistics and Education* 7 (2), 107–128.

Riley, R.W. (1998) Statement by the US Secretary of Education Richard W. Riley on California Proposition 227, April 27. On WWW at http://www.ed.gov/PressReleases/04-1998/unzst.html.

Rimalower, G.P. (1992) Translation, please. *Training & Development*, February, pp. 71–76.

Rimer, S. (1992) Words no longer escape them. *The New York Times*, July 6, pp. B1, B4.

Riverside Press-Enterprise (1998) Riverside plan irks Prop. 227's Unz. July 25. On WWW at http://www3.humnet. ucla.edu/people/macswan/RPE4.htm.

Robinson, E.V.D. (1910) *Commercial Geography.* Chicago: Rand McNally and Co.

Rodriguez, G. (1999) *From Newcomers to New Americans: The Successful Integration of Immigrants into American Society.* Washington, DC: National Immigration Forum.

Rodriguez, R. (1982) *Hunger of Memory: The Education of Richard Rodriguez.* Boston: David R. Godine.

Rohter, L. (1993) Puerto Rico votes to retain status as commonwealth. *The New York Times*, November 15, pp. A1, B8.

Ronjat, J. (1913) *Le développment du langage observé chez un enfant bilingue.* Paris: Champion.

Rose, J. (1994) Such a daughter, such an étrangère. *The New York Times*, September 29, p. C10.

Rose, P.I. (1989) Asian Americans: From pariahs to paragons. In J.S. Frideres (ed.) *Multiculturalism and Intergroup Relations.* New York: Greenwood Press.

Rothfarb, S.H., Ariza, M.J. and Urrutia, R.E. (1987) *Evaluation of the Bilingual Curriculum Content (BCC) Pilot Project: A Three Year Study, Final Report.* Miami: Office of Educational Accountability.

Rounds, K. (2000) Clippings: We hear Austria is a nice place to emigrate to. *Ms.*, April/May, p. 34.

Rúa, P. J. (1992) *La Encrucijada del Idioma.* San Juan: Instituto de Cultura Puertorriqueña.

Rubin, A.M. (1996) Service obligation delayed in National Security Fellowships. *Chronicle of Higher Education*, March 1, p. A43.

Rubin, A.M. (1997) Applications to National Security Education Program are down. *Chronicle of Higher Education*, March 14, p. A40.

Ruíz, R. (1988) Orientations in language planning. In S.L. McKay and S.C. Wong (eds) *Language Diversity: Problem or Resource?* (pp. 1–25). Cambridge: Newbury House Publishers.

Ruke-Dravina, V. (1965) The process of acquisition of apical /r/ and uvular /R/ in the speech of children. *Linguistics* 17, 56–68.

Rushdie, S. and West, E. (eds) (1997) *Mirrorwork: 50 Years of Indian Writing, 1947–1997.* New York: Henry Holt and Company.

Ryan, E.B. and Carranza, M.A. (1975) Evaluative reactions of adolescents towards speakers of Standard English and Mexican American accented English. *Journal of Personality and Social Psychology* 31 (5), 855–863.

Sahagun, L. (1998) In any language, the fight is on over bilingual instruction. *Los Angeles Times*, April 16, p. A5.

Salt Lake Tribune (2000) Judge delays English-Only from becoming state law. December 2. On WWW at http://ourworld.compuserve.com/homepages/JWCRAWFORD/SLT9.htm.

San Diego City Schools (1982) *An Exemplary Approach to Bilingual Education: A Comprehensive Handbook for Implementing an Elementary-Level Spanish-English Language Immersion Program.* San Diego: San Diego City Schools.

Sandlin, S. and Franck, M. (1999) Bilingual education has partial victory: Ruling dismisses APS bias claims. *Albuquerque Journal*, May 19.

Sandmeyer, E.C. (1939) *The Anti-Chinese Movement in California.* Urbana: University of Illinois Press.

Sandoval v. Hagan (1998) 7FSupp 2d 1234 (MD Ala.).

Schlesinger, A.M. Jr. (1992) *The Disuniting of America: Reflections on a Multicultural Society.* New York: W.W. Norton.

Schlesinger, J.M. (2000) Clinton pushes goals to keep economy solid. *The Wall Street Journal,* February 2, p. A3.

Schmid, C. (1978) Majority and minority relations in a multicultural society: The case of Switzerland. PhD dissertation, McMaster University.

Schmid, C. (1981) *Conflict and Consensus in Switzerland.* Berkeley: University of California Press.

Schmid, C. (1992) The English Only movement: Social bases of support and opposition among Anglos and Latinos. In J. Crawford (ed.) *Language Loyalties: A Source Book on the Official English Controversy* (pp. 202–209). Chicago: The University of Chicago Press.

Schmidt, R. Sr. (1998) The politics of language in Canada and the United States: Explaining the differences. In T. Ricento and B. Burnaby (eds) *Language and Politics in the United States and Canada: Myths and Realities* (pp. 37–70). Mahwah, NJ: Lawrence Erlbaum Associates.

Schofield, J. (2000) Translating success. *Maclean's,* May 1, pp. 54–56.

Schumann, J.H. (1975) Affective factors and the problem of age in second language acquisition. *Language Learning* 25 (2), 209–235.

Schumann, J.H. (1978) *The Pidginization Process: A Model for Second Language Acquisition.* Rowley: Newbury House Publishers, Inc.

Schürch, E. (1943) *Sprachpolitische Erinnerungen.* Bern: Haupt.

Schwirtz, M. (1999) Miami. *Mediaweek,* April 12, pp. 17–20.

Seligman, E.R.A. (ed.) (1930) *Encyclopaedia of the Social Sciences* (Vol. 2). New York: The Macmillan Company.

Selinker, L. (1972) Interlanguage. *International Review of Applied Linguistics in Language Teaching* 10 (3), 209–231.

Shady, M. and Gerken, L.A. (1999) Grammatical and caregiver cues in early sentence comprehension. *Journal of Child Language* 26, 163–175.

Sharwood Smith, M. (1981) Consciousness-raising and the second language learner. *Applied Linguistics* 2 (2), 159–168.

Shebala, M. (1999) Council slams door on "English Only." *Navajo Times,* July 22.

Sherman, P.E. (1904) Immigration from abroad into Massachusetts. *New England Magazine,* February 29, 675–676.

Shumway, N. (1988) Preserve the primacy of English. In J. Crawford (ed.) *Language Loyalties: A Source Book on the Official English Controversy* (pp. 121–124). Chicago: University of Chicago Press.

Siao, G.W-T. (1988) 1,000 Chinese books given to Monterey Park Library. *Asian Week,* September 16.

Siegel, J. (1997) Using pidgin language in formal education: Help or hindrance? *Applied Linguistics* 18 (1), 86–100.

Simon, P. (1992) *The Tongue-Tied American: Confronting the Foreign Language Crisis.* New York: Continuum.

Simon, R. (1993) Illegal residents not just from nearby nations. *The Los Angeles Times,* November 26, pp. A1, A42.

Simon, S. (1999) In insular Iowa town, a jolt of worldliness: A torrent of diversity has been a shock to tiny Postville, which was all white, all Christian for 150 years. *The Los Angeles Times,* January 26, p. 1.

Simons, M. (1993) Provençal leading a revival of Europe's local languages. *The New York Times,* May 3, pp. A1, A8.

Singleton, D. (1989) *Language Acquisition: The Age Factor.* Clevedon: Multilingual Matters.

Sklarewitz, N. (1992) American firms lash out at foreign tongues. *Business and Society Review* 83 (Fall), 24–48.

Skow, J. (1990) World without walls. *Time*, August 13, p. 70.

Skutnabb-Kangas, T. (1981) *Bilingualism or Not: The Education of Minorities.* Clevedon: Multilingual Matters.

Skutnabb-Kangas, T. (1990) *Language, Literacy and Minorities.* London: The Minority Rights Group.

Skutnabb-Kangas, T. (2000) *Linguistic Genocide in Education – Or Worldwide Diversity and Human Rights?* Mahwah, NJ: Lawrence Erlbaum Associates.

Skutnabb-Kangas, T. and Toukomaa, P. (1976) *Teaching Migrant Children's Mother Tongue and Learning the Language of the Host Country in the Context of the Socio-Cultural Situation of the Migrant Family.* Helsinki: The Finnish National Commission for UNESCO.

Sleeter, C.E. and Grant, C.A. (1987) An analysis of multicultural education in the United States. *Harvard Educational Review* 57 (4), 421–444.

Smith, G.M. (1998) Non-English driving tests reinstated in Alabama. *The Atlanta Journal-Constitution*, June 6, p. C5.

Smith, M.E. (1935) A study of the speech of eight bilingual children of the same family. *Child* 6, pp. 19–25.

Snow, C.E. and Hoefnagel-Höhle, M. (1978) The critical period for language acquisition: Evidence from language learning. *Child Development* 49, 1114–1128.

Sontag, D. (1993a) A fervent "no" to assimilation in new America. *The New York Times*, June 29, p. A10.

Sontag, D. (1993b) Study sees illegal aliens in new light. *The New York Times*, September 2, pp. B1, B8.

Soto, L. (1995) Atlanta Almanac: Backers of official English face vote today. *The Atlanta Journal-Constitution*, February 27, p. B2.

Southworth, F.C. (1985) The social context of language standardization in India. In N. Wolfson and J. Manes (eds) *Language of Inequality* (pp. 225–239). Berlin: Mouton Publishers.

Spencer, T. (1999) Voyage for freedom ends in deaths of Cubans on boat. *Times Union*, November 26, p. A3.

SPLC (1998) English-only driver's test violates law. *SPLC Report*, June, p. 3.

SPLC (2000) Center lawsuit wins rights for immigrants. *SPLC Report*, March, pp. 1, 4.

Spring, J. (1998) *Education and the Rise of the Global Economy.* Mahwah, NJ: Lawrence Erlbaum Associates.

Stamps, D. (1998) English as a second priority. *Training*, February, pp. 53–58.

Staples, B. (2000) The Republican Party's exercise in minstrelsy. *The New York Times*, August 2, p. A24.

Steinberg, J. (2000) Arizona teachers look to end of bilingual era: Conference examines new state measure. *The New York Times*, December 18, p. A12.

Stephens, M. (1978) *Linguistic Minorities in Western Europe.* Llandysul: Gomer Press.

Strapp, C.M. (1999) Mothers', fathers', and siblings' responses to children's language errors: Comparing sources of negative evidence. *Journal of Child Language* 26, 373–391.

Sung, B.L. (1990) *Chinese American Intermarriage.* New York: Center for Migration Studies.

Swaffer, J. and Woodruff, M. (1978) Language for comprehension: Focus on reading. *Modern Language Journal* 61, 27–32.

Swain, M. and Lapkin, S. (1991) Additive bilingualism and French immersion education: The roles of language proficiency and literacy. In A.G. Reynolds (ed.) *Bilingualism, Multiculturalism and Second Language Learning*. Hillsdale, NJ: Lawrence Erlbaum.

Tagliabue, J. (1998) The World: Achtung! English spoken here; In Europe, steps toward a common language. *The New York Times*, July 19, Sect. 4, p. 1.

Takaki, R. (1993) *A Different Mirror: A History of Multicultural America*. Boston: Little, Brown and Company.

Tasker, F. (1980) Dade Countians vote for a halt to bilingualism. *The Miami Herald*, November 5, p. 16A.

Texas (1999) *Texas Administrative Code, Title 16: Economic Regulation*. West Group.

Thernstrom, A.M. (1990) Bilingual miseducation. *Commentary* 89, 44–47.

Thernstrom, S. (ed.) (1980) *Harvard Encyclopedia of American Ethnic Groups*. Cambridge, MA: Harvard University Press.

Thomas, B.P. (1952) *Abraham Lincoln: A Biography*. New York: Alfred A. Knopf.

Thomas, R.R. Jr. and Gregory, T.A. (1993/4) A diversity perspective on the language challenge. *Employee Relations Today* 20 (4), 363–376.

Thomas, W.P. and Collier, V.P. (1995) Language-minority student achievement and program effectiveness studies support native language development. *NABE News* 18 (8), 5, 12.

Tierney, J. (1999) Polyglot city raises a cry for English. *The New York Times*, August 16, p. B1.

Times-Picayune (1998) Louisiana leads nation in teaching French, June 27, p. A3.

Toner, R. (2000) Platform strives to reach right and center. *The New York Times*, August 1, pp. A1, A16.

Toohey, K. (1998) "Breaking them up, taking them away": ESL students in grade 1. *TESOL Quarterly* 32 (1), 61–84.

Toth, J. (1991) Bilingual pupils held to do well. *The Los Angeles Times*, February 12, pp. A1, A18.

Totten, G.O. (1960) Bring up children bilingually. *American Scandinavian Review* 48, 42–50.

Towne, E.T. (1916) *Social Problems*. New York: Macmillan Co.

Trombley, W. (1980) Bilingual education holds strong political overtones. *The Los Angeles Times*, September 7, pp. 1, 5, 6.

Trombley, W. (1986) Norman Cousins drops his support of Prop. 63. *The Los Angeles Times*, October 16, pp. 3, 22.

Troyna, B. (1992) Can you see the join? An historical analysis of multicultural and antiracist education policies. In D. Gill, B. Mayor and M. Blair (eds) *Racism and Education: Structures and Strategies* (pp. 63–91). London: Sage Publishers.

Trudgill, P. (1972) Sex, covert prestige, and linguistic change in the urban British English of Norwich. *Language in Society* 1 (2), 179–195.

Trueba, H.T., Cheng, L. and Ima, I. (1993) *Myth or Reality: Adaptive Strategies of Asian Americans in California*. Washington, DC: The Falmer Press.

Tucker, G.R. (1975) The development of reading skills within a bilingual education program. In S.S. Smiley and J.C. Townet (eds) *Language and Reading*. Bellingham, WA: Western Washington State College.

Uchitelle, L. (1994) The rise of the losing class. *The New York Times*, November 20, Sect. 4, pp. 1, 5.

Unz, R.K. and Tuchman, G.M. (1998) Initiative statute: English language education for children in public schools. *NABE News* 21 (4), 12–14.

US Census Bureau (1999a) Quarterly estimates of the US foreign-born and native resident populations: April 9, 1990 to July 1, 1998. On WWW at http://www.census.gov/population/estimates/nation/nativity/fbtab001.txt.

US Census Bureau (1999b) Foreign-born resident population estimates of the US by sex, race, and Hispanic origin: April 1, 1990 to July 1, 1998. On WWW at http://www.census.gov/population/estimates/nation/intfile3-1.txt.

US Commission on Civil Rights (1988) *The Economic Status of Americans of Asian Descent: An Exploratory Investigation*, Publication No. 95. Washington, DC: Clearinghouse.

US Department of Labor (1999) 20 million jobs: January 1993 – November 1999. At http://www.dol.gov/dol_sec/public/media/reports/20mill/main.htm.

US English Update (1994a) US English Foundation. *US English Update* XI (1) p. 6.

US English Update (1994b) State update. *US English Update* XI (1), p. 3.

US English Update (1994c) US Senate joins in effort to stop INS. *US English Update* XI (1) pp. 1, 4.

US English Update (1994 d) US English takes on the IRS. *US English Update* XI (1) pp. 1, 2.

US English Update (1995) Federal update: Q&A with Congressman Bill Emerson. *US English Update* XII, p. 3.

US English Update (1999) Texas town declares itself America's first "Spanish-only city." August 13. On WWW at http://www. us-english.org/press/spanishcity.htm.

US English Update (undated) Race for the presidency: Where the candidates stand. *US English Update*, p. 2.

USA Today (1997) News from every state. August 21, p. 12A.

Valette, R.M. (1964) Some reflections on second-language learning in young children. *Language Learning* 13 (3 & 4), 91–98.

Valdés, G. (1998) The world outside and inside school: Language and immigrant children. *Educational Researcher* 27 (6), 4–18.

Valdman, A. (1997) Introduction. In A. Valdman (ed.) *French and Creole in Louisiana* (pp. 1–23). New York: Plenum Press.

VanPatten, B., Marks, M.A. and Teschner, R.V. (1992) *Destinos: An Introduction to Spanish*. New York: McGraw-Hill, Inc.

Vélez, D.L. (1986) Aspects of the debate on language in Puerto Rico. *The Bilingual Review/La Revista Bilingüe* 13 (3), 3–12.

Verhovek, S.H. (1995) Mother scolded by judge for speaking in Spanish. *The New York Times*, August 30, p. A12.

Vernon's (1986) *Texas Codes Annotated, Election Code* (Vols 1–2). St Paul, MN: West Publishing Co.

Vernon's (1997a) *Texas Codes Annotated, Education Code* (Vol. 1). St Paul, MN: West Publishing Co.

Vernon's (1997b) *Texas Codes Annotated, Civil Practice and Remedies* (Vol. 2). St Paul, MN: West Publishing Co.

Vira, R. (1965) *India's National Language*. New Delhi: International Academy of Indian Culture.

Vuko, E.P. (1997) Teacher says: Take the "foreign" out of languages; The sooner the kids start, the easier it goes. *The Washington Post*, October 20, p. C6.

Walker, R. (2000) Some Canadians seek their right to French schools: Small rural Francophone communities are seeking funding for French schools. *The Christian Science Monitor*, 7, March 9.

The Wall Street Journal (1995) Dole urges schools to offer regular classes in English. September 5, p. A16.

The Wall Street Journal (1999) Tony & Tacky: Duking it out. May 14, p. W15.

Walsh, M.W. (1992) A sign of the times in Quebec. *The Los Angeles Times*, February 21, pp. A1, A10.

Watkins, S.C. and Robles, A. (1994) Appendix B: A tabular presentation of immigration characteristics, by ethnic group. In S.C. Watkins (ed.) *After Ellis Island: Newcomers and Natives in the 1910 Census* (pp. 357–410). New York: Russell Sage Foundation.

Wells, S. (1986) Bilingualism: The accent is on youth. *US News & World Report*, July 28, p. 60.

Weinstock, S.A. (1969) *Acculturation and Occupation: A Study of the 1956 Hungarian Refugees in the United States*. The Hague: Martinus Nijhoff.

Wenden, A.L. (1998) Metacognitive knowledge and language learning. *Applied Linguistics* 19 (4), 515–537.

Wernick, A. (1993) But don't play politics with 'em. *The Daily News*, August 15, p. 35.

West's (1977) *West's Louisiana Statutes Annotated, Revised Statutes* (Vol. 2). St Paul, MN: West Publishing Co.

West's (1982a) *West's Louisiana Statutes Annotated, Revised Statutes* (Vol. 13). St Paul, MN: West Publishing Co.

West's (1982b) *West's Louisiana Statutes Annotated, Revised Statutes* (Vol. 24). St Paul, MN: West Publishing Co.

West's (1987) *West's Louisiana Statutes Annotated, Revised Statutes* (Vol. 1). St Paul, MN: West Publishing Co.

West's (1989) *West's Louisiana Statutes Annotated, Revised Statutes* (Vol. 16C). St Paul, MN: West Publishing Co.

Whitaker, R. (1998) International Academy produces proud parents, worldly students. *Detroit News*, March 30, p. D4.

Wildavsky, A. (1992) Finding universalistic solutions to particularistic problems: Bilingualism resolved through a second language requirement for elementary schools. *Journal of Policy Analysis and Management* 11 (2), 310–314.

Williams, C.R. (ed.) (1924) *Diary and Letters of Rutherford Birchard Hayes* (Vol. 3). Columbus, Ohio: Ohio State Archaeological and Historical Society.

Williams, E. (1996) Reading in two languages at year five in African primary schools. *Applied Linguistics* 17 (2), 182–209.

Willig, A.C. (1985) A meta-analysis of selected studies on the effectiveness of bilingual education. *Review of Educational Research* 55 (3), 269–317.

Wilson, Pete (1993) Illegal aliens are milking us dry. *The Daily News*, August 15, p. 35.

Wilson, Pila (1999) Why English is delayed until the fifth grade in Kaiapuni Hawai'i. On WWW at http://www.olelo. hawaii.edu/OP/orgs/hk/kekuamoo/0199/whydelay.html.

Wink, J. (1991/1992) Immersion confusion. *TESOL Matters*, 1991 Dec/1992 January, pp. 14, 17.

Wolfson, H. (2000) English-Only as hot issue. *Associated Press*, July 7. On WWW at http://ourworld.compuserve. com/homepages/JWCRAWFORD/AP26.htm.

Wong, A. (1977) Nixon "ping-pong" ball lands in Monterey Park. *Monterey Park Progress*, September 28.

Wokeck, M. (1991) Harnessing the lure of the "best poor man's country": The dynamics of German-speaking immigration to British North America, 1683–1783. In I. Altman and J. Horn (eds) *"To Make America": European Emigration in the Early Modern Period* (pp. 204–243). Berkeley and Los Angeles: University of California Press.

Wolfram, W.A. (1969) *A Sociolinguistic Description of Detroit Negro Speech*. Washington, DC: Center for Applied Linguistics.

Wolfson, N. (1989). *Perspectives: Sociolinguistics and TESOL*. Cambridge: Newbury House Publishers

Wong Fillmore, L. (1992) Against our best interest: The attempt to sabotage bilingual education. In J. Crawford (ed.) *Language Loyalties: A Source Book on the Official English Controversy* (pp. 367–376). Chicago: The University of Chicago Press.

Wood, D.B. (1999) In Mexico, US industry finds uncertainty: American and Mexican officials compromise on controversial tax plan, but long-term issues remain. *Christian Science Monitor*, November 1, p. 3.

Woodrow, K. (US Census Bureau) (1990) Undocumented immigrants living in the United States. Paper presented at the American Statistical Association, Anaheim, CA.

Xia, N. (1992) Maintenance of the Chinese language in the United States. *The Bilingual Review/La Revista Bilingüe* 17 (3), 195–209.

Yang, J. and López, R. (1995) English Plus bill introduced in Congress. *NABE News* 18 (8), 1.

Yniguez v. Mofford (1990) 730 FSupp 309 (D Ariz.).

Zangwill, I. (1939) *The Melting-pot: Drama in Four Acts*. New York: The Macmillan Company.

Zhang, K. and Xioming, H. (1999) The Internet and ethnic press: A study of electronic Chinese publications. *Information Society* 15 (1), 21–30.

Zavodny, M. (1998) The effects of Official English laws on limited-English-proficient workers. Federal Reserve Bank of Atlanta, *Working Paper 98–4a*, December. On WWW at www.frbatlanta.org/publica/work_papers.

Zepeda, O. and Hill, J.H. (1992) The condition of Native American languages in the United States. In R.H. Robins and E.M. Uhlenbeck (eds) *Endangered Languages* (pp. 135–155). New York: Oxford.

Index